According to

THE ROLLING STONES

MICK JAGGER

KEITH RICHARDS

CHARLIE WATTS

RONNIE WOOD

EDITED BY DORA LOEWENSTEIN AND PHILIP DODD
CONSULTING EDITOR CHARLIE WATTS

WEIDENFELD & NICOLSON

CONTENTS

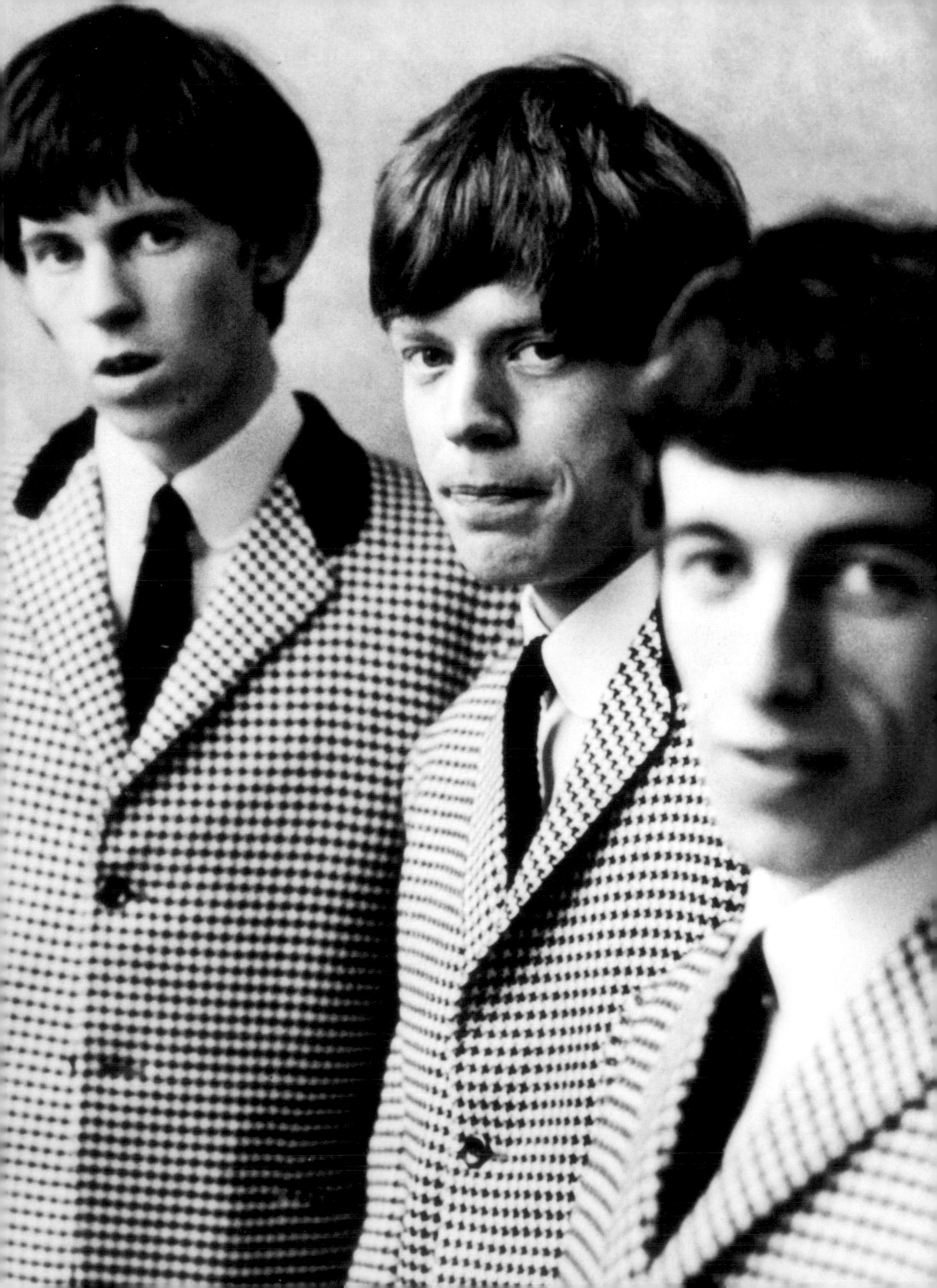

PREFACE

by Dora Loewenstein and Philip Dodd

With the announcement of the *Forty Licks* album and tour, there was no question that, at last, the Rolling Stones were ready to acknowledge the full extent of their history, their back catalogue and their influence. The album, released in Autumn 2002, brought together highlights from the previous four decades of the band's music-making, songs that had punctuated the many moods of that period and each of which held a particular memory for those of us who grew up listening to their music. But significantly, *Forty Licks* contained four new tracks. For the Rolling Stones, as conscious as they might be of the past, remain equally and resolutely a band of the present and the future, a true working band. There is no one else out there who can claim the same duration of commitment, energy and success.

It seemed like a good time for the Stones to tell the history of the band the way that they see it, the way that they remember it. The new generations of fans coming to the shows on the *Bridges To Babylon* or *Forty Licks* tours are often impressively familiar with the Stones' music, but may well be far less aware of the band's history and pre-history. That was the impetus for *According To The Rolling Stones*.

Here was a chance to get beneath the surface and understand what makes the Stones operate so well as a group of musicians who can still sell out stadiums around the globe. To explore what inspired them to become musicians in the first place and the events which had an impact on their musical and personal development. And to understand how the support of a long-lasting, loyal entourage of musicians, tour personnel and business advisers has helped the band not only survive creatively but also become pioneers within the music industry in terms of record deals and stadium tours.

We were looking for answers to questions that lie at the heart of the Rolling Stones. How have they continued to refresh and renew themselves to maintain a feeling of edgy dynamism despite their status as international cultural icons, admired and lauded with accolades worldwide? What is the alchemy between Mick and Keith that generates the creative tension which, like a never-ageing elastic band, propels the Stones ever forwards?

The first and most important decision was to allow the Stones the space to tell their story. We arranged a series of interviews during the *Forty Licks* tour – following the band from San Francisco and LA to Melbourne and Tokyo – to give the four principals the time between interviews to reflect, cogitate and mull. Two fellow interviewers were invited to help provide fresh lines of enquiry and new avenues to explore: Rob Bowman, a Canadian academic with an encyclopedic knowledge of blues, R&B, soul and rock, and Tim Rice, who understands as well as anyone the theatrical aspects of the rock spectacle.

Once through the door into the Stones' private on-tour worlds – each hotel suite customised for its inhabitant – they were, as expected, charming, generous, witty and funny, genuinely enjoying the memories and the stories. The whole process reaffirmed that the Rolling Stones have keen and inquisitive minds.

As will be clear to anyone who reads this book, the Rolling Stones do not bend to anyone or anything. They have a strong identity and a definite line to tread. They are far from malleable: they will not accept anything if they feel they are being presented with a *fait accompli*. As an outsider, you can try to second-guess what the Rolling Stones will do or say, but you will usually be surprised.

Throughout the work on this book, they have always been right on the button, questioning, deliberating and then supplying a positive and ingenious solution to any query, whether about the cover design, text or photo selection. Such is the depth and purpose of their involvement in this book, an indication of the level of professionalism and commitment that they have exercised throughout their career, the very essence of their survival.

We have tried to capture as much as possible of that essence – the character, vibrancy, vitality and humour of each of the Stones' voices, the individual elements that together create the personality of the Rolling Stones: Mick's sense of showmanship, Keith's love of history, Charlie's down-to-earth strength and solidity and Ronnie's affable, optimistic humanity.

To illustrate their story, we selected over 300 photographs. There are iconic images from the great photographers who have worked with the band in the past forty years – a long and prestigious list including David Bailey, Anton Corbijn, Michael Cooper, Dezo Hoffman, Gered Mankowitz, Jim Marshall, Terry O'Neill, Norman Seeff, Pennie Smith, Mario Testino and Val Wilmer. Equally, there are photos drawn from the Stones' own family archives or taken by their immediate entourage. Each photograph is, deliberately, given air on the page to breathe, as we wanted the whole book, in both conception and design, to be clean, open and readable.

The Stones' story falls into twelve chronological chapters. At the junctions between those chapters are essays by key participants in and observers of the Stones' career over the last forty years, ranging from Atlantic Records founder Ahmet Ertegun and Giorgio Gomelsky, the creator of the Crawdaddy Club, to the band's current co-producer Don Was and Sheryl Crow, who has supported them on both the *Bridges To Babylon* and *Forty Licks* tours. Each piece gives the mirrorball another twist, shedding a different light across the history of the band.

At the back end of the book are corralled those details which will clarify and expand their story, information that provides background explanations to the Stones' narrative without holding it up in full flood: a who's who, a chronology and a discography.

Above all, this is the history of the Rolling Stones *according to* the Rolling Stones. This is not an obsessive day-by-day account of every gig, every ticket stub, every B-side. It reflects the way the Stones themselves recall what they have done and what has happened to them, fluxing and flowing through the events and the emotions that have stayed strongest in their individual and collective memory. History and memory are notoriously grey areas, but it is hard to argue with the guys who were actually there.

The interviews for According To The Rolling Stones *were conducted during the* Forty Licks *tour, between November 2002 and May 2003, by Philip Dodd, Rob Bowman, Tim Rice and Dora Loewenstein.*

Music is a language that doesn't speak in particular words, IT speaks in emotions And if it's in the bones, IT'S IN THE BONES

Keith Richards

CHASING THE SIGNAL

1

Mick with guitar on an early family holiday.

MICK: I was always a singer. I always sang as a child. I was one of those kids who just *liked* to sing. Some children sing in choirs; others like to show off in front of the mirror. I was in the church choir and I also loved listening to singers on the radio – the BBC or Radio Luxembourg – or watching them on TV and in the movies. I loved all those early rock'n'roll singers. I don't know who they were; they were all just pop singers. I wasn't really that obsessed with them – I didn't care who or what they were – and I didn't make any value judgements about whether they were tacky or not. I just used to listen to them all. Eventually, though, as you do, I gravitated towards a number of singers who were really quite good, like Buddy Holly, Eddie Cochran, Elvis Presley and Chuck Berry. I put together a band with some friends, and on Saturday nights I would go out and do gigs, sometimes simply with pick-up bands who were playing in some hall or other, singing Jerry Lee Lewis tunes or country music.

The band I had with my friends, Little Boy Blue and the Blue Boys, was more like a skiffle group. In England in the late 1950s we had all those singers like Lonnie Donegan. I used to play guitar and the group would sing skiffle, but I don't remember performing that kind of music in public very often. The two things – rock songs and skiffle – were quite different. Skiffle was more like a coffee-house version of folk music.

Among the various people we used to play with was a kid called Dick Taylor. Dick was a guitarist who lived locally to me, and much later on he played for that band called the Pretty Things. There was a time when we – Dick, Keith and myself – played in the back room at Dick's house, trying out all kinds of rock music and some kind of rhythm and blues, Chuck Berry mostly. We played everything and anything – that's how you learn.

> *I had a number of friends who had their own record collections, so we used to go round to their houses and listen to them there. It was all a bit like trainspotting.*
>
> *Mick*

I remember seeing Chuck Berry in the movie *Jazz On A Summer's Day*, which was a very seminal picture – a great documentary about the Newport Jazz Festival shot by the fashion photographer Bert Stern, in a very interesting style which I thought was a different way of looking at things.

I didn't get to see Muddy Waters at that point. Muddy did tour in England, but he mainly played up North, as far as I know; he certainly didn't play London very often. The first Muddy Waters album that was really popular was *Muddy Waters At Newport*, which was the first album I ever bought, but there were many other things I was listening to. The really popular blues singers in England at the time were those people who used to tour here regularly, like Big Bill Broonzy, Sister Rosetta Tharpe and Leadbelly. They used to come and tour around in caravans, and whenever they toured they would also appear on television, so it was possible to see them on a regular basis. Since the UK only had a choice of two television channels, the odds were pretty good that you weren't going to miss a show if it was being broadcast. You had the TV on and there it was – you're just gonna see Big Bill Broonzy. I also had a number of friends who had their own record collections, so we used to go round to their houses and listen to them. There was one particular schoolfriend who lived close by. He was a little older than me and something of a blues purist. He liked Broonzy and Leadbelly, so I used to go over and listen to his records. It was all a bit like trainspotting.

You could also get hold of records directly from Chess Records in Chicago. I had come across a mailing address for them in some magazine or other. And when I had the money I would send off for records from them. They were really quite expensive for those days, because American record prices were higher than they were in England, and also to actually get them mailed out across the Atlantic cost a lot. Plus, you didn't even know if you were going to like the record when it arrived. You'd never heard it. So deciding what to order was a major decision. I knew I liked Chuck Berry, of course, and I'd order his records, because in those days they only released the singles. They would release those 7-inch extended-play records, like a sampler. You might have four tracks on one of them, and they would be a rather tantalising selection, so you'd go, "Oh well, I like that". That's how you bought them. Eventually they turned up in a cardboard package, not brilliantly wrapped. There were a couple of breakages; these weren't 78s, they were LPs, and they were pretty sturdy, but I did get one or two that were broken.

I also used to listen to a lot of jazz, the kind that Charlie likes. I had one friend who was very into jazz and he introduced me to the world of modern jazz. This was when all records were like gold dust, so you would bring your records over to one another's house and play them to each other. It was, "I'll play you my Big Bill Broonzy and my Chuck Berry and then you play me what you've got, and let's see if there's anywhere that our tastes cross over". He used to play me things like Jimmy Giuffre, who also appeared in *Jazz On A Summer's Day*, Chet Baker, who was very hip, and Gerry Mulligan on baritone. Dave Brubeck was also very popular; you'd often see him on the television in England – he was somebody a lot of people liked. And by a strange coincidence, when we walked down to the B-stage on the *Forty Licks* tour, we played a sample by Joe Morello, Dave Brubeck's drummer, of Nina Simone singing 'Let's Get Together'. All of that was my friend's taste: jazz music that was quite popular, not cool jazz. Everything had to have its own little pigeon-hole – there was cool, mainstream and traditional.

Chuck Berry was inducted by Keith into the Rock and Roll Hall Of Fame, January 1986. Keith: I lifted every lick he ever played.

KEITH: When I was growing up there was a feeling in the air that things were really changing. You could put that down to the fact that World War II had effectively finished in about 1957 or '58, rather than 1945, in terms of the effect it had on the population of the UK. This is all in retrospect, of course.

In the early 1960s Harold Macmillan used to say, "You've never had it so good". I don't know about that, but certainly before that time you grew up in the middle of all

the bomb sites and the rubble left over from the War. London had enormous buildings, but then you could turn a corner and suddenly there'd be three acres of nothing – and the streets were full of horseshit because there were hardly any cars then. I really miss that about London: horseshit and coal smoke, mixed with a bit of diesel here and there. A deadly mixture – it's probably what turned me onto drugs!

I had grown up on rationing. I remember going to school and being given a medicine bottle full of orange juice once a month and the teachers would say, "That's your Vitamin C"; you didn't feel you were missing out because that was the way things were, although there were lots of kids with rickets who hadn't got enough Vitamin C or milk. Candy was also in short supply. I was almost beyond the "I want my sweets!" stage, but when I was a kid you got one little bag of sweets a week and that was it. A lot of wheeling and dealing went down; the things people would do for a lemon drop! However, we didn't feel deprived because we didn't know any different.

The other thing about my generation was that this was the time that they stopped conscription, the draft. I had grown up expecting to be called up to do National Service. It was just part of life. At 11 years old, you took the 11-plus exam; at 16 you would do your GCE, and then at 18 you would get your hair cut and peel spuds for two years or become a fighter pilot – unless you could come up with a very bad cough, blind yourself, shoot your toe off or feign madness. But conscription came to an end in 1960, a year or so before I was 18, and at the same time there was all this new music around and even a few cars on the roads that weren't black.

The music came across the airwaves and suddenly it felt as if the world was actually changing. Things went from black and white or grey to full Technicolor: no army, there's rock'n'roll music and as long as you've got a bit of bread you can buy anything, you don't need to queue. All of these things combined created a very strong thing in England for our generation. It was a breath of fresh air and a promise of real possibilities, instead of the prospect of simply following in our fathers' footsteps, which was pretty gloomy.

I was fortunate that I came from quite a musical family and that my mother brought me up on the best that the BBC had to offer. I thought everybody played the piano or sang because that's what my family did. The first time I got applause was singing 'Bewitched, Bothered And Bewildered' at the age of four at Christmas. I grew up listening to Sarah Vaughan, Billy Eckstine, Ella Fitzgerald and Louis Armstrong. The flipside of that was that they also broadcast the British pop scene, where what you would be hearing was Billy Cotton shouting "Wakey, wa-aa-key!" and lyrics like "How much is that doggie in the window?" or "You're a pink toothbrush, I'm a blue toothbrush". I can still reel off the 1950s Top Tens, but it was intensely boring. So that's why Chuck Berry and Elvis were, to us, so startlingly different. The music got called rock'n'roll because it had gone white; otherwise it was rhythm and blues.

I have no doubt that I first heard Chuck Berry, Elvis and Little Richard on my transistor radio courtesy of Radio Luxembourg or the BBC. That's certainly where I first heard 'Heartbreak Hotel', 'Good Golly, Miss Molly' and 'Tutti Frutti'. And Chuck: I didn't know if he was black, white or indifferent at the time, especially with his material, which is such a beautiful mixture of hybrid stuff. You want the best rock and roll band in the world? Chuck Berry's band – Johnnie Johnson, Ebby Hardy and Willie Dixon. The first record I bought, or nicked, was 'Good Golly Miss Molly', but I didn't have anything to play it on. Radio Luxembourg was really the only station playing those songs. You could hear some of them on the BBC, but only if they were big hits and had been released in England so that they were given "needle time", as the BBC used to call it.

To get any kind of signal at all for Luxembourg you had to go all around your bedroom with your tranny. I'm sure I was supposed to be asleep, so I was trying to do this underneath the sheets. The station would keep going off into ads for watches or the Irish sweepstakes, but every now and again you would get something special. So I always had to search for the signal; it kept moving around the room with every damn song or else it would disappear in the middle of 'Heartbreak Hotel' – that's what they meant by "heartbreak". You'd keep chasing the signal and then it would come good just at the end

The Stones sit at the feet of the master, Howlin' Wolf. The legendary bluesman, who had previously recorded 'Little Red Rooster', was an invited guest on their Shindig! *special, filmed in Los Angeles in 1965, along with the similarly venerated Son House.*

Mick, pictured in the 1970s, with another major influence, Chuck Berry, whose 'Come On' provided the Stones with their first single in June 1963. Since then, their paths have crossed on numerous occasions, while Keith played a major role in the 1987 biopic Hail! Hail! Rock'n'Roll.

of the song – "da da" – and then there'd be this ad and you'd be like, "Shit!", because only the ad would be totally clear. But that was all part of the quest.

Then you had to start finding out where the hell these guys came from. I've worked with more American musicians than I have English, really, and their take on this is completely different. Bobby Keys is exactly the same age as me, almost to the hour – and for him, growing up where he did in Lubbock, Texas, meant that he was just around the corner from Buddy Holly; you could hear Buddy from the garage. So to Bobby, rock'n'roll was more of a gradual thing; you could already get country music, swing and rhythm and blues on the radio, so it wasn't such a drastic difference. What *was* drastic about the change in America was the fact that Elvis Presley and Buddy Holly turned up and these were white guys performing this music. Whereas in England and Europe it was the music itself that had the most impact rather than what the performers looked like. You might have thought to yourself, "That guy is obviously black", because you could tell by his style of playing, but you didn't give a damn. It was just, "Give me some more". For example, nobody knew that Jerry Lee Lewis was white for ages; we only heard about it through the grapevine; nobody realised he was a blond Welshman from Louisiana. You'd go to a record store and there would be a picture of Chuck Berry, and then you knew.

The other part of the quest was going back and discovering what these guys had done before. "Is this his first record? Just because it's the first one *I've* heard doesn't necessarily mean it is." Once you get into that, it becomes a lifelong thing. From Chuck Berry, you go and find Muddy Waters and then Robert Johnson, and then on through jazz and Buddy Bolden, until eventually you end up in the caves, where some caveman's banging one rock against another. I'm still following the trail on that one. The history of music is fascinating. It's one of those great clichés, which unfortunately are always true, that the more you find out, the less you know.

CHARLIE: At home I grew up listening to the great American crooners, mainly because those were the kind of records that my father was playing – Frank Sinatra and Billy

Charlie acquired his first drum kit at the age of 14 – a present from his parents. The legend 'Chico" on the bass drum is Charlie's tribute to drummer Chico Hamilton, whose performance on 'Walking Shoes' by Gerry Mulligan inspired him to take up the drums.

Eckstine, who was a fabulous crooner and the first artist I ever saw. When I started buying records, it was jazz for some reason, which I never ever had any difficulty listening to. When I was twelve I heard a record called 'Flamingo' by Earl Bostic and immediately wanted to be a saxophone player, and then I heard 'Walking Shoes' by Gerry Mulligan, with Chico Hamilton on drums, and decided I wanted to be a drummer, and that idea seemed to stick. The first albums I bought were by Johnny Dodds, Duke Ellington and Charlie Parker. I thought they were all the same thing, but then I started to read that they came from different places and eras and I became a serious fan.

At the same time a guy who lived next door to me, David Green, was the bass player in a band. Together we learned to play in skiffle groups and things like that, and we both played in the first band that we were actually employed to be in, a jazz band, when we were about sixteen. Then I played in various bands, performing Dixieland stuff, or doing weddings and bar mitzvahs with accordionists. I just played with everybody; playing was what I liked to do. I really wanted to be Phil Seaman, but I played all these other things because I knew that was how he had become Phil Seaman, working with dance bands and all that. I was also involved in instrumentally led jazz things, which were all very imitative, I might add, including the drummer. I was part of a Thelonious Monk-style group when I first met Alexis Korner in a coffee bar; he sat in with us on electric guitar.

Through listening to records – which is how I learned about R&B later on – I got to know Charlie Mingus and how I learned to play like – no, let me put it another way – how I learned to imitate Kenny Clarke, and also by going to see them play, which is why I still always prefer to see jazz players playing live.

I also worked with Chris Barber, who in his day was very avant-garde within traditional jazz. Whereas Ken Colyer was a fabulous revivalist – he and Cy Laurie played just like the Preservation Jazz Band, they were seriously copying the New Orleans style – Chris had a completely different take on traditional jazz. His band had great players like Monty Sunshine and his wife, Ottilie Patterson, and his banjo player was Lonnie Donegan, who became the skiffle star and had hits in America and England. Chris Barber had a connection with the Marquee Club, where Harold Pendleton would book American musicians including blues players like Sonny Terry, Brownie McGhee and Big Bill Broonzy, and Chris would play bass behind them. My idols were people like Phil Seamen and Tubby Hayes, rather than Chris Barber, but I did like his band. Cyril Davis, who was fabulous on harmonica, and Alexis Korner would take the Sonny Terry and Brownie McGhee roles with Chris. They asked Chris if they could do a night in the Marquee, and Harold Pendleton said yes, they could have Thursday night, which was the worst night at the club for jazz. At the same time Alexis Korner was doing some jamming and for some reason, through a friend of mine, Alexis asked me to play in their band.

KEITH: I started tinkering about on guitar. My grandfather, Theodore Augustus Dupree, my mother's father, was a musician – the Duprees came out of the Channel Islands; the Richards are Celts, the Welsh. Gus liked to sing, he played guitar, saxophone, violin and piano, and when he got bored with his seven daughters he'd take the dog for a long walk, and go singing on Primrose Hill. He taught me the love of music, the sheer love of it.

Gus had an upright piano, and on top of it there was a Spanish guitar, a very nice one. Whenever I went to visit him, I knew where it was and I just presumed it was part of the furniture. I only found out years and years later, in fact soon after Gus died, that he put it there deliberately. My family said, "Oh, he only put that up there when he knew you were coming round" and there had been a period of about five or six years before he had said to me, "Well, now you can reach it, you can take it down". It's uncanny, as if he had his eye on me as a guitar player before I knew it. He put it up there like some kind of unreachable icon.

Gus must have been checking me out every time I went round there because I'd keep looking up at it, even when he had made me some nosh. For some reason it was always the guitar that attracted me. I'd say, "Can I really touch it, Grandad?", and all of that. He'd say "Oh, are you interested in that?" and he'd bring it down. I began fiddling around with it, and then it was a matter of knocking on Mother for fifteen quid to buy a Rossetti, a beautiful guitar, made of wonderful plywood… Still, I learned the game on that trusty old thing. It was the only guitar I had for ages. It went out of tune a lot and when any of the strings broke, I had to wire one string together about three times to make a new one. I became very good at improvising by making these hooks to make the string longer by adding on another piece of string, and I learned how to glue the bridge back on when it fell off. It sounds ridiculous, but I did learn all about guitars.

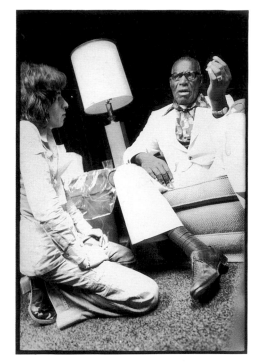

Bassist Bill Wyman in conversation with Howlin' Wolf. Bill and Charlie were able to repay a debt by forming the rhythm section for his London Sessions *album, released in 1971.*

Art school was where I was really introduced to the possibility of what was going on amongst other guitarists. It was a very diverse place, where you could suddenly hear a lot of nice playing because the age range of the students was between 15 and 18, which makes a lot of difference at that age. Jazz was obviously very big: the really hip ones were into Mingus and Monk, and then there was the whole traditional jazz scene, where everybody had a big black sweater down to their knees and the chicks wore black stockings. That was the only alternative for people going to art school, otherwise you had to go out to one of the ballrooms with a bouffant hairdo and listen to Nero and the Gladiators, who were probably a much better band than most of those trad bands. At the same time, going to see music in a ballroom meant you had to mix with all the different kinds of people who went there.

Then you had the Mods. I have no idea how those guys managed to afford their clothes – we never even had enough for cigarettes – but they were completely into it. They would have a suit or a jacket made up on a Monday and it would be totally out of fashion by the next Monday. Plus they were saving up for their scooters with all those little furry bits on the aerial. In other words, art school was a very diverse scene. There was also a folk element – and that's where the guitar comes in. Guys like Wizz Jones, who was a really good guitar picker, occasionally came round to the art schools, if they wanted a cup of tea. People like Wizz would sit in the john at the school and pass the guitar round. I learned a lot of licks in

The history of music is fascinating. It's one of those great clichés, which unfortunately are always true, that the more you find out, the less you know.

Keith

that john just from guys passing through. In a way it's probably not that much different from what Robert Johnson did, only it was Wizz Jones who was in the john. We'd go, "Okay, let's cut life class and go to the john". I didn't do very well at life class, but I became a much better guitar player.

From there on everything started to open up, because you had English rock'n'roll getting going. First of all it was with people like Tommy Steele, who was a great singer, but really not very rock'n'roll. And then there were your Helen Shapiros, all very tacky and lightweight. There was nothing of any substance coming out. Everything was basically covers of American songs, anyway, and it was just a matter of who got the TV time or whose record was obviously better, and whether it was hip or something like 'Itsy Bitsy, Teeny Weeny, Yellow Polka Dot Bikini'.

I was also listening to country music; that was perhaps a slight influence from my mother, but also at that time my grandfather was playing on American airbases as part of a real 'Turkey In The Straw' country band – all the double-stopping fiddle stuff I heard him play. And Hank Williams' songs were always around. He was so big that everybody would cover them, usually very badly, but when I heard Hank's original versions from time to time, it helped me to join up the dots. When I came to America I realised that on the other side of the scale from the McDonalds and the H-Bomb was an international sort of music that had come down through jazz and blues and country, all to do with the fact that there are so many different kinds of people in the States.

At the same time you had these anomalies, like Eddie Cochran and Buddy Holly. To guys of my age at the time, if you were the least bit interested in music, Buddy was the one, because he sang and he was very self-contained. Elvis was fantastic, but because Buddy had glasses and looked a bit like a bank clerk, you could say to yourself, "Well, it's not just for guys who look like Elvis", because otherwise it was sort of unattainable. What Buddy did was to level things out and say, "Hey, if you've got any good songs in you, you can do it". Of course later on I found out that Elvis was the real mama's boy backstage. It was Buddy who got the bitches over the fucking table; he never used to go on before he'd had a couple. It was totally the other way round from the images that people had of them.

And there was Chuck Berry, who plays the electric guitar in a way that means you can sound like a whole horn section – which will save you quite a few bucks come pay day, and put a lot of horn players out of business. Chuck is a beautiful mixture. It's something you can't put your finger on, but Chuck puts together a wonderful combination of rhythm and country. He does it better than anybody, and his lyrics are absolutely brilliant: succinct, original, witty, so cutting and filthy.

I also loved Scotty Moore's guitar work with Elvis. Those Sun recordings were like a real anchor. Eddie Cochran fascinated me too – there was another one-man powerhouse – as well as Jerry Lee Lewis. In the UK it was like, "Oh, somebody's coming over to do a tour" and the news would all be about the teddy boy riots, which was fascinating, but I was thinking, "Where's the music?" And that's rock'n'roll, I suppose – it's a name for something that's been around forever, and every now and again gets its name changed.

RONNIE: My mother was very artistic with her fingers – she'd create this incredibly detailed crochet work – while my dad had a 24-piece harmonica band which toured the race-tracks of England – Goodwood, Epsom, Sandown; the band would be by the winning post. It was a hell of a job when they all came home. They had a flat-bed truck and they'd lose most of the musicians on the way back from the gig when they turned a corner. They'd stop off at pubs along the way home, and my dad would busk away on the piano, basically bullshitting his way through songs – he was a big bluffer. But he was a very good entertainer, my dad; he sang and he told jokes and was very theatrical. Keith used to like him a lot and he and Charlie really enjoyed being with him at my wedding to Jo. He was on top form there. So my parents never put me off following my music, even when it was quite outrageous at the time and I had long hair. They would say, "Oh, if you want to look like that, go ahead".

I really caught the music bug from my two elder brothers. Art is ten years older than me and Ted, the jazzer, is eight years older, so they fed me a diet of either Jelly Roll Morton, Bix Beiderbecke or Louis Armstrong and his Hot Seven, which came from Ted, or Fats Domino, Little Richard, Howlin' Wolf and Jerry Lee Lewis, which was from Art. I'd go, "Oh, my brothers like this, I'll listen to it". They also had various bands with their fellow school and college pals. There was a guy called Lawrence Sheaf who played the guitar just like Big Bill Broonzy; they were the ones who first motivated me on the guitar.

Our house was in Whitethorn Avenue, a little council house near Heathrow. It used to rock every weekend; it literally used to rock. There would be about 30 or 40 people in there, in this tiny house. The piano was wedged halfway through the door, with people climbing over it and under it, mucking in with art students – they were rocking parties.

Various members of the groups that Art was playing with at the time would take me, while I was still in short pants, to see English R&B and blues pioneers like Alexis Korner, Long John Baldry and Cyril Davies. Art used to sing in the Cyril Davies Allstars. There were great people playing in the band, like Nicky Hopkins on the piano and Bernie Watson – usually known as "Strawberry" – on guitar, Ricky Brown on bass and Carlo Little, the drummer. Carlo had the first leopard-skin drum kit, which he used to play with Johnny Kidd and the Pirates and Screaming Lord Sutch, and he also had some connections through which he used to get these imports from America. I remember really getting off on things like Howlin' Wolf and Muddy Waters, including Muddy's first EP with 'Little Brown Bird' on it – there are some classic little slide and guitar licks on it. Carlo got me my first copy of 'Blue Feeling' by Chuck Berry, which had a lap steel guitar on it, and that was a real innovation to me.

Later, when I had my first group, the Birds, we worked with Franklin Boyd up in Savile Row, who had a publishing company which handled Tamla Motown, so we got lots of early imports. And I also had a jazz period when I used to learn pieces by George Benson and Wes Montgomery, and listened to a lot of Jimmy Smith and Jimmy McGriff, as well as some Grant Green. It was a wonderful form of groundwork. Just a little bit out of everyone's book. So the whole thing grew out of listening to everybody else's records. That's how Mick and Keith first got close as well, on the train coming back from college. They noticed each other's record collection and it was, "Hey, you've got Muddy Waters. You must be a good guy, let's form a band".

A very young Ronnie (far left) in the Birds (a shortened form of Thunderbirds), a London band he joined when he was just 16. After playing the capital's Mod circuit and issuing three Decca singles in 1964–5, the band split up in 1966, with bassist Kim Gardner (Ashton Gardner and Dyke) the only other member to make a name for himself.

AHMET ERTEGUN

Ahmet Ertegun founded Atlantic Records in 1947 (he is still co-Chairman and co-CEO). With his partners Jerry Wexler and Nesuhi Ertegun, he made Atlantic one of the world's leading independent R&B, jazz and rock record labels. In 1970 the Rolling Stones approached him to distribute their own record label through Atlantic Records.

In the early '60s, there was a tremendous excitement engendered by many British groups whose music was heavily influenced by early American black blues and more recent rhythm and blues. It was the same music that had inspired Elvis Presley several years earlier, and it suddenly brought forth a whole stream of new bands from England who were devoted to this music. Many of them were just doing square copies of black music, in much the same way that white American singers in the '50s had been doing square copies until true originals like Elvis began to interpret and reinvent this music with authenticity and real feeling.

It wasn't until the Beatles broke very big that US audiences were shaken up by this new wave of British artists. But it is important to remember that the Beatles' first records came out here in the US on a Chicago-based R&B label, Vee-Jay, before they moved over to Capitol. And they brought something very important and fresh to the interpretation of American black music. Ultimately, they made their reputation primarily as a pop group, but they paved the way in America for an entire generation of blues-based British bands — pre-eminent among them being the Rolling Stones.

The Stones were, in essence, much closer to the spirit of black music and at the same time more revolutionary and controversial in their approach. I was a fan beginning with their earliest records. I appreciated the fact that they loved the blues and R&B music that I loved, which was evident by the songs they wrote and the songs they picked to cover. And I knew immediately that they had the same love of American black music that I did, only they had something that I didn't personally have, which was great musicianship and a great voice.

When the Beatles arrived in America, they were met by thousands of teenage girls, and when the Rolling Stones arrived, there were thousands of screaming kids as well. But the Stones were also quickly embraced by a whole different group of people. I went to the first big party that was given for the Stones in New York, which was at Jerry Schatzberg's studio downtown on Park Avenue. Jerry was a fashion photographer who later became a film director and producer. It was also Baby Jane Holzer's birthday, and the whole Andy Warhol gang was there that night. It wasn't goo-goo-eyed teenagers, but rather it was young, hip, intellectual, cutting-edge people. And they appreciated the Stones as an artistic, rebellious group that was doing something else, something different from the other pop groups of the time.

The Stones were more outspoken and anti-establishment than many of their fellow artists. They were fearless, and there was a lot of talk surrounding them — a mystique which included all sorts of exploits in fields that were considered forbidden, especially in their early days. Whether they were justified or not, they were attributed to them at the time.

It got to the point where I would go to a Rolling Stones gig just to hear the introductions to the songs — they would give you such a big kick because you knew what was coming up. It was that kind of excitement, that kind of adrenalin. I became friends with Mick, Keith, Charlie and everybody else in the group, as well as with people like their terrific pianist Ian Stewart.

This friendship brought about one of the most important days of my life. In the autumn of 1969, I was in Los Angeles and I happened to drive past a studio where there were hundreds of kids hanging around outside, and that's how I found out that the Stones were in town.

I was staying at a bungalow at the Beverly Hills Hotel, and the next morning, somebody knocked on the door of my suite. I opened the door, and there was a roadie standing there who said, "The Stones are recording". And I said, "I know they are". He continued, "Mick said if you'd like, you can come by the studio, and they'll play you some of the stuff they're doing".

So I went by the studio that evening. They all gave me big hugs and greetings. They played me a new version of 'Honky Tonk Women' that they were working on and some other things. The producer, Jimmy Miller, was rolling joints, and they were all listening to music and everybody got high. But then I had to leave to keep a dinner engagement with a guy named Bill Drake, who programmed the records being played on dozens of radio stations. He was courted by every promotion person in America, but he liked me because we drank straight bourbon together.

So I went on to this meeting, and when I arrived at the house, there were all these guys from different record companies there vying for favours. And Bill said, "There are only two people in the world who can drink this good whiskey, and it's Ahmet and me". So he poured two glasses and went chug-a-lug, and I went chug-a-lug. Then we went to dinner and had more drinks.

I had made a date to meet Mick at the Whisky A Go-Go, where Chuck Berry was playing, so I called up the club and reserved a corner table. I was with Bill and a couple of girls, and when I said, "Listen, I've got to leave to meet Mick Jagger at midnight", Bill said, "Oh my God, Mick Jagger?!" So I said he could come with me.

Now, all four of us went to the Whisky and Mick arrives and the band was playing and it was very loud. We had a few more drinks and made jokes, and Mick started to tell me something over the noise. I could barely make out what he was saying, but I gathered that he was telling me that the band's contract with Decca was up and that they were interested in being on Atlantic, a label they had long admired. But by this time, I was really starting to slow down, considering all I had consumed that night, combined with a bit of jet lag. So as he was explaining all this to me, I fell asleep. And this girl kept shaking me and saying, "This is important, Ahmet, wake up", but I kept nodding off. So Bill and Mick picked me up and they walked me to my car and I was driven back to the hotel.

As it turned out, my apparent nonchalance served me well. Mick loathes pushy people, and he loved the fact that I fell asleep in his face. The next day, I met with him and the rest of the guys, and we started our negotiations for what was to be a fifteen-year association between Atlantic Records and the Rolling Stones. It was a period during which — between the Stones and Eric Clapton and Led Zeppelin — we nearly had a lock on British rock'n'roll. And we kept that going for a long time, with a large roster of UK bands that also included the likes of Yes, King Crimson, ELP, Roxy Music, Genesis, Bad Company, and others.

I think the Stones wanted to be on Atlantic because Chess was out of business. It was a choice between Atlantic and Excello. In all seriousness, they wanted to be on a funky, independent label; they really didn't want to continue with the big corporate label situation. Mick knew our catalogue very well — it was some of the music he grew up with, and he was a fan.

On the other hand, they were an enormous group who needed a major distribution network. We had a bit of both: we were able to give them the strength of a major, and the benefit of international, distribution, and at the same time the personal attention of an independent and the understanding and hands-off appreciation of their musical value and originality.

I also have to say that we were able to give them what was probably the most expensive deal that had been made up to that time — both in advances and royalties. Of course, as time goes by every major deal is eclipsed by the next one, but it was a very big deal nevertheless.

It was also a deal that was very different from our usual way of working. We very rarely signed artists who had already had significant success on other labels. We had signed a few established artists, but certainly none who had been as popular as the Stones. For example, when we signed Aretha Franklin, she had been on Columbia for five years, but she didn't have any great success until she came with us. The Stones, on the other hand, were the number one rock'n'roll group in the world at the time we signed them.

Needless to say, I was flattered and thrilled when they decided to come with us. I remember when, after that party where I first met them, I was telling my friends how great I thought they were, and how hip and different, and so on. And one of them said, "You can't compare these people with an artist like Frank Sinatra — a group like this, they're jumping around the stage now, but what are they going to do when they're thirty?" I would have been very happy to say, "Well, when they're thirty, they're going to be recording for me", but, of course, I couldn't have predicted that at the time.

As it turned out, some ten years later, we celebrated Mick's thirtieth birthday with a party on the roof of the St Regis Hotel in New York. For entertainment, we had the Count Basie Orchestra and Muddy Waters. That was probably the only time that Basie and Muddy played the same gig.

One day, I was in Washington, DC and I was staying at the Watergate Hotel. In the hallway, I happened to run into the great Russian dancer, Mikhail Baryshnikov. We were friends, so I said, "Listen, if you're not doing anything tonight, I'm going to see the Rolling Stones". He said he'd love to see them, so I took him to the concert. He was absolutely flabbergasted, and after the show he told Mick, "There are only two people who could dance the way you danced tonight. That's you and me!"

I believe that the secret of Mick's great charisma is his enormous personal charm, which comes across equally in one-on-one conversation or on stage in front of thousands of fans. When you talk to him, he is completely engaged and engaging, with an expression in his eyes that reflects real interest and true understanding. And then there is that extraordinary smile and the amazing contour of his mouth, which is utterly captivating. Mick emanates a genuine warmth and depth of feeling that infects all those around him. And when he's listening to music, or singing and dancing with the Stones, there is a look of elation in his face that comes from a very deep place in his heart.

Mick, of course, has long been a great sex symbol, for both men and women, but, far more importantly, he's a great singer. He has the ability to change his voice and his approach from one song to another, which is something you rarely hear people talk about. He uses all sorts of different voices, he sings falsetto, and it's all done with a purpose – there's meaning in everything he does.

Musically, what sets the Stones apart from everyone else, besides the great catalogue of songs written by Mick and Keith, is how fabulous and original their arrangements are. Keith's guitar-work has always been both incredibly subtle and completely unmistakable, and whether it has been with Brian Jones or Mick Taylor or Ron Wood, he has created a musical interchange unlike any other. The way the guitars work together, and with the rhythm section, is completely unique – it's such an amazing groove, and it's not a copy of anyone that preceded them. Of course, it's influenced by the great blues and R&B grooves from the past, but they've taken it to a completely new place.

At the centre of that groove is Charlie, who is one of the greatest drummers that I have ever heard. The only other musicians I know who have had the same kind of feel as Charlie does are the great jazz drummers like Dave Tough, Big Sid Catlett and Jo Jones. It's all a matter of having a sense of time and Charlie Watts is one of the very, very few, if any, drummers in rock'n'roll who really have that sense.

The soul of the group has always been Mick, Keith and Charlie, and of course Bill Wyman was very important during his many years with them. The group today sounds to me as good as it ever has, maybe even better. They have kept on going because there has been no reason for them to stop. I don't know how long Mick wants to continue, but to me, when you're in the audience in a big hall, he looks just the same as he did when he was twenty-two. He's in great shape and he's very limber, and the whole band sounds fantastic. The Rolling Stones are the longest-standing circus of all time.

All music is connected
especially in a little place like
England. Nothing comes from
nothing at all.

Mick Jagger

A PEBBLE IN
THE POND

2

KEITH: By the time I met Mick on the train at Dartford, I'd already heard one or two tracks by Muddy Waters, but I didn't actually own any of his records. Mick had a copy of *The Best Of Muddy Waters* – which is *still* probably the best of Muddy Waters. Within a few days of seeing each other, I either went over to Mick's place or he came over to mine. And almost inexplicably, from that one meeting between Mick and myself, with me wanting to know where he'd got his records from, and then as we listened to them together, we realised that we were really in touch – which we still are now, in this weird, bizarre, night-and-day method of ours. When it comes to music, if we work on it together, there's something that just happens. I don't know how or why: I leave that to the mysteries of alchemy…

We started listening to records and playing a bit, and Mick said that he'd been singing in a band that was doing Buddy Holly numbers at school hops and stuff like that, although I never saw him performing any of those. And then he said, "I've got a mate called Dick Taylor who's got a spare house we can play in", and I said, "Dick Taylor?" I was going to art school with Dick, who was also a bit of a guitar player and who had gone to grammar school with Mick. Suddenly there was an extra connection between us, one of those coincidences. Dick's mum and dad had gone away on holiday for a couple of weeks, so we said, "Why don't we get together round there and knock it out?" Another friend called Bob Beckwith came too – he had an amplifier, which really made an important difference, and he had a Grundig tape recorder: you could hear how bad you were and still think you were fantastic.

So without really saying, "Let's start a band" or anything, we just began to have fun playing together and figuring out how it was all done. And at the same time Mick was already getting records from Chess while we were still waiting for them to be released in England. I didn't know that you could do that with Chess Records, but Mick was much more organised.

Mick was in contact with a guy called Dave Godin, who lived up the road in Bexley Heath. He was a real collector, a great aficionado, and so we started to go round to his house. There were all these records; we just went, "Jesus Christ!". It was like a treasure trove. That was the moment you realised how much there was to explore and how much further you could delve in. Those were the days when you could knock on somebody's door and say, "What's the title of that Chuck Berry song?" or ask about some T-Bone Walker B-side – something really obscure – and they wouldn't know, but they'd say "Oh, come in and have a cup of tea and have a look", or "Let me look through the list", and they'd have filing cabinets of the stuff.

It was an expanding thing. I think the meeting between Mick and me was like what happens when you throw a pebble into a pond and the water just ripples outwards. It still is a fucking big pond. It's like, "Look at all that water and that's just the top"…

MICK: Alexis Korner used to play in this club in Ealing, and I would go there on Saturday nights, for a laugh. It was full of all these trainspotters who needed somewhere to go, just a bunch of anoraks. The audience was mainly guys – most of whom were pretty terrible – and the girls were very thin on the ground. That was the initial audience for the kind of music that Alexis was playing and then it expanded a bit. We used to get other people coming down there and the whole thing got going. I used to go every weekend and do a number. It was so close to where I lived anyway, it was nothing, just a ten-minute tube ride away.

KEITH: Throughout his entire life Alexis had a passion for the blues and, damn, the man was on the radio and everything. If you were on the BBC, now come on, you'd risen to almighty heights – getting on the radio? I mean, wow! Alexis's band was like an informal school; the number of musicians that he turned round and encouraged is huge. Alexis was a good guitar player, but he was also completely dedicated to his music and he was dedicated to encouraging other people into it. You never got the elbow from Alexis. There were times when he might say to you, if you had a problem, "I think you should forget about it, if only because it's making your life too depressing", but otherwise he was always encouraging. From Alexis's point of view, he had led an uphill fight to get the blues and R&B accepted, and suddenly it burst wide open through bigger flood gates than he could ever have expected, with his half-hour radio programme once a week on the BBC's Third Programme.

> *When it comes to music, if we work on it together, there's something that just happens. I don't know how or why: I leave that to the mysteries of alchemy.*
>
> *Keith*

CHARLIE: Alexis was the musicologist. Alexis knew everything about music. He had started off as a disc jockey and had hundreds of records. He used to live with a guy called Charles Fox, who was the spokesman for the avant-garde and presented radio programmes where he would play records by people like Albert Ayler. Their apartment was on two floors in Moscow Road, off Queensway, and the rooms were stacked with all these albums they had been given.

Alexis played this music called R&B, which I'd never heard of, and he had Dick Heckstall-Smith on saxophone, a very modern player, and a harmonica player called Cyril Davies who I'd never heard the likes of. A year or so after I'd joined Alexis, he had one of the most avant-garde jazz bands of the time, a bit like Charlie Mingus's band (Alexis would love me to say this: Mingus was one of his favourite jazz musicians because of his real blues roots), with Ginger Baker on drums, Jack Bruce on bass and Graham Bond on organ. Cyril had left by then, and it was a very weird band. Alexis had a fantastically eclectic taste in music. It really was about one step away from rock'n'roll in its spirit; one of the greatest bands ever put together.

KEITH: Mick had heard about Alexis Korner and the Ealing Club. He managed to blag his dad's car – which was always amazing to me because we never had a car. It seemed as if we had been piddling about with the guitars round at Dick Taylor's house forever, but it was probably only a matter of four or five months. At that time I wasn't looking at myself as a guitar player. I was just very interested and I enjoyed playing – I'd done a few school gigs with a friend of mine called Mike Ross, playing country songs. But Alexis was such a great guy, he would ask anybody who could play, "Do you want to take over for ten minutes while I have a drink?", and you'd get up there quivering and ankle deep in sweat. It was a terrible place, really.

We knew as soon as we walked on that everyone went crazy, but nobody wanted to give us a gig. It wasn't because we weren't any good, but because we weren't playing the "right kind" of music.

Mick

CHARLIE: I have a very clear memory of being at the Ealing Club and playing with Brian and Keith. The calfskin on the drums would go as dead as a doormat because there were so many people in there – the ceiling used to drip. They put this thing up like a tent above us and as the evening went on it got lower and lower and if you touched it a stream of condensation would come running down your back. And you couldn't hear a bloody thing.

Brian, Charlie and Keith in their early Ealing Club days.

KEITH: The Ealing Club was like a sub-basement that went down underneath Ealing tube station. There were glass paving stones which leaked like shit, and the condensation in the club was probably the worst I've ever come across. That's why I can still work those joints now, from all the practice I had there. You were literally stepping in an inch of water in the middle of all the electrics. It's a miracle more people weren't fried down there! The club belonged to this Lebanese or Syrian guy, who was a mean little ferret, but all right in his own way – you got to know your archetypal London club manager, the ones who'd say, "You're playing or I'll break your neck".

Ealing was basically full of aficionados. You didn't go down there to get laid, and if you tried to, it was probably somebody else's old lady, anyway. In any case, it was a very male-orientated scene at the time. Later, as the crowd began to grow, there were more females coming in and also guys were bringing their girlfriends along, but at the beginning it was very much boy's stuff, almost like a trainspotters' or stamp collectors' club. It was a very

small scene and the way it exploded so quickly was beyond anybody's expectation. We didn't really know it was happening, it just did. From there the ripples got bigger. We had gone down to the Ealing Club and there we found Alexis Korner, Brian Jones, Paul Jones and Charlie Watts. Ian Stewart came into the picture, and of course there was Cyril Davies on harmonica.

MICK: I'm a Little Walter fan, but I can't remember when I first started to play harmonica. In the early days, there was obviously a competitive aspect between me and Brian, in the same way that Keith was competitive with Brian on guitar. The thing about Brian was that he did play a lot of instruments. He used to play the clarinet, although I never actually heard him, certainly not with us, especially as the clarinet was a sort of no-no instrument out of trad jazz – you wouldn't ever want to pick up a clarinet with a rock band – but I know the clarinet had been his main instrument. And he played recorder on 'Ruby Tuesday', which I think was one of the few times he ever played a wind instrument on a Rolling Stones record. But Brian *was* a wind instrument person, so to speak. In the beginning, I think Brian was a better harmonica player than me, and then I got better than him, although that's very subjective because he had a completely different way of playing.

RONNIE: When I went down to see Art sing with Cyril Davies, Mick Jagger would be in the front row. He'd ask Cyril, "How do you bend a note?" and Cyril would say, "Well, you get a pair of pliers…"

MICK: Cyril Davies was the only harmonica player I could see play live. There wasn't anybody else, unfortunately, although Cyril was a really, really good harmonica player. Much better than I could ever be. That was his thing. He used to sing, but not particularly well. I learned an enormous amount from Cyril, but he wasn't an expansive person, he was very gruff, almost to the point of rudeness.

It was from Brian, Mick and Keith that I first seriously learned about R&B. I knew nothing about it. The blues to me was Charlie Parker or Johnny Dodds playing slow.

Charlie

First of all I did figure out that you had to have loads of harmonicas in different keys, which was very expensive; you had to have them because otherwise you were stuck. And you also needed reeds because they would often break and frequently be badly made. Then I wanted to know how you played harmonica, but Cyril refused to tell me. So I just observed him. I used to chat to him and in the end he got kind of used to me, but the harmonica is not an instrument that is very easy to teach, because you're not sitting there with a keyboard, saying, "Oh, Mick this is how you play, you put your finger on there". With the harmonica you can't really show someone what to do in their mouth… I'm sure there are books and tutors that you can buy, but what I did was to sit around with my one harmonica listening to records by Jimmy Reed, who conveniently only plays in a couple of keys, so there were only two or three variations. That's really how I learned to play – playing along to Jimmy Reed records.

KEITH: The first time that Alexis invited Mick and me up on stage to do a couple of numbers, I suddenly realised we were going to do 'Roll Over Beethoven' – now that was definitely not up Alexis's *strasse*. So I started "duh, duh, duh" and I saw Alexis deliberately break a string so he didn't have to play. Although he had this fantastic eclecticism, he didn't want to be part of rock'n'roll. Cyril Davies was also very anti at that time, although he changed his mind within a few months. Cyril would say, "This is not a rock'n'roll club", and so I'd have to take on this tough panel beater.

MICK: In England and in America there was a division of people who liked a certain kind of jazz. In the same way that for some people modern 20th-century art is a non-starter, for other people any jazz that had been recorded after World War II – or whatever the particular date it was that they had in mind – was the same. All these clubs like the Ealing Club or the Marquee had been traditional jazz venues putting on Dixieland bands. I never liked that music personally, although it was very popular in England: Acker Bilk, that kind of thing… The musicians played the arrangements exactly as they had been written in the old days. They were quite good musicians, but all they ever played was this stuff.

KEITH: At this time there was a huge strain between what we were doing and traditional jazz music, which basically represented the whole London club scene. All the clubs and pubs were locked up within a few promoters' hands and suddenly I guess that they felt the chill winter coming in and they realised that there would be no more 'Midnight In Moscow' or 'Petite Fleur' for them. They had become a little bit complacent, and at the same time there was a growing realisation in my generation that not everything had to be in the same bag – there was a nice fluid feeling amongst people that things were changing. But some of those older people really didn't want to move with the times. It was a very bitter fight, especially when we had no resources. Some of those musicians – who shall remain nameless and who are probably dead anyway – really resisted. You'd get taken round the back and shown a razor and they'd say, "Take this fucking rock'n'roll shit out of here, my son". We didn't feel that we were trying to push a hole through their right to make a living; it was just like, "Hey, give me a little elbow room, man, all I want to do is play as well".

MICK: Chris Barber was very influential, because Lonnie Donegan was in his band and also because Chris was the person who brought Muddy Waters to England. I think Muddy Waters had toured England previously with his electric band, which went down like a lead balloon, apparently. All these places like the Marquee Club were traditional jazz venues and so they had this aesthetic that you could only play *this* kind of music with *this* kind of line-up in *this* kind of way. Cyril Davies was exactly the same about blues. It was, "Blues is like this and harmonica playing is like this, and da-da da-da". I didn't know what they were on about really, because I was just interested in music as a whole. I didn't really give a shit: if I liked Tab Hunter singing 'Red Sails In The Sunset', I went out and bought the record. I'm still the same now really; most musicians are. But some of these people were seriously purist, and they thought that the Rolling Stones in the early days was a rock'n'roll band, which we *were*. We knew as soon as we walked on that everyone went crazy, but nobody wanted to give us a gig. It wasn't because we weren't any good, but because we weren't playing the "right kind" of music. We were like Muddy Waters with the Chris Barber Jazz Band. We weren't playing the right music in the right place at the right time.

KEITH: I think the trad jazz guys must have saturated their own market – there were just too many of them around – because within a few weeks of us starting to play and doing the intervals with Alexis at the Marquee, we got the main gig – mind you, that was only £50 if you were lucky, and that had to be shared out amongst the whole band – and the trad jazz bands found themselves out of work, which was the time when we experienced a lot of that aggression.

CHARLIE: When Alexis's band was offered the Thursday night gig at the Marquee, I wasn't in the country, I was working as a graphic designer in Scandinavia. So it was like, "Alexis Korner, who's he?" A friend of mine said, "You've got to come back and do this", so I said, "I don't know him really, I've met him a couple of times, what's this band?" I arrived back having finished my work – at which time I might add I actually played with Don Byas, when he sat in with this student band from the Conservatory – and did a rehearsal with Alexis. That's where I met my wife Shirley, because two of the guys in the band, the piano player Keith Scott and Andy Hoogenboom, the bass player, were from Hornsey Art School, which is where Shirley was studying, and she came down with Andy and his wife.

Cyril Davies played what I later learned was "Chicago blues". Chicago for me was jazz played by Eddie Condon and Dave Tough. The music Cyril was playing with Alexis was coming from folk songs out of the Mississippi Delta. So I was playing it without knowing what the hell it was.

Alexis saw his band as being able to play anything, anything at all. Then it all became a bit difficult because although he

> *Edith Grove — oh dear, what a dump, a beautiful dump. There was nothing much to eat, but that didn't matter: at least we could buy some records.*
>
> *Keith*

*Charlie playing with
Cyril Davies and Alexis
Korner.*

was creating this new sort of music, he effectively cut his right arm off when Cyril, who was the star of the band, left him.

Cyril's big argument with Alexis was that Alexis wasn't playing Chicago blues, and Alexis couldn't see that. I loved both of them, but I was not going to sit in the middle of them arguing about the band; there were also a lot of things going on about the money and that sort of thing. I wasn't going to get involved. I was just the drummer in the band, two quid a gig, and – knowing nothing about the music they were playing – I couldn't even join in the arguments because I didn't have a clue what they were talking about.

In the end I left Alexis because he was heading off in a different direction, and I could feel that I wasn't up to it. I said, "Ginger Baker should do this", and he took over from me. Ginger was seriously strong in those days, ahead of a lot of people. I remember the drum kit he used to play with Alexis – he had made it himself out of clear blue plastic, very avant-garde.

I'd met Brian through Alexis, maybe even before – and I had also met Mick through him. Alexis didn't have a regular singer. There was Cyril Davies, but he wouldn't do certain songs, or didn't want to, and we had an American GI called Ronnie Jones and a couple of other Geno Washington-type singers. Mick Jagger was another one who Alexis would call upon to sing with the band. They were like sit-in singers. I remember going with Alexis to play next door to the Hilton at Londonderry House. The Marquis of Londonderry was a friend of Mick's, actually, and he loved jazz. Mick was the singer, and the guest of honour was Benny Goodman, who sat in and played with us.

I knew Keith from when he and Brian would sit in at the Ealing Club. Alexis had this

incredible habit of breaking strings, so he'd have to go off and change a string, and it would be Brian and Keith up there doing their thing.

KEITH: Edith Grove – oh dear, what a dump, a beautiful dump. It was so inconvenient to keep going back to Dartford from London, and we thought that if we could scrape just a few quid together we could afford it. There was nothing much to eat, but that didn't matter, at least we could buy some records. I think it was probably through living together that winter that we suddenly really felt like we were a band without even knowing it. It's not as though it was somebody's big idea that: "We will now form a band and I hereby state…". It just came together.

CHARLIE: I went to live with Brian and Keith at their flat in Edith Grove. It was a ridiculous household. Brian and Keith used to be hilarious together, but it was actually Mick's flat, so it was, as usual, on his head whatever we did. It's funny how things don't change that much. It was always more of a family than a band. I was looking for a job – I was what actors call "between engagements" – and slowly we got more work. I started to like R&B a lot because I spent a lot of time sitting around with Brian and Keith listening to it. I had never liked Elvis until Keith played me the Sun Records material – I loved that; and then the early stuff with D.J. Fontana on; I think that's fabulous.

KEITH: We didn't make any money. We were spending a year or so begging, borrowing and stealing. We went round picking up old beer bottles, me, Brian and Mick, and we'd take all the empties back, which was how we'd scrape through the week, or buy a new guitar string.

Although Mick and Keith wrote 'Sitting on A Fence', standing on a wall was another desperate attempt to ring the changes for an endless stream of publicity shots. The photograph on the next page, those on page 45, one on page 58 and the two on page 59 were taken during the same extensive session.

Since we didn't have any gigs and nothing much to do, Brian and I started developing this interweaving way of playing two guitars. It became obvious to us when we listened to Jimmy Reed. The two-guitar thing on Jimmy's records is so laid out, so stark and beautifully consistent – he hardly changed his sound at all in 25 years – that you could understand how to use it on other things rather than just copying Jimmy Reed. Brian and I had nothing to do during that damn cold winter of 1962–63 except shiver in our overcoats and figure out Jimmy's stuff. From there we moved on to Little Walter and Louis and David Myers, who were members of his backing band – and then, of course, the Muddy Waters stuff along with Jimmy Rodgers, Howlin' Wolf and Hubert Sumlin. We listened to the team work, trying to work out what was going on in those records; how you could play together with two guitars and make it sound like four or five.

We thought, "If we can get that down, we've really got something different going". In English bands you had one hot picker and another one who just strummed. There was no attempt to make a cohesive sound out of the two guitars; it was "You're rhythm, you're lead" and never the twain shall meet. What we heard, after listening to Jimmy Reed, Chuck Berry and Muddy Waters and all the blues players, was that it should be seamless, that you shouldn't ever hear the joins – like good editing.

CHARLIE: It was from Brian, Mick and Keith that I first seriously learned about R&B. I knew nothing about it. The blues to me was Charlie Parker or Johnny Dodds playing slow. And Chuck Berry I learned mainly through Mick, funnily enough, with the lyrics. Mick was the first guy I had met who could sing the lyrics all the way through on songs like 'No Money Down' or 'Jaguar And The Thunderbird' – he could do it now I'm sure, if you asked him…

KEITH: I originally met Ian Stewart, along with Brian, at the Ealing Club. Stu was the only one of us who had any financial means and any organisational capacity. Stu was another person like Alexis, in a way. He was very full of enthusiasm for his music and for anybody else who wanted to share it, and also he could play so much better than any of the rest of them when it came down to straight boogie-woogie piano.

CHARLIE: Ian Stewart was a great catalyst for the jazz blues in this band. Stu had taste that never changed throughout his life. He came to the music from a different angle to Alexis, or Keith. He was from the school of Count Basie playing boogie-woogie, which Stu loved, playing very straight ahead, in a loose way. The period he lived through underwent a hell of a lot of changes, particularly in jazz, but he never budged. He had terrific convictions. Even living through the excitement of John Coltrane and his quartet, Stu never budged, even then. In the same way, his taste with the Rolling Stones never moved away from the Ealing Club, and he would criticise us endlessly if we did.

KEITH: Stu was frustrated because he didn't really have anyone to play with, so I think it was really his idea for us to rehearse. I don't think Brian, Mick or I thought of it. We were just hanging around, having no deliberate ideas at all. So it was Stu who said "For 15 bob we can rent the Bricklayers' Arms", and he and Brian organised it. The rest of us were all just try-outs as far as Stu was concerned.

When I first went to rehearse, I remember going into the Bricklayers' Arms and saying to the landlady, "I've got a guitar". She goes, "Upstairs", and I went up to the first floor, turned the corner and heard this beautiful Albert Ammons-style piano. I'd just gone up one flight of stairs and suddenly I was in Chicago. And there's Stu playing the upright piano, looking out of the window – he was watching his bike, I realised, which was tied up to a parking meter – and at the same time playing the most beautiful Albert Ammons stuff. He didn't even hear me enter. I just stood there and listened, and I think from that minute I've always felt that the Rolling Stones is actually Stu's band. I was listening to him and thinking, "Jesus Christ, this is making me nervous, he's out of my league".

At the beginning there was quite a little tussle, I think, between certain factions amongst us, including Brian and the other guys involved in the rehearsal: Geoff Bradford, who was an accomplished guitarist, and Brian Knight, who was a good blues shouter and a friend of Art Wood's – everybody's connected one way or another. Stu encouraged me to play the Chuck Berry stuff, while the other guys wanted to play strictly Howlin' Wolf or Leadbelly and bluesy material. So you had that traditionalist blues thing going. I once saw this fought out in the Manchester Free Trade Hall between an audience who watched Muddy Waters play acoustic guitar for an hour, applauding magnificently, only to boo him off when he came on with his Chicago band.

There was no drummer at the time, we couldn't afford one. Mick Avory and Tony Chapman did come along, but it would just be for the one night. Tony Chapman was there because he knew Bill Wyman and it was his amplifier... But we weren't even thinking of gigs. We were still just playing together.

Drummers are the most expensive people in town, and also the very rarest, which makes them kind of hard to get. Charlie had been playing with Alexis Korner. Alexis had to let Charlie go because he had an audition with the BBC and they wanted Alexis to use Ginger Baker. This was because Ginger already had one of their union licences or something. Charlie had left Alexis's band and joined Ronnie's brother Art Wood's band. There were negotiations going on with Charlie via Stu: "If you can guarantee me – I forget how many – regular gigs, and if you can offer me more money, then I'd rather play with you guys than with the Art Wood band". He said he'd really love to play with us, but it would cost him too much to drag his drums across town.

RONNIE: Charlie was the drummer in my brother's band, and he said to Art, "I've got an offer to join this interval band called the Rolling Stones. What do you think I should do?" Charlie thought it would only last a week or two or something, but Art said, "Yeah, go for it. If you want to join this band, we'll give you a hand over with your kit" and Art physically helped Charlie shift his drum kit from the Marquee across to Ken Colyer's club or somewhere in Wardour Street – and since that moment there's been no looking back for Charlie.

CHARLIE: For me it was just another job offer, to be honest. I was in three bands already when I joined the Rolling Stones. None of them had any work happening, though. I still go past the place where I used to rehearse with them, which is now an off-licence. It used to be a pub, not the Bricklayers' Arms, but another one in Edith Grove, on the corner. We'd go and get fish and chips from the shop next door – that place is actually still there. The rehearsal room was on the corner. I have no idea why I was asked to go along. I'd never met Bill Wyman before; I just remember going to rehearsal for the first time and him being there with this ridiculously big amplifier – which really was the only reason that he was in the band, according to Keith – with some funny green vinyl stuff stuck all over the cabinet. Bill has tiny hands; he was a very un-bass-guitar-like person and his bass guitar was really small, too.

KEITH: Charlie didn't know any of the repertoire, but then who did, except a few guys in Chicago? Jimmy Reed becomes essential in this story as far as the Stones are concerned. Brian and I were listening to the two guitars working, and Charlie was listening to Earl Phillips – what a drummer – and hearing how subtle he was. From listening to his playing, Charlie saw his way clear to play a backbeat rock'n'roll and still swing with his own identity. It wasn't just a matter of playing rock'n'roll, bang. All of the best rock'n'roll records had people like Earl Palmer on them; they were all jazz drummers. You didn't just pull a switch and find that a rock'n'roll drummer had appeared overnight. Drummers like Earl Palmer and Slam Stewart had been playing that shit forever; it was just a matter of simplifying it. So I think for Charlie it was while he was listening to the subtleties of Earl Phillips playing behind Jimmy Reed that he saw that there could be different approaches to playing R&B, that you could be your own man within this framework. And I think that's what turned Charlie on.

CHARLIE: Keith and Brian turned me on to Jimmy Reed and people like that. I learned that Earl Phillips was playing on those records like a jazz drummer, playing swing, with a straight four. Freddy Below, on the other hand, played shuffle, which is what they did in Chicago. So on a lot of the Chuck Berry songs, which we turned into "straight eight" rhythms – which is what Chuck Berry played – Freddy Below was playing "four, four, swing", and the mixture when it hits right is incredible, but if it doesn't, one of you is going to be out of sync. So we learned to play the Freddy Below way.

> *Drummers are the most expensive people in town, and also the very rarest, which makes them kind of hard to get. Charlie said he'd really love to play with us, but it would cost him too much to drag his drums across town.*
>
> *Keith*

MICK: You were so adamant that blues was the music for you, you wouldn't listen to anything else. It was like, "Jazz, I'm not going to listen to this crap". Charlie liked all that kind of stuff too, but then Charlie had been playing for Alexis Korner and he had never played rock'n'roll before, I don't think. It was another world, but he understood what shuffles were because they are also there in jazz. We used to have these other drummers, including Tony Chapman, Mick Avory and Carlo Little, who always comes up with this story about how he could have been a millionaire and all that crap. Carlo used to play these great fast eights, just like the early days of power drumming. The kind of thing that John Bonham used to play later on with Led Zeppelin. All the American drummers – D.J.Fontana or J.M.Van Eaton, the drummer with Jerry Lee Lewis's band – were much lighter players. They came out of traditional country music backgrounds and did these little shuffles, whereas the drummers with Little Richard came from a kind of jump music background – "babadoom, babadoom" stuff – which they played very hard, and which formed the basis for drummers like Bonham and Keith Moon.

When we played with Carlo Little he would put all this stuff into the band. It was very exciting to play it, but Charlie had no knowledge of that and so he just played with more of a jazz feel. And that's why the Rolling Stones was a more interesting band than bands like Freddie and the Dreamers, Herman's Hermits, the Searchers or the Hollies. We were

Brian pictured outside a watering hole in Richmond, south-west London, in early 1963. The Station Hotel, where the Crawdaddy Club was hosted, was a more regular haunt. The local Richmond and Twickenham Times gave the band their first write-up that April, which began, "a musical magnet is drawing the jazz beatniks to Richmond". Brian carried the clipping in his wallet for months afterwards.

very different from them. I'm not denigrating them – they were what they were, and sometimes they did things very well – but they were playing one kind of music, whereas we had a much broader, much deeper, musical background.

KEITH: There's no such thing as a rock'n'roll drummer. There are only drummers. Sometimes you wonder about what you've spawned: guys with three bass drums and five million cymbals... This thing is supposed to fly, to move and to swing. It's not supposed to just hit you in the head. To have a drummer from the beginning who could play with the sensibility of Charlie Watts is one of the best hidden assets I've had, because I've never had to think about the drummer and what he's going to do. I just say, "Charlie, it goes like this" and we'll kick it around a bit and it's done. I can throw him ideas and I never have to worry about the beat. He's always been like that. It's a blessing. It's only on the few occasions when I've had to jam with a bad drummer that I realise how lucky I've been all these years.

MICK: The Rolling Stones played blues, but we also played Ritchie Valens if we wanted to. To my mind, playing Little Walter and Ritchie Valens was all the same. It's not the same kind of music, but we made it the same. It was just a laugh. So if you look at the Rolling Stones' back catalogue you'll find that it's very varied, whereas a lot of the people we had to deal with in fact had very narrow viewpoints. They were all involved in the BBC and they were very snobbish about rock'n'roll – with some reason, because what they understood as British rock'n'roll had consisted of very bad American covers, often done, to be honest, by people with very little talent, but who looked very cute. There's nothing wrong with cute, but they were not particularly good at what they did and tended not to have any kind of career potential. Cliff Richard was one of those people, in fact, but he did have some talent and lasted, whereas the others didn't. So these blues purists we knew didn't really recognise Elvis as a talent that had any meaning to their world, although in reality he kind of straddled it all. And we were doing the same thing, in a way.

KEITH: We decided to put an ad in *Jazz News*, because the only place you could aim at with R&B were these little jazz clubs, which was the big alternative music scene at the time. If you didn't go to the ballrooms in your beehive, you went to jazz clubs. And also *Jazz News* had far cheaper ad rates than *Melody Maker*. Brian was on the phone talking to them: "We'd like to place an ad. We're available for work, and you can call us at..." The voice on the other end of the line obviously said, "What are you called?" Panic. *The Best Of Muddy Waters* album was lying on the floor – and Track One was 'Rollin' Stone Blues'. So the band's name was picked for us by Muddy Waters.

CHARLIE: They hung their hat on this label called "R&B" because Brian would sit for hours composing letters about R&B. The letters would go on forever – he used to write to *Melody Maker* telling them that in this black and white advert it must include the description "R&B"; it couldn't be just a band. Brian was very instrumental in pushing the band at the beginning. Keith and I would look at him and say he was barmy. It was a crusade to him, a) to get us on the stage in a club and be paid half-a-crown and b) to be billed as an R&B band. It was a bit like saying, "We don't play New Orleans music, we play bebop". Nobody knew what he was talking about except a few maniacs who owned all the albums, but once the movement started you suddenly found there *were* other people out there, like a band in Newcastle called the Animals, who, when they played Chuck Berry and R&B, were bloody good.

Thursday nights at the Marquee, at the time Alexis Korner took over, was the club's down night, when they would usually only get 100 people in the audience. Whereas on Sunday nights, when Johnny Dankworth played, there might be 900. Within about a month of Alexis starting on those Thursday nights, Harold Pendleton had 950 people packed in there; he wasn't allowed to admit any more. I think it was because people liked the players, and you could dance to the music.

But then the Rolling Stones went from 900 people to a thousand at Ken Colyer's jazz club on a Sunday afternoon at Studio 51 in Great Newport Street. Every week that we played, there seemed to be more people, and it just grew bigger and bigger. I'm not saying that it didn't need pointing in a few directions along the way, by Giorgio Gomelsky and then Andrew Oldham, but it did accelerate all the time.

KEITH: Giorgio Gomelsky was the promoter behind the Crawdaddy Club at the Station Hotel in Richmond. Up until then I think we were just copping gigs on the phone. People would call up and say, "Do you want to come and do a gig at the Red Lion next week?" Stu was also doing a lot of fixing, but that was just on a very local basis. It was Gomelsky who organised us and made those Sunday nights at the Crawdaddy an event, rather than just being a pick-up thing, so that we started getting a name.

Giorgio was very much like Alexis, desperately in love with a certain kind of attitude, a dedicated non-conformist, which didn't go down at all badly with me, or any of us. He was the kind of guy where you could go round to his apartment, have some very strong coffee, smoke some Sobranies and map out plots, because he was plugged into the club scene. He had contacts that we didn't, and he was really good at organising and making something of the Stones, even though it was still on a very small scale. Giorgio was the one who focused it by saying, "Well, we've got to get one place and make it happen there, and then you can build on that", and he understood that people would then come to you instead of you having to go to them.

CHARLIE: Giorgio hired the pub for £10 at the weekend. He was like Alexis, but whereas Alexis could do it with music, Georgio did it with words. He had boundless enthusiasm and could talk for hours – which is nice – but the reality is that he was the one who booked us in there. Then it took off and Giorgio could

> *When we played at the Crawdaddy, I think we were initially just a change in the menu, but then it became like the plate of the day.*
>
> *Keith*

see it build. He knew exactly how many people were actually turning up each week – we could sense it more than see it – he was the one who'd got his eye on the till.

KEITH: Given that era in London, unless you went down to some of the West Indian clubs in London – places you visited either not knowing what the club's name was or wondering how you ended up there – you couldn't get much more tribal than what was going on at the Crawdaddy, and then gradually at other venues like the Ricky Tick Club in Windsor or Eel Pie Island. We actually became a West London band, because that's where the gigs happened to be, and when you're that age coming from Southeast London, West London feels like the other side of the horizon. I guess a lot of it had to do with Stu coming from Surrey and also that many of the art schools were based in West London, at Twickenham, Richmond and Kingston, and they didn't want any more Dixieland jazz shoved down their throats. The students were probably already there; they just went along to their usual hang-out. I always wonder how much depends on your local pub and who's appearing that night: what's more important, the pub or who's appearing? Usually you hang where your hang is and see what's on, so I think that we were initially just a change in the menu, but then it became like the plate of the day.

To me it seemed more that the crowd who were already there just grew bigger. If you wanted to let yourself go in West London in the early '60s, I guess that's where you could really let your steam off. It was sweaty. It was hot. There were so many different people involved: some of our first fans were little chicks from the East End, which was another of our enclaves. We didn't play down there that often, although we had regular gigs for a while in Dalston and Walthamstow and places like that. A great hard core of Cockney chicks followed us around – I still remember one or two. They were probably our first female fans.

> *The Crawdaddy is where I realised that Mick could actually work a stage about the size of a rug better than anybody in the world – except for maybe James Brown.*
>
> *Keith*

CHARLIE: There was no space at the Crawdaddy. That's why Mick used to shake his head and all of that, because he had no room to move. He shook his head, which became a joke, simply because he had nowhere to dance. He basically had to dance on a table. And he used to have his maracas going as well.

I like to think we became popular – and this is feedback from Shirley and other people who knew us way back then – because we played music to dance to, which was a massive appeal to the young people. In addition, we weren't bad looking and I think Mick's gyrating was amazing. It still is, but it was especially so when he was dancing in a space the size of a tabletop.

KEITH: On Sundays we used to play at Ken Colyer's club in Soho for an hour-and-a-half or so in the afternoon – which was always a great gig – and then we'd drive straight down to the Station Hotel in Richmond and you'd think it was the Queen's funeral or something. There would be double lines queuing around the hall just to get into this one little room; there was sweat hanging from the rafters. We'd play from 7 to 11 with a couple of breaks of ten minutes here and there. We'd probably do two ten-minute versions of

A sequence of publicity shots.
Charlie: Brian was a lot of fun then, he was really funny in those days.

On stage at the Crawdaddy Club in Richmond, where the band regularly drew full houses. It was at the Crawdaddy that the Beatles met the Stones en route home from recording Thank Your Lucky Stars *at Twickenham TV studios nearby. This early-1963 visitation was reciprocated at the Royal Albert Hall.*

'Pretty Thing' and people would think it was all one piece. You really got your chops together there. They wanted their music all the time and you'd better deliver, it was like, "Waiter, give me some music".

The Crawdaddy was our training ground, where Mick and I learned how we could screw something up royally, and at the same time nobody would know it except us. It's where Charlie and I learned how to throw ideas up in the air and then go, "Whoops, that one stuck. Never mind, I've got it", how to pick up beats and how to cover the lead singer. At the time you're not even aware you're learning that shit, it's only later on you realise that this was one of the important places. And the Crawdaddy is where I realised that Mick could actually work a stage about the size of a rug better than anybody in the world – except for maybe James Brown at the time. The bigger the stage you give Mick, the harder it is to control him, but he can work with a coffee table if that's the only room there is available. Mick could make an awful lot out of a couple of square feet and that was what always impressed me; the fact that he was able to work in that confined space and still make it pop.

MICK: In those early gigs the one thing that audiences liked to do was participate. Even now in a really big place they like to participate in a small way, and in a smaller place they can participate a lot. They could do what they do now – "Oh yeah!" – and wave their arms, and they loved all that. That's what people still like to do when they go to a show and that's what I like doing with them. I'm not very good as an entertainer when they're all sitting down.

The audience had their own dancers. From this ragged collection of anoraks who made up the audience in the early, early days, they very quickly became a rather chic, well-dressed audience, college people, the art school crowd, and they had their own little way of dancing and wearing their hair really short. They had their own fashion, which changed very quickly, and they had their own dances, so we could look at them and go, "Yeah, OK, that's kind of interesting". And then when we used to go out to the provinces, we used to look at the audience and go, "Fuckin' hell!"

KEITH: England is so small. Maybe it's that very compactness about the country that made things take off – and you can't discount World War II as a factor for the generation that I belong to. When I didn't want to go to school I hid in a bomb site, and it was no different in Liverpool than it was in London, whereas in America the difference between Boston and LA is like a lifetime or maybe even a light year. The Beach Boys would never have made it in Boston.

There was a definite buzz in the air, just the fact that three or four of us had actually managed to put a band together and that we had started playing places. For me, the first time we struck out on our own marked a great change in my life, and at the same time the Beatles were beginning to make their mark. It was a definite turning point; even at the time you were able to take it on board, but what you did not realise, and could not realise, was how big a turning point it was. The only equivalent for me was 1956, when I first heard rock'n'roll.

It had grown from Stu putting out a few whispers here and there to Giorgio actually organising things, though not even on a semi-professional level, because he was a dedicated amateur. He was one of those great Russians, and he hated capitalism. He had to grow into it and he didn't grow into it very gracefully. It wasn't really his scene. Everything was on a very loose basis; nobody knew how big this thing was going to get. Giorgio could handle a few London clubs, but at that time nobody saw a market anywhere north of Watford. You wouldn't want to go there and catch something nasty. Beware the dragons and yokels!

One of the earliest publicity shots, turned into a postcard by Andrew Oldham for press purposes.

GIORGIO GOMELSKY

Giorgio Gomelsky founded the legendary Crawdaddy Club in Richmond, the springboard for the Rolling Stones. He went on to produce the Yardbirds, Julie Driscoll, John McLaughlin, Gong and Magma, among others. In the late 1970s he moved to New York.

I got to London from the Continent on a dank, dark and smoggy winter night in January 1955. I was twenty-one at the time and bent upon a very particular mission. I grew up during the troubled days of World War II all over Europe and lived my early teenage days under various restraints, which led to a pronounced inclination towards rebellion, an intense dislike of repression and exploitation and a strong identification with the underdog. It was during World War II that in a friend's attic I came across American pre-war jazz recordings hidden away, because, of course, it was forbidden to listen. When I heard Duke Ellington's 'Rockin' in Rhythm' and 'Caravan', something made me feel like a conspirator in an insurgency. I guess in those distant, pulsing sounds we heard the hope and promise of liberation from repression and suffering. That music became a means for me to explore, understand and describe the world; a tool of knowledge, a form of participation and social action.

After the war I became an inveterate jazz fan and proselytizer. Around 1954 I collaborated on a weekly radio jazz show and by 1955 I convinced the emerging TV department to let me make a documentary about the jazz scene in England. Thanks to a few dedicated musicians, jazz, trad jazz and skiffle had emerged in the early '50s. (As everybody knows, the Beatles' first attempts at music were as The Quarrymen, a skiffle group.)

Alas, by the late '50s the music business had reverted to a pale version of imported white and commercial American rock'n'roll, ruling the waves with Elvis imitators like Cliff Richard, Tommy Steel and Marty Wilde. Trad was dying out and skiffle was co-opted by the record companies.

By 1962 it became clear to me that the music scene was in a rut and a new twist was needed. Blues was the answer. Its simple, repetitive rhythms and chords and colourful lyrics provided an understandable communal message, and, although it clearly reflected a different social reality, it still dealt with the life of the underdog.

This is where I first met up with the Stones. From the mid-'50s on, Chris Barber had managed to bring over to England such blues greats as Memphis Slim, Big Bill Broonzy and Muddy Waters, whom no one had ever seen before. He also started replacing the skiffle segment in his shows with a blues set featuring Alexis Korner and Cyril Davies, who formed the first British blues outfit, Blues Incorporated. Sometime in 1962 they got a Thursday residency at The Marquee, and it became the epicentre of the nascent London blues scene.

Now, most jazz clubs didn't have liquor licences, so during the breaks people would sneak off to the nearest pubs. One night I was holding forth about the need to inject new energy into the scene when I heard a soft-spoken, lisping but firm voice behind me saying "Giorgio, you gotta come hear my band. Iths the betht blueth band in the land, weally!"

It was Brian Jones. He and his band certainly qualified as underdogs, so I decided I would help them at the earliest opportunity. I looked around for venues to promote "rhythm & blues" bands, as we decided to call them. My idea was to go as far away from central London as possible, convinced that the music itself had sufficient power to attract an audience.

One of the venues I found was the Station Hotel, just across from the last stop of the Richmond Underground District Line, about a half-hour outside London. It was a pub with a back room where, as in many others around London, promoters could put on music "clubs" and keep the door money to cover their expenses and pay the bands. Rents were cheap, but if the "club" didn't make it and the pub didn't sell booze, you'd soon be thrown out.

One Sunday the band I had booked didn't show up. The publican wanted to cancel our arrangement and I had to literally beg for another chance. This, then, became the opportunity to help Brian and his lot. I knew they had a firm dedication to the blues and were a keen lot, determined to spend whatever energy they could muster to prove themselves, and could be trusted to show up.

But there was a problem. It was Sunday night, and the ad for the gig had to be delivered to Melody Maker by Monday afternoon. It read:

RICHMOND, Station Hotel

Tidal waves of R&B sounds

From ROLLIN' STONES

The adventure had begun. I felt the Stones were given a raw deal by the jazz and music business establishment and I made it my new "mission" to change that. I spent the last pounds I had printing leaflets, visiting all the music pubs, making phone calls to friends and the press, beating the BRRB (British Rhythm & Blues) drum. Much was depending on next Sunday's turnout.

When the day came, I threw a peremptory look out the window and got a shock: it was snowing. This was a very unusual occurrence in London. No one was equipped to deal with that, and I wondered if Ian Stewart's rusty old Volkswagen bus would make it down to Richmond. I shouldn't have worried. (I have to say, during their stint at the Crawdaddy the Stones were of the utmost punctuality, come hell or high water.)

Alas, by opening time an audience totalling three people had braved the weather! Brian said to me, "Giowgio, there'th three people in the audience and six of uth' on stage. Should we bother to play?"

I knew this was going to be a very critical moment — for them, for my mission, for the blues in London, for the rest of humanity even!

"Brian," I answered, "how many people you think could fit in here?"

"A hundred perhaps?"

"Okay," I said. "Play as if there were one hundred people here, and they'll come..."

They seemed relieved someone had made a decision, and play they did, not just one set, but the customary two 45-minute ones. I knew then they had the substance to mark their presence on the scene and turn on a new generation to the blues and its rich reflections of life. (This is also why I rarely went to see them in later years. I had witnessed perhaps one of their best performances ever, at the very start of their career.)

At the end of the evening, I spoke to our three punters and asked them if they had enjoyed the evening.

"Man, it was great. This is our music."

I asked them if they knew two people each to bring along next week. If so, they would get in free.

So, the following Sunday, nine people showed up. The publican, who by this time had noticed our determination but still doubted this "blues thing" would ever get off the ground, complained again about the attendance.

"Look," I told him, "we've tripled the audience, and will do so again next week". And we did. The nine people each brought two friends, so (including the nine who got in free) we went to twenty-seven, and the week after to over seventy. In nearby Kingston there was an art college, so I posted a flier on the students' bulletin board, and the week after dozens of them showed up.

At first, most of this new audience was boys, blues fans and collectors. Some were budding musicians, like the soon-to-be Yardbirds and Eric Clapton, who often showed up with hard-to-find albums under their arms, so we started employing them as DJs between sets.

Slowly a pattern for the evening emerged. The first set was a kind of warm-up; new songs and arrangements were tried out, almost like a public rehearsal. Then there was a 45-minute break and everyone went to the bar to partake in a jar or two. Since we had to be out of the place by 10pm, the second set would start around 9:15. By now everyone was well tanked-up and the music more intense. The idea was to get our audience to participate in some way. But how do you dance to this music? Mostly they were just standing there gaping. The band ended up with an infectiously pulsating extended version of a Bo Diddley song, either 'Pretty Thing' or 'Doin' the Crawdad', but no one was moving.

This puzzled me. Perhaps it was shyness, or they needed some kind of an example they could follow. One night when the band was really giving out, I signalled to my friend and assistant Hamish Grimes to get on a table so everyone would see him and start waving his arms over his head. Within seconds the whole crowd was undulating. This was perhaps the single most important event in the development of the Stones' ability to build a link between stage and floor, to connect and become joined to an audience, to bring about something resembling a tribal ritual, not unlike "a revivalist meeting in the deep South", as Patrick Doncaster described it a few weeks later in the *Daily Mirror*. No one had seen anything like this in the sedate and reticent London of 1963. It was exciting and foreboding. It heralded that a drastic social-cultural turn was on the books.

Over the next few weeks more punters came. The word of mouth worked like a dream. The place got so popular people had to stand in line from two o'clock in the afternoon to get into the place five hours later. It got so crowded that the boys who wanted to bring their girlfriends had to carry them into the room on their shoulders.

The breakthrough had happened. Now we had to go to the next step, spreading the news. A young journalist working for the very conservative *Richmond & Twickenham Times* managed to get a whole page about the club past his editors. The *Daily Mirror*, the biggest newspaper in the land, gave us an amazing plug. Unfortunately, this alarmed the pub's owners, the huge Ind Coope Brewery, and we were given notice that the Crawdaddy's days at the Station Hotel were over.

That same day I got news that my father had passed away in Switzerland, and the next day I was on a plane. Enid Tidy (my lady at the time) and Hamish Grimes, with the help of Harold Pendleton – by then convinced of the legitimacy of the undertaking – found a new home for the Crawdaddy on the grounds of the nearby Richmond Athletic Association, which could accommodate nearly 1000 people, three times the size of the Station Hotel.

The Stones continued their residency there until they went on to bigger and better things. Other bands cut their teeth at the Crawdaddy, notably the Yardbirds. BRRB was now firmly established, and soon the whole world would know about it. The music scene in England was turned around. Thanks to the Beatles, huge markets were opened up, Swinging London happened and an entire new generation of creative people came to the fore. Blues enjoyed a worldwide renaissance; the old bluesmen became folk heroes and for a while at least were able to get some recompense for what they had given the world.

Forty years later, what does it look like? There is something beyond scale in the unprecedented length and perspicacity of the Stones' career. There's also an enigmatic, slippery yet fateful part; sometimes success can set you apart from the rest of humanity. Attempting to make total sense of it is like holding sand in one's hands or watching a train hurtling past you in the night.

For my part, I'm glad they endured, and not too surprised about it. If nothing else, it is a celebration of loyalty to a youthful inspiration, of being "mates for life" in a manner so distinctive and endearing of the English character. Besides, more selfishly, it validates the sagacity of my having been of some assistance to them when few if any believed in their relevance.

But perhaps it could also be the time to "close the circle". A few weeks ago I went to a benefit concert for one of the great surviving blues guitarists, Hubert Sumlin. Like many other bluesmen, he's still traipsing around the country in an old jalopy, driving hundreds of miles between gigs and often struggling with health problems due to age and no medical insurance. I remembered how Giuseppe Verdi, the great and hugely successful Italian composer, made sure that a substantial amount of his wealth should be used to establish a museum and retirement home for old opera singers, musicians and conductors. Some one hundred and twenty years later, Casa Verdi is still going.

I think it would be wonderful, timely and appropriate for the boys from South London to contemplate doing something similar for the music which from the far-away Delta of the Mississippi animated their youth and so richly compensated them.

3

LIKE LIGHTNING

I loved playing with Keith and
the band — I still do — but
I wasn't interested in being a
pop idol, sitting there with girls
screaming. It's not the world
I come from. It's not what I
wanted to be and I still think
it's silly.

Charlie Watts

The band in Paris, with the Arc de Triomphe looming in the background. Their concert at the Olympia in October 1964 saw an estimated £1,400-worth of damage done by fans, 150 of whom were arrested. Three days later it was off to New York for a second US tour, where equally exuberant fans brought Times Square to a standstill.

KEITH: The whole attitude in London changed over the winter of 1962–3 and during that following year, although you only became aware of that in retrospect. If you were there and part of it, everything just happened in slow motion. And things were also beginning to change in the rest of the country, although we had no idea about what was going on in Liverpool, for example.

RONNIE: I never got to see the Stones at the Crawdaddy, but I did see them at various other venues, like the Ricky Tick Club. Leo Clerk, the manager of my first band, the Birds, had a club called the Cavern in Windsor where the Stones played. I joined the queue and watched them all fall out of this van that Ian Stewart was driving – they were all wearing orange-coloured tab shirts. Alex Harvey and his blues band were on before them and Alex went on and on; he must have played for about four hours before the Stones appeared. He kept doing 'Take Some Insurance Out On Me Baby', the Jimmy Reed song. He must have played it about five times in a row – and meanwhile the audience was just waiting for the Stones to come on.

In those days they were playing on those old kind of pub stages, which were very cramped anyway – and with a piano and a drum kit there was hardly any room. From where I was standing the band were all mixed up in the heads of the people bobbing up and down.

Mick would just be moving on the spot, more or less. Brian or Keith might have been sitting on a stool. You'd never see Charlie, of course – just a couple of sticks every now and again.

There was definitely a buzz around Richmond. All my friends would be talking about this band that played Chuck Berry and Bo Diddley numbers – 'Route 66', 'Cops And Robbers' and things like that – and they had a gang who would just follow them around. I went to the Richmond Jazz & Blues Festival and I remember seeing the Stones' tent. It was like a big elephant heaving up and down. I thought, "That sounds good", so I walked in and got into the spirit of it. And I was the last one out of the tent as well, watching them do their stuff. They had a certain flavour and a certain way of handling the songs which appealed to and attracted women as well. That was a big vibe: if you were going to a public affair where the Stones were playing, you were sure to find some great women in the audience, which made it extra special!

CHARLIE: We weren't as loud then as we are now. No bands were; volume has taken off over the years. Nowadays bands won't go out without somebody to mix the sound. In those days we'd never heard of a sound engineer: the first amplified drums I ever heard was Mitch Mitchell with Jimi Hendrix, when they put a vocal mike over Mitch's kit. With the Stones, we used to do songs like 'I'm Moving On' – which Brian used to play a choo choo train slide on – and because I couldn't hear myself I used to ride right on the rim of the cymbal, which makes it go really loud. It was the only way I could hear myself.

KEITH: I used to be good friends with Wayne Fontana, Eric Stewart – a lovely guitar player – and Tony Hicks from the Hollies, but we also had a very good rapport with the Beatles. The first time I saw them was at the Station Hotel – they were very cool guys in black leather overcoats, which we were very jealous of. I think we and the Beatles were surprised by each other, because we didn't know they were working away up in Liverpool and they didn't know what we were doing down in London. Although it was not exactly the same thing, partly because we were more blues-orientated, there was an awful lot of crossover. We could all meet around Little Richard and Chuck Berry, Buddy Holly, Eddie Cochran and Carl Perkins.

One of the things that impressed us about Andrew Oldham when he approached us at the Crawdaddy was that he'd worked for the Beatles and Brian Epstein – it wasn't that he pitched it that way, it was just that everybody kind of knew. And the minute he started talking, we thought, "This is a very sharp boy". We didn't think we had anything to present, but Andrew made us think about the Rolling Stones as a viable unit and how to

> *The first time I saw the Beatles was at the Station Hotel — they were very cool guys in black leather overcoats, which we were very jealous of.*
>
> *Keith*

sell it. What I thought I had learned at art school was how to play guitar, but when I think about it, I realise that I had also learned the subtle art of advertising. Some of the teachers worked in agencies and came to the school one day a week; we'd think, "Wow, he works at a real advertising agency – he can probably spell Madison Avenue".

Andrew pulled together the innate talents within the band. He turned us into a gang, in a way, a sort of conspiracy. And he broadened our horizons. Our biggest aim at the time was to be the best blues band in London and that would have done it for us. But Andrew

> *Andrew Oldham always was sharp, and very smart: he used to wear all those little suits with tiny, short jackets. He had great taste and style, which reflected on us, I think.*
>
> *Charlie*

Mick takes time out from a Ready, Steady Go! *television recording to be photographed by Val Wilmer, best known for her portraits of black music legends.*

said, "What are you talking about? Look, I've just come from working with these four berks from Liverpool. You can easily do this". He had the experience – even though he was just as young as we were – but he was very precocious: a sharp fucker and a right little gangster. Also he really wanted to be one of the band. At one time he called himself "the sixth Rolling Stone", so as well as the management side, he thought of himself as part of the gang.

MICK: Andrew was a publicist for Brian Epstein, although we didn't know that. He probably said, "I am the Beatles' publicist" – how about that as a line? Everything to do with the Beatles was sort of gold and glittery and Andrew seemed to know what he was doing.

CHARLIE: He was the best, Andrew. I liked him. When Andrew got his own office in Regent's Park, I used to live down the hall – my apartment was at one end of the hallway and his office was at the other end. Andrew was very smart, he used to wear all those little suits with tiny, short jackets. We all got on with him, and we all liked what he was saying, he was very good at channelling our feelings. And he could see the possibilities, otherwise we'd have still been schlepping round the clubs, playing in Bournemouth for ever and never moving on. Andrew saw himself as being something bigger than an entrepreneur or an agent in London, and in those days bigger meant being Phil Spector and having artists like Gene Pitney or the Everly Brothers singing with you. He didn't see why he couldn't be big in Hollywood.

He always was sharp. He had great taste and style, which reflected on us, I think. We were in the world of the Beatles because of our age, because we were a guitar band and

Andrew Oldham dressed the band, briefly, in matching houndstooth-check jackets for a photographic session. Keith:You want to make a record no matter what it takes, even to the point of wearing houndstooth suits. I never saw guys lose jackets quicker in my life.

The publicity photographs here and on the opposite page were taken at an extensive session. Other photographs from the same session are on pages 37, 38 and 45.

because everyone wanted to be that popular, but we were a totally different band. We were a live band for a start – much better than they were live – and Andrew, compared to Brian Epstein, was younger and he looked much hipper; he reflected what London was like at the time. That doesn't mean to say he was cleverer than Brian, because no one has matched the popularity that the Beatles still maintain. No one's achieved that, apart from Elvis, Frank Sinatra and Bing Crosby. Brian set all that in motion, but then in another way Andrew set up the Rolling Stones for forty years.

KEITH: Andrew worked with Eric Easton, a very nice guy, who was extremely well-established in the music business. If you opened any *Melody Maker* or *NME* at the time, you'd see an ad for "Eric Easton Management Inc, Personal Management Agency etc". Eric and Andrew were a funny combination, these two total opposites, but in a way it was a magical one because Eric had the established connections and Andrew had his recent whizz-kid status from working with Brian Epstein.

A Stones fan at Ready, Steady Go! *proudly displays Keith's autograph on her cheek. Such adulation could be dangerous: Mick was mobbed on the show while the band were promoting 'The Last Time' and "was stamped on by scores of stiletto heels".*

Keith and his Gibson Les Paul. Unlike many guitarists, he has no signature instrument, favouring both Fenders and Gibsons over the years, alongside more exotic specimens such as a transparent Dan Armstrong.

Then Andrew got the deal at Decca Records – like lightning. The beautiful thing was that Dick Rowe at Decca had turned down the Beatles. Was he going to say "No" twice? So we knew we had them over a barrel before we even started negotiating, which is why we could do it the way we did it, having artistic control, recording for our own company, and leasing Decca our tracks, so that when we were recording we didn't have a little bloke in a brown coat coming round telling us, "I think there should be more violins on it".

I wasn't aware then how radical that deal was – I just knew that at the time it was important to me: I did not want to be signed up with a record company and be told I had to play 'Apache'. I didn't realise quite what an amazing fissure that put into the establishment, because those monolithic empires, EMI or Decca, were just like the British Empire or the Bank of England to me. But Andrew educated us really quickly that the people who were running these institutions had no idea what was happening, that they'd really lost touch. These companies had made weapons in the war; making records was really a tax break. That's why there was a red button called "Missiles Fire" on the mixing board at Olympic Studios in London. They had got it straight from the RAF, and hadn't even bothered to put "record" on it instead.

We met Sir Edward Lewis, bless his old soul, who'd run Decca forever and had done wonderful things. He was there with these three little old men and he didn't even know what was going on; he should have been at home in bed. I hate to say it, but we were Nazi-

NAME .....Martyn..Hill..

ADDRESS ..10, Parkinson House,....
....Frampton.Park.Estate,.
...Hackney, London,.E.9....

NO ...6006..................

DATE OF ENROLLMENT) 14/6/4

ANNABELLE SMITH,
93–97, REGENT STREET,
LONDON, W. 1.

1, Little Argyll st
London
W.1.

A Rolling Stones Fan Club card from 1964. Unlike the Beatles, registering as a Stones fan was something of a statement: 11 boys were suspended from a Coventry school in May for having "Mick Jagger haircuts", while even weekly music paper New Musical Express *sneeringly described them as a "caveman-like quintet".*

like in our brutal attack on Decca, saying: "This is what's going to happen" and they crumbled. That was one of Andrew's most important contributions.

Andrew also realised how you could stir it up and how easily you could manipulate Fleet Street. He would call a few of the papers and say, "Watch the Stones get thrown out of the Savoy", and then he'd say to us, "We'll just go dressed as usual and try and get lunch" – and of course with no ties you'd get chucked out of the Savoy and there's the press with their story: "The Stones thrown out of the Savoy". Just silly little things like that.

The decision that Ian Stewart would not be part of the Rolling Stones just got sifted down to me. I was still only the guitar player, like a hireling. I had no sense of hierarchy. I think it was Brian who laid it to Stu, although it's not really important. In the end it was Stu's decision to stay with us – he said, "I'm here as long as I can still play piano, and we'll hang together in the band and I'll not be in the pictures". Nobody knew that the Stones were going to be what they became, but, knowing Stu, maybe he saw greater things than any of us ever perceived. He might have realised that in the way it was going to have to be marketed he would be out of sync, but that he could still be a vital part. I'd probably have said, "Well, fuck you", but he said, "OK, I'll just drive you around". That takes a big heart, but Stu had one of the largest hearts around. In any case there were very few good pianos on stages in those days. If there wasn't a microphone on it, you couldn't hear it anyway, unless you were Little Richard. I think Stu was bemused by the whole rock'n'roll circus. He enjoyed it without having to be torn apart, sign autographs and go to photo shoots. He was in every respect the kind of Rolling Stone he wanted to be because he could be totally anonymous, but still be along on all the good shit.

MICK: It was obvious that Ian Stewart didn't fit the picture. He was still playing piano when we wanted him to; he didn't play on everything, anyway, because we were playing electrical instruments and he was playing an unamplified upright piano in a noisy club. You couldn't hear it. I'm not dissing him as though he wasn't part of the whole thing, but there were a lot of numbers which he didn't play on. It was plain that Ian didn't want to be a pop singer.

KEITH: Our earliest recording sessions had been with Glyn Johns at the IBC studios – he had the keys so he'd let us in at night. Glyn was very friendly, but very secretive; he kept worrying about whether the night watchman was going to come round. It was a very surreptitious session. Glyn was another Ian Stewart connection. They used to share an apartment together. It was filthy, underwear and baggy pants hanging all over the place – disgusting. Not like Edith Grove, *we'd* leave them on the floor; that was called the carpet. In fact very few of us had underpants; underpants were a sheer luxury.

MICK: Although I don't think Andrew was, in the real sense of the word, a record producer, he did fulfil a lot of the roles. In any case, as far as recording was concerned, nobody in England knew what they were doing, in my opinion. Everyone was making it up as they went along. If you ask me, "What do you look for in a record producer?", picking the song is part of it. Andrew wasn't always right, of course, but no one is always right. He would help pick tunes, so if Keith and I wrote ten tunes, Andrew would say, "I think this is the most commercial one", and that's the major job of a record producer. The other job is to get the band to play as well as possible. Andrew was very enthusiastic and it was my role, along with him, to make sure the band was playing enthusiastically. He would tell me, "Hey, Mick, get out there and fire them up", because I used to like being on the other side of the glass as well. And the other job of a producer is to hire people to record the music properly, which he sort of vaguely did. When we went to LA and recorded there, whether he got that by luck or judgement, it was a good call.

CHARLIE: Andrew had a good pair of ears, a bit like Phil Spector. That's all Phil Spector did really: he heard it and did it the way he heard it. It wasn't Bacharach and David. In fact I've never ever thought of Andrew as a record producer, although to be honest, I was much more interested in what I was doing and my booth and what we were going to play than what Andrew was up to. When we first met Phil Spector – when he came and joined us in the studio in February 1964 – I thought he was a really nice, quiet guy, and the same with Gene Pitney, but don't forget they were just people who I'd met, I wasn't actually in awe of them like Andrew was. I was more in awe of Dizzy Gillespie than them. Andrew loved to drop Phil's name. Phil might have played some maracas or a tambourine, or told Andrew to move the microphone somewhere or move somebody around.

KEITH: Andrew could hear the beat and he could hear the electricity and the enthusiasm coming off it – and if that makes a good producer, then he was a great one. Maybe he's not a producer in terms of a Quincy Jones, but then Quincy Jones has never produced the Rolling Stones. We didn't even know what a producer was, to be honest. We just figured there had better be somebody behind the glass who was in contact with us apart from the engineers, because we knew even less about them. Later on we got to work with "hall of fame" engineers like Dave Hassinger, who know more than the producer does sometimes. I've gone behind a producer's back many times: "Hey, he wants to change the guitar sound – pretend you have, he won't know".

CHARLIE: I don't bother even now with mixing sessions. I've never bothered with them because most of the time we've had fantastic engineers. We all had records that we liked and that we'd want to sound like that so, for example, you'd have tambourines on everything like Phil Spector did. Andrew never came across to me as particularly a producer. It was more of a social thing, he was guiding what we did because we used to be together a lot. But he was definitely there and he always had suggestions.

Mick performs in front of his own image in February 1965.

We did a funny cover of a very good song, which was 'Come On'. I suppose we thought it was commercial; I don't really remember ever being involved in that.

KEITH: The first single was Chuck Berry's 'Come On'. It was middle ground, but it was also very, very pop. We threw it in along with a couple of Bo Diddley songs and I think it was chosen because it was so obviously more chart-orientated. We did listen to Decca's feedback, obviously – not that it was particularly interesting. It might have been Andrew Oldham along with a few people like Dick Rowe making the decision. It really didn't matter to us; we just wanted to put it out. Then the record did so much better than we had expected and suddenly we were being told to wear the houndstooth check jackets. That one track did it. And then, when you're sitting there in that terrible jacket on *Top Of The Pops* and going, "It's not quite the vision I had", Andrew would say, "Well, I tell you, I've seen Muddy Waters in some ridiculous suits" – anything to make a record. We were hip blues players, and the next minute we're on *Thank Your Lucky Stars* or *Juke Box Jury* and you've done it because you want to get into the studio, you want to make a record no matter what it takes, even to the point of wearing houndstooth suits. I never saw guys lose jackets quicker in my life.

We might have expected to make a small dent in the charts and then maybe slowly work our way in as we learned the game and all of a sudden we were in the Top Ten, and on *Top Of The Pops*. We all looked at it and went, "It's all going to be over in two years", because nobody had ever lasted. The Beatles thought the same thing. But the weirdest thing is that LPs

> *When the Stones were on* Thank Your Lucky Stars *or* Ready Steady Go!, *I would race home from college to see them. I'd be sitting there, saying to myself, "I'm there, I'm in this band, they're playing exactly the same shit I'm playing".*
>
> *Ronnie*

The Stones, like the Beatles, were accorded the rare honour of forming the entire panel on television pop show Juke Box Jury. *This appearance, recorded on 27 June 1964, was followed by a* Top of the Pops *slot promoting their latest single 'It's All Over Now'.*

Photograper Terry O'Neill captures the loneliness of life on the road, framing Brian in one of the transport cafes with which the band had become all too familiar during their first, hard-working days travelling the country.

started to become important. Before then an LP was something you might buy for Christmas if you'd really liked the guy for twenty years – Frank Sinatra or Duke Ellington. Elvis or Buddy Holly could sell a few, but unless you had a body of work, an LP was usually a retrospective of what you'd done. And if you were a British recording artist, you went into the studio to record one or two hits and ten fillers. The Beatles and us went in to cut every track as though it was going to be a single; obviously not all of them would make it, but you'd work at them, not just put everything into two songs – and that changed the face of recording, the way people thought of records and made longevity as a band a possibility.

RONNIE: It meant everything for a band to have a record in the charts and I remember 'Come On' did pretty well. I think it's brilliant – I like the original by Chuck Berry and 'I Want To Be Loved', the B-side. And then they were on *Thank Your Lucky Stars* or *Ready Steady Go!* I would race home to see them. My mum did an interview once saying, "Ronnie was always obsessed with this band, the Rolling Stones. I didn't understand, but all I know is that he wanted to get home to see the Stones on *Ready Steady Go!*" They were the band, the one I wanted to be in. I'd be sitting there, saying, "I'm there, I'm in this band, they're playing exactly the same shit I'm playing. That's my band".

CHARLIE: Eventually, by June 1963, we had to move out of the Station Hotel in Richmond because of the crowds. It got too big for the pub. It could have been that the pub didn't like the noise – which I don't think it was – or that they didn't like that crowd of people, any one of a hundred reasons. I think we were told the facility was better in the other place, the Athletic Ground, or maybe Giorgio Gomelsky got it cheaper.

MICK: Everything happened quickly. But you had to be quick in those days because there was so much going on and you could get lost in the rush. There were so many bands around in those days, nearly all of them terrible and most of them sort of manufactured – and some were just bad, and not even manufactured. Nearly all the bands were from the North of England. There was this 'Mrs Brown, You've Got A Lovely Daughter' side to them, which is a fascinating aspect. Keith and I will talk about this music hall thing, the vaudeville influence that lay behind all these groups like the Beatles and, to a certain extent, ourselves, although a lot less as far as we were concerned because the North of England was so much further behind London culturally at the time – that wasn't really a bad thing, they just were. So all those young groups had been brought up knowing about music hall, going to it with their parents, so when bands like the Hollies actually got up on stage they'd behave like vaudeville entertainers. They were not cool.

There weren't as many bands in London – the Dave Clark Five and us – but in the North there were thousands, they were coming out of fuckin' everywhere. And they weren't like us – we could play every number that Chuck Berry ever wrote and they used to play 'Roll Over Beethoven' and that was it. If they played Motown they only played 'Money'; mind you, so did we. Everyone did. We thought we were the only people who knew that tune and when we went to the North of England we discovered everyone had done it. It was really funny. We did some Otis Redding and Solomon Burke's 'If You Need Me' and 'Hitch Hike' by Don Covay. I loved the Supremes and we all loved Marvin Gaye – definitely the hippest artist at Motown. But the Beatles did a lot of Motown so we stayed away from it. And anyway I was never a huge Motown fan until we'd become well known.

CHARLIE: We used to always start with some Jimmy Reed songs even late in this period. We'd go and play at the ballrooms and the show would be a Jimmy Reed number, then a Bo Diddley number, and the kids had never heard of these things. A lot of bands then would do more commercial R&B, like Coasters material, and they hadn't even heard that, let alone where we came from with these Muddy Waters songs. Brian was on a bit of a crusade to do that. I think we thought we were the hippest thing going, that the music we were playing was the way it was going to go or the way it should go.

KEITH: We kind of got thrown in at the deep end on our first UK tour, with Little Richard, Bo Diddley and the Everly Brothers. It doesn't take long to get the hang of their attitude and also the first thing you realised was that everybody's the same everywhere. There might be a difference in language or accent here and there, but on the road you learn real quick. There are certain basics that need to be taken care of and it doesn't matter whether you're white, black, brown or yellow, it's got to be taken care of. It's a very fast university.

That first tour lasted six weeks; we started off just ending the first half, doing two or three numbers, and by the time we got back to London the Everly Brothers couldn't hold down the top spot, which to me was kind of embarrassing. It happened so swiftly. We did a tour of England, I'd never been around that much of England before: Blackburn, Leeds, Barnsley, Wigan; they were still real *Coronation Street*-type towns, unbelievable. And then there were the birds: there's nothing like 3,000 chicks throwing themselves at you to turn a guy's head, especially that randy lot I work with… We just had our tongues hanging out and would take any old slag down the coal hole for a quick one before we go on. Terrible stuff really, but fun times.

CHARLIE: I remember a turning point when we went to the Royal Albert Hall for a NME Poll Winners' Concerts. They had created an R&B award because they didn't know what category to put us in. We turned up early and saw the Beatles' van. It was covered in lipstick and we all thought, "Blimey, that's what our van should be like"! We had exactly the same van but no lipstick. But it only took a few months before it happened.

Police escorts and back entrances were the order of the day on tour in the US when it came to ensuring safe arrival at concert venues.

RONNIE: People used to read their own thing into each member of the band. Mick was the hard-to-get-at lead vocalist. Brian was even more mysterious, and that's what made the audiences keep coming back, to find out a bit more about them each time, to get a little nearer. There was so much general craziness and pandemonium that surrounded them, the shows never lasted long: it was always quite a feat to see more than two songs being played… I didn't follow them around after that. I'd got the message and I thought I'd let them go around the big wide world and do whatever they had to.

My band was called the Thunderbirds. We had a little residency in our local community centre, at a club called the Bird's Nest, and we had our own little following going. We were only just starting out and the Stones were already well known. I always used to compare the fees, like the Stones were getting £70 for a gig or £150 on weekends, and it was like, "Wow!" Then our band started getting £50 midweek and £75 at weekends and then we got over the £100-mark for a gig and we thought, "Yeah, we're going to be up with the Stones", and then we found out they were getting £300. That's where I lost track of them. They weren't seen for dust, but we kept plodding on in the Birds.

KEITH: Our first album reflected what we used to play at the Crawdaddy – a regular diet of Jimmy Reed, Bo Diddley, Muddy Waters, with some Slim Harpo. The album was basically the cream of the set! We cut the album in a room full of egg boxes, using a two-track Grundig. The only concession to professionalism was that the tape recorder was hanging on the wall instead of sitting on a tabletop. So it was like, "Oh, this is recording". In ten days we'd done it, boom, and then it came out and we'd sold 100,000 in a week – which was phenomenal – but by then I'd seen the big studios with all of the gleaming knobs, so in comparison that first studio looked like bullshit, but it was a funny thing that we chose eventually to record it in this room full of egg boxes. I was probably more comfortable there. It was cheap, and also not intimidating, none of those guys in brown coats walking around with stopwatches, and it probably had something to do with our deal with Decca, which was us saying, "Hey, we don't even need your studio".

We would sit around in playback and go, "Sounds good" or "Stop it, let's do it again" and then, "Yeah, that's it". It was either a yes or a no. We were using a two-track or four-track machine and there's not a lot you can do with that. To overdub you had to do what they call ping-ponging between the tracks, which was not a great thing because you actually lost generations of sound quality. That sometimes happened when you smashed the track together, which I later used to the max on things like 'Street Fighting Man' and 'Jumpin' Jack Flash', where it was all acoustic guitars totally overloaded and smashed into a tiny microphone going into a little Philips tape recorder.

From the mixes that we heard off Chess and blues records, the voice was really just part of the sound of the band and only barely raised itself, so that sometimes you had to say, "What was that?" I think that maybe because that was the way we heard it and the way we were used to it on stage, Mick's voice just sat on top and was almost just another instrument. Mick's voice was very hard to record in those days and they'd probably be ping-ponging it in any case. Also it intrigued people. They'd ask "What did he say?" and they'd talk about it. Of course the other thing is that half the time on those early records Mick was singing totally incomprehensible southern Negro lyrics to white kids.

On those early albums, Mick and Brian both played harmonica. It probably depended on how many guitars we needed on a particular number. I still think that Mick is probably one of the best blues harp players around and stays up there against just about anybody

America was a joke when we arrived, but by the time we left we had an audience and by the time we came back we had made a hit record there. It was all uphill, but the audience grew every time. When I first went there I wanted to go to New York and Birdland and that was it... New York was the home of what I dreamed I wanted to be, which was a black drummer playing in 52nd Street. Of course, I'm not black and the scene had gone by the time I got there, but New York was still a very hip jazz centre

Charlie

else you can name apart from Little Walter himself. Mick can phrase on harp so brilliantly. Sometimes I used to say, "Why don't you sing it like that sometimes?", and he'd say, "Oh, that's two totally different things", whereas my point is that they are exactly the same; it's just blowing air out except one is with words and the other is with notes. Billie Holiday was one of the best singers ever, and who did she copy? Louis Armstrong, who sang exactly the way he played cornet. Mick and I always argue about that.

If Brian was going to play harp, then there could only be one guitar, so it would probably be a decision that we only needed one guitar on this song, because then Mick would play the maracas. An interesting aspect about the percussion of this band was the Bo Diddley influence. Jerome Green, who played with Bo, was such a beautiful lush, a real Chicago lush, and such a sweet guy; all he did was play maracas. It was my job on the first tour to pull him out of the pub and say, "Hey, Jerome, get on before Bo docks your wages". He got kind of sick towards the end of the tour. I took him to the doctor and I had him in my joint recuperating for a week or so. So I was like his English minder. But Mick also studied Jerome. He didn't play the four maracas in each hand like Jerome could do, but a lot of moves are relevant, and the tambourine that Charlie used to put on the bass drum added another extra percussion thing.

CHARLIE: America was a joke when we arrived, but by the time we left we had an audience and by the time we came back we had made a hit record there. It was all uphill, but the audience grew every time.

When I first went there I wanted to go to New York and Birdland and that was it. I didn't care about the rest of America. New York was the home of what I dreamed I wanted to be, which was a black drummer playing in 52nd Street. Of course, I'm not black and the scene had gone by the time I got there, but New York was still a very hip jazz centre. One of the first bands I saw when I got to New York was Charlie Mingus's, with Danny Richmond on drums, and Sonny Rollins had just come out of hibernation and had his trio. Those were the days when Sonny used to start playing in the dressing room and then play to the walls all round the stage. It was fantastic.

I thought every jazz musician I liked came from New York, but of course they didn't, and then I came to Los Angeles later and I liked LA too – we used to practically live there at one time in the '60s: we'd be recording or something for three months of the year. I do remember San Antonio, because we met Bobby Keys and the Beach Boys at the State Fair Show there. Then I went to Chicago and fell in love with Chicago as well.

And we did some recording at Chess. Everyone the band loved had recorded there. Thank God we did go there, because we got a great engineer called Ron Malo. Keith still plays a Chuck Berry record every night in the dressing room. It's not something he does religiously, it just happens there are five records there and one of the best is a collection of Chuck Berry songs. I listen to it and still think, "Bloody hell".

When we went there Marshall Chess took us to see where they had the racks with all the albums they produced. I was interested in the jazz stuff – all the Argo label material – people like Al Grey and Ahmed Jamal. In those days there were some great jazz clubs in Chicago – the Persian Room and the Alhambra – and some great players.

I met a young dummer there called Maurice White, who was playing with an organ player and an albino guitar player, called Speckled Red, or one of those sort of names. I remember them being in this tiny room and the fantastic sound coming out of it and the lovely little drum kit Maurice was playing. It was a thrill meeting people like Muddy Waters, of course, but I was also looking for Vernell Fournier and Freddy Below – people like that.

The band pictured in 1964, the year in which they moved from all-night rave-ups at London clubs through ballrooms and town halls to the Empire Pool, Wembley (now the Arena). They are shown here in April, playing a Mod Ball.

Terry O'Neill shot a series of relaxed photographs of the band on the road. The lower photograph on this page shows Mick with Andrew Oldham, the ex-PR man for the Beatles, who, though just 19 when he first linked with the Stones, guided their early career as both manager and producer. By early 1968 they had taken control of their own affairs, leaving Oldham to concentrate on running his Immediate record label.

KEITH: Some people say I made up the story about seeing Muddy Waters painting the ceiling when we went to Chess. I've got no reason to make things up. The people who say it's not true weren't there. I remember the whitewash coming down and Muddy saying, "I love what you're doing with my music".

It was incredible to see the studio and the way they operated, and to realise, when you plugged in there and heard what was coming off the tapes, that certain rooms do have certain sounds. We cut a lot of stuff there – it was such a warm room to play in, although it's not just the room, it's also to do with the guys who are operating it.

CHARLIE: I know we had wanted to record in Chicago – it was the obvious thing for us to do – but I think Andrew would have been instrumental in setting that up. It was a great move. A classic example of where the studio engineers just plugged us into the board and you were off; they had the sound and everything. This was their own domain, their home, they worked there all of the time. It was just that it wasn't Chuck Berry playing, it was Keith. And when we left, back they all went to the bands they normally worked with.

The entrance to Longleat House, Wiltshire, provides the Stones with their most unusual gig to date, in August 1964. Over 200 fans fainted as the crush became intense, but the Marquis of Bath proclaimed it "a delightful day...so few hospital cases".

KEITH: There was a guy called Big Red, or something, playing in the B studio, storming blues stuff, a big, big albino black guy, with a Gibson that looked like a mandolin in his hands. Mick, Charlie, Stu and I went in to listen to him; it was a powerhouse band, but we didn't even think about asking any of the Chess artists to sit in with us. We were just happy to be in the room, that was enough and...why would they want to play with us? We were the new white boys in town. I don't think we would have presumed to think like that in those days as we were still apprentices. But it was a thrill to actually meet the guys,

and at the same time they gave us a lot of respect, probably because we were selling a lot of records, which always engenders a lot of respect!

MICK: I can't remember going to Chess – it's just like something I read about in books. I can remember meeting Muddy Waters later on at clubs: he was always asking me to get on the stage and I never wanted to, though Keith and Brian would jump up on stage.

CHARLIE: When I think about it in retrospect the fact that we actually walked on stage with Muddy Waters is something else; he was one of the great, great fathers and has played some of the best stuff ever. The funny thing was going to Chicago and playing our music which came out of the Chicago blues, and then going on to do a show to a load of white kids who had never heard of the music we were playing at them.

KEITH: I think we were all conscious of the fact that we were beginners. Obviously we were thrown into it. It was such a short time from just working the Crawdaddy to touring the States and working with the top bands or recording at Chess. I always had that feeling that we were trying to rise to the occasion. It was a massive time of soaking things up.

It wasn't just the black musicians. Suddenly you'd find yourself in Oklahoma listening to some incredible little country band in a bar and you'd think, "This is light years ahead of us, playing-wise, but they'll never get out of this bar". We were kind of learning; there was a lot of scratching our heads and thinking, "There are so many good bands here, what the hell are we doing?", and at the same time, "How come we're top of the bill?"

We have never thought of ourselves as the "greatest rock'n'roll band in the world" and that was especially true then. We didn't think anything much of ourselves. We just thought we were lucky to be there, so let's learn what we can. It was like being given extra tuition.

Mick and Keith respond to the questions of a US TV host. Charlie: It looks like I've borrowed Mick's roll neck or he's borrowed mine…

DAVID BAILEY

David Bailey was already making his mark as a fashion photographer in London in the early 1960s, when he first met Mick Jagger. Bailey was heavily involved in the visual presentation of the Stones, creating the album cover shots for *The Rolling Stones No. 2*, *Out Of Our Heads*, *Get Yer Ya-Ya's Out!* and *Goats Head Soup*.

It was Jean Shrimpton who introduced me to Mick Jagger, because Jean's sister Chrissie was going out with Mick, who was still at the London School of Economics. Chrissie told us about Mick and said, "He's great. He's going to be bigger than the Beatles". She had been over to see the Stones playing at Eel Pie Island and the Crawdaddy Club.

One day Mick turned up with Chrissie. He was already striking. I tend to react to people visually, and what struck me straightaway were his lips; I used to make Mick extremely angry by joking that his mother used to stick him to store windows while she went shopping.

I immediately liked the Stones when I first heard them, because I had always liked the blues. Here was a band playing songs like 'Little Red Rooster' by Willie Dixon, the kind of blues singles which I used to go out and track down in record shops like Dobell's in Charing Cross Road. In contrast, I thought of the Beatles as a boy band, a very manufactured group when they started out, whereas the Stones seemed to grow organically. The Beatles' haircut was old-fashioned — it only seemed "modern" to people who didn't realise it had been around for a long time — and I personally didn't find lyrics like "I want to hold your hand" that interesting.

Shortly after we met, Mick asked me to take him to a "posh" restaurant. I think he liked my lifestyle, especially all the girls, although I was then much more of a bad boy than he was. In fact, Mick lived with me for a little while when he had nowhere to stay in London; this was the 1960s, of course, and my place was pretty much an open house. I decided we should go to a place called the Casserole down on the King's Road. I remember that Mick paid, which was unusual in those days because back then he never paid for anything. I told him to leave a tip and he said, "Leave a tip? What the fuck for?" I said it was normal practice and suggested he leave a ten-shilling note, one of those old brown banknotes. Mick put the ten-bob note on the plate, but as we were putting our coats on, I noticed his hand slip out and pop the ten shillings back in his pocket.

The first proper portrait of Mick ever published in America was one of mine. I offered it to the British magazines, but they said, "No, who is this guy? We don't know who he is", so I sold it instead to Diana Vreeland at *American Vogue*. She said, "I don't care who he is, but he looks great and we'll publish it". *Glamour* magazine then decided I was an expert on British bands. I told them they had to get the Stones, but they decided to go with the Dave Clark Five or a group like that, which Mick was really pissed off about. Middle America was extremely square.

Later I introduced Mick to Andy Warhol, who I already knew. The first time I took Mick to meet Warhol at Baby Jane Holzer's, Mick sat down and stuck his feet up on her favourite lattice Chinese table. I thought "Fuck, she's not going to be pleased", because I wouldn't have done something like that, but Mick could get away with it because the Stones were the cool group. Andy Warhol and I had acquired the rights to Anthony Burgess's *Clockwork Orange*. The plan was that I would direct the film and Andy would create some silk screen sets. We both wanted to use the Stones, but Andrew Oldham wanted more for the Stones than the entire budget of the film, so that project went down the chute.

I loved Andrew Oldham, thought he was terrific. I wouldn't have wanted to cross him – he was a worrying little fucker – but he was possibly as important to the Stones at that point as what they were doing themselves. The meeting between Andrew and the band was very significant. Andrew had a broader range of references, he read more widely and he knew what was going on a little more than the Stones.

On a handful of occasions I went out on tour with Mick, when the band were playing college gigs. It was not a lifestyle I would have wanted to embrace. And I was never impressed with their groupies – I had the edge then; photographers were still more desirable than rock'n'roll musicians. But there were riots; lots of over-excited little girls running round with autograph books. I had a new E-Type Jag at one point and Mick came along for the ride. He got totally annoyed because these fans were jumping all over the car writing messages in lipstick on it – "I love you, Mick".

Once we went out in Jean Shrimpton's Mini, while Brian was in his Humber, the sort of car a vicar would drive. After the gig it was always, "Let's go before Brian comes". There was a lot of animosity, particularly between Brian and Mick. Brian wanted to keep the Stones more purist – whatever that means – while Mick saw an opportunity to go more commercial. I did actually like Brian, but he was very spoilt, and his accent was posher than the others.

There was no question that Mick was the leader of the band. Brian was too sulky and moody, while Mick would just get on with it. When we did the cover shot for *Out Of Our Heads* – the close-up of their five heads – I deliberately placed Mick at the back because I felt they wanted to give the impression of being more democratic.

I always thought that Keith was in a world of his own. Keith was always Keith. Keith has always been to me the personification of rock'n'roll. He has never changed, he's never given a fuck, he's straight down the line. And he stuck to his guns more than the punks ever did. I loved it when they asked him to perform at the concert for Princess Diana and he said, "No, sorry, didn't know the chick". He never compromised and he's now in a position where he doesn't have to compromise.

I got on very well with Charlie because he had worked as a graphic designer. He knew who Irving Penn was and a little bit about my own work. And of course he was more jazz-orientated, and I had been listening to a lot of jazz — when I was fourteen I really wanted to be Chet Baker.

Bill was always a placid character. I only really got to know him much later on; he turned out to be more interesting than I had thought he was going to be. Bill hated people swearing, particularly in front of his wife, Diane. If you said "Shit" or "Fuck", he used to turn round and say, "Sorry, Diane". Of course, the more he said that, the more everybody swore.

I was also doing some work with the Beatles at the time. The Beatles were great, but they seemed "square" — a good word that has sadly fallen out of use. Jean had bought the Beatles' first release and I thought it was naff; they didn't really become interesting until the time of *Abbey Road*. But there was more to it than the Stones simply being cooler than the Beatles. They were more charming. All of the Stones were charming. Ringo was OK — he never took much notice of anything — but Paul was always very earnest and protective of his image. I didn't particularly like John, although he had very definite opinions and knew where he was going — but even he ended up sitting around in his white robes in his bedroom with Yoko, being worthy. And George had his Hari Krishna. The Beatles took themselves so seriously. The Stones could always laugh at themselves. And the Stones were never silly. Although Mick ponced around in an ugly frock at the Hyde Park concert, with all those butterflies, it looked all right on him.

Later I worked with the Stones on the cover for *Goats Head Soup*. That was the shot where I put a scarf over Mick's head and said "I'm going to make you look like Hepburn". I think he thought I meant Audrey Hepburn, while I actually meant Katharine Hepburn in *The African Queen*. It was Bianca Jagger who got that one through because she said "Oh, it's great, Mick", while he was saying "Oh no, we're going to look like a bunch of poofs". The establishment also helped enhance the Stones' image. The biggest mistake the government ever made was busting Mick and Robert Fraser. They should have busted a dustman or a postman and then nobody would have wanted to smoke dope, but busting Mick was the biggest advertisement for dope ever.

The Stones are still cool. Before he died Joe Strummer said to me, "Bailey, I'm worried that I'm too old to be doing all this". I told him it was a racial thing, because if he was black and ninety years old nobody would care. But because he was white and middle class, he was suffering from the concept people have that older white people can't play rock'n'roll. But if he was a BB King or a Willie Dixon or John Lee Hooker, nobody would think twice. Joe said, "You've made it much better for me. I'm going to carry on doing what I'm doing". And the Stones still are.

4
INTO THE PRESSURE COOKER

You had two months between
one hit and the next.
Immediately we had written one
hit song, there was suddenly
a terrible increase in pressure:
Where's the follow up?
It was relentless.

Keith Richards

A group portrait by Gered Mankowitz, whose distinctive photographic style would become a part of the Stones' mid-1960s image. This shoot was for the cover of Between The Buttons.

Former convent schoolgirl Marianne Faithfull is put through her vocal paces by Mick before Gered Mankowitz's watching lens. She burst on to the scene in 1964 with a hit recording of the Jagger/Richards' composition 'As Tears Go By', having been added to Andrew Oldham's management stable after a chance meeting at a party.

KEITH: One thing I can never thank Andrew Oldham enough for – it was more important to the Stones than anything, and probably his main achievement – was that he turned Mick and me into songwriters. It would never have occurred to me to try unless he had forced it on us, brutally speaking. He'd say, "Look at the other boys, *they're* writing their own songs".

For a while Mick and I thought we'd do it just to keep Andrew happy, but then the songs started to crop up. The first one we wrote was 'As Tears Go By'. That was the song where Andrew locked us in the kitchen in my flat up on Mapesbury Road in Willesden. He said, "You've got to try". He put a guitar in the kitchen and locked the door and we stayed there all night. Six weeks later it was in the Top Ten, sung by this ex-nun with these enormous gazongas, bless her heart. That was encouraging, as it was our first song. It was amazing that anybody picked those songs up. We'd say "We've got this one; it's really a puerile pop song", but Andrew would say "It's got a nice melody" and then he would call back, "Guess what? Gene Pitney's recording it". So we felt, "Well, this isn't so difficult, is it?"

At that age, if we had four days off from doing shows, it seemed like there was nothing to do and if it was raining, you didn't want to go out. So we just used to hang at night. Mick lived downstairs, I lived upstairs and all we did in those days was either listen to music or play it. If we got lucky, we got laid, but apart from that…

MICK: Keith likes to tell the story about the kitchen, God bless him. I think Andrew may have said something at some point along the lines of "I should lock you in a room until you've written a song" and in that way mentally he did lock us in a room, but he didn't literally lock us in. One of the first songs we came out with was that tune for George Bean, the very memorable 'It Should Be You', which Charlie tries to tease me with because I can't remember all my own words; it's my claim that I can sing part of any song and Charlie sometimes tests me when he's got all the books out. It's quite funny – he doesn't know, I could be making it all up.

CHARLIE: From my point of view Andrew was the one who pushed Mick and Keith into writing songs – but that doesn't mean to say that one day they wouldn't have decided to do it themselves. Andrew told them to write some songs for some artists he had and I'd play drums on the sessions. He used to love having a tambourine on the snare drum or the bass drum, so you'd always get a lot of tambourine. He made Mick and Keith start writing 'As Tears Go By'. Maybe because it was supposed to be for this blonde girl who'd just come out of a convent, Mick immediately went into an early English style – that music was the very, very beginning of flower power; there were a few bands, like Pentangle, who played that stuff.

MICK: We were very pop-orientated. We didn't sit around listening to Muddy Waters; we listened to everything. In some ways it's easy to write to order. If you say to me, "I've got this girl, she sings like this, and can you write me a ballad about some starlight at 100 beats a minute, then I know exactly what I'm going to do. So Keith and I got into the groove of writing those kind of tunes; they were done in ten minutes. I think we thought it was a bit of a laugh, and it turned out to be something of an apprenticeship for us. It was fun, and Andrew made it very light-hearted. Because none of these artists were any good. They were all kids that Andrew was trying to pick up, because he was trying to invent this Phil Spector character, and we all knew they were useless. He'd say, "Come on, write one for this or that bloke", and you knew it wasn't important and your career didn't depend on it, or he'd say, "Hey, go and write this one for Gene Pitney – we'll all make a bit of money". It was all done for extra money on the side, and very much tongue-in-cheek.

KEITH: The amazing thing is that although Mick and I thought these songs were really puerile and kindergarten-time, every one that got put out made a decent showing in the charts. That gave us extraordinary confidence to carry on, because at the beginning songwriting was something we were going to do in order to say to Andrew, "Well, at least we gave it a try, you can't do everything". But in a very short space of time, writing became at least equally as important as playing. I thank Andrew for that, because the minute you start to write about things, it turns you into another person. You start, without realising it, to observe things in a different way, and you begin to look at life as little vignettes for ideas. You end up with a much more sharpened set of receptors. Andrew made you feel that there was no limit, and he gave us something to aim for as well.

CHARLIE: In those days Mick and Keith would be up late sitting on the bed in

> *'As Tears Go By' was just what we were able to come up with. It was easier to write a simple pop ballad than a great rock song like 'C'mon, Everybody'.*
>
> *Mick*

Andrew Oldham orchestrates a press shoot.

Keith tunes up in Los Angeles, 1965, the year that saw the band's third and fourth tours of North America. They also recorded at Chess and RCA's Hollywood studios, bringing their music back to its roots, and were welcomed back to the Ed Sullivan Show. *However, this took place behind closed doors after previous audience unrest.*

Keith's room playing a guitar and I'd be sitting on the other bed banging a phone book or something – and that only really stopped in the 1970s. Brian wasn't a writer, really, so suddenly the band was going off in a direction he couldn't hold on to. Brian loved being what one would call a "star".

KEITH: On our tours of the States we were mainly working with black acts. When you went down south you noticed a big difference. Suddenly the black guys were more uptight. They'd stop and sit at one end of the bar and you'd think, "What have I done? I was talking to you yesterday." And then you'd see the signs coming up as soon as you got south of Washington DC. When you were dying for a pee in some restaurant in Carolina, you'd get there and it would say 'Coloureds Only' and you wondered who was being discriminated against. America in those days was far less homogenised than it is now. We used to say that anywhere round the edges was cool, but once you got in the middle you didn't know what was going to happen. There was such a difference in attitude between the big cities – Chicago, New York, LA, New Orleans – and the rest of the country.

The *TAMI Show*, which we went to record in October 1964, had never been done before and it's never been done since, but at the time you didn't realise this was an experiment, and that they were trying things that had never been done before. They were using new sound systems and new ways of shooting things. The acts included James Brown, Marvin Gaye, Chuck Berry, Solomon Burke, the Supremes, Martha and the Vandellas, and Jack Nitzsche, who had already worked with us, was in charge of the orchestra. It was really kaleidoscopic, and then we had to follow James Brown, the tightest machine in the world! That did make me a little tight. Thank God the audience was mostly white. However, everybody else was just as nervous, I realised later, because they were being filmed, although in a way you were also a little removed from the gut-wrenching feeling, because there was so much other activity going on. It was like, "Cut here", "Next act". To us what was great was to walk down a corridor and bump into every damn soul star in the world: "Yo, Solomon! Yo, Marvin!"

MICK: What was interesting about the *TAMI Show* was that there was a huge list of acts, not only all these black acts – Chuck Berry, Marvin Gaye, the Supremes – but a lot of

*Mick photographed by
Gered Mankowitz.*

white acts too – the Beach Boys and Jan and Dean – everybody who was popular in LA at the time, basically.

We weren't actually following James Brown because there were hours in between the filming of each section. Nevertheless, he was still very annoyed about it, so I tried to explain to him that it wasn't really a show, that it was just a TV programme and it could be cut up and edited in any way, that he might end up at the beginning if they saw fit to put him there. I said, "That's television".

I was a great admirer of James Brown, not only for his movements. For a long time I only heard his records. Then I used to go and see him at the Apollo Theater in Harlem, with Charlie normally. I had a lot of different reasons for doing this. First of all, I was very interested in him, and then the more interested I got, the more I started looking at him from a sociological point of view, because I found this whole culture fascinating. I thought, "This is odd". I'd never seen housewives smoking pot before; they'd sit in the back room parlour at the Apollo, older women with their kids, and just smoke pot. So I got the picture that nobody really cared and that it wasn't like a concert where you would turn up, pay for your ticket, go in, see the show and leave. This was more like an old-fashioned movie show where the films would keep running round and round, and you could go out and have a beer or something in between. I'd go out and see James Brown in the dressing room. I don't know if a lot of people hung around James Brown at that point. I think that probably came later – and I used to sit there and chat with him. He knew who I was, but he didn't really know me.

CHARLIE: Seeing James Brown play had a great effect on all of us. At the time he had the crown as the greatest entertainer around, and his show was unbelievable. The hippest one on the whole *TAMI Show* was Marvin Gaye, who was a lovely guy – fantastic.

MICK: When James Brown came to the *TAMI Show* I already knew the whole thing about James Brown and all the people like him, that you were always "Number One". Americans in those days – even now really – were always portrayed as very brash, completely the opposite of the way English people are: the English never want to trumpet themselves. It's not even reserved, it's beyond reserved – you never shout out about how good you are; you always underplay your strengths. You never say you're the best at what you do and you always have to have this slightly ironic tone about everything you do. Whereas James Brown is like, "I'm Number One, I'm the hardest-working man in showbiz", and I'm going, "Oh really, I thought that was just like a joke", and "How hard *do* you work?"

There's a distinctly African-American cultural aspect to this. It's how boxers walk into the ring with one guy holding their belts up, one guy telling everyone to stay out of the way and another guy singing their praises. It's what used to be done for the headman, the chief or the king. James Brown did the same thing, with Bobby Byrd and Danny Ray. They would come on and do all these big praise intros: "Here he is, the hardest-working man in show business, Mr Please, Please, Please", this huge build-up – and then you found, when you were talking to James Brown that he was repeating it to you.

I used to really enjoy this whole thing. Part of me was a big fan and the other part was detached, going "How different and how weird is this?" and trying to get into and under it a bit.

Of course I copied everyone's moves; you've got to learn from people. I first copied my grandmother and my mother and my cousins, and then I copied Little Richard. It

Mick inspects the furniture after moving into a flat in Harley House on London's Marylebone Road.

isn't really *copying* them, you just pick up things and you try and do steps you think are going to work for you. You say, "That's a move I like". Some audiences you have to work really hard, and a lot of that stuff comes from seeing James Brown and people like him, because they work the audience very hard, whereas other performers in white rock'n'roll, especially English bands, don't do that much. The people I learnt that stuff from were nearly all Americans.

KEITH: When Mick saw James Brown, he added some of his moves to his repertoire, just like anybody else, but I wouldn't even say it was particularly conscious. We were starting to play bigger and bigger stages, but Mick already had a lot of moves. He could do some really neat spins. So it wasn't as if he suddenly copied James Brown or anybody else. He would say, "That guy's incredible", but he wouldn't analyse it or take it to bits. Maybe in his own mind he did, but to me he wouldn't say, "I've got to get that move down". It was all very much by osmosis. It's just like being a guitarist. You watch somebody else and you hear a guitar lick, and without even knowing it you're up on stage – and suddenly without ever thinking, "I wonder how that's done", it just comes out. That's the way I like it, because it's a lot less hard work!

CHARLIE: Mick never had a problem in front of an audience. He was never like Brian. Keith's never really had a problem either, but Keith is naturally a shy person like I am. Mick is a very *private* person, but he's not shy and he's a natural entertainer. He's the best front man in the world – along with Michael Jackson (who was also as good at one time) – and that's saying something.

Brian's role, when we first started the band – or when he first started the band – had been very much as the leader, but he didn't have the capacity to go further than that, or the band went in a direction that he couldn't cope with as the leader. We didn't really have a leader, I suppose – it was just a band.

He was also the front man as far as using all the gizmos. No one had ever heard of a slide guitar – when John Lennon saw it, I remember him going, "Well, yeah". But slowly Mick became more dominant, especially once we were on television. In clubs you had hours to sit up there and get yourself across; on television you've got four minutes, and Mick was very good at that. Brian also got himself across as a personality, but it was just this little blond bloke next to Mick. So Brian really worked hard; he practised his 'Walking The Dog' backup vocal very hard. And he studied how he looked when he was playing the guitar – things like not getting his hand in the way of his face. He was very image-conscious. He spent ages getting his fringe right, and he used to count his moves out – they'd always be the same, whereas Mick is a natural; he was then and he still is. You can work hard at what you do, and Mick does, but there's a certain thing which makes you go, "Blimey!", and that's the natural thing. It happens every now and again with Mick, and you go, "Fucking hell!"

Brian was insecure and, much to his annoyance, embarrassed. It annoyed him because he wanted to be the centre of attention, but he wasn't. One of Brian's agonies and downfalls was that he wanted to be the leader and unfortunately he wasn't talented in that way. I think it helped make him unhappy, along with not being very well and doing the wrong things.

It was fantastic that 'Little Red Rooster' went the way it did; the drum part was like the fabulous Sam Cooke's version. I could hear Howlin' Wolf during the recording of *The London Sessions*; he was sitting on this bench with Eric Clapton and we were all standing waiting for Wolf to say "go". I was leaning on the drum kit looking at him and he was going, "And the drummer goes 'Boom'" – I thought, "Fuck, what have I got to do there?" Fortunately he just meant that was where to come in.

KEITH: We played on *Shindig!* with Howlin' Wolf. I've got to say that's probably because the producer of *Shindig!* was Jack Good. I think Jack saw the possibility, by asking us "Who do you want on?", and we said "Howlin' Wolf", because Jack certainly wanted to push things that way. Hats off to Jack Good for that, because he kind of used our leverage to do that. This was when we were starting to realise a certain sway to things. Before that we'd just been tossed in the wind and were just learning the game.

If you got a TV show, especially with American TV, you did it – it didn't matter what it was. You'd have to get up early and do these morning TV shows and the presenters would be going, "Oh, we've got these cute little things from England. Look, their eyes move and they talk, too. Let's ask them a question". You would be seething inside, but at the same time you were part of the game. When you start out, you think, "All I want to

After jetting from gig to gig in the States in their own plane, the band take propeller-driven transport to play in Belfast, September 1965. As ever, autographs are demanded by the stewardess and her colleagues. Next stop would be Los Angeles to record 'Get Off Of My Cloud'.

Brian and Mick en route to Marseilles in 1966. The gig they played on arrival resulted in eight stitches after a flying chair caught Mick in the eye. 85 of the 2,500 fans present were detained after "going bonkers...the kids even hit the police with their own truncheons".

Keith: It was rough, but you did learn how to write songs, to say something in a very short amount of time and to make it go from A to Z in two minutes, thirty seconds.

do is make a record and learn how records are made and then write some songs", but slowly you become more and more aware that if you want to do that, you have do all the other stuff – those TV shows and the photo shoots.

So I knew this was a very rare thing, that *Shindig!* was a high-rating TV pop show and the fact that we'd got Howlin' Wolf on it was a little triumph for us, one of our first triumphs. The only thing about Jack Good, who was so English, was that he stood there in his little bow tie and said to Howlin' Wolf, "I say, Mr Howlin', can I call you Howlin'?"

Watching Howlin' was an impressive thing – realising that the music, right in front of your face, sounded exactly the same as the record; an unbelievable tower of power. Physically Howlin' Wolf was so striking. Although there was a rumour that he had murdered a couple of guys, as far as I knew he was very gentle and kind. His wife still lives in Chicago and she hangs together with Muddy Waters' widow. On the *Bridges To Babylon* tour they both came backstage: two little sweet old ladies – Mrs Burnett and Mrs Morganfield.

CHARLIE: The *Shindig!* show with Howlin' Wolf was fantastic. We just thought it was the obvious thing to do. Jack Good had this strange sort of English commercial slant that meant it was totally logical to have this "Howlin' Chappie" singing a song. To have an American on the show was something else; to have a black American was a tremendous thrill.

KEITH: We didn't find it difficult to write pop songs, but it was *very* difficult – and I think Mick will agree – to write one for the Stones. It seemed to us it took months and months and in the end we came up with 'The Last Time', which was basically re-adapting a traditional gospel song that had been sung by the Staples Singers, but luckily the song itself goes back into the mists of time. I think I was trying to learn it on guitar just to get the chords, sitting there playing along with the record, no gigs, nothing else to do. At least we put our own stamp on it, as the Staples Singers had done, and as many other people have before and since: they're still singing it in churches today.

It gave us something to build on to create the first song that we felt we could decently present to the band to play. We were going to lay it on our own guys. It was not like fooling

Into The Pressure Cooker

somebody in Tin Pan Alley and letting them add a nice arrangement – we had to lay this song to the Stones. We hoped that Charlie wasn't going to kick us out of the room and that we'd get a smile of approval rather than a slight frown or that look of confusion that is even worse than an outright "No way". That's the hard bit, and that's why it took longer.

'The Last Time' was a kind of bridge into thinking about writing for the Stones. It gave us a level of confidence; a pathway of how to do it. And once we had done that we were in the game. There was no mercy, because then we had to come up with the next one. We had entered a race without even knowing it.

CHARLIE: I remember vividly making 'Satisfaction'. It was at RCA in Los Angeles, in the same studio where Duke Ellington recorded one of the greatest records he ever made, *Ellington Uptown*, with Louie Bellson on drums: that's the famous 'A Train' track. Dave Hassinger, the engineer, used to smoke Tiparillos constantly. He seemed a lot older, like a man, while we were still boys. And LA was like "Wow!". We used to go and eat at a restaurant like a Denny's, where they had copper pennies all over the table. Eating was part of the LA experience.

When we were working out drum parts, I might do it one way, and Mick or Keith would do it differently. I'm totally open to Mick or Keith's version and what they think. I'd say, "Right", and try to play it as well as I could to make the song work. That's about as much I would ever want to get involved in the composition, because you can have too many people writing and composing, and then there's a danger that nothing happens. If you're pulling at a piece of chewing gum too many ways, it just breaks. I've never been involved in the writing, ever. That was one of Bill's gripes! I was never interested.

KEITH: With 'Satisfaction' I got the fuzz tone and I thought we'd already finished all the tracks that we wanted to cut. So this was just a little sketch, because, to my mind, the fuzz tone was really there to denote what the horns would be doing. But Andrew spotted the spirit of the track and we were already back on the road before we heard that they'd decided that 'Satisfaction' was going to be the single. We had thought we were going to cut a better version. It was still not finished as far as we were concerned, but sometimes an artist's sketches are better than the finished painting – and that's probably one of the perfect examples. We hardly had a chance to hear the playback before we were touring again, then Andrew called us up a week or ten days later and said, "That last thing you did, 'Satisfaction', that's the single". Suddenly I was hearing it on the radio on every station and I thought, "I'm not going to complain", although I never considered it to be the finished article.

Then we were on a roller coaster. I remember after 'Satisfaction', which was a time of great triumph, a worldwide hit, Mick and I were sitting back in some motel room, in San Diego, if I remember rightly. We gave this big sigh of relief and it was exactly at that moment that there was a knock at the door and the phone started ringing and people wanted the next hit. It was a hard training ground, but if we had been allowed total artistic freedom, we probably wouldn't have written half of those songs.

As it went on we'd call up John, Paul or George about the single releases. Everybody was talking about the Beatles versus the Stones and all that crap, and yet between us, it would be, "You come out first and we'll wait two weeks". We would try never to clash; there was plenty of room for both of us. There was a time when 'Paperback Writer' came out and one of ours – 'Paint It Black' or something like that – came out before or after;

Charlie photographed by Marilyn Demick, one of the earliest Stones fans.

Mick with Paul McCartney. Charlie: The Beatles had a fantastic look, but they weren't very good on stage. They didn't do anything on stage — literally nothing: it was Paul going with his left hand and looking up and down and John nodding his head. Ringo moved more than anyone up there. The Beatles didn't swing live — but I suppose they didn't have to, they just sang 'Can't Buy Me Love'.

(Previous page) Keith photographed in the recording studio by Gered Mankowitz.

we had stitched it up with them. There would be surreptitious phone calls. It was, "OK, ours is ready, yours ain't"… "All right, you go first".

Being in the States gave us so many musical directions, just the fact of having more than one radio station. In England at that time there was the Light Programme, the World Service and the Home Service. In the States you'd get into a car just to listen to the radio, and raiding record stores was the other great thing. I'd go down to a store and find Charlie and Brian were already down there in the blues section; we were like starving men who had suddenly been let into a banquet.

We were listening to a lot of soul music at the time, but to us soul music was very sophisticated and required more instrumentation. I think we were just learning the roots and then compressing it sometimes because we wanted to. When we found how much more variety there was in soul music, we saw more and more of the connection between that and what we were doing. It was just a natural progression time-wise and music-wise from the blues.

MICK: Keith and I used to go to these shows which had everybody on the bill; they all did one number, and a mixture of what we would now call R&B and pop and rock, all on one bill. There'd be an Italian singer followed by Jerry Lee Lewis and then it would be Joe Tex. Anyone who had a hit could get into the show. It didn't matter – they were mostly good. One number from each person was a fantastic way of doing a show – inconceivable now, really – and they were all playing with the house band. It wasn't a pilgrimage for me, it was just whatever music was on.

RONNIE: It was always something new to look forward to; the treatment of how the Stones' latest record was going to sound. You never knew what it was going to be, what kind of way it was going to be presented or what their image was going to be: war-paint or just the hard, long-haired, scruffy, rock'n'roll London bit, which was always appealing.

Mick in France, 1966, photographed by Jean-Marie Périer.

MICK: Around 1966 we started writing these different kinds of music. Keith was writing a lot of melodies and we were arranging them in a number of different ways, but they were never thought out, except in the studio; there was no real planning behind any of that. We did all those songs in a couple of sessions at RCA; we were on a roll there: '19th Nervous Breakdown', which is not very good, really, and 'Have You Seen Your Mother Baby', which is not very good either.

'Mother's Little Helper' is a very strange record, like a music hall number, with an electric twelve-string on it, which made it very distinctive. It's very hooky all that stuff: 'Paint It Black', the Bo Diddley hook on '19th Nervous Breakdown' – very hooky and very pop.

CHARLIE: We've often tried to perform 'Mother's Little Helper' and it's never been any good, never gelled for some reason – it's either me not playing it right or Keith not wanting to do it like that. It's never worked. It's just one of those songs. We used to try it live but it's a bloody hard record to play, although we did perform it live on Ed Sullivan.

MICK: 'Paint It Black' is quite good and very different. It has that Turkish groove that was really out of nowhere and something to do with Brian helping the song move along by playing sitar, which gave that record a particular flavour.

KEITH: I must say in retrospect that actually what made 'Paint It Black' was Bill Wyman on the organ, because it didn't sound anything like the finished record, until Bill said, "You go like this".

CHARLIE: On 'Paint It Black' the drum pattern might have been suggested by Mick and I'd try it that way, or we'd be listening to a certain record at the time – it could have been anything like 'Going To A Go-Go'. Engineers never liked recording ride cymbals in those days. We all used to have the kind that Art Blakey used, with the inch-long or so rivets, so the cymbals would cover everything, and the engineers would go mad.

MICK: At this point I don't think Brian was necessarily shying away from guitar. He just enjoyed being a colourist and that was very effective. His guitar playing was good when he played slide guitar – that was a strength – but he wasn't much of a rock player, really. Keith could do the other parts and Brian wasn't really that needed, so he was more interested in playing the recorder or the sitar. Brian was more like an all-round musician rather than a specialist guitar player. It is great to have someone in a band who's doing that – now we have to have hundreds of people to do all those jobs, it's really boring. Brian was a very good dabbler. Ultimately that was not a good thing for him, but when he was on this musical dabbling he was good.

KEITH: Brian was a man of excess. He got into excess really quickly. The fame affected all of us – and it still does, no doubt – but it seemed that there was an extreme personality change which happened really quickly with Brian. It was as if he'd been given this substance, and the more he got of it, the more he wanted. He was always very intense, anyway, about anything that he wanted to do, but there seemed to be something additional within a few months or a year of starting out. This has probably got something to do with the fact that Mick and I were writing the songs. At the beginning he had considered himself the senior member of the band. I think he was a very jealous guy, which affected everything in his life, to the point of self-destruction. If something was his,

it was his – ask Anita. He probably felt that he was becoming a second fiddle to Mick and myself. At the point I realised this, I said to Brian, "Well, all you've got to do is write some songs, if that's what's bothering you".

But writing songs was not his forte. Also, writing songs by yourself is difficult. I've very rarely written songs alone: my idea of fun is writing a song with Mick or somebody else, bouncing ideas off each other, the interaction. My own ideas are only half a thing. I can yell them at the mirror or the wall and they will come bouncing back, but it's not a lot of fun talking to the wall.

I think Brian found himself being idolised in one way, as "the little blond wonder", but inside himself being very, very pissed off against Mick and myself and Andrew Oldham. Probably most of his hatred was aimed at Andrew and then it dissipated in bitter tiers down to Mick and myself. So without knowing it, he deliberately made himself unpleasant to be around. You're on the road 350 days of the year and suddenly you've got this guy who is the one cog in the machine who doesn't seem to be considering how the machine can help him; he's no longer a part of it. I have always thought that fame was something to live with and that we were famous because this thing we've got together works, but I think that for some weird reason Brian saw it as a stepping stone to something else.

If you've got to travel with somebody in a car for eight hours, do three gigs in the same night and then move on, you have to be a smooth team and support each other. But Brian either wouldn't turn up, or if he did he'd just make a lot of very snide remarks, and he also developed some very annoying personal habits like his obsession with his hair. When you're alone with the guy so much, you start to mimic him. Then Brian would get pissed off that we were taking the piss out of him, and the whole thing became compounded. After 'Satisfaction' Brian's unhappiness became much more noticeable and then he started being

Bill and Brian at work in the studio, by Gered Mankowitz, Los Angeles, 1965. The Jagger/Richards writing team proved too prolific for either to get a look-in. Bill did, however, contribute 'In Another Land' to Their Satanic Majesties Request, *and this was extracted for a US single.*

*Four photographs,
taken in 1965, seen
for the first time,
from an album
of photographs by
Marilyn Demick.*

DEC   65   •

Brian makes a "Nanker" face. This was a running joke within the group in the early Edith Grove days. The pseudonymous writing credit Nanker-Phelge, disguising some of the early work of Mick and Keith, remained in use as late as 1965 and covered some 14 songs.

Charlie: Brian felt marginalised and he wasn't strong enough physically to cope with being away on tour and going on stage regularly. There was a period in Chicago where Brian was in hospital and had to go home. That's when it started to go wrong with Brian. We actually did carry on performing, like The Who, with Keith, Bill and me playing the music behind Mick — and of course we've never been that type of band; we've always had a rhythm and a lead swapping around.

really excessive, first of all with booze and then the drugs, which he knew nothing about. Brian wanted to be different to the rest of us, but he didn't know who he wanted to be. So he'd be hip-hopping around with anybody who would flatter him, which became intensely irritating to Mick and me. Eventually your only defence when it became intolerable was to take the piss out of him in front of everybody else. It was really unforgivable, but that was the pressure we were under – and I think we all feel a bit ashamed of it. But Brian was just sitting in the back of the car drooling. And then he started to get sick and we were all trying to ask him, "Hey man, what's this all about?" Obviously he wasn't able to articulate it. It was too deep inside him – and then what happened is that suddenly in late '66, we were so exhausted that we couldn't go on the road. We were wiped.

It was a pressure cooker. There was no time off in those days. For three or four years we maybe had ten days or two weeks off in the whole year. At that age you've got non-stop energy and if things are working out and you're on the trail of something, you don't really notice how hard it is. It was high pressure.

MICK: Look at the schedule: it goes tour, tour, tour, tour, studio, studio, tour, tour, tour, studio, studio. The work was absolutely non-stop between the studio and the television appearances. The night of the gig there'd be an interview and then the *Scooby Doo Show* and whatever else. There was no time off.

Brian wanted to be the centre of attention, but he wasn't. One of Brian's agonies and downfalls was that he wanted to be the leader of the band and unfortunately he wasn't talented enough to be the leader.

Charlie

ROB BOWMAN

Rob Bowman is a professor of music at York University, Toronto, specialising in ethnomusicology and popular music. In 1996 he won a Grammy ('Best Album Notes' category) for his monograph in a ten-CD box set chronicling the history of Stax Records and wrote the definitive book *Soulsville USA, The Story Of Stax Records*.

Every creditable history of rock and roll spends an inordinate amount of time discussing the role of the Beatles, through songs such as 'Tomorrow Never Knows' from *Revolver* and later singles such as 'Strawberry Fields Forever', in introducing the notion of eclectic experimentation and "art" to the world of popular music. The Rolling Stones are always acknowledged in such works as the prime progenitors of what is nominally referred to as London R&B. They are consequently given credit for playing a seminal role in turning young white North Americans onto blues.

While true, this stereotypical account of rock history in the 1960s fails to acknowledge the fact that, while the Beatles were redefining the very nature of what popular music could be, the Rolling Stones were simultaneously forging an idiosyncratic style that drew less on European classical sources, but was just as eclectic, wide ranging and innovative. If the Beatles opened the doors to the world of progressive rock, between 1965 and 1968 the Rolling Stones helped forged the blueprint for modern rock itself.

When the Stones first came to North America in June 1964, they were virtual unknowns. Their first North American forty-five, a cover of Buddy Holly's 'Not Fade Away', had entered the Billboard charts a month earlier, peaking at a woeful #48 midway through the group's short fifteen-day tour. Already stars in the UK, when it came to America the Stones were starting once again from ground zero.

Audiences were sparse that first time around. With the exception of the opening show in San Bernadino and the closing shows at Carnegie Hall in New York City, the band found themselves playing to mostly empty houses. To add insult to injury, the group had to endure the patronizing remarks of host Dean Martin during their performance on the nationally broadcast *Hollywood Palace* TV show. The Stones, themselves, had wondered what it would be like to try and get over performing their versions of black American music for an American audience. What they hadn't counted on was the unremitting hostility and intolerance of many adult Americans.

Two weeks after the group headed back to London, their second American forty-five, the Jagger-Richards-penned 'Tell Me' entered the charts, followed a scant three weeks later by the band's cover of soul group the Valentino's 'It's All Over Now'. Both forty-fives topped out in the mid-twenties. 'Tell Me', also included on their first North American album, *England's Newest Hit Makers*, epitomised the early songwriting efforts of Mick and Keith. A decently crafted pop ballad, it had little to do with the Stones raison d'être, their love, infatuation and intoxication with black American music. 'It's All Over Now', on the other hand, was the first indication of a significant shift in the band's repertoire and consequent sound.

From their formation in 1962 the Stones had drunk most deeply from the twin wells of post-war blues, most prominently represented by covers of Jimmy Reed, Muddy Waters and Howlin' Wolf songs, and mid-fifties black rock and roll as epitomized by the one-two punch of Chuck Berry and Bo Diddley. One of the many wonders the Stones encountered on their first visit to the United States was American black radio. In 1964 that meant the sounds of soul and artists like Solomon Burke, Otis Redding, Don Covay, Irma Thomas and Sam Cooke. The Rolling Stones came to North America a blues band that could also play primal rock and roll. They returned home steeped in the sound of soul. The Stones would return to North America in late October 1964 for a three-week tour, near the beginning of which they taped the fabled *T.A.M.I.* show, headlining a bill that included such soul luminaries as James Brown and Marvin Gaye. These were heady days indeed.

In addition to the shift in the band's repertoire, as 1964 wound to a close there were other notable changes within the group. At the beginning of the year Bill Wyman and Brian Jones were singing background vocals. By early 1965, Keith Richards, consolidating his position as creative leader of the band, had become the sole vocal foil for Mick Jagger. Even more significantly, Jagger and Richards had begun to emerge as songwriters capable of writing music that drew authentically on the black idioms that had always resided at the core of the Stones' performance-oriented aesthetic.

January 1965's soul-inflected 'Heart of Stone', recorded in Los Angeles during that second American sojourn, was the first example of the Glimmer Twins' newly found songwriting prowess. The watershed moment, though, came a scant two months later when Keith and Mick, inspired by the Staple Singers, reworked the gospel standard 'The Last Time'. When recorded by the Stones and issued in late spring, the song promptly stormed its way into the Billboard Top Ten.

'The Last Time' was followed by the Stones first single to top the charts, the apocalyptic '(I Can't Get No) Satisfaction', written and recorded in May 1965 on the group's third North American tour. By late fall 'Get Off My Cloud' had provided the group with their second #1 smash. 'The Last Time', 'Satisfaction' and 'Get Off My Cloud' form a trilogy of sorts. All are riff-based compositions whose success rests on the unrelenting propulsiveness of their groove, Charlie Watt's swing approach to drumming, arrangements that juxtapose extraordinarily electric guitar riffs with more colouristic second guitar lines and, above all, Jagger's increasingly controlled, yet still ultra intense vocals. In the case of all three singles, the performances sound like they are on the edge of veering out of control, creating an aura of frenzied excitement simply unmatched by any of the Stones' contemporaries.

Up to this point in the world of pop the rule of thumb was, when this successful, simply repeat the formula until sales indicated that the audience wanted something different. The reason that the Stones remain a going concern some three years into the 21st century is that they opted for a different path. Beginning with 'l9th Nervous Breakdown', Richards' songs tended to feature much more distinctive and highly developed melodies that were complimented by (1) Jagger's similarly idiosyncratic lyrics and (2) extraordinarily sympathetic and disparate band arrangements. Late 1965 through early 1967 was an incredibly fertile and creative period for the band as riff-based soul-influenced composition gave way to melodically-based pop music of the highest order. To this day, I marvel at the sheer distinctiveness of each successive single: the Indian raga sound of 'Paint It Black', the music hall somewhat tongue-in-cheek 'Mother's Little Helper', the downright Elizabethan 'Lady Jane', the incredibly manic 'Have You Seen Your Mother, Baby, Standing in the Shadow?', the stoic 'Ruby Tuesday' and the barrelhouse piano-driven 'Let's Spend the Night Together'. When you factor in the quality of *Aftermath*, the group's first album comprised solely of originals, 1966 signaled a quantum leap forward for the band.

While the essence of these records clearly resides in the compositional breakthroughs of Keith Richards, their magic is partially a result of the continually evolving sense of the Stones as a performing ensemble. By the group's second North American tour in late 1964, Brian Jones appeared to be losing interest. Ostensibly the founder and, at least in his own mind, once leader of the band, Jones had difficulties reconciling his roots as a blues purist, his intoxication with stardom and, partially due to his inability to write songs, the fact that he was increasingly playing second fiddle to Jagger and Richards. Compounding his personal anxieties, Jones also had health problems, some of them undoubtedly physical and others perhaps more psychosomatic.

Surprisingly, the shift in the band's interests sparked renewed enthusiasm on the part of Jones and gave him a second life within the band. A quick learner with great musical facility, he promptly became the band's colourist picking up a panoply of different instruments at session after session. It's simply impossible to conceive of 'Paint It Black' minus Jones' lead sitar line, 'Ruby Tuesday' sans his exquisite recorder counter melody or 'Lady Jane' bereft of his winsome dulcimer. Other notable examples of Jones' multi-instrument abilities include the lead marimba part on 'Under My Thumb', the Japanese koto playing on 'Take It or Leave It' and 'Ride On Baby', the melotron on 'Please Go Home', the brass lines on 'Something Happened to Me Yesterday' and the harpsichord and sax on 'Dandelion'.

Jones wasn't the only member of the band who was blossoming creatively in the halcyon days of 1966 and early 1967. Bassist Bill Wyman contributed the unforgettable dive bombing bass runs at the end of 'l9th Nervous Breakdown', achieved a wonderfully distorted sound on 'Under My Thumb' and 'It's Not Easy', alongside Keith played bowed bass on 'Ruby Tuesday', added the bass slides to the beginning of 'We Love You' and came up with the organ line and tempo that, according to all concerned, transformed 'Paint It Black' from the ordinary into the extraordinary. Charlie Watts was equally creative, adopting a busier approach to his drumming, employing more cymbal crashes to mark the sections of songs such as 'l9th Nervous Breakdown', 'Paint It Black' and 'Mother's Little Helper', contributing militaristic fills on 'Ruby Tuesday', taking a brief drum break at the end of 'Complicated', adding finger cymbals to 'Back Street Girl' and propelling 'We Love You' and 'Dandelion' with surprisingly demonstrative tom-tom fills.

According to Keith Richards, much of this creative burst can be directly attributed to the ingestion of various psychoactive substances that were an integral part of the period for virtually all concerned. Equally important was the fact that the band had begun to cut back on the non-stop touring and recording schedule that had been their daily reality from early 1963 forwards. Drugs played an even greater role in the recording of the group's 1967 album, *Their Satanic Majesties Request*. While every member of the band remembers the sessions for the album as being incredibly fun, all are also painfully aware that as a musical creation the album was sub-standard.

All things considered, *Their Satanic Majesties Request* was a critical and commercial failure. Part of the problem was undoubtedly that mid-way through the sessions the group parted ways with Andrew Loog Oldham, their manager and producer since 1963. When the group headed back to the studio in early 1968 they had in Jimmy Miller a new producer in tow and a batch of songs that signaled a return to roots American music. This time, though, the roots weren't the post-war blues of Chicago and Chuck Berry rock and roll. They were pre-war blues, classic country and, to a lesser extent, gospel. The first batch of recordings heralding this new sound produced two singles, 'Jumpin' Jack Flash' and 'Street Fighting Man', and the album *Beggars Banquet*. Collectively these records lay out a sound and approach that would form the basis for their work through *Let It Bleed*, *Get Your Ya-Ya's Out*, *Sticky Fingers* and *Exile On Main Street* and, as such, represent the first rays of what is unanimously understood as the group's golden period.

The genesis of the band's rejuvenation lay in those age old tonics known as rest and relaxation. After a short three-week jaunt through Europe in March and April 1967, the group decided to take an extended hiatus from the road which ultimately lasted two-and-a-half years. With time on his hands for the first time since the band started and feeling that he had reached an impasse as a guitarist, Keith Richards began to explore the world of open guitar tunings favoured by many of the great pre-war bluesmen such as Robert Johnson and Reverend Robert Wilkins. These new tunings forced Keith to learn new chord voicings on the guitar and ultimately led him toward a new approach to composition. Once again relying on riffs as the basis for many of his new songs, Richards and the Stones forged a style that helped usher rock music into the modern era.

The moment I first heard 'Jumpin' Jack Flash' is indelibly burned into my psyche to the point that I remember it as if it was yesterday. It was June 1968 and I was about a month shy of my twelfth birthday. Headed to the local variety store to buy a butterscotch sucker, as per usual, my transistor radio was pressed tightly to my right ear, tuned to the local Toronto pop radio station.

Seemingly like a shot from outer space, the opening chords of 'Jumpin' Jack Flash' came flying out of my transistor speaker with a force and bite the likes I nor anyone else had ever heard before. It would be years later that I would learn that Keith had played the part on an acoustic guitar that he had compressed and distorted beyond recognition by putting it through one of the very first cassette tape recorders. All I knew that fateful June day was that my head was nearly taken off by the sheer sonic force that emanated from my tinny transistor. In those first few seconds, nine bars before Mick's vocal entry, I knew the Stones were not only back but they, and by extension rock and roll, had entered a new epoch.

Thirty-five years later, after having heard the original recording who knows how many hundred times and having witnessed the group play it over the course of dozens of live shows, 'Jumpin' Jack Flash' remains an elixir just as potent as it was on that day in June 1968. It has not only stood the test of time but, like the band itself, it has seemingly transcended and defied the very logic of time. It remains one of the greatest moments in the history of rock and roll.

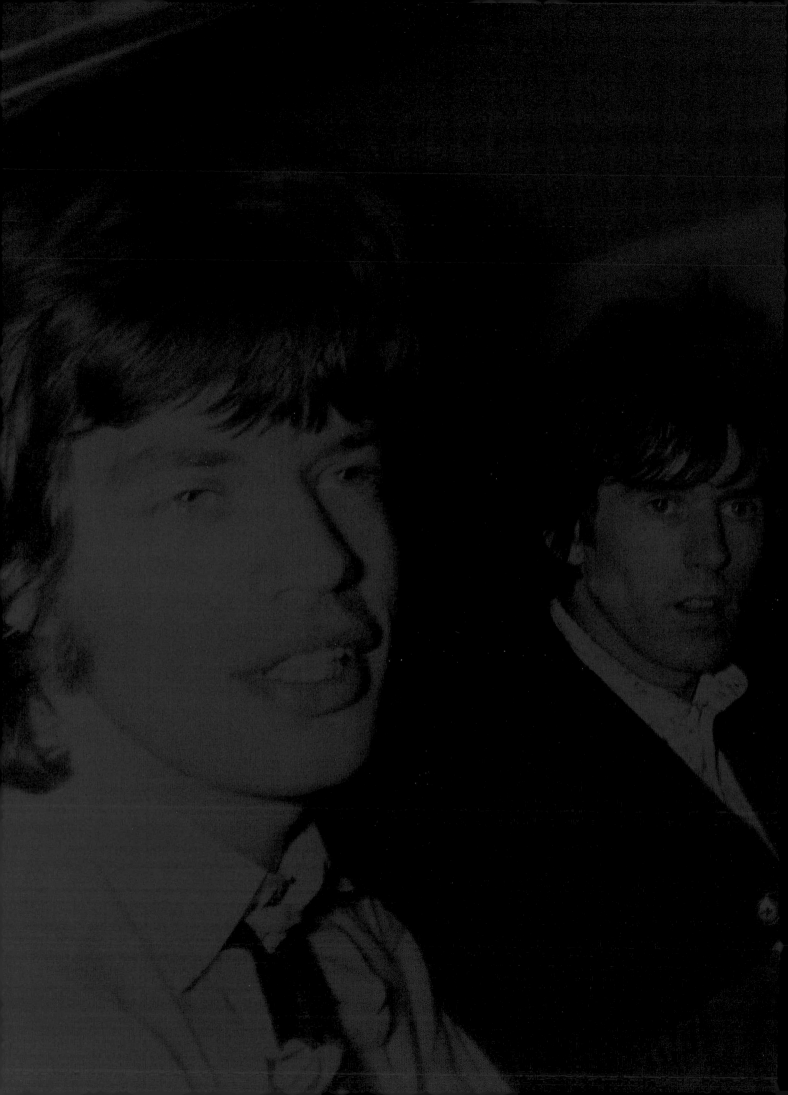

There were too many things going on. We wanted to move on from being a pop group. We wanted to be more grown up. On the other hand we wanted to take loads of drugs & have lots of girl friends.

Mick Jagger

CLOSING OF THE CURTAIN

5

*As the 1960s entered
its psychedelic phase,
the Stones' collective
image became more
hedonistic. Their 1967
release,* Their Satanic
Majesties Request, *was originally available
in a Michael Cooper-
designed cover
incorporating a
three-dimensional
image that could only
be manufactured by
two factories in the
world and rumoured to
cost $1 apiece.*

KEITH: When we got busted at Redlands, it suddenly made us realise that this was a whole different ball game and that was when the fun stopped. Up until then it had been as though London existed in a beautiful space where you could do anything you wanted. And then the hammer came down and it was back to reality. We grew up instantly.

There was a realisation that the powers that be actually looked upon us as important enough to make a big statement and to wield the hammer. But they'd also made us more important than we ever bloody well were in the first place. Hence you got the "Who breaks a butterfly on a wheel?" piece – which from *The Times* was a pretty heavy editorial. I think it's still considered one of their boldest editorials.

At the same time nobody knew how long this little "summer of love" would go on for; you were just trying to milk this good time for all it was. If we'd still been on the road, perhaps we wouldn't have got busted, but something else would have happened. It was the closing of the curtain on that period. The prefects had told us they were not going to put up with our behaviour and the fact that they considered your influence on the public to be of significance made you wonder what they were scared of. Before this, I'd never thought about the authorities or anything like that. Who gave a shit? You just carried on – make sure the water comes on and stop people running red lights, that was their job. I pay my taxes and there you go. But after this you suddenly realised that there was a determined effort to bring you down.

CHARLIE: There were a lot of drugs being taken at that time, but it was a very fashionable thing to do. It was quite common for musicians to take LSD and then bring a bottle of Jack Daniels on stage.

KEITH: I had started to hang out with Brian again, and I made a very conscious attempt to re-cement my relationship with him when he wasn't working and the pressure was off. I used to live across the road from him. I was enjoying Brian's company while he was relaxed and we were still playing together in the house. Then, just after we got busted, a trip to Morocco sounded good, but it didn't work out that way – and things got ugly again. I pulled the old Bentley out, and Brian and Anita and myself sat in the back playing sounds. Brian fell ill and we had to put him in a hospital, so it was Anita and me in there. Of course, amazing things can happen in the back of a car – and they did. Brian caught up with us in London, and there was a tearful scene. That was the final nail in the coffin with me and Brian. He'd never forgive me for that and I don't blame him, but, hell, shit happens.

A case could be made that Brian had an acid trip that he never quite came back from – I'm only surmising that – and after that everything was all a bit fragmented within him; the bits just kept moving further and further away from each other.

MICK: *Their Satanic Majesties Request* was a really fun moment, and there were some good songs on it: 'She's A Rainbow' was very pretty. Nicky Hopkins on piano was very much in evidence on that record. '2,000 Light Years From Home' was a good track; we performed that live quite a lot, but the studio version was actually a bit too long and not focused enough. There's a lot of rubbish on *Satanic Majesties*. Just too much time on our hands, too many drugs, no producer to tell us, "Enough already, thank you very much, now can we just get on with this song?" Anyone let loose in the studio will produce stuff like that. There was simply too much hanging around. It's like believing everything you do is great and not having any editing – and Andrew had gone by that point.

CHARLIE: *Satanic Majesties* was a very druggy period – though not for me, and I'm not saying that as an excuse. I was never into drugs much at that time, only later on, although I was probably the first one who smoked, but I wasn't into any of the other things. At the time it was acid, which opened up a lot of possibilities, but nothing we did was nearly as radical as what musicians like Albert Ayler and Sun Ra were doing, as far as I was concerned.

I don't know if much good came out of *Satanic Majesties*. We had a go at anything we wanted to do – and most of the time we did it ourselves. Later on it all became very serious and if you wanted a tabla on a track, you'd ask an Indian musician to come in and play it – nowadays you would just sample the greatest tabla player in the world and play it on a keyboard. In those days if you wanted a tabla you had to try and play the thing, which is what we all did. Mick would be banging away on something, I'd be banging something. It was, "Let's play this song all together".

It was actually a lot of fun rather than a musical revolution. I don't think the songs are as good as a lot of music we did before or after, not by a long way, but that happens. It wasn't one of our great records, although it was a very interesting time. Sometimes you listen back to some music later on that is really quite good and which you've forgotten about – but I don't think that's true of *Satanic Majesties*.

> *I can remember virtually nothing of the Satanic Majesties sessions. It's a total blank. God knows what the sounds were like. We were pretty much the way we look on the cover!*
>
> *Keith*

KEITH: I can remember virtually nothing of those sessions. It's a total blank. We were pretty much the way we look on the cover! The thing I remember most about making *Satanic Majesties* is that cover. We went to New York with Michael Cooper and met a Japanese guy who had a camera that could produce a 3-D effect. We built the set on acid, went all round New York getting the flowers and the rest of the props; we were painting it, spraying it. We were just loony, and after the Beatles had done *Sgt. Pepper*, it was like, "Let's get even more ridiculous".

We were also fighting these legal battles, which was just one of the reasons why the record is so weird. Your mind is totally taken up with all this other shit and at the same time you're still trying to carry on with your vacation, so in spite of the fact that the hammer had come down, it was like "I'll carry on being nuts for a bit". So really it was a very stoned time, a lot of which came from the concussion of the hammer, although in fact the whole impact of the hammer only took effect on the next record.

MICK: The reason Andrew Oldham left was because he thought that we weren't concentrating and that we were being childish. It was not a great moment really – and I wouldn't have thought it was a great moment for Andrew either. There were a lot of distractions and you always need someone to focus you at that point, that was Andrew's job. Also Andrew didn't seem to know exactly what he wanted to do: he wanted to be this, that, and the other. He thought he would make lots of money in business, but he'd spent all his money on peripheral projects.

KEITH: Andrew did kind of disappear around the time of the drug bust, but I wouldn't say that he was the first thing on our minds at that point. When you get busted, you're not really thinking about who, why and what. You're just thinking, "How do I get out of this?" But his absence did add to a sense of where we were going or not going, and that it wasn't where he thought he wanted to go. So probably his not being with us when he went into the shadows contributed to a growing distance between us.

CHARLIE: I always look upon Andrew as an entrepreneur more than a manager, although maybe it's the same thing. I don't think we really needed a manager, to be honest.

KEITH: There is a change between the material on *Satanic Majesties* and *Beggars Banquet*. I'd grown sick to death of the whole Maharishi guru shit and the beads and bells. Who knows where these things come from, but I guess it was a reaction to what we'd done in our time off and also that severe dose of reality. A spell in prison at Wormwood Scrubs would certainly give you room for thought!

I was fucking pissed with being busted. So it was, "Right we'll go and strip this thing down". There's a lot of anger in the music from that period.

'Jumpin' Jack Flash' and 'Street Fighting Man' came about because I had become fascinated by the possibilities of playing an acoustic guitar through a cassette recorder, using it as a pick-up, really, so that I could still get the crispness of an acoustic – which you can never get off an electric guitar – but overloading this tiny little machine so the effect was that it sounded both acoustic and electric. Technology was starting to increase in sophistication, but I just wanted to reduce it back to basics.

I bought one of the first cassette machines – a must for a budding songwriter – and then day in, day out recorded on it. Then I began to get interested in the actual sound of the machine, how close you could put the microphone to the guitar and what effect you

Brian and guitar. A troubled personal life and a seeming detachment from the band and their music meant that he had little musical contribution to December 1968's Beggars Banquet, *the final Stones album released during his lifetime.*

Brian and Mick in the studio.

Mick in classic frontman pose. The Stones had all but ceased performing in Britain during the mid-1960s, an unbilled spot at the NME Poll Winners Concert in May 1968 their first in Britain for nearly two years. The arrival of Mick Taylor would help re-establish them as a road band par excellence.

could get out of it. After all, everything's electric, even anything you hear played by Segovia has gone through a microphone and some form of electronic stimulation before you hear it. That little box was always with me; it was like my notebook. The first time I figured the technique out, I was playing into it, strumming away and I crashed out. I listened back to the tape the next morning and heard the guitar getting closer and closer to the microphone, and was intrigued by the possibilities.

When we were in the studio I would bring in that little Philips cassette recorder, get a wooden extension speaker, plug that into the back of the recorder, shove a microphone in front of the speaker in the middle of the studio and record it. We would all sit back and watch this little microphone record the cassette machine in the middle of the studio at Olympic, which was the size of Sadler's Wells. Then we'd go back, listen to it, play over it, mash it up and there was the track.

MICK: I remember the recording session for 'Jumpin' Jack Flash', and not liking the way it was done very much. It was a bit haphazard – and although the end result was pretty good, it was not quite what I wanted. The fidelity wasn't that great; it wasn't quite as in your face as it could have been. What *was* a watershed moment was creating a promotional film for it, which was very much groping in the dark compared to the way music videos developed.

CHARLIE: 'Jumpin' Jack Flash' was recorded at Olympic; we were doing it deliberately for a single. Keith is playing my floor tom-tom on it to give the "boom-da, boom-da" sound. Now you'd just programme it and loop it or something daft like that. The sound on 'Jumpin' Jack Flash' is very close together, because we do sit close to each other in the studio, much to most engineers' amazement nowadays. Nobody does that any more, really.

'Street Fighting Man' was recorded on Keith's cassette with a 1930s toy drum kit called a London Jazz Kit Set, which I bought in an antiques shop, and which I've still got at home. It came in a little suitcase, and there were wire brackets you put the drums in; they were like small tambourines with no jangles. The whole kit packs away, the drums go inside each other, the little drum goes inside the snare drum into a box with the cymbal. The snare drum was fantastic because it had a really thin skin with a snare right underneath, but only two strands of gut.

> *When we first started out we wanted to be a blues band and then we became more pop-oriented — because we wanted to be popular and to get played on the radio — and then we started to become more of an eclectic band.*
>
> *Mick*

Keith loved playing with the early cassette machines because they would overload, and when they overloaded they sounded fantastic, although you weren't meant to do that. We usually played in one of the bedrooms on tour. Keith would be sitting on a cushion playing a guitar and the tiny kit was a way of getting close to him. The drums were really loud compared to the acoustic guitar and the pitch of them would go right through the sound. You'd always have a great backbeat.

'Street Fighting Man' is a funny song to play on stage in an era when you don't fight in the street any more. To play the song is fantastic, but the lyrics are very much about the events of 1968 in Paris, which is when Mick wrote it. It was political: not that it was going to change the world, but it was extremely influenced by what was going on; a very strong song about what was happening at the time.

KEITH: Mick was writing most of the lyrics. Sometimes I might have suggested what the theme was going to be, maybe even the first verse and then I'd say "Where do we go from here?" The working-class lyrics came from Mick, but I think that was *his* reaction to the hammer coming down. It was a period when I wouldn't know what he was going to come out with next. Take 'Sympathy For The Devil', for example: lyrically that was all his. I was just trying to figure out whether it should be a samba or a goddamn folk song.

CHARLIE: 'Sympathy' was one of those sort of songs where we tried everything. The first time I ever heard the song was when Mick was playing it at the front door of a house I lived in in Sussex. It was at dinner; he played it entirely on his own, the sun was going down – and it was fantastic. We had a go at loads of different ways of playing it; in the end I just played a jazz Latin feel in the style that Kenny Clarke would have played on 'A Night In Tunisia' – not the actual rhythm he played, but the same styling. Fortunately it worked, because it was a sod to get together.

MICK: There were definite pressures to get some kind of focus. The technology had moved on somewhat. On our early records, to achieve what we wanted to do had required too much layering – we used to call it "ping-ponging", going from one track to another – so we ended up with a very messy sound, a bad signal-to-noise ratio, basically. What started as a great rhythm track ended up as this sort of mush, but by the end of the '60s, there were a lot more tracks available and you had more choices about what was possible without losing all the fidelity. Jimmy Miller had produced a record with Traffic, which I liked very much: it sounded very good. So we decided we wanted to get into a groove with this new sound.

CHARLIE: Jimmy Miller made a significant contribution to the band at that time. That was because he had a great set of ears and he was a musician, a percussionist, who could and would join in, and he happened to be in London at a time when there were a few good bands around, including Traffic. Jimmy was very, very good; the nearest we've been recently to working with him is Don Was.

KEITH: Jimmy Miller was one of the most simpatico producers I have ever worked with. He could handle a band – especially this band – and give everybody the same level of support. He was a great drummer in his own right, so he could talk to Charlie on equal terms, and he had a very good rapport with Mick. He didn't mind any idea that came up. He loved improvisation. I don't think I could have done 'Street Fighting Man' without

Charlie and former art student Shirley Shepherd married in secret in Bradford in 1964 and have been together ever since. They are pictured here with daughter Serafina, born in March 1968.

Charlie: I've still got the chair – I bought it from a business partner of Wolf Mankowitz, the photographer Gered Mankowitz's father. I've had it for 40 years.

Keith presides at a mock drugs trial in 1969. The outcry against Mick and Keith's drugs convictions in June 1967 culminated in a Times newspaper leading article, headlined "Who Breaks A Butterfly On A Wheel", by editor William Rees-Mogg. This indicated a shift in British society's attitude towards rock counterculture, or in Times-speak "the new hedonism" as opposed to "traditional values".

him. Mick would get impatient with my experiments sometimes, but Jimmy gave me a lot of encouragement saying, "Let's take this down the line and let's see where it goes".

MICK: There was a kind of country and blues roots feel to tracks like 'Prodigal Son'. You just let certain parts of you out when you wanted to. When we first started out we wanted to be a blues band and then we became more pop-oriented – because we wanted to be popular and to get played on the radio – and then we started to become more of an eclectic band.

As far as country music was concerned, we used to play country songs, but we'd never record them – or we recorded them but never released them. Keith and I had been playing Johnny Cash records and listening to the Everly Brothers – who were *so* country – since we were kids. I used to love country music even before I met Keith. I loved George Jones and really fast, shit-kicking country music, though I didn't really like the maudlin songs too much. And to me all these old rockers were really converted country singers; Jerry Lee Lewis is the most obvious version of that, but you could also hear it in Gene Vincent and Ricky Nelson.

The country songs, like 'Factory Girl' or 'Dear Doctor' on *Beggars Banquet* were really pastiche. There's a sense of humour in country music anyway, a way of looking at life in a humorous kind of way – and I think we were just acknowledging that element of the music. The "country" songs we recorded later, like 'Dead Flowers' on *Sticky Fingers* or 'Faraway Eyes' on *Some Girls* are slightly different. The actual music is played completely straight, but it's me who's not going legit with the whole thing, because I think I'm a blues singer not a country singer – I think it's more suited to Keith's voice than mine.

KEITH: To me 'Factory Girl' felt something like 'Molly Malone', an Irish jig; one of those ancient Celtic things that emerge from time to time, or an Appalachian song. In those days I would just come up and play something, sitting around the room. I still do that today. If Mick gets interested I'll carry on working on it; if he doesn't look interested, I'll drop it, leave it and say, "I'll work on it and maybe introduce it later".

The Lennons join Keith, Mick and Brian on the set of Rock And Roll Circus, *the music extravaganza filmed for television at Wembley Studios in December 1968. Despite an all-star cast list, including the Who, Eric Clapton and Jethro Tull, it would remain unseen for nearly three decades.*

CHARLIE: On 'Factory Girl', I was doing something you shouldn't do, which is playing the tabla with sticks instead of trying to get that sound using your hand, which Indian tabla players do, though it's an extremely difficult technique and painful if you're not trained.

KEITH: When we had been in the States between 1964 and '66, I had gathered together this enormous collection of records, but I never had any time to listen to them. In late 1966 and '67 I unwrapped them and actually played them. It was like an incredible blues archive; suddenly I had time to study music again and listen to it. For the first time since 1963, it seemed, I could sit down with the guys and listen to music, and listen to it again. For the previous three years, I had either been writing a new song or learning how to play it or recording it. Now I had the luxury of becoming a listener again. Somebody has to make the music, but the real joy of music is listening to it. I was able to refuel and re-evaluate, and there was a lot of different music around, not just the blues stuff, but some Indian music and gypsy music. I started to listen to more classical music and more jazz than I had done for a long time.

A lot of the country music came from just travelling around America. If you were playing in the mid-west in 1964 or '65 you weren't going to hear much else. There's a wonderful simplicity about it – it's another form of the blues – and then there's this lovely white Formica, plastic bit on the top. The Everly Brothers are pure country and they made some of the best rock'n'roll records of all time: 'Wake Up Little Susie', 'Bye Bye Love' and 'Cathy's Clown'.

So I was listening to what other people were doing, having a chance to sit around, talking to people like Robert Fraser, Christopher Gibbs or Michael Cooper, and we also had a chance to see the Beatles. There was more contact between members of the Stones and the Beatles than ever before, ever since they'd given us 'I Wanna Be Your Man'. At that time they were saturating everything. The Beatles could do no wrong; not that they thought so, but as far as the general public were concerned. Everything they did was getting better and better and more mind-blowing – whether it's true or not in retrospect

The release of Beggars Banquet *in December 1968 was celebrated by a feast in the Elizabethan Rooms of London's Kensington Gore Hotel. Guests included Lord Harlech, while footage of the invitation-only event made it onto the national television news.*

The Daily Mail *lamented the fact that these "apostles of present-day grooviness [resorted to] the oldest gag in show business — custard-pie throwing".*

(Top and centre) Brian and Charlie relax the day after the Beggars Banquet *reception.*

(Bottom) Mick, Keith and Charlie peruse pictures from the Rock And Roll Circus. *Just one number from the show, 'You Can't Always Get What You Want', made it into a 25th anniversary TV retrospective, 25X5, before the project finally attained video and audio release in 1996.*

is another thing – but they were also like us, under overwhelming pressure to come up with something, trying to readjust to a changing society.

MICK: Brian wasn't really involved on *Beggars Banquet*, apart from some slide on 'No Expectations'; that was the only thing he played on the whole record. He wasn't turning up to the sessions and he wasn't very well. In fact we didn't want him to turn up, I don't think.

KEITH: Brian's trouble wasn't musical. There was something in him that meant that if things were going well, he'd make sure it screwed up. I know the feeling: there's a demon in me, but I only own up to having *one* of them; Brian probably had *45* more. With Brian it was all self-consuming pride. If we'd been living in another century I'd have been having a duel with the motherfucker every single day. He would stand on his little hind legs about some piece of bullshit and turn it into a big deal – "You didn't smile at me today" – and then he started to get so stoned, he became something you just sat in the corner.

> *Brian wasn't really involved on Beggars Banquet... He wasn't turning up to the sessions and he wasn't very well. In fact we didn't want him to turn up, I don't think.*
>
> Mick

CHARLIE: I think Brian's self-esteem had gone down a lot by then. Keith was very dominant at that time – and also Keith had gone off with Brian's girlfriend. Brian was at a very low ebb and I don't think he ever got over it. I don't mean that he held it against Keith; it was what happened and that was that.

I think Brian lost interest and was more interested in being a pop star than a player – a lot of people are. It was also a phase when a lot of people were leaving bands and starting their own. Brian was the first of us to meet Bob Dylan and Jimi Hendrix and all those people; he was moving in that circle of people – he went to New York and met Allen Ginsberg and that crowd. Brian always had aspirations of being a singer and a leader of men and he wasn't either of them.

He had certainly worked the hardest at the very beginning on selling the band – before Andrew took over. Brian was a very good, adaptable guitar player, but he was no Jimi Hendrix, or Jeff Beck or Mick Taylor – that special talent. If you are just a very good player and you try to be a virtuoso, it becomes very difficult.

KEITH: We were quite happy that Brian wasn't around on *Beggars Banquet*, because when he wasn't there we could really get on with our work. And of course by then there was the whole situation with Anita, which was probably the final nail in the coffin as far as Brian and the Stones were concerned. By this point he was deliberately determined not to be part of what we were doing. He was going off into all these grandiose ideas: "I'm going to write and produce, I'm going to make films". It was complete fairyland.

He was a pain in the arse, quite honestly. We didn't have time to accommodate a passenger. This band can't carry any dead weight – no band can – and at the same time it was almost as if Brian was trying to screw the Stones up by not being there. He was so self-important, maybe because he was so short. I mean, why would a guy buy a Humber Super Snipe if he couldn't see over the steering wheel?

MICK: Keith and I went to Italy, and Keith had this idea for 'Midnight Rambler', so we just starting changing the tempos within the tune. Melodically it remains the same thing, it's just a lot of tempo changes. We worked on it with acoustic guitar and harmonica, just jammed it, went through the tempo changes and had it all organised by the time we had to record it for *Let It Bleed*.

CHARLIE: Jimmy Miller played drums on a couple of tracks on *Let It Bleed*, including 'You Can't Always Get What You Want', which I subsequently copied. That's how good Jimmy was at hearing songs. He wasn't a great drummer, but he was great at playing drums on records, which is a completely different thing. 'You Can't Always Get What You Want' is a great drum track. Jimmy actually made me stop and think again about the way I played drums in the studio and I became a much better drummer in the studio thanks to him – together we made some of the best records we've ever made, including 'Honky Tonk Women'. One-sixth of those songs was Jimmy, for me. Mick might say, "That's rubbish; you did it all yourself", but that's the way I feel. Jimmy taught me how to discipline myself in the studio. He would show me things and tell me more. He was a very good producer for our band. He was also very fortunate in one way because he was on a high – literally – and he'd got Mick and Keith at an extremely creative period as well.

MICK: 'You Can't Always Get What You Want' was something I just played on the acoustic guitar – one of those bedroom songs. It proved to be quite difficult to record because Charlie couldn't play the groove and so Jimmy Miller had to play the drums. I'd also had this idea of having a choir, probably a gospel choir, on the track, but there wasn't one around at that point. Jack Nitzsche, or somebody, said that we could get the London Bach Choir and we said, "That will be a laugh".

RONNIE: Before I joined the band I couldn't believe that Charlie didn't play drums on 'You Can't Always Get What You Want'.

MICK: We did 'Gimme Shelter' in a big room at Olympic Studios, and then did the over-dubs in LA with Merry Clayton. In London Keith had been playing the groove a few times on his own – although I think Brian was still around at that point; he might even have been in the studio actually – but there was no vocal. The use of the female voice was the producer's idea. It would be one of those moments along the lines of "I hear a girl on this track – get one on the phone".

CHARLIE: We've never played an intro to 'Honky Tonk Women' live the way it is on the record. That's Jimmy playing the cowbell and either he comes in wrong or I come in wrong – but Keith comes in right, which makes the whole thing right. It's one of those things that musicologists could sit around analysing for years. It's actually a mistake, but from my point of view, it works.

RONNIE: I met Brian one night by the radiator in Olympic Studios. Nicky Hopkins said, "I'm going to introduce you to my friend Brian", but Brian was not making much sense. He was sitting there going, "Urgh, urgh". I could understand the way he was with all the drugs going on around him.

MICK: Keith and I went to tell Brian that he was no longer in the band. I think he wanted

it. He wasn't there in his mind. Nowadays, you could say, "Brian, you have to go to this centre in Arizona for a couple of months to clean up", but in those days that wasn't as obvious an option. And naturally he didn't want to do it himself. He didn't seem to be very interested in staying in the band. He'd made his contribution to it. People are different. Not everyone wants to be in a rock band for forty years. You've got to want to do it. Some people are not psychologically suited to this way of life, and Brian was one of them. He really wasn't cut out to do this.

CHARLIE: Brian left us no choice in the decision. It wasn't like Mick Taylor leaving when he was playing so fabulously, and you thought, "What is he leaving for?" Brian wasn't in the Stones any more, or he physically wasn't up to it and so his head or heart weren't in it any more. He was more interested in being at home, the first home he'd ever had, and he was trying to get a band together with Mitch Mitchell. Everybody made the decision, but it was almost made by itself. We didn't suddenly turn round and say, "You missed a session, you're fired".

It was a decision made over quite a long period of time, ever since the time Brian had come home from the States long before we'd finished one of the tours. It was never right from then on. I think his not being in the band hurried his death along, but in any case he wasn't a very strong person – in fact he was very frail.

KEITH: We made a band effort. Mick, Charlie and I drove down there together to see him at his house. It was like going to a funeral, really. We were all very quiet. We went through these suburban lanes and then out into the country. We turned up at Brian's house and said, "Wow, nice joint". It was A.A. Milne's place. I looked around and thought, "I can understand how he could write *Winnie The Pooh* around here".

Then we got to talk to Brian. In a way it was weird, because he knew what was coming. We were saying to him, "How do you feel about this? We're going to go back out on the road and you're in no condition to join us, man. We're going on, are you going to come on board again or not?" We offered him the chance to stay, but it was an offer that we knew was going to be refused. He wasn't going to come back; it was already a foregone conclusion. It was just a matter of how he took it. It was kind of sad because Brian kept talking about the plans that he'd got: "Yeah, thanks for coming, but I'm playing with so and so, and I've got all of these projects and I'm writing this". He was going to go out on the road with Jimi Hendrix; he had millions of schemes.

We were asking him, "Are you all right, man?" I mean, the three of us don't take the trouble to drive down to somebody's house if we don't care about them, even if it *is* to tell them "You're fired". But he kept talking about what he was planning to do, so we said, "Well, we wish you well, pal". But at the same time we knew we had to fill the gap, because we were getting ready to go back into business.

RONNIE: I had been working the circuit up and down England and I'd bump into people like Jeff Beck. I also met Rod Stewart – our favourite band was the Small Faces and when Steve Marriott left them in the lurch, we thought, "That's a crime, we can't have that", and so we joined that band to keep them together. Ian Stewart gave us a rehearsal place in Bermondsey, which was the Stones' rehearsal studio. That's where Ronnie Lane took a phone call from Mick, who said, "Would Ronnie Wood join the Stones?" and Ronnie said, "No, he's quite happy where he is".

MICK: I just made a phone call to John Mayall. He said, "I've got this guitar player. You can have him, and he can come down right away". And he turned up with this guy Mick Taylor almost the next day. It worked and we thought, "Well, OK", and suddenly we had this gig at Hyde Park coming up, so we just went with him. There wasn't a big audition process, because he seemed to fit in really well and there was the pressure to do the gig. Maybe if we'd not had a gig coming up for six months, we'd have tried lots of others, but we just had to get on with it. I'm sure that if he hadn't worked out, we'd have changed him, but he seemed to fit in really quickly.

KEITH: I don't think we'd have gone down to see Brian if we hadn't already been looking and found somebody, but I don't remember now if that was the exact order of events, or whether we'd actually decided that it was going to be Mick Taylor. What prompted us was the fact that we were going to do this concert in Hyde Park and so we had an urgent need for a new guitar player. I guess that I had always hoped that Brian might get it together, optimist that I am – you can put a blindfold on and give me the last cigarette and I'll still hope they won't shoot.

Mick knew about Mick Taylor. He came in and played, and we said, "Well, that's it". We were going back on stage, Mick had come and played with us and we thought he was damned good and full of beans, why not keep him?

The last thing I'd wanted was a carbon copy of Brian, and after all Brian hadn't been playing guitar much recently, so I'd had to do all the parts, and I'd had to play with myself – I still do, but that's neither here nor there!

Mick Taylor turns up and plays like an angel, and I wasn't going to say no. I thought I'd let the guy develop, because by then I thought I was an old hand – I was all of 25 years old! That's what four years on the road would do to you. You came out at the other end and you were already 50; you'd seen a lot of things.

CHARLIE: Brian didn't live long enough to do a lot of things he was talking about or thought he could do. Whether he could have done them, I don't know, but he never had the chance. He was incredibly young when he died, when I look back on it. I look at pictures of my wife and myself at Brian's funeral and I just think, "Bloody hell". We were so young.

KEITH: God, that guy's timing was always dodgy. And still the mystery of his death hasn't really been solved – but that's another story. I don't know what happened, but there was some nasty business going on. Did he have an asthma attack in the pool, or was he shoved under? It wouldn't surprise me: Brian could really piss people off. What really killed Brian, though, was not getting the mixture right between the music and the fame.

The gig at Hyde Park was so bizarre. On the one hand it was as if the band was starting all over again, but instead of it being at the Crawdaddy Club or somewhere like that, we were breaking in a new guy for the first time in front of the biggest crowd we'd ever played for. In a way it was easy because we couldn't do any wrong, but we didn't know that. There was a very volatile audience and on top of everything we were having to deal with the fact that Brian had not just left the band, but left the planet. There were conflicting emotions: not only was it "Here come the new improved Rolling Stones", it was also a funeral. We had to turn the event into a memorial as well as a celebration. To try and do the two things at the same time meant walking a very thin tightrope. It was a big day for all of us. Then to get into the gig we were in an armoured car with the cops for

Mick on stage in Hyde Park, July 5 1969, with Mick Taylor behind. It was the 20-year-old ex-Bluesbreaker guitarist's first gig with the band, and the Stones' first for some 14 months. Granada TV later broadcast a seven-song selection from the afternoon's set.

As the Stones launched into 'I'm Yours, She's Mine', 3,500 butterflies were released from cardboard boxes in a symbolic gesture. Some 400 fans had later to be revived from heat exhaustion.

The gig in Hyde Park attracted an audience estimated at between 250,000 and 500,000, who were warmed up by the Third Ear Band, King Crimson, Screw, Alexis Korner's New Church, Family and Battered Ornaments. Fifteen tons of debris were later cleared up by fans, who were promised a free record for every three sacks they managed to collect. It was said the music could be heard half a mile away, against the wind, at Marble Arch. Somewhat nearer at hand were VIP guests Eric Clapton, Ginger Baker, Donovan, Paul and Linda McCartney, Mama Cass Elliott and Pink Floyd's Dave Gilmour.

an hour just trying to reach the stage. It was a very hot day, the sun was beating down and I thought, "Is this what it's like to be a soldier? Bloody hell, thank God I don't have to wear a helmet".

MICK: To be honest, Hyde Park didn't really feel that difficult. It was a bit of a challenge, to go and play for all these people. I think we were pleased to get out and play with somebody else, because we'd been like a horse with three legs. Now we had another guitarist, and we could say, "Play this", and he'd play it. That was the good part. The bad part was that Brian wasn't there any more, which was really sad.

Brian didn't live long enough to do a lot of things he was talking about or thought he could do. Whether he could have done them, I don't know, but he never had the chance.

Charlie

RONNIE: There was a sea of people at Hyde Park, and I was walking around the outside wondering how I could get into this band, when a car pulled up, and who jumped out? Mick and Charlie! They came up and said, "Hello, Ronnie, nice to see you. When are we going to see you again?" And I said, "Sooner than you think…"

CHARLIE: I remember going to see Allen Klein at the Dorchester, going to pick up my silver trousers which Shirley's girlfriend had made for me, the huge crowd – and Shirley being hit by a flying sandwich! Also we had a huge number of drummers for 'Sympathy for the Devil'. I think we met every African drummer in London. From that day on the strangest people have come up to us and said, "We played with you at Hyde Park".

It was a lot of fun. Most of the time I'm not too good at having fun at a gig – I'm too worried – but this was a lot of fun, and the first gig with Mick Taylor. He was amazing and looked fabulous in those days, with his long hair; a very romantic period. Mick also looked fabulous with his Byron-style dress on – and it was a peak period for Keith too: he had a great look.

RONNIE: The Stones were just like tiny little ants in the distance. To catch up with what really went on I had to watch the film of the concert later. I spent most of the day fighting off lots of sloppy, drunk, stoned people. If you were a musician trying to hear the music being played it was quite a pain in the neck because of all the other people. You'd be saying, "Shut up, we're trying to hear the music". I was excited for the band. I knew Mick Taylor was a wizard. I loved his guitar work and to this day I still try to reflect his melodic passages because he created trademark starting points. You have to include his licks in

Brian Jones' funeral took place in his home town of Cheltenham on 10 July 1969. Bill, Keith and Charlie attended, Mick being about to commence shooting the film Ned Kelly *in Australia.*

Brian photographed beside George Harrison's swimming pool.

The Stones in late 1969, with Mick Taylor. The rest of the year after the Hyde Park concert would be spent in the States, mixing the forthcoming Let it Bleed *and touring amphitheatres and raceways. Returning home after the tragic final date at Altamont Speedway, California, they played two end-of-decade gigs at London's Lyceum.*

Charlie: Mick and I look like two kids lost at a party.

Mick Taylor made his reputation playing guitar with local band the Gods. John Mayall selected him to replace Peter Green in his Bluesbreakers, and he stayed with them for two years and as many albums before receiving the call from the Stones.

order for a particular solo to go somewhere else in your own way. I always pay tribute to a lot of his licks. Whenever I play 'Honky Tonk Women' I can hear his contribution. When they first played that at Hyde Park, he'd already put his stamp on it, and on me. I thought, "Yeah, this guy's going to work great with the Stones, and I'm very pleased for him".

KEITH: Hyde Park was important, not because of the musical content but because it was one of the largest gatherings ever held in London. There was a powerful feeling that there were a lot of us, that things were changing, that we had something to give. By then we were being leant on aggressively by the authorities, so to us it was a great show of solidarity. It must have made them tremble a bit down the road in Whitehall.

Getting the balance of the occasion right was more on my mind than whether Mick Taylor was coming up to the mark: he probably played better than I did! We were very rusty. None of us had been on stage for quite a time and PAs and monitors were still in the experimental phase – or non-existent. In those days you just started and what you could hear you had to live with, but you had no idea if the audience was hearing what you could: we just pumped the shit out of the PA. We are very good at working a crowd – how good we actually sound is another thing. Hyde Park was one of the most abysmal-sounding shows we've ever done, but it was also one of the most important. I guess that day was a turn of the page.

CHRISTOPHER GIBBS

Christopher Gibbs (second from right) was part of the London art milieu in which the Stones became involved in the mid to late 1960s. He was a participant in many aspects of their lives at the time, having Brian, Keith and Mick to stay in Morocco, being present at the Redlands drug bust and creating decors for the film *Performance*.

I first met the Stones through Robert Fraser. We had been at Eton together — I'd been kicked out and he hadn't, through some startling injustice — and we had stayed friends, both dealing in art, sometimes buying things one from another. Robert had a gallery in Duke Street, off Grosvenor Square, and lived in Mount Street. He was blessed with a set of sharp antennae for what was happening in music, dance and clubs, and in fashion and art.

Robert's antennae picked up the Rolling Stones. He had lived in America and had a very good ear for black music, which is what made him jump. He first alerted me to the existence of the Stones, who were playing at Richmond and Eel Pie Island, when they swam downstream and emerged into the life of central London, showing up in Soho eateries like Mrs Beaton's Tent, which is where I think he may have glimpsed them for the first time.

Robert knew a lot of avant-garde film-makers and used to show late-night film shows where directors like Dennis Hopper, Kenneth Anger and Bruce Conner would show their own movies, while much dope was consumed and people — me included — would lie about on the floor, making the right kind of noises when the wrong sort of things happened. Robert liked the idea of a salon, and having groovy young people, and groovy old people, in one room together, all enjoying one another. He was a collector: he used to lure round up-and-coming poets and musicians (of course, this was also to do with thinking about selling them a Magritte). Although, at the time I met them, the Stones didn't have much money, they were lively, beautiful and charming. They were good to hang out with: merry company, funny, irreverent and open-minded.

I really got to know Mick when he wanted to have a house in the country. I am one of those people who reads *Country Life* every week and goes through every ad; and architecture and landscape have always been my passions. Robert, on the other hand, was a complete townee — he got rather nervous whenever he saw a green field — so I seemed to be the logical person to help Mick find somewhere. By chance there was this house near Newbury, appealingly called Stargroves, which had belonged to the family of my friend John Michel, painter, writer and mystical mathematician. It was a very nice place in a wonderful position, with wild country beyond it, but quite easy to get to from London.

On one memorable visit just before the house was bought, Mick, Marianne Faithfull, Terry Southern, Mason Hoffenberg, Robert and I drove down to Stargroves, stopping at various hostelries along the way for a little sharpening up — a joint here, a line there, a drink there, nothing to eat — and arrived at the house to meet the then-owner, a rather buttoned-up chap called Sir Henry Carden, who obviously thought we were a gang of ragamuffins, but who was extremely pleased to find someone who wanted to buy this dilapidated Victorian house complete with stable yards, kitchen gardens and lodge.

We used to head off in a gaggle on trips around Britain and Ireland, particularly with Mick and Brian; sometimes Keith. Keith was very close to Mick, graceful and rather shy. He always struck me as being extremely intuitive about what was going on in people's heads, with a tremendously sensitive sympathy that allowed him to pick up on what somebody might be feeling or going through. I never regarded Charlie — the most charming and gentlemanly — as a gang person. He was quite self-contained, sophisticated and elegant.

Brian, though, was the epitome of chaos, which was very difficult to avoid. It was like a great spider's web all around him, ensnaring anyone who got near.

He was incredibly self-obsessed, demanding and impossible, but in those days he just about got away with it by being charming. He charmed people through music; he was not seductive in the same way as Mick. It was his way of communicating with people: he'd make you listen to a song or wring the music from an unfamiliar instrument.

Mick has a wonderfully searching intellect. He has always been open to what is going on around him, but he is also quick to get to the nub, the juice of the thing — and then he likes a good dollop of what turns him on. He has a most extraordinary discipline for someone who, to a large degree, is at the mercy of his senses.

We went on a lot of jaunts to Ireland — I took Mick and Marianne to stay with Desmond Guinness at Leixlip, which was the beginning of a long alliance — and there were trips driving. I remember being taught to drive by Mick. I had never learned to drive and he said, "That's ridiculous, of course you must", so I learned with Mick as my instructor, dodging enormous haywagons on small country roads. There were travels all around England and Wales, climbing up mountains, looking at churches and houses, during which I was usually the guide; the Stones gave each adventure a completely different edge. It was great fun.

On one trip we arrived at Leixlip on a day when a great event was taking place at Kilkenny Castle. The Butler family, the Marquises of Ormonde, who owned the Castle, had gathered together all the people called Butler who were descended from them. We headed over there with Desmond Guinness, and the people at Kilkenny were far more excited by seeing the Rolling Stones than Butlers young and old wearing little labels saying which branch of the family they came from. The Butlers were pretty fed up. We had made them into "second-page men", they said, complaining to Desmond about our bad behaviour.

I went to Tangiers with Brian and Anita Pallenberg; we stayed in the Minzah Hotel. They had a fight and Brian broke his arm; when he went to hit Anita he struck an iron windowframe instead, snapping his arm, so that we had to put him in a nursing home. On the steps below the Minzah we discovered Ahmed Hamifsah, who became a friend for life. Decades ago he used to send hashish stitched into slippers, and he became hugely successful, surrounding himself with beautiful Norwegian girls. His tiny shop with a shoe box of jewellery swiftly grew up and down the steps with assistants and brass beds covered in velvet mattresses. He with his pipe festooned in jewels was soon busted, and he became a bearded holy man, his forehead calloused with the marks of constant prayer.

We also had a Marrakesh life: one Christmas we rented a house with a large garden and lots of peacocks. Paul and Talitha Getty had just bought a place in Marrakesh, Bill Burroughs was in town, and together we stormed about the place. We later stayed chez Getty – a very beautiful, sprawling house with several courtyards. We would climb up on the roof, where we could see the snowy mountains above and the gardens below, full of palm trees, squawking birds and fish in tanks. A lot of music was played, and musicians brought in from the Djemaah El-Fna, that great un-square square full of sounds and stories.

And then there was the bust at Keith's house, Redlands. A group of us had stayed there the night before, and then had a day out on the shingly beach in the Witterings. We were all full of acid and nonsense, and on the way back we drove in a van and tried to visit Monkton, the house of Edward James, the surrealist poet, up in the woods above West Dean, which Robert Fraser was very keen to see. But although we drove a long way through trees protected with iron guards painted in strange stripes of purple, green and yellow, the gates were locked (by an odd coincidence I later became a trustee of the Edward James Foundation and was involved in selling this house we never got to see).

That night the police came. My impression was that it had to be an arranged thing. There were one or two innocent creatures caught up in the bust, including a youngster called Nicky Kramer, thought very wrongly to have something to do with the set-up. There was nothing remotely wicked about him – he was a sweet, fey, amiable loon. The infamous David Schneiderman, on the other hand, was a Pied Piperish character. Who the hell he was, and where he came from, nobody knew: he had just popped up. He was able to tune into everybody's wavelength and was seductive, satanic, the devil in his most beguiling of disguises. After the bust he vanished as devils do, in a puff of smoke, and was never seen again.

The occasion was very dream-like, and to a certain extent a great surprise to me, because I was strangely innocent about heroin. I didn't know that any of my friends had ever taken heroin or would think about doing such a thing. What Mick had in his pocket was what anyone who was trying to do all kinds of things at once would have had – a few Mother's Little Helpers – but what Robert had in his possession was a complete shock to me.

It was a bust on quite a big scale. They had usually happened in London flats with a couple of coppers from the Chelsea squad. At Redlands, this great horde of rustic West Sussex policemen descended on us. The whole event had a rural ring and was quite surreal, heightened by efforts of various friends of friends of friends to buy off the police and the papers. This was never going to work. I went to visit Robert Fraser in prison; when he came out, he was very, very troubled. I can also remember the new bite to the Stones' music that emerged from that period. Keith's attitude was to express his defiance through the music. It came through in the pain and the wit and the bite of the songs. The music was always his voice.

Brian got busted again and came to stay with me in Cheyne Walk in Chelsea, creating absolute chaos and burning holes in the sheets. It was a nightmare. I couldn't wait to be rid of him. He was cracking up and the band had definitely fallen out of love with him. He was terribly damaged and going through hell and bringing everyone down there with him. When he bought Cotchford Farm, I went down a few times, sold him some things and tried to help a bit, but I could see that it would not do much good. Brian was beginning to be very chippy and angsty and impossible to handle.

William Burroughs and his collaborators Bryon Gysin and Ian Somerville had a flat together behind St James's Square. They were very into apomorphine revulsion therapy, and I know that there was talk of Brian doing that treatment, but whether he did, or whether he went to the Priory a couple of times I don't know.

The Stones and their activities – like the film *Performance* which I was involved in – were a kind of crucible into which energies were poured and enflamed. Some were utterly consumed and some came through. I come from very sturdy, hardworking, good citizen stock and although I had naturally kicked against that as hard as I could, I had inherited useful survival genes. So, although I took most of the drugs in the book and tried out all kinds of other experiments and stayed up all night, I would go straight to work at nine in the morning, carry on with my business and my life and go back to play.

Mick had that kind of discipline in spades, as well as an ability to edit out the unnecessary. Sometimes that required a ruthless element, that might mean friends and attachments were expendable in the end game. However, everybody needs anchors, and the impression I have is that Mick also needs the framework; he has always been close to his family and his girlfriend or wife of the time, enjoying a real closeness, even if he was going off in three different directions at the same time. Keith learned how to develop that editing instinct, Charlie didn't need it, but Brian was incapable of it, which was his downfall.

Robert Fraser rang me at four o'clock in the morning to tell me that Brian was dead. Mick called next day to talk about what he might read at Hyde Park. We discussed using Wordsworth's 'Intimations Of Immortality' as well as Shelley's 'Adonais' – "Life, like a dome of many-coloured glass, Stains the white radiance of Eternity".

The Stones went off on tour to the States and then they moved away to France, and everything changed. There had been a period when I saw them virtually every day for three or four years. It was a time when they tuned into a whole world of people who came from a different way of life but who had things they could share and enjoy. Of course, the Stones brought a huge amount into the lives of everybody they had anything to do with – they certainly opened my own eyes to no end of possibilities.

This band wouldn't still be going if we didn't have a loyal following. Fortunately a lot of people have always wanted to come and see us. It's one of the things that's helped us over all the bad periods.

Charlie Watts

THE FIRST RESURRECTION

6

KEITH: This band has been like a phoenix. And the 1969 tour of the States was our first resurrection. We felt we were a new band; we were starting again. I think we figured that this marked the beginning of a new chapter, and we were wondering whether people would accept the Stones without Brian Jones. The '69 tour was essentially a continuation of the Hyde Park gig – we knew that we really had to tighten up and get our stage chops together, but at least we had a working unit again.

CHARLIE: I call that tour "the Led Zeppelin tour", because it was the first time we had to go on and play for an hour-and-a-half. I blame it on Jimmy Page. Led Zeppelin had come to the States, and they would do a twenty-minute drum solo and endless guitar solos. Two or three hours on stage was what we heard they did, and it became something of a norm for anyone doing a concert. And the Grateful Dead had Jerry Garcia playing for hours.

KEITH: When we first started playing gigs, the entire set only lasted twenty minutes. Nobody expected a rock'n'roll band to have more to say than that. On our first tour with the Everly Brothers, they did play for nearly forty minutes, but they were top of the bill. Otherwise it was the turnaround of acts that was important, and everybody gave it their best shot. There was no padding. I don't think in our first year we ever finished our projected twenty minutes. You went out, got yelled at, and either the cops closed it down or a riot broke out.

In 1969 the set was getting on for two hours. People had bought the Stones records and now they actually wanted to listen to the music – which we'd been dying for them to do ever since we left the Crawdaddy Club. The first rudimentary monitors and PAs were coming in, which allowed the audiences to listen. We had actually got used to *not* playing, because we knew you couldn't overcome 3,000 screaming chicks with the equipment we had. So we hadn't played consciously live for quite a long time, which meant we had to start re-learning our stage expertise.

CHARLIE: Physically, we didn't know how we were going to feel at the end of 'Satisfaction' if we'd been playing for two hours before we got there. And we had to learn the shaping of a performance. Chip Monck, who had done the lighting at Woodstock, and Bill Graham were very good at helping us understand the shape of a show: the start, the finish and an encore, because we had never, ever done encores. We used to do whatever it was and go home – which was probably just down to youthful arrogance.

MICK: Before the 1969 tour the shows were very short and you never knew the size of stage you would be getting – it could be the size of a postage stamp or a large theatre. On the '69 tour there was a consistent size of stage and I was able to perfect some movements, knowing that in a particular number I would be doing this or that move. It was the first time that the repetition and the continuity of the shows gave you the ability to work something up; before then it had been very haphazard. I imagine that the tour started off rather shakily, but as time went on, the ideas began to flow, and I had the whole length of the show to work my performance.

In 1969 the set was getting on for two hours. People had bought the Stones records and now they actually wanted to listen to the music — which we'd been dying for them to do ever since we left the Crawdaddy Club.

Keith

Tina Turner was on that tour, but I didn't consciously copy any moves from her. She always says I did, but she's a woman and the movement involved is totally different. However, I would be out dancing all the time off stage, going to clubs and picking up whatever moves were going on in there.

CHARLIE: The show at Altamont came right at the end of the tour. We came into Altamont by helicopter, got out and saw oceans of people completely out of it, mostly kids who were really bombed out and girls with hardly anything on. It was like Woodstock in a way – it was the fashion of the moment, but it was the end of the fashion. If Woodstock started it, we stopped it.

The event was not out of control, it was controlled, very much so. I was in a tent talking to a couple of the Angels. The tent flap wobbled and one of them whacked the flap with a billiard cue – there was probably some kid's head behind it. But you had to carry on talking; you couldn't say to guys like that, "Hey, don't do that" because – and I may be making excuses – I think they'd been drinking and taking whatever all day, like everybody else there.

When we went through the backstage area it was full of people. A lot of them were fucked up and the Angels made a razor-sharp line for us to walk through. I felt very worried as we walked to the stage. It was an event waiting to go wrong. I remember seeing a Harley-Davidson parked right in front of the stage. There were half a million people there, and the bike got knocked over – the Angel who owned it went berserk at the crowd, and I just thought, "What a stupid place to park".

The Angels also did something that would never have happened normally: they were actually on the stage with us. Mick, Bill and Keith could hardly get out of their way. As things began to get worse they moved out in front of the stage. Their argument was that by doing all this, they saved Mick's life. They were certainly very strict about it.

I didn't see the stabbing, and wasn't aware of it until later on when we saw the footage for the documentary. I think it was Rock Scully, the Grateful Dead's manager, who asked the Angels to handle the security because they had a great fan base. We knew nothing about the San Francisco area, and it was also an era when the police were thought of as "the pigs". The Chicago riots had happened recently, and there had been a lot of images of the cops beating people up, so you thought that if you had cops in charge it was going to be worse. As a result we, the Stones, ended up with a kind of contract out on our lives at one point, because the Angels said it was all our fault and one of their guys was going to be sent down for the killing.

What happened at Altamont was not what we played music for. We had, yet again, got into another fine mess.

KEITH: We owed the record company a live album of the tour which became *Get Yer Ya-Ya's Out*. It's about as un-tampered with as possible, given the technology and the material available at the time. There's a bit of touch-up here and there, a couple of spots on one or two tracks where something failed or cracked out and that we brushed over, but it was a pretty accurate reproduction of that tour.

MICK: This was the period when we set up Rolling Stones Records. In the end we didn't do as much with it as we could have done. It's hard to get the right people

involved to do the business, and of course you have all your stuff to do: writing and touring. I would have become more involved, but the Rolling Stones was a full-time job. I couldn't run a record label as well. But it was fine as a vehicle for our own albums; *Sticky Fingers* was the first.

CHARLIE: During the tour of the States we went to Alabama and played at the Muscle Shoals Studio. That was a fantastic week. We cut some great tracks, which appeared on *Sticky Fingers* – 'You Gotta Move', 'Brown Sugar' and 'Wild Horses' – and we did them without Jimmy Miller, which was equally amazing. It worked very well: it's one of Keith's things to go in and record while you're in the middle of a tour and your playing is in good shape. The Muscle Shoals Studio was very special, though – a

Jim Price on trumpet, Bobby Keys on sax and Nicky Hopkins playing on tour in 1970. Ian Stewart stands behind Nicky Hopkins (also pictured below left). Jim and Bobby were hired as the horn section when their gig with Derek and the Dominos fell through. Bobby played a solo on 'Brown Sugar' on the Sticky Fingers *album.*

Nicky Hopkins at Mick's wedding in Saint Tropez in 1971.

great studio to work in, a very hip studio, where the drums were on a riser high up in the air, plus you wanted to be there because of all the guys who had worked in the same studio. I just placed my drums in the place where Roger Hawkins used to have his kit.

MICK: At the end of the '60s I had a little more time to sit around and play my guitar, writing songs rather than just lyrics for the first time. I'd written songs before then, but they were little things like 'Yesterday's Papers'. Now I could take it more seriously. 'Brown Sugar' was one of those songs. I wrote it in Australia, somewhere between Melbourne and Sydney, while I was in my trailer filming *Ned Kelly* – I had a whole bunch of time out there. I was simply writing what I wanted to write, not trying to test the waters. People are very quick to react to what you write, but I just write what comes into my head.

CHARLIE: Mick started playing the guitar a lot. He plays very strange rhythm guitar; he plays up on everything, very much how Brazilian guitarists play, on the up-beat. It is very much like the guitar on a James Brown track – for a drummer it's great to play with.

Sticky Fingers was the first time we added horns – that was the influence of people like Otis Redding and James Brown, and also Delaney and Bonnie, who Bobby Keys and Jim Price played with. It was to add an extra dimension, a different colour, not to make the band sound any different. And on stage I imagine we all must have liked playing with horns. I've always liked horns, although there is a danger that they can make

Mick overtakes horse-riding bandmates in the South of France, where the Stones had taken up residence in April 1971, largely for tax reasons.

everything sound like a show band. But coming from the love of jazz that I have, I love having them all around me.

RONNIE: I was still seeing the Stones from time to time. Record company parties were always big on the scene. You'd hop along Oxford Street from one record company to another, drop into their Christmas party – and over the years you built up little cliques.

I would bump into the Stones at odd times – Rod Stewart and I used to go and ask their advice every now and again. We went up to Chester Square once to ask Mick about a record deal that we didn't know whether to get involved with or not, and he gave us some advice on that. Years later, when I was living in Malibu, Steve Tyler from Aerosmith would come over and he'd ask Mick, "What do we do when we go to Australia?" and Mick would tell him, "If you're playing in the open air and it's a midday or afternoon show, make sure you have a canopy over you because the sun is too hot, you'll get sunburn and fatigue" – simple, friendly advice like that, which he's given to many bands. He was always running out and spotting new talent, as he still does, and giving them advice, which I always thought was very sweet.

The first time I got together with all of them was after Brian's time, when we were recording in Olympic Studios. I was in the studio with Stevie Marriott, and the Stones would be recording in the big studio, so we used to hang a little bit there. And then when Mick got married to Bianca, I got an invite to go down to the South of France with my first wife, Krissy. If I close my eyes I can see Ringo, Jimmy Miller, me and Krissy, Nicky Hopkins, Bobby Keys, Bill and his girlfriend Astrid. Bianca was always wonderful.

CHARLIE: The period in 1971 and '72 was both exciting and difficult, because for tax reasons Rupert Loewenstein had made me sell my house in England and move over to France. I'd bought a house which I was hardly in since it was being done up, so I was living in Keith's house more than my own.

KEITH: We were forced onto our back foot by the whole tax thing. In England we were stymied and we suddenly felt the whole weight of this dead empire coming down on us.

Keith and son Marlon (far left) with family friends.

So the only thing to do was to go away and reconstruct everything, and say, "We're all going to do this boys, we're going to move out – let's be a family". In a way it was energising, which is, I guess, why *Exile On Main Street* ended up as a double album.

CHARLIE: I couldn't speak French, but my life was fine, although it was very lonely for Shirley. Mick and Bianca would be in San Tropez or Paris, Bill was renting houses left, right and centre in France and Keith had Nellcôte. Everybody had a great time, but it was also very stressful, because the people who weren't in the band could go shooting off to London every now and again, and we weren't able to do that, of course. The only one who wasn't worried by that was Keith, who was being supplied in his mansion with the band working downstairs. It must have been heaven for him.

KEITH: Nellcôte was a great house, and it wasn't too showy. It was in the bay at

Mick and Bianca on honeymoon in Venice, 1971, after their May wedding in St Tropez. Press interest, both at the ceremony itself, and afterwards, was such that the couple spent time at an Italian castello which could be reached only by sea.

Villefranche, and had been built by an English admiral called Byrd. There was a cave and steps down to his own private boating dock, so I bought a speed boat. I thought I'd splash out, I might be in jail the next year, so let's have some fun while I'm free! I think we'd sucked the South of France dry…

We hadn't intended to record in my house. We did look around for studios around there once we'd all decided that was what we were going to do – but although there are plenty of very good French recording engineers now, at that time in the South of France in the early 1970s, there weren't too many. There were no studios with good rooms to work in, the equipment was shabby and nobody felt comfortable in any of the places we looked at. I had this basement, which was really very ugly, but it was the biggest one of all the houses we had down there, and we also had our own mobile recording truck. So we said, "Why don't we just forget about looking for a studio. Let's bring in the truck and work around the problems; at least this way we don't have to ask interpreters every time we want to turn it off or on".

CHARLIE: The recording at Nellcôte is what I really remember about *Exile On Main Street*, because the other tracks on the album were off-cuts, which we took down there and over-dubbed. The drums were recorded down in the wine cellar. I had just moved to France and I used to have to drive from where I lived, through Nîmes and Aix-en-Provence to where Keith was. In those days they didn't have the *autoroute*; you can do the journey in four hours or so now, but in those days it was a six-and-a-half or seven-hour drive along these little roads. I couldn't do it every day, playing and then going home, so I used to have to live at Keith's, but he was always upstairs and I'd be out in the day. Or I would go over and live with Mick for a while because they had both taken big houses, which gave me the option of going back to Mick's at night instead.

> *A lot of the recording was done in the way Keith likes to work, which is playing it twenty times, then letting it marinate over another twenty goes, very much like a jazz thing. Keith is like a jazz player in many ways.*
>
> *Charlie*

Jimmy Miller lived in a house above Nellcôte somewhere; I remember him being in this weird place up there. Keith's house was the only one on the end of this point, a magnificent house, a fantastic Edwardian mansion, which some Italian bloke had bought and re-done completely. Stu had the piano in one room, I'd be down in the cellar, and they'd move the guitars around.

Gram Parsons was also down at Nellcôte. He was a lovely guy and he worked well with Keith. I was a friend of Gram's, but I didn't know him very well. I love Hank Williams and Bob Dylan's *Nashville Skyline*, but the whole Nashville thing I'm not that enamoured of. I'm not a great lover of stetsons and Nudie shirts. But I think for Keith the songs are very interesting, and some of those country players are just fabulous if you're a guitarist. I can enjoy Buck Owens and Bob Wills' swing band and George Jones, but it's not something I am particularly good at. I suppose Elvis Presley had a great country band.

KEITH: When I started to hang with Gram, it did alter my relationship with Mick. He may have been a little bit jealous, because Gram and I were working together a lot and playing a lot of country music, which Mick is just as intrigued by. I don't know if Mick felt

shunted aside because Gram and I were really tight for a while. I'd got to know him in the period where we had a year or so off the road. There was quite a release from being stuffed in the car with the same four guys – one of whom, of course, was Brian, who had been a pain – and so when I came out of that bubble I was able to make a lot of friends in a short period. You don't think about it at the time, it's what you do and you love doing it. There's always something interesting around the corner.

I met Gram Parsons in 1968, when he was with the Byrds. They had come to England to play in the clubs; it was when they had *Sweetheart Of The Rodeo* out and just before they were due to go to South Africa. I met him at a club, where we started talking. He asked me, "What about this South Africa thing, have you ever played there?", and I said, "No, we don't go there, it's worse than Georgia". We spent the night talking and the next day he left the Byrds. They went to South Africa without him.

Gram showed me the mechanics of country music. The guy is amazing. He never had a hit record; if you look in the charts you'll never see his records and yet he's one of the biggest names in country music. I always ask why? If he hadn't been a silly sod and croaked, God knows what he would have done. Yet at the same time I think he achieved most of what he was going to do anyway; in the short time he had he crammed it all in. Gram changed the face of country music without anybody even knowing it. After he died, there was this whole different aspect of country music, which pervades to this day. As far as that level of influence goes, Gram was like Jimi Hendrix, except that Jimi was obviously far more successful in his day – although Jimi did breed a whole generation of very bad feedback-loving guitar players!

Gram knew songs that I'd forgotten or had never known. He introduced me to a lot of players, and he showed me the difference between the way country would be played in Nashville and in Bakersfield – the two schools – with a completely different sound and attitude. But apart from that he was just a very special guy. He was my mate, and I wish he'd remained my mate for a lot longer. It's not often you can lie around on a bed with a guy having cold turkey, in tandem, and still get along.

CHARLIE: What you have to remember is that when Keith was in his drug period, the time was his. What that meant was that you could get somewhere at a particular time, but Keith wouldn't be there: you could make a record, but he wouldn't be on it. In fact we did one called *Jammin' With Edwards,* which was a whole period when Keith didn't show up. At gigs you used to have to wait for him for two hours to go on. Nowadays, if we're five minutes late everyone goes mad, but then it was much milder. Everyone would sit from 9 o'clock until 11 or 12 and they would happily wait, but that was what a lot of musicians did then. Keith wasn't the only one doing it. There were a few people like that – it's just a lot of them haven't survived. But by working at Keith's house, Keith not being there for the recording was a problem we could generally avoid.

A lot of the recording was done in the way Keith likes to work, which is playing it twenty times, letting it marinate over another twenty goes, very much like a jazz thing. They call it "working on Keith time". Keith is like a jazz player in lots of ways. He knows what he likes, but he's very loose and he would never tell you what to do. You have to work

Keith warming up before a performance.

Keith photographed by Ed Caraeff on infra-red film in a Los Angeles hotel.

The Stones' personalised airliner on tour in the United States, 1972.

(opposite) On tour: whiling away the time on board between cities.

it out for yourself, or you'll say to him, "Is that it? I think I should do this" – and he'll say, "Yeah, yeah", whereas Mick loves to control it all, which is fine in another way.

MICK: *Exile On Main Street* is not one of my favourite albums, although I think the record does have a particular feeling. I'm not too sure how great the songs are, but put together it's a nice piece. However, when I listen to *Exile* it has some of the worst mixes I've ever heard. I'd love to remix the record, not just because of the vocals, but because generally I think it sounds lousy. At the time Jimmy Miller was not functioning properly. I had to finish the whole record myself, because otherwise there were just these drunks and junkies. I was in LA trying to finish the record, up against a deadline. It was a joke. Of course I'm ultimately responsible for it, but it's really not good and there's no concerted effort or intention.

I don't like going into the studio without knowing what's going on. I'm a singer. It's all right for bands; they can stand there and jam their butts off, but a lot of it is just a waste of time. It's very boring, and then it's much more difficult later on to make up the songs. I can do it, but it's not my chosen method.

Exile is really a mixture of bits and pieces left over from the previous album recorded at Olympic Studios and which, after we got out of the contract with Allen Klein, we didn't want to give him: tracks like 'Shine A Light', and 'Sweet Virginia'. Those were mixed up with a few slightly more grungy things done in the South of France. It's seen as one album all recorded there and it really wasn't. We just chucked everything in. As long as people like the album, that's fine. It's just that I don't particularly think it's a great album.

The thing about *Exile* is that everyone loves it, but I don't really know why. There aren't any real hits on it, apart from 'Tumbling Dice'. And although it's great to listen to, it isn't that great when you try and play songs from it. There are a lot of tracks on that double album, and only a handful of songs you can perform: 'Tumbling Dice', 'Happy', 'All Down The Line' and 'Sweet Virginia', which is a nice country tune. So there's a good four songs off it, but when you start to play the other nineteen, you can't, or they don't work, or nobody likes them, and you think, "OK, we'll play another one instead". We have rehearsed a lot of the tunes off *Exile*, but there's not much that's playable.

CHARLIE: We always rehearse 'Ventilator Blues'. It's a great track, but we never play it as well as the original. Something will not be quite right; either Keith will play it a bit differently or I'll do it wrong. It's a fabulous number, but a bit of a tricky one. Bobby Keys wrote the rhythm part, which is the clever part of the song. Bobby said, "Why don't you do this?" and I said, "I can't play that", so Bobby stood next to me clapping the thing and I just followed his timing. In the world of 'Take Five', it's nothing, but it threw me completely and Bobby just stood there and clapped while we were doing the track – and we've never quite got it together as well as that.

KEITH: *Exile* was a double album. And because it's a double album you're going to be hitting different areas, including D for Down, and the Stones really felt like exiles. We didn't start off intending to make a double album; we just went down to the South of France to make an album

and by the time we'd finished we said, "We want to put it all out". We could have cut it in half and released a single album and then made another one, because double albums were very unpopular with record companies: the fact that you have to charge more is just one of the reasons why you shouldn't make a double album.

When the record came out it didn't sell particularly well at the beginning, and it was also pretty much universally panned. But within a few years the people who had written the reviews saying it was a piece of crap were extolling it as the best frigging album in the world.

The point is that the Stones had reached a point where we no longer had to do what we were told to do. Around the time that Andrew Oldham left us, we'd done our time, things were changing and I was no longer interested in hitting Number One in the charts every time. What I want to do is good shit – if it's good they'll get it some time down the road. *Exile* proved that point of view. Also it's the way to sustain a band so that it can expand itself, otherwise you're just trapped into that pop cycle.

I can say that from *Beggars Banquet* through to *Exile* was a consistent body of work, mainly because it was done with the same guys. It's not surprising that when you lose key people who you work with making records, there will be a period where you go, "Whoopsadaisy". We've always had an influx of incredible producers and engineers who want to work with us – I can't understand the attraction really. With *Exile On Main Street* Jimmy Miller's name is written in gold in rock'n'roll heaven. Working under the most bizarre conditions and knowing the characters that he had to deal with, Jimmy was a joy.

For *Goats Head Soup*, Jamaica was one of the few places that would let us all in! By that time about the only country that I was allowed to exist in was Switzerland, which was damn boring for me, at least for the first year, because I didn't like to ski – and then I got to get out on the slopes and it was great. We were on the back foot all the time, being

Stevie Wonder was the opening act on the 1972 tour, affording Jagger and Taylor the opportunity for a little moonlighting. Wonder, like the Stones themselves, had just taken control of his own career, renegotiating his contract with Motown and paving the way for such classic albums as Talking Book *and* Innervisions.

(overleaf) Four portraits by Norman Seeff.

shunted from pillar to post. Nine countries kicked me out, thank you very much, so it was a matter of how to keep this thing together – we'd go wherever. It was a matter of finding out who would have us for any given amount of time and there would be a lot of crap about visas and all of that, but we were determined to make the album, wherever we ended up recording it: see you at the North Pole! I'd rather be in the warm than the cold – hence Jamaica probably – and also it started to become a kind of adventure.

Jamaica – oh, the music island! We were hearing interesting sounds coming out of Jamaica, plus they had cheap studios. Dynamic Sound in Kingston was an amazing place: the drum kits and the amps were nailed to the floor. Jamaica's a wonderful place, kind of free and easy. I'd been there on and off in the 1960s, but only for a visit. After *Goats Head Soup* I've lived there whenever I can. I have family there – villages welcome me with open arms. They like music and they like musicians and as long as you don't get your head chopped off with a machete, you're all right! I think there's a certain power of influence that comes up from the roots in Jamaica. It kept me there – I didn't leave.

The album itself didn't take that long, but we recorded an awful lot of tracks. There were not only Jamaicans involved, but also percussion players who came from places like Guyana, a travelling pool of guys who worked in the studios there. It was interesting to be playing in this totally different atmosphere. Mikey Chung, the engineer at Dynamic, for example, was a Chinese man – you realise how much Jamaica is a multi-ethnic environment.

RONNIE: My real involvement with the Stones started in 1974, when my ex-wife went down to Tramps. Keith was trying to escape from a drug dealer and Krissy said to him, "Ronnie's in The Wick in Richmond". "Why don't you come back to see him because he's making an album?" Keith's going, "Anything to get out of here. I've got to get away from these people". He came over to see me, and four months later he was still there! He was fabulous: the police waited exactly two weeks too late to bust him. They had the place under surveillance, and then they swooped, only to find that Keith had left two weeks earlier. In those four months, that's when we got really close.

I had been working on my first solo album – *I've Got My Own Album To Do* – and during that time Mick Jagger used to come round and help me. The place was always full. Mick would bring David Bowie over. You'd have Greg Allman and Paul McCartney and people were queuing down the stairs: Keith Moon, Ringo – it was, "Oh no, not more drummers, get out of here!" We had Kenney Jones in there, Andy Newmark, Jim Capaldi – it was nuts.

When I was writing 'I Can Feel The Fire', Mick gave me a hand on the song, and he said, "Help me on this one. I've got this chorus with these verses for 'It's Only Rock'n'Roll'." So we went through that with Bowie and me singing the background vocals on it and Willie Weeks on bass. Andy Newmark had fallen asleep or gone away. Either way we didn't have a drummer, so we woke Kenney Jones up in the middle of the night. The session came together with odds and ends, but we got the basic track cut. Then they took it all over to Island Records, where Keith wanted to pull all of my guitars off.

KEITH: I was surprised when I heard 'It's Only Rock'n'Roll' because what they put on was actually David Bowie and Mick Jagger doing the song, since Mick had gone over to Ronnie's and dubbed it with Bowie. The Stones tried to re-cut it, but in the end we said, "Keep the original, and we'll over-dub, because it's got the feel".

RONNIE: With a song like 'It's Only Rock'n'Roll', you can't really get into who wrote which note. We were bouncing ideas to and fro. Mick had the chorus already and it was trial and error, like most songs are. You shape them up and before you know it, you've got your chorus, your verses, your middle eight and where the solo is going to be. The song moulds itself pretty quickly and you've got the basic one down on the tape anyway. It was like 'Maggie May' – that was just an album track with Rod Stewart. I played all the instruments and afterwards I thought, "Oh, that was a good album track". I had no idea that it was going to do so well.

Mick said, "I've got a deal. You can keep 'I Can Feel The Fire' and I'll keep 'It's Only Rock'n'Roll'". I had no bargaining power, so it was OK. We were writing songs together and Mick would take some ideas and structures which would obviously become a Jagger/Richards song. I didn't mind going through years of all that first. It was my apprenticeship.

KEITH: We were starting to do sessions for *It's Only Rock'n'Roll*, ten days here, a week there – a lot of it was then done at Stargroves, which was Mick's place. Things get a little blurry here. I have to go by the producers and how they died. Jimmy Miller was still there for *It's Only Rock'n'Roll*, because I remember him being down at Island Studios in London, but by then Jimmy was down to carving swastikas into the desk, bless his heart. He had assumed that anybody could adopt my lifestyle after a while, but he hadn't realised that my diet is very, very rare.

CHARLIE: I think that Keith was pretty out of it for some of that period, which shouldn't have helped, but maybe it did. Maybe that was where the creative energies came from. I don't know, because although I was very close to Keith, I was never a part of that aspect of his world, and he would never push it on me. It was like with Gram Parsons – I was very unaware of what they were doing. It was just what they did. It wasn't like being at a swimming pool: "Hey come in and join us".

KEITH: At the end of 1974 Mick Taylor told Mick Jagger that he was leaving the band, and Mick Jagger told me. I thought he was a fantastic player. But at the same time there was a certain lack of camaraderie, shall we say. It's not Mick Taylor's fault – he's a very sweet guy – but it was just that we're very volatile people in this band and if there is somebody who just sits there, it's like, "Come on, let's put a firecracker under his arse".

RONNIE: I felt pretty sorry for Mick Taylor when they started dressing him up and playing with his hair and putting silly hats on him. I felt that I had been quite lucky: I would have probably been on the needle if I'd had joined at that time, the amount and the intensity of the dope that was surrounding the band. I don't know if I would have been strong enough to have been able to fight it off. Because lots of people have fallen by the wayside trying to keep up with them.

MICK: Mick Taylor was very much a stand-still chap. Perhaps a little bit too static and unemotional, though he was a great player.

KEITH: The thing that disappointed me about Mick Taylor was that leaving the Stones was a chance for him to go on and do something else and he didn't do shit. He thought he was going to be a writer, a producer, that he'd take it as far as you could – but unfortunately he never got it.

RONNIE: I was there when Mick Taylor handed in his cards. It was at a party thrown by Robert Stigwood. I was sitting right next to Mick Taylor and Mick Jagger, and Mick Taylor was saying, "Mick, I'm leaving the band". Mick Jagger's going "What?" and Taylor said "I really am leaving the band, right now", and he got up and left. Mick turned to me and said, "What am I going to do, Ronnie? Oh no. Would you join?". So I said, "Yeah, of course, but I don't want to split the Faces up". He said "No, don't worry", and I went, "Well, ring me if you get any ideas". Mick said "Can I ring you if I get desperate?" – "Sure, yeah" – about a year later he did, when Rod Stewart had just left the Faces, so it was perfect timing.

Charlie: I've still got that shirt. I couldn't play in it – all the ruffles came down my wrists and I'm trying to get rid of them here.

Recording of Exile On Main Street, *the band's second album release on Rolling Stones Records, was begun in summer 1971 using the mobile studio at Keith's villa. In December they moved to Los Angeles' Sunset Sound, new guitars having been purchased in Nashville to replace eleven stolen in France. The music spread over a double (vinyl) album, and has since been acclaimed as some of the band's best work. At the time, however, they risked critical opinion that the material didn't justify the more expensive format.*

Exile On Main Street *is not one of my favourite albums, although I think the record does have a particular feeling. When I listen to* Exile *it has some of the worst mixes I've ever heard. I'd love to remix it.*

Mick

MARSHALL CHESS

Marshall Chess grew up in the environment of Chess Records, the company founded in 1950 by his father and uncle, Leonard and Phil Chess, which released records by the great bluesmen of Chicago and early rock'n'roll artists including Chuck Berry and Bo Diddley. In 1970 he became president of Rolling Stones Records.

In the spring of 1964 Andrew Oldham contacted me at Chess Records. Andrew wanted to know if the Rolling Stones could come to Chicago and record in our studios. At that time the only people who were allowed to record there were the artists on the Chess label — musicians like Muddy Waters, Howlin' Wolf, Sonny Boy Williamson or Chuck Berry. For the Stones to do so would be a massive exception to the rule. But — in my early twenties — I knew the Stones were performing material by our artists, so I became their champion within Chess, and after a certain amount of cajoling, I persuaded the family to give me permission to let them come.

The building on 2120 South Michigan Avenue — an address the Stones immortalised in the instrumental track they recorded there — was a narrow two-storey building, with a parking lot from which a door led straight upstairs to the studios. Keith remembers arriving and seeing Muddy Waters painting the studios. I can't quite believe it, because I can't imagine Muddy putting on overalls, but that's the beauty of different people's memories. It is certainly possible that Muddy might have helped the Stones lug some equipment from the parking lot into the studios, because he was that kind of a guy. The blues musicians like Muddy weren't too interested in the Rolling Stones, but they did like the fact that they were covering their songs, and that, as a result, more and more people, particularly white people would become aware of their music.

While the Stones were in town, I did the guided tour, showed them round the Chess operation, took them to see the archive. I had just acquired a brand-new

Porsche convertible and one night gave Brian Jones a lift back to the hotel the band were staying in. Brian had shoulder length hair, longer than anyone else in the band, and we had the Porsche's top down. At one intersection we stopped for a red light, and a bunch of Midwesterners took great delight in shouting, "Homo, homo!". That was the Mid-West in 1964. We didn't have people in Chicago who looked like the Stones. At Chess we had some pretty strange motherfuckers on the label, but we never had anyone who, like the Stones, drank straight from a bottle of Jack Daniels in the studio rather than nipping to the bathroom for a drink or a toke. This was new even to us.

I had been helping out at Chess since I was ten years old. It was as though my father ran a grocery store - it just happened to be a record company. One of my first jobs was sending out records by mail. We had some customers in the UK and Europe, and I don't think it's a trick of memory that I recall being in the shipping room and packing up a box for one M.P. Jagger of Dartford, Kent.

After I finished school, I spent some time in Europe, setting up Chess's European division, expanding Chess into new markets. In 1966 the company moved to a new, much larger, building in Chicago which contained three studios and our own record pressing plant. I produced a couple of hits: the Rotary Connection, a psychedelic rock outfit featuring Minnie Riperton, sold a quarter million copies of their first album. *Electric Mud* was a Muddy Waters album including his cover of 'Let's Spend The Night Together'.

Then, out of the blue, my father and uncle sold Chess Records in the fall of 1968. They owned the number one black radio station WVON and wanted to diversify into black TV. They were also, as a white-run company releasing albums by black artists, taking a lot of heat from civil rights groups. I was devastated. In fact, I freaked out - this was the company I was being groomed to take over. My father and uncle offered me my share of the sale - a million dollars - so I could set up my own record label. But then the bottom fell out of that dream. My father died in October 1969, and he died without a signed will. Some vast percentage of his estate went to the government in taxes. There was no million bucks. The new owners of Chess, a West Coast corporate, seemed only in budgets and forecasts, whereas the company had always been focused on creativity. I was very depressed - so I quit.

Within three weeks I had a call from an old friend, Bob Krasnow (later president of Elektra Records). He'd heard I had quit, and said the Stones were coming out of their deal with London/Decca: "Let's get together and try to set up a deal with them". I knew Bob well enough to talk straight, and I told him there was no room for both our egos in a set-up like that. But I thought I might try on my own.

I'd met Mick Jagger at the Ad Lib club in London and had his phone number. I called him up and he answered. I explained that my life had changed, that I was sitting around doing nothing and had backers to start a label. I told him I'd heard there were changes afoot in their career too and he said we should speak, but that he had passport problems and couldn't travel to Chicago. So I flew over to London, and turned up at the Stones' office at the appointed hour, only to be told by Jo Bergman in the office that Mick was in Ireland; this was my introduction to the fact that the Rolling Stones operated in a different time-frame. I was mad - this was not how I was used to doing business - and Jo knew it.

One of the best things about my relationship with the Stones was that I was not a groupie, I was not a starfucker and I treated them like a Chess artist. And when I met Mick at his house in Cheyne Walk, he did seem nervous. The house was beautiful, a whole different reality for me: he had Persian rugs, oriental furniture and while we talked he danced to Clifton Chenier's 'Black Snake Blues'. He told me the Stones wanted to start a label but they didn't want a manager; Prince Rupert Loewenstein had just begun working with them and was going to handle the money. I went down to meet the band in a rehearsal studio in Bermondsey. I saw a copy of Muddy's *Electric Mud* album hanging on the wall – the big centrefold of Muddy in a white robe – and took it as a good omen. Because of my new understanding of Rolling Stones time, I told them I had to know in two weeks or I was going to start my own label. Astonishingly, on the fourteenth day a telegram arrived, and the adventure began.

My first job was to finish off putting together *Get Yer Ya-Ya's Out*, their live recording off the 1969 tour, and their last recording for Decca. I recall playing 'Cocksucker Blues', accompanied by the Stones' lawyer Paddy Grafton Green, to a panel including Sir Edward Lewis. Not surprisingly they flipped out and declined to release it as a single. I liked that. I knew I would like working with the Stones.

I had recently got divorced, and the Stones and Rolling Stones Records became my life. For a while I lived in Keith's house in Chelsea, upstairs in the maids' quarters. On my first visit I was greeted by the sight of a floral painted grand piano being played by Gram Parsons. I got a certain amount of teasing because I was wearing jeans. The Stones had only ever seen me in my sharp record company exec guise, wearing a suit and tie. I was already entering the world of the Rolling Stones. It was an opportunity for me to break my own chains.

A distribution deal was signed with Atlantic Records and I helped Prince Rupert who – though a formidable negotiator – was then learning about the music business. I'd known the Erteguns since I was a baby: Ahmet came to my bar mitzvah. It was a great deal, one of the highest royalty deals that had ever been struck with Atlantic.

These were exciting days. We had to come up with a logo for the label. I had to go to Rotterdam for a meeting with the band, flew in to Amsterdam and hired a car to drive there. On the way I passed a Shell petrol station. In the States the company's stations had the word Shell. In Europe there was only the yellow shell symbol, so when I got to the meeting I mentioned how neat it would be to have no type but just a logo. When the tongue and lips idea came up I hired numerous artists who produced every possible variation until John Pashe finally designed the one that endured.

Sticky Fingers hit Number One in the UK and the US. 'Brown Sugar' topped the US charts and was Number Two in the UK. It was a great start. The pressure was on. Ahmet Ertegun had told me, "The Stones take too long. I need a record every twelve to eighteen months". On the other hand, for the first time there was a co-ordinated approach to the Stones' career. With Peter Rudge handling the tours, Prince Rupert the financial aspects and myself executive producing the albums, there was a concerted strategy.

The tax position meant a re-location to the South of France. For me the *Exile On Main Street* sessions at Keith's house, Nellcôte, meant a lot of work, building a kitchen in the house, constructing the Rolling Stones mobile studio with the help of Stu, Alan Dunn, Andy Johns, Glyn Johns and Olympic, trucking it down to the South of France and figuring out how to make it all work, and taking a lot of flak from the accountants because it was costing so much.

There followed a series of intense moments. The American tour of 1972: a wild tour captured pretty accurately on *Cocksucker Blues*, the film I produced that was shot by the realist photographer Robert Frank — although it missed out the lighter, funnier moments that offset the more negative, heavier aspects.

Goats Head Soup: watching the ambience of Kingston directly affect the mood of the album, the hot weather and the sultriness seeping into the soul of the record. We used to book studios for a month, 24 hours a day, so that the band could keep the same set-up and develop their songs in their free-form way, starting with a few lyrics and rhythms, jamming and rehearsing while we fixed the sound. It amazed me, as an old-time record guy, that the Stones might not have played together for six or eight months, but within an hour of jamming, the synergy that is their strength would come into play and they would lock together as one. Atlantic did not want to take 'Angie' as the single off *Goats Head* — they really wanted another 'Brown Sugar' rather than a ballad — and there were some heated arguments before we all agreed on that choice, another US Number One.

On the 1973 tour of Europe I played trumpet with the Wonderlove brass section on the last three numbers (my lip was too soft to play more) of the last eight dates. On the 1975 Tour of the Americas I would find myself, a mid-West Jewish boy, hanging out with the likes of Rudolf Nureyev and Man Ray. I was also busted, along with Mick and Keith, by the Providence, Rhode Island, police, after Keith had lashed out at some unrelenting photographer.

All these experiences enriched my life, but by 1976 I was worn down. It wasn't the Stones, it was me. I had realised that all the people kissing my ass were doing it not because of who I was, but because of the band. Girls would fuck you only because they wanted you to introduce them to the band. I ended up with my ego sucked dry. I was disenchanted with my own soul. I had been abusing multiple substances — I only had to look in the mirror to see the effects. Despite albums and singles going to Number One, I was not happy with myself. I felt I had to make a break or die.

I had had a love affair with the Stones, a hot love affair. But like all affairs, it cooled. And in 1977 I told them that I was going to leave. While we were in Switzerland, I had a dinner with Mick in Montreux and explained all the reasons. They asked me to help out on *Some Girls* but the week before I was due to start, Keith was busted in Toronto, and that marked the end of my work. Suddenly the phone calls from the sycophants stopped. In fact, nobody rang. After seven years of seeing the Stones every day of my life, living with their ups and downs and intimate lives, everything stopped abruptly. Over the following years I cleaned up, had a family and lost touch completely.

On the *Bridges To Babylon* tour I decided to go and see the Madison Square Garden show. Keith met me and took me into the Garden's lavish dressing rooms. Keith's wife was there and Ronnie's family. I said, "OK guys, give me your attention for five minutes. I always felt that things ended wrong between us. I had that dinner with Mick and then it just ended. It's been bothering me for 18 years." And Keith, bless him, just said, "What the fuck are you talking about, Marshall? You were there. And now you're here." And you know what? He was right.

It wasn't so much
a question of being a
wizard on the guitar.
You also had to be
quite a magician to
be able to live with
the Stones.

Ronnie Wood

THE NEW BOY

7

Ronnie Wood joins the band, initially on a temporary basis, as the Stones pose in front of the Alamo national monument during their 1975 tour. He celebrated his 28th birthday on the opening date before an audience of 15,000 at the Louisiana State University.

RONNIE: I got a phone call from Mick while I was out in Los Angeles. I had been laid low by some kind of smog-related illness and I couldn't physically move – luckily the Faces were taking a break from being on the road, or else we had come to the end of a tour. Mick said, "We're desperate. Could you please come out to Munich?" and I went, "Yeah, as soon as I get back on my legs, I'll be there" – and that was it.

KEITH: We were running the auditions to find a replacement for Mick Taylor. There were some fantastic guitarists coming into town. Wayne Perkins was a beautiful American guy and an incredible player – he was as good as Mick Taylor, if not better – and Harvey Mandel was another American, another brilliant player. Then Ronnie Wood comes in, who's English – and we all looked at each other. This is an English rock'n'roll band, after all, and that was basically the criterion. It wasn't about who could play the sweetest notes. It was all to do with who could perform "the ancient form of weaving" with me, and who I could communicate with. A band is a mixture of many things, but a lot of it has to do with whether you are able to live together every day on the bloody road.

MICK: We tried out loads of people. It was quite difficult, and we really weren't very good at trying them out. We were useless – hopeless, to be honest. When we tried out bass players after Bill left, we were much more organised: we just sat in one room and tested dozens of them.

CHARLIE: We started the auditions and went to Rotterdam, where I met Kenny Clarke, which was the highlight of the whole bloody thing for me, that and playing with Jeff Beck. Jeff would have got the job, I think, but he never turned up again! He came, played an audition, left the next morning and nobody knew where he'd gone. Maybe Keith didn't like the way he played or maybe they didn't get on in the way that Keith wanted. The thing about Ronnie, apart from the fact that he is a very good guitar player, is that he's very sociable, and an extremely likeable person. Jeff Beck is too, but Jeff's a much more complicated person than Ronnie. If you're on tour, you can't have a Jeff Beck with you for only four days a week, you need him for seven – and Ronnie's a seven-day-a-week guy. I think that is perhaps what Mick and Keith thought was great about him. Forget the guitar playing, because you've got to be good to be asked to do the job – and Jeff Beck is probably the best guitar player to come out of Europe, along with Martin Taylor. Jeff would have been much more rock'n'roll than Mick Taylor; we'd have had the old foot going and everything, but Jeff would have been much harder to know.

Jimmy Page also came and played with us at that time. Harvey Mandel did a great job with us when he came in the studios, as did Wayne Perkins, but I think the problem with Harvey or Wayne joining this band is that they were American. I think we all felt that at that time it was better for us to choose an English guy. That doesn't mean that if in 1969 we'd wanted Jimi Hendrix to join us after Brian left, and if Jimi had wanted the job, that we'd have said no. But in general Ronnie's Englishness was an important factor.

RONNIE: I think you had to be able to live with them, with the Stones. When I first walked into the studio where the auditions were going on, I said, "OK, play this song – it goes like this" and Charlie said "Oh, he's bossing us around already!" That was his first line to me.

CHARLIE: I hate making comparisons between guitarists. It wasn't a question of who was "better", but for this gig I think Ronnie was much better suited. And in addition Ronnie is a great asset with Mick and Keith, since he's very good at remembering what we do in each song. Because Keith plays a bit like I do – and this is not being rude about him – he doesn't really know where it's going necessarily, and he doesn't want to know. So if someone asks, "What key was that in?" and Keith goes, "Oh, it was in B flat" or whatever, Ronnie will say "No, we did this, and the middle goes da, da, da".

Ronnie's analytical, but he's not great at concentrating. He can solve a problem, but solving it time and time again is not interesting to Ronnie! He's fantastically quick, he's very good and he's usually right, so he is a very good musician in that way. Playing with Ronnie is as interesting and as much fun as playing with Mick Taylor, it's just that with some of the songs and in some of the moments they contained, Mick could turn them into something else, so that when you hear them back they're beautiful, because that's what he was like. But those moments don't arise, and have never arisen with Ronnie in the band, because with the way he works with Keith those same spaces don't appear. We do different things with Ronnie in the band, and he is fabulous at doing them. I don't know how good Brian Jones was as a

> *I think that it was important for the others to have a sense that someone would be able to live and survive with them through all the ups and downs of being out on tour along the long road ahead.*
>
> *Ronnie*

guitarist, because I'm not a guitar player, and so I don't really know his capabilities, but what was good about Brian is what's good about Ronnie, except I think Ronnie's better at it.

Brian was a good all-round guy to have in a band because he could play any instrument. His concentration was limited, but it was a little better than Ronnie's – Ronnie's attention span is about a minute, Brian's was like *two* – and like Ronnie he could have a go at everything. Brian would play a recorder, an autoharp and a piano on one song. In those days in the studio you didn't have programmes. Now you can have Artur Rubenstein playing piano with you or at least the touch of him, whereas then you either had to ask Artur Rubenstein if he'd like to play with you or you had to try and copy him. There was one song on which Bill and Brian or Keith were trying to play the cello. One of them was holding the cello and the other one was doing the bowing. It was like amateur hour, but it was great fun. Brian was a great one at being able to do that and Ronnie also has that capability. If you leave Ronnie with an instrument for a day, he will be able to play something on it; whether it's a trumpet, a saxophone or an accordion – he'll get something out of it. He is better than Brian was at playing slide guitar, and also the laptop steel, which is a bloody hard instrument to play, having to work those pedals with your feet. And he now plays a sitar guitar on 'Paint It Black'. Ronnie loves playing all those instruments, which is a great asset for the Stones.

> *After I joined the Stones, my dad, Archie, didn't call me Ronnie, he called me "Ronnie Wood of the Rolling Stones".*
>
> Ronnie

RONNIE: I had always been a huge Mick Taylor fan. I'd known him really well back in the early days, well before he joined the Stones, when he was playing with a band called the Gods, and I was playing with the Birds. He used to be too nervous even to go on, and he'd say, "Ronnie, play my bit for me". I'd go, "Mick, come on, you're a brilliant player", and in any case I didn't play a Les Paul like he did. But he'd say, "Please, Ronnie, take my guitar and do my show. You've got to go on". And he'd push me on stage. I'd do his set for him and then I'd go and play a set with the Birds.

Mick Taylor always underestimated his talent. He thought he was a terrible guitar player. He's the same to this day. We got a letter from him backstage on the *Forty Licks* tour, saying, "I've got no confidence, I'm really depressed and short of cash. Give my love to Ronnie". Keith summed it up when he said, "That's all part of what goes with leaving the band", because Mick is one of the few people who's ever left this band alive!

Ronnie Wood at home, at The Wick, Richmond Hill. He had beaten off competition from Jeff Beck, Clem Clempson, Mick Ronson, Rory Gallagher, Peter Frampton, Harvey Mandel, Wayne Perkins and Ollie Halsall (depending on which music paper you had read) to secure his place in the Stones.

CHARLIE: We made some of the best music we've ever made with Mick Taylor. I thought the chemistry worked fabulously, and musically it was a peak period, which may not be all down to him, it might equally be the songs that Mick and Keith were writing, but the combination worked. As a lead, virtuoso guitar, Mick was so lyrical on songs like 'Can't You Hear Me Knocking', which was an amazing track because that was a complete jam, one take at the end. He had such a good ear, and I would help push him along. On 'Waiting On A Friend' he went into that Santana style of playing. It was incredible, and it really worked. He was a fabulous guitar player.

Mick wasn't a difficult person to have in the band, but he was very young when he was

with us and he was a totally undisciplined soul. He was no workhorse. He hated doing anything twice. If you didn't get Mick the first time, you could forget it. You had to come back the next day and get him first time again. Keith, on the other hand, gets better and better each time he does another take. Mick wasn't a great one for going into the studio the next day to put a solo down or to work on overdubs like Mick Jagger does. It was just one of those things. He was a great one-off guy, a natural.

However, I don't think Keith thought that Mick Taylor was as wonderful to work with as Ronnie. Keith loves working with Ronnie. And Ronnie is very good at one thing that Mick Taylor was totally useless at – basically showing up and playing for the next thirty years.

RONNIE: Nicky Hopkins we've lost, Jimmy Miller we've lost, but Mick Taylor is still alive and kicking and wearing a big fat suit!

KEITH: Mick Taylor was a beautiful player, so beautiful. A brilliant blues player. I would

Charlie in the mid-'70s.

A portrait of Charlie by David Bailey.

never knock the man's musicianship – he used to wipe me away. He had all the licks down, but where was his heart?

I had already been playing with Ronnie off and on, on the side, for a couple of years, and I'd say, "What a shame we can't do this with the Stones, Ron". It was so much fun to play with Ronnie, and Mick Taylor was not a barrel of fun – he doesn't know any Max Miller jokes!

And with Mick Taylor I wasn't playing in the way that I wanted to. For me it seemed to be heading back more and more towards the lead guitar/rhythm guitar split, which has never been my thing. I have always been much more interested in "the ancient art of weaving", as Ronnie and I call it. And Ronnie understands what that is all about. It's like the Bayeux Tapestry: playing together in a way where you can't tell what is rhythm guitar and what is lead guitar and where you can pick it up, flow it around and bung it across to the other guy. Where somebody will say to me, "I love that lick you do", and I can answer, "Well, actually, I didn't do that, Ronnie did it!"

It's about the guy you're playing with. You've really got to be into each other in a certain way, even though sometimes you might end up hating each other's guts. I've played with the best players in the world; some are simpatico and some ain't, and some are too technical and can never sit back. I'm here to abolish the difference between rhythm and lead guitar, because to me it should all follow on seamlessly, but then of course I've been doing this for decades. I think I have been very lucky to play with Ronnie because he is one of the most sympathetic players I know, though Lord he can be erratic – but that's what I love about him. It pissed me off at the time when Mick Taylor left, but then, whatever happens, happens. Ronnie created a completely different relationship, which carries on to this day, and it has grown. I must admit that on the *Forty Licks* tour Ronnie was playing the best that I had ever heard him.

CHARLIE: When Mick Taylor announced he was leaving I was not surprised, because I always felt that he was capable, not necessarily of better things, but certainly of different things, which is what I thought he wanted to go on and do. I think we were all angry, because he simply upped and left... but that's Mick Taylor, one realises now, that's what

he's like. So for me, his solo career has been a big disappointment. Mick had told me that he wanted to do his own solo records and I was always in favour of him doing that.

Mick Taylor took me along to meet John McLaughlin, who at the time was playing in Lifetime, which consisted of Tony Williams on drums, Larry Young on keyboards and John McLaughlin on guitar – just the three of them. I'd already seen Tony playing with Miles Davis, but I'd never seen Lifetime. We went to listen to them in New York and it was fantastic. Mick said he was doing this solo album and I told him, "Don't sing, just play – and use people like Tony, or Elvin Jones, or ask Ginger Baker to do it with you. Get people who you wouldn't normally think of working with". This was in the days when record companies would give people like Nicky Hopkins and Mick Taylor a lot of money – maybe a million or half a million dollars – just to make a solo album. And they'd go away and take it all deadly seriously and see themselves up there like Elton John or Bob Dylan. Now Nicky Hopkins wasn't Elton John. Nicky was a fabulous piano player, but his album ended up with him trying to sing proper songs, instead of doing those little piano melodies that he used to play. And Mick Taylor's solo effort was the same. I only found out years later that he was quite messed up at around that time, which must have had a lot to do with why he was very unproductive after he left us.

> *I have been very lucky to play with Ronnie because he is one of the most sympathetic players I know, though Lord he can be erratic – but that's what I love about him.*
>
> Keith

I certainly wasn't disappointed when Ronnie joined, although I never knew Ronnie was joining, in a way. I wasn't aware that Ronnie was the chosen one. He sort of played with us and then did a tour with us. I certainly do still tend to think that Ronnie only joined the Stones a couple of years ago, but it's actually a hell of a long time. He's a wonderful person to have with you, a very light personality, and he's a great guy to be on tour with. He's a lot of fun – he's daft as well – but he's a nice person.

RONNIE: I had always wanted to work with Keith. He was one of my favourite guitarists, and *Get Yer Ya-Ya's Out* was always the Faces' favourite album. We used to play the record before we went on stage, to get vibed in.

Keith and I both love Robert Johnson, Earl Hooker and all the people that had played with Muddy Waters. We've both got a lot of Barbecue Bob in us; that old steel guitar-picking style. Backstage, when Keith and I are working out on our guitars before a show, we often go into those old 1920s, down south, guitar-picking things and it comes across in the songs. I have an old 1947 Gibson semi-acoustic and Keith has an old blond Gibson semi-acoustic.

Keith always loves to have a sparring pal on the guitar – and generally in his everyday life. I think he really misses Gram Parsons. I never knew Keith when he was hanging with Gram, but from what I gather they hung very similarly to the way Keith and I do. I met Gram's daughter at one of our shows in LA, and because I could see, looking from afar at the relationship between her and Keith, how touching it was, I gave her a hug and said "I'd love to have met your dad", and she said "He'd have loved to have me meet you". We got quite weepy, it was very sweet. I'm sure I've helped to keep something going along the lines of the interplay that Keith must have had going with Gram.

Being that sparring partner was something of a change for me because I had been the

Keith models in 1975. That year the band was top of Performance *magazine's list of audience-drawing power, based on the figures provided by US promoters.*

only guitarist in the Faces. I'd play rhythm and lead and I was also the band leader, calling all the shots and all the cues. So it was actually quite a relief for me to be second in line for the cues, because Keith would call all the musical changes in this band. It's quite a cushy job for me, in a way. It was easy for me to say, "OK, Keith's at the helm here, and I know when I've got to do this, come in here, I've got the solo here or he's got the solo there or we'll be weaving the guitars together". It worked out – and it still does work out – pretty well.

I'm carrying more responsibility nowadays because I'm seeing things clearer and playing better, and the whole band is much more of a powerful fighting unit than it's ever been. There were times when we used to bluff it, get stoned out of our brains and just go for it – "Eyes down and meet you at the end!" Looking back on those days I think, "Oh my God, how did I ever play that, how did we even get through it, let alone trying to remember the set list or what town we were in or what year it was…"

CHARLIE: On the 1975 tour of the States, Ronnie wasn't really in the band. We were still in the process of trying to poach him off the Faces, and, as soon as he'd finished our tour, he went straight off and did another one with them. His wife didn't see him for two years, I don't think!

RONNIE: In 1975 I did two tours with the Faces, with the Stones' tour of the States in the middle. I remember Keith especially saying, "We'll never formally announce you as being in the band, we'll just keep them guessing" – and that situation went on for years and years, to the point where no one asked any more. I was very happy to be with the Stones because there was no future for the Faces. When I did the tour with them in autumn 1975 we were hanging on to the threads of the band. I would have carried on because I wouldn't have wanted to be the one to fold the band. At the time it would have just been perfect for me to carry on juggling my commitments with both bands, never stop working, great! But in the end the Faces did fold and Rod Stewart had left, so it was not

Ronnie, Mick and Keith harmonise on the Stones' 1975 US tour.

Mick in a pre-show stadium, 1975.

like being on loan any more.

When we launched the 1975 Stones tour, we hired a flat-bed truck to play on and promote the tour, and drove it round the streets of Manhattan. We'd all said, "Where did we get this idea from?" and Charlie had told us, "It's an ancient jazz thing from Harlem – they used to do it in the old days".

So it was nine o'clock in the morning in New York City; there we were going down Fifth Avenue and I saw Shep Gordon – who was Alice Cooper's manager – walking along with his briefcase. Shep had helped Groucho Marx find a way out of all the problems that he had in his later life after his involvement in that quiz show *You Bet Your Life* – Shep got Groucho his money back before he died. I met Groucho once, when I went over to his house with Ahmet Ertegun. We rang the doorbell; ding, dong, the door opened, and there was Groucho. His first words to me were, "That's the silliest haircut I've ever seen" and then he growled, "Follow me". As he was walking along with his cane he was going, "Are you a man or a chicken?" I was just keeping my mouth shut, and walking behind with Groucho, while he kept turning round and insulting me: "What the hell are you doing in my house?"

We passed Shep Gordon, on his way to his office and we were playing "bam, bam", coming round the corner: here's the Rolling Stones and Billy Preston on the back of a truck, with me in my band jacket from an endangered species. I like fighting for endangered species and there I was in this Thomson's gazelle-skin jacket. My daughter still teases me about that jacket.

The first gig I played with the Rolling Stones was on my birthday, June 1st. I had a sea of thoughts going through my head along with all these songs that I had had to learn. I thought, "Whoooah, here we go, in at the deep end". It was very exciting, a real challenge, and luckily I have always loved a challenge. It's still a bit that way because this band keeps changing.

I was more concerned with paying a good homage to – and making a good representation of – all the things that Mick Taylor had laid down during the period while he had been with the band; his melodies and his virtuosity. If I am playing a song like 'All Down The Line' it's a tribute to Mick Taylor's playing, and if we play 'Can't You Hear Me Knocking' I'm doing Mick Taylor, only now I can take it off somewhere else.

I always thought that I would never be able to play like Mick, while he thought he was no good – he thinks I'm far better than him and I'll say, "Come on, Mick, get out of here", but he honestly believes that. I didn't dwell on it too long. I knew that I had it inside me to play things my way, but to add the flavour of Mick Taylor as well is cool.

On the tour I was immediately struck by the level of the Stones' organisation. They had things like set lists and daily sheets pushed underneath your hotel room door that told you what was happening, when the sound checks were and things like that, and there was a support band and a case of champagne. That was something I had never been used to. With the Faces it had always been "Yeah, we'll just give out champagne instead of having a support band", and we'd be sitting around in the dressing room asking each other, "What songs are we going to play tonight? What are we going to open with?" It would be

*Looking at photographs
of a performance.*

*(opposite) Ronnie by
Christopher Sykes.*

that rough. The Stones always had some structure in the way they were going to present themselves. I loved it.

MICK: The 1975 tour was different from the ones we had done before because we had a new lighting director called Jules Fisher, who is still very much around. We had started off with Chip Monck, who was our first lighting director, on the 1969 tour. 1969 was the great watershed tour because that was when we started hanging the sound and therefore hanging the lights. On the 1972 stage we had quite a complex light show and one of Chip's things was that we hung mirrors up. We had a mirror that came up in the front of the stage and we put very big lights at the back and bounced all the lights off the mirror. That was one of Chip's special numbers. Then we changed lighting directors for the 1975 tour and brought in Jules Fisher in 1975. During this period the whole arena show started as an industry for us, and I think for everyone else. I'm not a great historian of the rock business, but I think Pink Floyd were the only other band doing this level of things as well.

Before this period there was no real rock tour industry, and so we had to take people out of other work – we took people out of *Holiday On Ice* for the travelling shows because everything had to be rigged. We hired all the riggers off *Holiday On Ice* and Disney, because there was simply no rock'n'roll pool of talent and experience. That was something that eventually developed with people like Chip Monck, and the whole idea of loading up the stuff and trucking it around was unheard of – which sounds really funny now – no one had ever done that before. It was something that had to be learned. The other shows that were doing this weren't rock shows, but it was a very similar procedure: they had to get a lot of stuff in and out of the ice hockey arenas, which were exactly the kind of venues that we were playing in the United States.

CHARLIE: Billy Preston was on that 1975 tour. He was, and still is, fabulous, especially with his own band, which, rather madly, we incorporated into ours – we had half his band in ours. Billy did some great things with us – he was at his best during that period, with his gospel piano stuff. Mick also wrote some excellent songs with great melodies with him around that time.

*(overleaf) Scenes from
the 1975 tour of the
US photographed by
Christopher Sykes and
Ken Regan. Shown here
travelling with the band
are (page 190 bottom
right) Charlie's wife
Shirley and daughter
Serafina, (page 191
middle right) Billy
Preston, keyboards, and
Ollie Brown, percussion,
and Bianca Jagger (page
191 bottom far left).*

Ronnie, Stu and
Charlie in flight.

The last time I saw Billy was when I was working on a movie score. We were working on *Bridges To Babylon* and Billy played on a couple of songs of ours and so I went next door and did some work with him. Since then I heard he worked with Eric Clapton and got into some kind of trouble, I don't know what. I've never ever seen that side of Billy. Whenever I've met him or been with him, he's been a lovely, charming man.

RONNIE: Billy was one of the sweetest guys you could ever meet. And we also had Ollie Brown playing percussion on that tour – Ollie *E.* Brown, if you don't mind, the man in the stacks, the tallest man in the world.

MICK: We've always had a keyboard player on board, sometimes more than one. Right back in the early days, we had Stu as our road manager and he played the piano as well. Then we had Nicky Hopkins, Billy Preston and others. You have to have a keyboard player because so many of our songs require them, and I couldn't imagine doing those songs without having keyboards. That doesn't mean that every song needs a great keyboard part, but a lot of them do, especially the slowies. And also the keyboard player quite often has another function, which is helping with the musical arrangements and keeping the whole thing on an even keel.

The 1975 tour contained lots of props along with all the new things that Jules Fisher had added, which were things that he had done on Broadway: projected surfaces and painted cloths. We had two versions of the lotus stage, one of which was a great opening using what was called a Venetian curtain, a cylindrical curtain. In a few large cities, when we could afford it in those days, the leaves of this lotus folded up and at the beginning of the show the stage was completely covered with a kind of sheath of gauze. I had to get inside the lotus, climb up a ladder and hang on like grim death to one of the petals, which then opened to reveal the band playing. It was a very pleasing shape, which was shunted down well into the front half of the hockey arena so that we were really amongst the audience. At the other venues on the tour we couldn't afford to have the stage moving, but the lotus shape was still out there thrusting into the audience, not these rather geometric shapes that people do now and that we still do – just like rather boring rectangles.

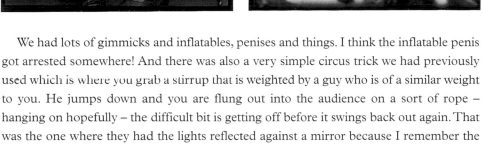

Charlie and Shirley Watts backstage.

Bill cuts a celebratory cake at the end of a tour that reached 27 cities, saw the Stones play 45 gigs and gross nearly $13 million. Two months later, in October, the band would reconvene in Montreux to commence the recording of Black and Blue.

We had lots of gimmicks and inflatables, penises and things. I think the inflatable penis got arrested somewhere! And there was also a very simple circus trick we had previously used which is where you grab a stirrup that is weighted by a guy who is of a similar weight to you. He jumps down and you are flung out into the audience on a sort of rope – hanging on hopefully – the difficult bit is getting off before it swings back out again. That was the one where they had the lights reflected against a mirror because I remember the rope had to go out and bang into the mirror frame.

CHARLIE: Because of our personality we were eventually forced to play in these places like Wembley Stadium. In fact I preferred playing Wembley Stadium to Earl's Court. I

Charlie and Mick, with Stu in the background.

Mick — and Bill — with clockwise from top: Andy Warhol, George Harrison, Billy Preston and Elton John, Bob Marley and Peter Tosh, and Howlin' Wolf.

thought it was horrible in Earl's Court. Mick and I went to see Elton John playing there and he was great and everyone loved it. We played there and it was bloody awful. I don't know why. It was really awful.

RONNIE: After I joined the Stones, my dad, Archie, didn't call me Ronnie, he called me "Ronnie Wood of the Rolling Stones". He came to the show in Wembley in 1982 – one of the only gigs that he ever came to, and there was my dad in his wheelchair, going "That's my boy, Ronnie Wood of the Rolling Stones". He was the first to arrive and the last one to leave Wembley Stadium. He went down each row of the seating area, shook hands with everyone, kissed all the girls, sat them on his lap with the one leg that he had left and he was saying, "I could still give you three yet, darlin'" to all the good-looking girls.

By the time we released *Black And Blue*, I was settled in. Although the others were learning things from me, because we were all bouncing ideas around, obviously I was learning from the more experienced boys. And they were a mine of information; they still are.

Backstage, 1975.

I didn't get a songwriting credit, apart from on 'Hey Negrita', which was credited as "Inspiration by Ron Wood". There were a lot of "inspired" days like that – for 'Melody' it said "Inspiration by Billy Preston". There were a number of people who took umbrage, like Billy, or who said, "Thank you and fuck you" and who'd never see the Rolling Stones again. But I thought, "OK, I have to keep plodding along, they're older than me, and I'm still the new boy. I'll always be the youngest member of the band, so I'll put that down to experience. One day I'll get my fair share". Sure enough, it took a long time, but it did happen. And in any case, who better to be an apprentice with than the band that you always wanted to be in. I've never felt bad about it, and I've never been a businessman either, so I'm lucky enough to be blessed with being able to play guitar.

I have learned that to make sure you get a credit on a song, you have to have a combination of persistence and good timing. I think that Mick Taylor would have chickened out by saying, "Oh, I haven't got the time to follow it through and keep on pressing my case", but you have to keep pushing at the right time, when there's a little lull, where there's a gap.

CHARLIE: The reggae influence on the songs on *Black And Blue* came primarily from Keith. In the 1960s I used to have a lot of ska and Blue Beat records. When they came out as 45s I'd get them. They were my brother-in-law's, in fact: he'd send them to me or he used to bring them over when he came to stay with us and he'd give them to me.

(opposite) Keith with his son Marlon, his eldest child with Anita Pallenberg. Named after actor Marlon Brando, he is now in his thirties and a father himself. Keith's coat was a present from Charlie.

(previous pages) Ronnie in the studio by Ken Regan.

Playing reggae is like playing backwards, but a beautiful, fantastic rhythm, I suppose it's one of the last unique little rhythms, a quirk that it happened in a way. It's like all those Latin American rhythms you get – they're forever playing something on a cowbell and it turns into another kind of dance or there's a girl with a slightly bigger arse than before, and it's become a rumba. There are a hundred names for all these rhythms that are essentially banging a cowbell, as Mick would say. He would say that it must be hell to be a drummer in one of those bands, not because of their playing – because the music's beautiful – but because of the knowledge you need to have of all those endless variations on the rhythms, the things that have to be done in a particular way if it's going to be that kind of a dance. In my band I have a Brazilian percussionist, and it's wonderful, you just say, "It's more like a samba or whatever," and he can play it. It's amazing.

But reggae was a whole little rhythm that was dreamt up out of the blue – it's flared and died out now, I think. Well, they ruined it. People like Sly and Robbie became so proficient at playing that the whole thing became like a machine, and then indeed they started using a machine and, in terms of the actual recording technique rather than the musical technique, the beauty of all the Barrett Brothers type of playing was diluted because the sound became so clean. The great thing about early reggae is that it was such a weird sound. It was an engineer's music, not really a band playing.

Mick was certainly into reggae. I had all those records in France with me when we moved there and when we were recording the tracks for *Exile On Main Street* at Keith's house. Mick used to have them as well. I'd play him 'Cherry Oh Baby' or he'd play one to me. And *The Harder They Come* was an album Keith listened to a lot. There was one tour we did that I called the *Harder They Come* tour because he played the album every night on the bus. I could sing every song. I couldn't play many of the licks the drummers played, but it's a fantastic album; a great example of reggae at its best.

RONNIE: Reggae was part of my compendium of different styles, along with a bit of jazz, a bit of blues and a bit of soul. I listened to quite a lot of reggae with Eric Clapton – I used to hang out with him in that period. In the 1970s Keith and I would go to the clubs and we'd take along our own reggae music, for instance, and we'd go up to the DJ and

ask him to put our music on so that everybody would be dancing to Toots and the Maytals or something. We would do that at every club and get our favourite music played and we'd be rocking. It was like having a massive party everywhere we went in the world – New York, London, all across Germany, and Europe in general. Keith used to have a whole other angle on clubs. We used to score as well, so the word would come that this or that club was where to go for this or that stuff, so let's take the music along. It would be one big party and when the stuff showed up, it would be even more of a party!

I played with Bob Marley at the Oakland Coliseum when I lived in Malibu. One of his guitar players, Al Anderson, had had his guitar stolen so I brought a guitar up to the Coliseum for him, and Al said, "Come and play with us". I went in to see Bob and said, "So far, Bob, you're the only member of this group who doesn't know that I'm playing with you!" He didn't say a word; he just looked at me as if to say, "Well, if you can cut it, it will be all right, but if you can't, you'll be off". After a couple of songs on stage I got the "You're all right" look and so I played right through to his encore, which must have lasted an hour.

So all of us, independently and together, were into reggae, and it was also a mood of the time. I had this particular lick that I took into the studio and the others said, "What are we going to start with?" and I said, "I've got this song". Charlie was sitting behind his kit, so he was already into it and then Keith and Mick both got into the motion of it. That was 'Hey Negrita', which came together very easily. The key to getting a song across in this band is never to try and write all the words. If you've got the rhythm, you're lucky! Let Mick write the words and then you're in with a chance.

KEITH: With *Love You Live* it wasn't that we wanted to make a live album, but we owed the record company one and we didn't have one really good basic recording. You have to work with what you're left with. The trouble with live recordings is that you're up there playing and you have no say about what's coming off the recording heads onto the tape. So either there was something that was not very well played, or it wasn't well recorded or somebody lost the tapes. Live recordings are always a toss of the coin, and that was especially true then. Nowadays technology has made it easier to capture a band on stage, but at the same time live albums are strange things because if you select the best sound off the sound board, you might well have a very good-sounding record, but it doesn't sound live any more and you just raise the level of the audience at the end! It's a fine balance between the sound and the atmosphere in the venue because the beauty of recording on tape is that you actually *can* capture an atmosphere and spirit on tape. It's quite amazing, but it can be done and that's why people like music – it's the reason why they like to listen to records.

Canada was the crunch. The shit hit the fan big time. I was looking at the possibility of having to do seven years in jail.

Keith

RONNIE: We had to record the show at the El Mocambo club in Toronto to add an extra side of material to *Love You Live*. I remember the cut-out palm trees on stage and Maggie Trudeau, who was my guest. We had a laugh, but the gig was a bit of a mist: we had so many songs to remember and I don't think we had a definitive set list until the last minute. There was a lot of humming and hawing and although I can't remember what songs we played, when somebody shows me the list, it always looks great to me!

CHARLIE: The El Mocambo was one of our club gigs, which I think are usually pretty dire, because there are too many people in them; it becomes really uncomfortable, and we generally play too loud as well. Way too hot and way too loud. The gig at the Mocambo itself doesn't stand out in my mind, but I do remember having dinner with Mick and Mia Farrow and Ronnie being with Margaret Trudeau and nearly falling down the lift shaft. And I remember Mick running to me saying, "Get out, get out, we're going to get busted". I always felt awful because we actually did disappear and leave Keith there. It was terrible really. I have always wondered why did we leave him? It was total paranoia at being roped into a bust that had nothing to do with me, and feeling it was really to do with Anita and Keith. I felt very, very bad about that and Stu stayed behind with Keith and he never, ever forgot that, Stu. He and Keith made some great sides while they were stuck there: a great version of 'Confessin' The Blues' and 'Run Rudolph Run', with just the two of them.

KEITH: I was asleep when I got busted. It was just another day, I had been at rehearsal, got back to the hotel and passed out. My next memory is being woken up and dragged by these two very big people who were slapping me awake. You can't be arrested if you're not awake, so they were splashing water. I woke up thinking, "I'll wake up in a minute." I'd rather have had the nightmare. Canada was the crunch. The shit hit the fan big time. I was looking at the possibility of having to do seven years in jail. At least I faced it. It's the only thing I'm proud about in all of that period – that I faced up to it and said "OK, that's it, and it's all over". The reason that Anita and I didn't stay together is because she didn't, and I'd gone. I was looking down the bad end of the gun. Bill Wyman was the first one who actually went out and scored shit for me. He'd never done that in his life, but he did it, because I had asked the Mounties when they busted me, "Give me a gram back, because otherwise you know what I've got to do – I've got to go out and get some more, and you're going to follow me and bust me again". And they wouldn't do that, naturally enough, the cops are not like that.

At the end of the day you don't mess with me. There's no point in doing it. I'm only a guitar player, I write a few songs. I'm a troubadour, a minstrel – it's a long-established profession. That's all I do. I don't have any big aspirations. I'm not Mozart. But the only reason the cops became interested in me was because they thought that I *was* that important, and that was really what shocked me.

I said to myself, "OK, the experiment will now come to an end. This is a laboratory, and we're closing the laboratory down". Before that I had just thought, "Hey, what you do to yourself is your own business". I wasn't responsible for the guy in the schoolyard who was selling shit to kids. They try and lay that on you: if you take drugs, then you're turning on some school kid. My attitude had been like Baudelaire – "Let's see what this stuff does" – but the reason I'm still alive is because I made sure that if I was going to do anything, it had to be top-quality stuff, I wasn't going to compromise. But then the good stuff got harder and harder to find. Wherever I went people would track me down.

I simply realised I couldn't cover all the bases, so it was, "Boom, OK, fine, I really needed that, it's time to snap to". I was fucking my band up, I was fucking my family up, I was fucking myself up – fucking *everything* up – and the experiment had gone on just a little too long. I had done it to hide, to hide from fame and being this other person, because all I wanted to do was play music and bring my family up. That was the only way that I could shield myself. With a hit of smack I could walk through anything and not give a damn and not have to feel embarrassed or put upon. It may be a cheap way out of the problem, but it's still damn expensive.

So I brought it to an end. It's no big deal: it's not like having your kneecaps shot – though it's never easy to clean up. People that don't know about it write about "the horrors of cold turkey", but when you've done it ten or twelve times, it's not so horrific. I would never interfere with anyone else's problems, though. Never, ever. Anybody can do what they want and I'll clean up my own corner: Area A is where you eat, Area B is where you sleep and Area C is where you crap. I would never dream of telling anybody else what to do and I never saw anybody doing anything to threaten the band, except me.

CHARLIE: I wasn't worried about the future. I didn't really care and I've never cared. It's not something I sit and worry about. If it all ended tomorrow – I don't mean if we all die, but if we simply stopped playing – that would be all right, I'd do something else or play with somebody else. I've never worried about the band stopping. If it does, it does.

As far as taking drugs was concerned, I had never really taken drugs. I used to take speed, but the stuff I took was like slimming pills, and so I always felt, "It's nothing to do with me", or "I don't know what I could be charged with". I was always implicated, and so was my family. We were always searched or picked out by certain people because of what I did for a living and the associations I had. In the '60s it used to be the long hair and then it became drugs as well. It wasn't until the '80s that I actually did that myself, but up until then it was never anything. So my whole defence would have been, "Well, I don't take them and because Keith does, it doesn't mean to say *I* do". But of course there were all the implications for the band – our career went on hold.

It wasn't something I sat and worried about, or blamed Keith for, because I think what he was doing was much more of a problem to him than it was to me. I think Bill was

Playing a club venue again after many years. The El Mocambo Club, Toronto, March 1977, recording live to make up a side for the album Love You Live, *with Margaret Trudeau in the front row at Ronnie's invitation.*

I still tend to think that Ronnie only joined the Stones a couple of years ago, but it's actually a hell of a long time. He's a great guy to be on tour with. He's a lot of fun – he's daft as well – but he's a nice person.

Charlie

much more upset about the imposition on his life than I was. I suppose I should have been, but I wasn't.

RONNIE: When Keith was going through all of those problems, we tried not to look on the dark side. I just kept my fingers firmly crossed, hoping that everything would work out. There was very little we could do, other than just continue going through the paces. I suppose we always had a little bit in reserve in those druggie days where there was a possibility that some country's immigration department might not have allowed Keith in, although we couldn't have imagined the band without Keith. But if there had been a problem, we'd have been obliged to get round that somehow. I would have been part of the band, but I don't know what we'd have done for the other guitarist! When I heard that if we would perform a gig for the blind in Canada with the New Barbarians it would help Keith, it was "Yeah, let's go, let's do that" and it sure helped.

Charlie practises.

Ronnie and John Belushi on the set of TV's Saturday Night Live, *October 1978. A couple of years later, Belushi starred as Jake Blues in the R&B spoof* The Blues Brothers. *He died young in 1982.*

Rehearsing for Saturday Night Live, *for which the band acted as both hosts and musical attraction when opening the fourth season. Guests included Carrie Fisher (Princess Leia from* Star Wars) *and New York Mayor Ed Koch.*

The Stones perform on Saturday Night Live. *Their screen appearance came as some respite in a month in which they took severe criticism over the tongue-in-cheek lyrics of 'Some Girls', and faced Keith's court case.*

KEITH: Over the two years that the court case dragged on, every time I'd come up for a hearing to Toronto, they'd all be there, crowds of people with placards, saying, "Hey it's not fair, let Keith go". And then there was a blind girl, bless her, from Montreal, my blind angel. I had known this girl for a couple of years. She came to as many gigs as she could; she'd say she was determined to make it to the next show and of course we were worried

about her. I'd speak to the truckers and ask them to drop her off at the next show and to make sure she got there safely. And to me, that was it. She came forward and went to the judge's house, after office hours and at night, knocked on his door and told him this story. Two days later I had the next hearing and it was, "OK, you're sentenced to perform a concert for the blind", which we gladly did. That's why I love Toronto, because they solved the problems in a nice way.

CHARLIE: Keith got saved by some blind girl he knew. And he still sees her. He never forgets. He's a wonderful bloke like that.

PRINCE RUPERT LOEWENSTEIN

Prince Rupert Loewenstein was a director of the London merchant bank Leopold Joseph when he met Mick Jagger in 1968. He was invited to manage the business affairs of the Rolling Stones in 1970. He successfully organised their intricate and complicated finances and has been their financial adviser for the past 33 years.

In late February 1977 I was in Los Angeles to negotiate new distribution deals for Rolling Stones Records with a number of interested companies, since the contract with Atlantic Records was coming to an end. I arrived in my room at the Beverly Hills Hotel to be greeted with many a bottle of champagne sent by the various people competing for the contract; among them were a magnum of Dom Perignon from Robert Stigwood, who at that time was working with Polygram, and a bottle of Korbell to which was affixed a note saying, "Sent by Ahmet Ertegun and Atlantic Records". Only later did I hear that the Korbell had actually been sent by Robert Stigwood as a joke. A day or so after I arrived, when I was busy negotiating the deals, I had a telephone call from Mick Jagger telling me that Keith Richards had been arrested in Toronto, charged with drug peddling — and that this would soon be announced on television worldwide.

After a moment or two of anxious reflection I then had to telephone all the suitors, who one by one dropped out of the race, leaving only Ahmet Ertegun, with whom we, of course, renewed the arrangements for America, and we still managed to sign up with EMI for the rest of the world. But the news about Keith was, of course, a most serious blow, since clearly it significantly reduced our bargaining power.

That we continued the Stones' relationship with Atlantic was neither a hardship nor a disappointment. The joy of working with Atlantic after the band's sad experiences with record companies and managers in the 1960s had been enormous. Atlantic was still very much the child, albeit a most grown-up one by then, of Ahmet Ertegun, who had sold Atlantic, the company that he had started with his brother and some friends, to Warners, Steve Ross's company. Originally his company had been Kinney Services, which I believe had been his then father-in-law's parking lot and funeral parlour company. This later acquired Warners, a company that after many mergers, acquisitions and reconstructions is now called AOL Time Warner. It is notable for being the company that has had the largest US corporate loss in history: larger than the national debt of many countries joined together ($98.7 billion, including asset write-downs of $99.7 billion in 2002).

Notwithstanding his sale, Ahmet had remained very much in charge, even on a day-to-day and, dare we say it, a night-to-night basis. Many was the recording session that he attended – occasionally asleep, but more often awake – to encourage his artists, for it was as his artists that he saw them, with a nod or a wink, a laugh or a frown.

His wisdom and enthusiasm were of great help to the band in their new recording career. In those early days with Atlantic, which started with the release of *Sticky Fingers* in 1971 and continued with great success with *Exile On Main Street*, *Goats Head Soup* and *Black And Blue*, it was interesting to note that the bulk of the sales of the records took place in the USA. The "rest of the world" was certainly a less important market. This became even more apparent with the release of *Some Girls* in 1978, which remains the Stones' best-selling album.

Meanwhile, proceedings against Keith continued. However, we were fortunate that the mills of justice ground with their customary slowness and the sentence was only delivered in October of 1978 after the triumphant release of *Some Girls* and the attendant tour of the United States. Naturally, from the point of view of the band, the future had been rather cloudy – it was technically possible, but in reality impossible, to imagine the Rolling Stones without Keith alongside Mick and the others – but luckily the sentence was more lenient than had been feared, since, of course, imprisonment was the likeliest possibility. Keith was obliged to perform a benefit concert in aid of the Canadian Institute for the Blind ("Why not for the deaf?" he said), but was allowed to return to the USA for treatment and work could be resumed.

I first met the Stones in late 1968. Mick and I were introduced by Christopher Gibbs, a friend of mine who asked me whether I would be able to look after the financial affairs of his friend Mick Jagger and the Rolling Stones. At that time I had not heard of the Rolling Stones, though I did recall vaguely disapproving of William Rees-Mogg's article in *The Times* about Mick Jagger's arrest in Sussex. However, I was quickly educated by my wife and was under the impression that a large fortune could be administered at my bank.

I then met Mick at his house on the Chelsea Embankment and we "clicked", though it was then quite apparent to me that there was no large fortune to be administered, but instead that they were experiencing a fraught and difficult time, having become involved in a series of contractual entanglements that had to be unravelled. I was then a director of a small merchant bank, and managed to persuade my partners that the financial problems of a prominent rock band were no different, in essence, from the problems of any other financial organisation that sought advice in the City of London.

Of course the lifestyle of such a band was different from that of the chief executives of, say, ICI or British Aluminium, though the human problems encountered were not all that dissimilar. Even, we gather, politicians can have complicated emotional relationships and gullibility and over-enthusiasm are not unknown even in the most elevated corporate circles. However it was hard at that time to convince City bankers and solicitors of this, and indeed the much-publicised antics of rock stars did little to help when the Rolling Stones' early contracts had to be interpreted by a series of judges.

Shortly after I encountered Mick, Bill, Charlie and Keith, Brian Jones, whom I never met, died; at the same time we were giving a dance in our London house where everyone was asked to wear white. I remember Mick wearing a somewhat bucolic white smock, which he also wore at the memorial concert tribute which the Stones paid to Brian Jones in Hyde Park a day or two afterwards. Mick, as I remember it, brought Marianne Faithfull to our party and she chose to wear a black dress. She was at that time a beautiful young woman with a fetchingly innocent air.

By 1970 it became clear, once we and our solicitors had examined their contracts, and what passed for their accounts – trunkfuls of papers, which had to be shipped from the Stones' and their lawyers' offices – that the band had a burden of debt, which they would only be able to repay through future earnings if they left the United Kingdom. It should be remembered that in those days, before Lady Thatcher's administration, income tax took 83 per cent of all incomes earned above £24,000 per annum and a further 15 per cent of investment income above £2,250 per annum.

The Rolling Stones exiled themselves to France, where they worked and settled in the Alpes Maritimes. Charlie Watts and Bill Wyman made the fortunate decision to buy houses in the South of France, whereas Mick and Keith, alas, only rented houses, spectacular though they were. In those days France was not yet a haven of state socialism as was England and, as one fears, is going to be the case for all of us in the European Union.

During those early days I had frequently to fly down to Nice to have meetings with the band, since they were then settling in to such a new environment, and indeed, working hard recording *Exile On Main Street* in the splendid villa which Keith and Anita Pallenberg had taken. My own working life was much taken up with conducting a series of law suits (and legal settlements) on their behalf against their former management and record companies, which necessitated endless discussions and sessions with lawyers both in London and in America. However, the result of the law suits, etc., was by and large successful: their prime result was that the Rolling Stones were free to record and compose without being shackled by their old arrangements.

Money was still short in the period ending 1978, since debts had to be repaid and the cost of their financial obligations and, indeed, their own life-style had to be covered. However different the Stones were in character, none of them lived frugally.

The ten years that followed 1978 definitely marked a transitional point for the Stones, and the fact that they overcame their youthful problems and matured into the highly professional, but still enthusiastic, group that they are today is a noteworthy fact. Luckily, individuals differ one from the other and the different characters and make-up of each person in the band produce tensions which later can resolve into harmony: I have often thought that my own role in the organisation has been a combination of bank manager, psychiatrist and nanny.

The next few years saw the release of *Emotional Rescue*, *Tattoo You* and *Undercover*, whose sales, while reassuring, never matched those of *Some Girls*. However, 1981 and 1982 did see the first large-scale tour, playing to over two million people in the USA and one-and-a-half million in the rest of the world. Up to then, touring had been a secondary interest for the Rolling Stones, as for so many other leading bands. Tours were not financially very remunerative and "working the record" was seen as a way to heighten public awareness of the new releases. Indeed it must be said that Ahmet Ertegun never even thought that touring increased record sales. He had the strong belief then, and continued to hold it later, that record sales depended on the quality of the music and the amount of times the records were played on the radio.

Moreover, before the 1980s no money was made from merchandising, and corporate sponsorship, which lifts the publicity of the tour to much greater heights through the massive advertising of the companies involved, had never happened. The Rolling Stones were the first band to have a corporate sponsor in 1981 (Jovan). One of the main reasons for the modest remuneration enjoyed by the artists was that they, with their strongly (if naively) held views about providing cheap tickets, affordable by everybody, played into the hands of the promoters. This of course resulted in the quite disproportionate profits made by "scalpers" in contrast to those paid to the artists.

The Rolling Stones have, I think, been among the trail-blazers, whereby the difference between what is actually paid for tickets and what is accounted for and paid to the artists has significantly lessened. On top of that, now in the United States and alas only two or three other countries, the net revenues received by the artists bear a much more realistic relationship to the money paid for merchandise than in the old days.

In the last twenty years the Stones' record sales have shown a different pattern: many more have been sold in the rest of the world than in the USA, although the overall volume of sales falls short of the hopes kindled by the great success of *Some Girls*. However, the band is fortunate in that the last few tours have been so successful, underlining the Rolling Stones' great popularity.

To sum up, I have witnessed, as we all have, amazing changes in our world over the last forty years. A significant turning point in cultural life occurred in the 1960s and this coincided with a significant political change brought about, as is so frequently the case, as an aftermath to a world war. Rock music was a symptom of a new secular evangelisation, where the prohibitions of the decalogue were subordinated to the gospel of fulfilment of the individual's desires. The Rolling Stones' enormous popular success is a tribute to their ability to capture this taste and to gratify its expectations.

The changes in technology have also affected the basic economics of the enterprise. Remuneration, instead of coming from the sale of what used to be shellac records and are now CDs, will soon change and the public will find that, by subscribing to a licence fee or paying a modest sum to download a song, it will be able to call up any recording in any language at any time and at any place. While this trend has already started, it will still take a few years to take over the marketplace. It will dramatically change the cast of characters who will survive, and the attributes of those who will dominate the popular music industry in the future.

What will not change is that some performers, like the Rolling Stones today, in their live performances, will be seen to have star quality and consequently will continue to attract large crowds. It will also be realised that many attractive songs could provide potent advertising slogans and catchy tunes which could help the great corporations in selling their wares. The Rolling Stones have strength, professionalism, great musicianship and, what is possibly the most important of all, that star quality which is so lacking in our disquieting age.

You can make a very strong case
that the large stadium show
is not an American art form at all,
and that it was really the Rolling
Stones and Pink Floyd who invented it.

Mick Jagger

PUSH AND PULL

8

*The band by
Dimo Safari.*

RONNIE: *Some Girls* is one of my favourite Rolling Stones albums out of the ones that the band has made since I've been with them. In many ways, *Some Girls* was a celebration of getting Keith back, but I was also enjoying the interplay with Mick. I was having a lot of fun hanging out with Mick and being involved in shaping up the songs, as much as with Keith. Whereas Keith was saying to me, "Hey, come over to my side a bit more, you don't want to hang with the vocalist". I had to play the whole thing very carefully!

KEITH: For *Some Girls*, Mick hooked us up with Chris Kimsey as the engineer, and found a very good studio in Paris, which turned out to be somewhere that we felt very comfortable working in. I practically lived there for the best part of six years. I woke up once after falling asleep under the mixing desk and discovered that the band of the Parisian police force were doing a session in the studio. I popped out from under the desk: "That was nice, very nice – I'm out of here".

A lot of the good stuff was done, as it always is, when we nailed the right team to work together in the right room. In theory, you can make a record anywhere as long as you've got the right guy to do it with and he's brought the right microphones along. There's one aspect of recording technology where some company is always bringing out something new, and because of that people get antsy and always want a new formula to make it work – that's when you get synthesisers, and the internet, things that really should have been kept secret! A synthesiser is fine for a song-writer who is working away in his back bedroom, but don't try and make records with one.

CHARLIE: A lot of those songs like 'Miss You' on *Some Girls*, and later 'Undercover' and things like that, were heavily influenced by going to the discos. You can hear it in a lot of those "four on the floor" rhythms and the Philadelphia-style drumming. Mick and I used to go to discos a lot. A great way to hear a dance record is by listening to it in a dance hall or disco – I used to go to dance halls to look at the drummers when I was a kid. In the 1970s, of course, there were some fantastic dance records out. As dopey as their clothes might have looked, the actual records that Earth, Wind & Fire released, for example, were fabulous. It was a great period. I remember being in Munich and coming back from a club with Mick singing one of the Village People songs – 'YMCA', I think it was – and Keith went mad, but it sounded great on the dance floor.

We weren't going to clubs every night of the week, but if we were playing or recording somewhere, we might go out a couple of times a week. Mick would find us a club to go to. I never danced by the way, I just used to sit there while Mick danced. I never, ever dance, as my wife will tell you. If you're a drummer, everybody always thinks that because you play this particular instrument you can dance. The only drummers who really do dance are usually the South American and Cuban players.

We would go there to listen to records as well, and I used to play them at home – well, I didn't, but Shirley used to play them an awful lot. When you're writing or working on a song, whatever you're listening to becomes part of the mix. It's like when you listen to the radio, if you're listening to Shostakovich you're either going to switch off from whatever you're doing or his music is going to seep in there. Mick liked to have some rhythm while he was playing, making a song up, or getting a song into another shape.

MICK: For me, going to a club is the same as never being able to read a book unless you're thinking about making it into a movie. There's a part of you that says, "Why can't you just go out and enjoy yourself?" But I think it's absolutely essential to do that, for me anyway, because otherwise you could be listening to new records and everything that's happening musically, but you wouldn't be able to see the way in which people are reacting to those sounds. In any case, listening to new records isn't really the same thing, because when you go to a club they don't only play what's been released in the last couple of weeks. When you go to a club, you'll usually find that they're playing a very eclectic mix, and so you get to see people reacting to all kinds of different things.

> *It was very hard juggling these plates and making sure one didn't come crashing down on your head. I suppose if Charlie had pitched in as well we'd have had some almighty group argument and exploded into oblivion.*
>
> *Ronnie*

KEITH: Mick was always far more interested than me in the pop scene. In the late '70s there were some very interesting things going on with the disco beat – you had that whole "four on the floor" thing, four beats in a bar on the bass drum – and also punk was happening, so there was this intriguing juxtaposition.

*Keith gets dressed
before a performance.*

*(opposite)
Mick by Terry O'Neill.*

RONNIE: Mick has a history of checking out what the kids are listening to, whether it was during the disco era or funk, or whatever. He always keeps one eye and one ear on what they're listening to and how we might be able to apply it to what we do and how we might put our stamp on it. We used to go out together, sampling the flavour of what was in the air at the time. Just being with Mick in the clubs is quite an experience, anyway, because he attracts all the female go-getters there, so it's always interesting to sit there, be a fly on the wall and watch what's going on. From Charlie's point of view I know that's what he would have done – had a little laugh.

Keith's not a flavour-of-the-month person. He's not a great trend follower: Keith knows what he likes. Mick is always interested in what's new, which is very good for the band because it gives us this push and pull. When they are apart, like when they were doing their solo albums later on, Keith doesn't get the push and Mick doesn't get the pull, although Keith does seem to be happier in his pull… So Mick would get the sounds in, and Keith and I would pump them out.

KEITH: My attitude has been never to aim anything at any audience: "It's 'I like this – fling it out'."

CHARLIE: The punk stuff was really the mood of the moment. Mick is a great flavour-of-the-month person, so we had gone from playing the "four on the floor" rhythms on 'Miss You' to trying to be Johnny Rotten, who was trying to be us, in a way. That was fine with me, because it's really all the same thing. Writing those songs is the difficult part. I find it interesting, and so I do have to keep up with contemporary rhythms. I don't mean Jack DeJohnette's playing – although I naturally listen to him – but more how it has filtered down from somebody like Tony Williams to the street. There are some drummers in New York, like Terreon Gully, who are playing fabulous stuff.

RONNIE: Those punk songs were our message to those boys. We never sat around talking about punk, but you couldn't avoid it. It was on the news all the time with the Sex Pistols and the Clash and all the other punk bands. It was something that was in the air exactly in

the same way that disco was when 'Miss You' came around: we didn't get together and say, "Let's make a disco song". It was a rhythm that was popular and so we made a song like that. Funnily enough, I saw the guys from Green Day backstage on the *Forty Licks* tour: they made some records that reminded me of 'Respectable' and 'When The Whip Comes Down' from *Some Girls*. We also threw in a bit of Bakersfield country with 'Far Away Eyes'.

Sugar Blue played harmonica on 'Miss You' and 'Some Girls'. He was somebody that Mick or Keith found playing on the street. The thing that blew my mind was what that guy could do, because I play a little harmonica. I know how to suck and bend, blow and bend like Jimmy Reed, but if you gave a harmonica to Sugar Blue, he could play in C, C sharp, C flat, B, A and F, all on the one harmonica. The way he bent it was unreal. If you're Sugar Blue, it's like being a guitar player and folding the guitar neck in half and playing both halves and still getting something out of the instrument. What he played was the impossible, and I've never met anyone like him before or since. The sad thing is that he's probably back on the street vamping like he was when Mick and Keith first came across him, not realising the quality of what he does. He obviously knows he's great, but he doesn't know how valuable he is. The thing is with someone like Sugar, he's like one of the Meters – Zigaboo or George Porter – he's just there playing, going, "I don't know how good I am, all I know is I can do this". Meanwhile I'm standing there thinking, "How the hell did you do that?"

Ian McLagan, my old sparring partner from the Faces, also came over to Paris. I still insist the Faces were the best bunch of midgets you would ever, ever come across. Kenney Jones, Ian McLagan and Ronnie Lane were the impeccable midgets. Mac was, and is, very valuable: he has the piano-playing spirit of Nicky Hopkins and Ian Stewart and – from more recent times – Chuck Leavell. Mac has his own band and has been working with Billy Bragg, a man who'd rather preach than play, but the great thing is, as Mac said to me, "It's a gig".

KEITH: When I returned to the fold after "closing down the laboratory", I came back into the studio with Mick, around the time of *Emotional Rescue*, to say, "Thanks, man, for

Ron with his father, Archie, backstage at Wembley in 1982.

shouldering the burden" – that's why I wrote 'The Beast Of Burden' for him, I realise in retrospect – and the weird thing was that he didn't want to share the burden any more. Mick had grown used to running the show – and I slowly became aware that he resented any interference.

RONNIE: The sessions for *Emotional Rescue* were back in Paris. The great thing about working in Paris is that you are always close to great restaurants, so you can keep the old fires stoked up with all that good food, which is half the battle. In some of the places that you find yourself stuck in for work, it's awful, not that you see much of the surroundings, but you just get very fed up surviving on room service.

The Pathé-Marconi studio proved to be a good testing ground for producers like Chris Kimsey, who'd worked on *Some Girls*, and later Steve Lillywhite, because it was somewhere that we knew well. If we had a new guy come in to work with us, it would be like saying, "OK, you're in our front room". Nevertheless, the studio had a rather cold atmosphere, and it was quite bland and strange out there in the suburbs of Paris. We used to pile out of Keith's Bentley into the studio and plough past the collection of French dealers who would be hanging around and who used to converge on the studio.

There was one bar called Vesuvius. It was upstairs; a little jazz bar that was really quite funky. I used to go and get stoked up there before going along to the session. I remember that in Paris Keith was very adamant about working above and beyond the call of duty. At about four o'clock in the morning, just when everybody was getting really tired, after we'd really done well and cut a couple of basic tracks, Keith would say, "Right, now we're going to do this", and we'd all go "Ahhh…" while Bill would be hovering in the doorway. Keith's catchphrase of the time was, "Nobody sleeps while I'm awake". There was one night when I'd actually managed to get out of the studio one night and climb into bed thinking, "Oh my God, I'm so tired". It didn't last. Keith climbed over the fence outside, jumped into my garden, broke into the house. In my sleep I could hear the door bursting open, boom, boom, crash, bang, and in they came, right up to my bedroom – "Nobody sleeps while I'm awake" – and I was dragged back into the studio. So they were a slave-driving bundle of sessions, but we did get an amazing amount of work done.

'Dance Part I' was one strong riff where Mick immediately took the bait, literally got up and danced to it, which was the whole idea of the track: it's a catchy riff. That was an example of a song that originated without words, just a groove with various changes, but never a chorus. We did have various alternative mixes going at the time, but I can't really tell the difference between 'Part I' or 'Part II' or 'Part III'. It was just a novelty, the 'Part I' bit, I think.

For *Tattoo You*, Mick and Chris Kimsey realised that there was a lot of great music that we had recorded in the past that had never been released, particularly from all the material we had amassed during the *Emotional Rescue* sessions. So they went back and started sifting through it all, and eventually got to the point where they got up to here with it, and said, "Let's not go any further", and used songs like 'Waiting On A Friend'.

KEITH: 'Waiting On A Friend' is one of those songs that you write sometimes, and when you hear it back you say, "What was that really about?" At one level it's just a nice song and I don't think there's ever any pointed meanings. Very few things that we've ever written have had anything to do with what is actually going on, for the simple reason that we've got so much to hide!

RONNIE: 'Black Limousine' came about from a slide guitar riff that was inspired in part by some Hop Wilson licks from a record that I once owned, mislaid for years, found again and finally lost again. But I always remembered what I had heard on it. And there was another guy called Big Moose, who I've never heard of before or since. I had this one 45 that Eric Clapton gave me which had him on. He was an old slide guitar guy who had one particular lick that he would bring in every now and again. I thought, "That's really good, I'm going to apply that" – and so subconsciously I wrote the whole song around that one little lick, building on it, resolving it and taking it round again. I always take a leaf out of the book of these one-shot wonders.

That was something that clicked musically straightaway with the guitars and drums and Mick, and then we immediately got into sparring about the lyrics for it, since it was obviously crying out for some words. Once again the riff was taken care of and I let Mick do the words. Keith is more of a one-man riff writer – "That's my riff, get your hands off. Help me on it by all means, but this is my song" – whereas Mick is a little more open about it if you go to him with the first idea. Clearly, if someone's got the initial idea for a song, it's basically theirs and if either Mick or Keith come into a session armed with a riff and the words all the way through a song, then it's pretty much a closed shop. I could go to them with fully finished songs, but it's much harder for me to get the whole song as my song, and telling them how to sing it – because Mick's got his own style and that's why I let him interpret it in his own way. It's only fair really.

But I let that song slip through my fingers. I fought until I was blue in the face to get

Ronnie in an Ovation guitar case.

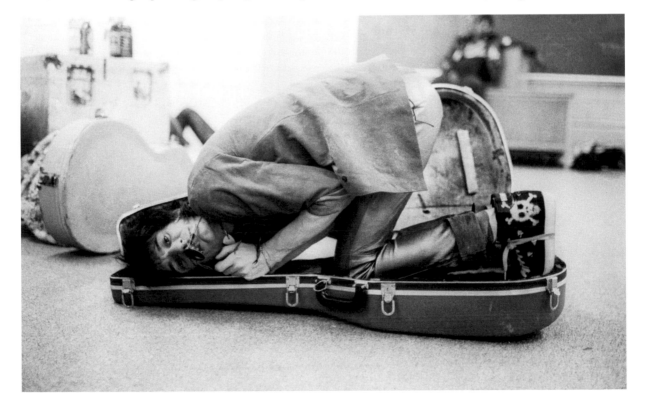

*Keith's daughter
Angela (left).*

the credit, going on and on: "I wrote that, I wrote that". One of the lessons I had to learn was that if you want to get a credit, it has to happen there and then in the studio, as you're recording it. As far as 'Black Limousine' was concerned I didn't go about it professionally enough to get a credit, so I let it go.

I don't know why 'Start Me Up' was missed off the selection for *Emotional Rescue* or *Some Girls*, because that's when we recorded it. It's strange. I think maybe we were saving it for a single. I have the impression that it was a riff that Mick brought along, like 'Don't Stop' for *Forty Licks* – very much a Mick kind of idea, although in the end 'Start Me Up' became a Mick and Keith-welded song with contributions from both of them. It was one of those genuine collaborations between the two of them, with a little magic from both sides happening instantly.

MICK: On the 1981–2 tour we worked with a Japanese designer, Kazuhide Yamazari. Those were daytime tours; there were no night-time shows. Most concerts that took place outdoors at that time were played during the day, probably because it was cheaper, I don't know. So we had the bright, bright primary colours, which were designed by Kazuhide and we had these enormous images of a guitar, a car and a record – an Americana idea – which worked very well for the afternoon shows.

*Karis with Elizabeth
on her lap, Mick with
James, and Jade.*

RONNIE: There was one moment on tour where Mick Taylor came and played with us on a show, but he was so loud – I don't know if it was out of nerves or what – that Keith was about to wring his neck. I had to try and block Keith's path a few times during the songs. He was going, "I'm going to kill him". I don't know how the two of them managed to make it work as long as they did.

CHARLIE: With the bigger stages, the others all just moved further out. Mick has always done that; he has always done what he does. It was just that the runways and the areas have got bigger, sometimes through his own choice in designing the stage – "We'll have this, that and the other" – and sometimes because of the physical situation. But essentially it's the same thing as being on that little stage in the Crawdaddy Club, where he used to wiggle his arse. It's the same arse wiggling, except I never see him sometimes when he goes off on the wings. On the *Voodoo Lounge* tour, where we had huge wings, I never saw Mick half the time, he was always off round the corner.

RONNIE: On those first stadium shows – zoom, you'd see Mick go running a mile out to the sides. I used to do a load of running instead

of playing. Since then I've enjoyed playing more than running about and climbing everywhere. There had to be changes in our way of presentation, but underneath everything there was always the club in us, to carry us through even stadium shows. It's such a big, massive thing, a lot of what you are doing is disappearing up into the air and so you don't really know what's reaching the audience. It becomes a bit confusing. You can't be out there watching what you're doing, so you don't really know how it's coming over.

KEITH: The bigger shows are harder to play, even though we do it most of the time, because you're so locked into lighting systems, computers. You should never believe that there's such a thing as freedom of communication – the more the communication there is, the more confusing it becomes. And the more constricted you are just by the size of the operation. When we play on a B-stage or at a club venue, for us it's just like coming back home, sweating it up a bit. You can be as free and loose as you want, and if you screw up, so what, you just say, "Shut up, start again" and that's how you get the looseness into the band.

CHARLIE: That was the period when Mick and I started getting seriously into stages. Because we were playing in football stadiums we had to think big. When you're out there in this vast stadium, you are physically tiny up on stage, so that's why on the 1981–2 tour we had those coloured panels and later we started using devices like the video screens. We became very aware of not being seen, of just being there like ants. Mick is the one who *really* has to project himself over the footlights. And when the show gets that big, you need a little extra help, you need a couple of gimmicks, as we call it, in the show. You need fireworks, you need lights, you need a bit of theatre.

KEITH: At the time of *Undercover* we were using some sequencers and synthesisers. For a while you always think that things are going the right way and then you get things like the synthesiser – a machine that should have been left in the back room to work things out

Jo Wood, Jerry Hall and Patti Hansen, soon to be Patti Richards, in 1982.

(opposite) Keith married Patti Hansen on his 40th birthday, 18 December 1983, in Mexico. Mick, the only other member of the band present at the secret ceremony, was best man.

on. That damn machine. In the '80s you could tell every time it cropped up on a record. Luckily, its worst days are over now. Everybody grew sick of it, but it's an example of what you're continually having to deal with in the music business, juggling with technology as well as the audiences, which keep changing all the time, too.

RONNIE: Synthesisers and sequencers are not Keith's cup of tea. I did find working with sequencers awkward as well, but I didn't say, "Oh, I'm not doing it", I used to go, "Are you sure?", but I'd go along with it. We don't want too much of that, although a hint of it is fine. But Keith hated all of that technology. Whereas Mick has always been the experimenter, keeping informed about what's going on; he is prepared to take it on board as he did when he brought in the Dust Brothers on *Bridges To Babylon*. It's something he has to go through. In this area Don Was has been a good healer. He meshes the two sides together very neatly and manages to keep Keith interested in the modern techno stuff as well as keeping the blues roots.

Keith didn't have many songs on *Undercover*. During this period there would be just the one token Keith song on every album. I think it was just something that Mick and Keith had going. It was something unwritten that was going on between the two of them, which I don't really understand. It is hard to nail what lay beneath it. Mick was not a very good drinker and drugger, and when he decided to quit or cut down his intake, generally change his personality and try and be a more responsible person, Keith didn't really like the change in him. Between the two things, the overuse and the cleaning up, there was some residual resentment, for some reason.

When I look at the *Undercover* album that becomes apparent. As soon as I see the list of songs on that record I think, "Whoops, this is not a balanced concept album, it's all over the shop". It is a mixture of salvaged songs and a couple that I am never conscious of having made it on to the album. I've got another one of my tender songs on there – 'Pretty Beat Up' – but 'All The Way Down' could have been a better song (we didn't explore its full potential) and 'Too Much Blood' was interesting mainly because we went out to Mexico to make a video. In terms of the musical peaks on that album, there really aren't

(previous pages)
Keith by Michael
Halsband.

The celebrated energy
of the band's
performance captured
by Ken Regan, and
opposite, by Denis
O'Regan.

that many. That was definitely a time of disruption – and not one that I refer to very often.

This was the beginning of a very disjointed period leading up to the release of *Dirty Work* – the first hint of the falling apart of the Jagger/Richards camp, the first sign that it was in danger of collapsing. There was terrible tension around and it's where I had to assume my diplomatic role a lot. Keith had this bee in his bonnet about anything that Mick did – he'd say "Aah, it's crap". Then Mick would be coming to me, asking "What's wrong with Keith? What have I done?", followed by Keith, who would be saying "What are you talking to him for?" and I'd find myself in trouble with Keith. It was very hard juggling these plates and making sure one didn't come crashing down on your head.

I suppose that if Charlie had pitched in as well we'd have had some almighty group argument and exploded into oblivion.

However, we did put in some wonderful changes on the song 'Undercover Of The Night', because Keith wouldn't get involved in the song. I remember it being just me, Mick and Charlie. I used to really enjoy playing that song with Mick and Charlie – we took it up into some wonderful adventures with all these different changes. It was really good. There was a great percussive and acoustic version, which is the kind of song it should be, really. The final polished, glossed-up version may have been Mick's vision of the song, but I know the funky version was one he loved as well.

Bill was always there for me, helping in the construction of a song. He'd know where the changes were and keep a note of them, in the same way that Chuck Leavell has done since he has been playing with us. Bill would also be helpful in that respect, but as far as any actual input to the creation of the songs, it would be fair to say that he never really put a great deal in. And he would kind of disappear whenever there was an eruption about to take place, which was definitely a very smart strategy on his part.

MICK: For me, doing a solo album or a Stones album is all the same, with one proviso: that when I'm writing for the Rolling Stones I don't mind if the song sounds like the ones the Stones do, whereas if I'm writing, but not recording, with the Rolling Stones, I don't want the song to contain too many of the clichés that one associates with the Rolling Stones, so I try quite hard to avoid them. Before the release of *Forty Licks*, I wrote 'Don't

Stop' in the same period that I was writing the songs for my solo album, and I just put it to one side and said to myself, "This sounds very much like the Rolling Stones to me. It might be very useful in the coming months, but I'll leave it for now and I won't record it because I think it's going to be better for the Stones". Yet it will all be part of the same song-writing session, because I'm not really writing to order.

The problem with song-writing is that at the time you have to think that the song is a good thing, and that at some point it's a wonderful creation, but at the same time it usually isn't wonderful. There are usually one or two things that should be left out, but it's very rare that you have some time to step back from the process, look at the song and think about it, and go "Wait a minute, that is good, but this could be better and that part shouldn't be there", because by the time you've finished the song it's usually late. You'll be on a tour, or on a deadline and the record's always imminent. But if you do think that you've written a good song, the next question is whether it's going to make a good record or not. It may be a great song, but it may not be very well recorded or played or sung and you might have missed the opportunity.

Keith signs a programme for Jim Callaghan, head of security for the band.

Chuch Magee, backline technician, is glimpsed behind Keith and Ronnie.

RONNIE: We didn't play at Live Aid, although Mick did his set with Tina Turner and the video with David Bowie. Keith and I ended up playing with Bob Dylan. The first time I ever met Bob was at the Band's studio, Shangri-La. Eric Clapton was there recording with the Band and I was on Sunset up in LA. I said, "I've got a feeling I should go back out to Shangri-La, so I got in the car and there was a phone call from the studio, saying, "You should be here now, man, Eric Clapton is here with the Band". I said, "I know that" – Rob Fraboni was engineering: he's Keith's favourite man to this day – and they said, "And guess who has just turned up and is playing your song?" I asked, "Who?" They said, "Bob Dylan", so I went, "Driver, put your foot down!" That's when I got 'Seven Days'. Bob said to me "You can have this song", and I ended up cutting it with Mick Fleetwood on drums. Every time I see Bob he says, "Hey, Woody, do you want to do 'Seven Days' tonight?" I say, "Well, you wrote it" and he says, "Yeah, but you can play it". Bob's wonderful.

Shortly before Live Aid Bob called me up and asked me if I wanted to do this "charity event" – of course, before it happened I had no real idea what Live Aid was going to become – and he came over to my basement studio in New York. "Let me show you some songs", he said. I knew the songs, but I'd never actually played the chords, so I said, "Look, we're digging in too deep here. Do you mind if I get Keith over?" Bob's going "Yeah, I don't mind, but I'm quite happy with just you" and I'm saying, "I've got to have my sparring partner, Keith".

So I rang Keith and he was like, "What do you want?" I said, "I'm here with Bob Dylan". "Bob who? Fuck you". I said, "He's working on some kind of project, and he's here in the studio with me now". I went back down to the studio. Bob asked me, "What are we going to do, man?" so I said, "Whatever you say Bob, let's go". We sat there playing all of this shit, and two hours later Keith arrived. "What the fuck do you want?" he asked again and I'm going, "Bob Dylan's downstairs". "Yeah, but he's got something to prove to me otherwise I'll knock his head off." I said to Keith, "Be nice to him, Keith, be nice to the man, he's Bob Dylan after all". "Yeah, well what the fuck's he doing with my guitar man. What's he doing messing with my Ronnie?" I said, "Just come downstairs, Keith, and have a look". Keith comes down: "Hello Bob, I love you". I said, "You two-faced motherfucker!"

As far as the show was concerned, we didn't really know what the hell was going on. I remember leaving my place on West 78th Street between Riverside and West End with Bob telling us, "We're on in Philadelphia, man". I said, "Come with me in this limo," but Bob didn't want to. "No, I'll take the truck with my daughter" – Bob's daughter was driving the truck. So I said, "Well, Bob, we'll follow you" and we drove off with Keith saying, "This had better be good".

Just before we went on at Live Aid – and this is the crown topper – we were walking up the stairs to go on stage at Philadelphia and Bob turned round and said, "Why don't we do 'It Ain't Me Babe', how about playing that one?" I said, "Bob, it's too late – we

Rehearsing at Longview Farm, Massachusetts, in September 1981, before the US tour.

At an after-show party in New Orleans, 1981.

Keith and Ronnie by Ken Regan.

Tina Turner opened for the Stones on selected dates of their 1981 US tour, giving her the chance to duet with Mick on 'Honky Tonk Women'. They would reprise their double act at Live Aid in 1985, this time performing 'State of Shock' and 'It's Only Rock'n'Roll'.

didn't practise that one, we did everything else in your catalogue and the Stones' catalogue". Then Bob bust a string during the gig. He looked at me and said, "Woody, what am I going to do?" I went, "Bob, you want my guitar?" and he said, "Yeah", so I gave him my guitar. This is the only night I didn't have a guitar roadie. I looked offstage: "Have we got another guitar?", they went, "No" and I said, "Fine, I'll wing it". I took Bob's guitar and started playing slide on one string. Everyone told me afterwards, "Oh, you were so fucked up", getting the guitar and playing on one string, and I said, "I was only trying to help Bob!"

After we'd played, the curtains opened and there was everyone in the cast. Keith and I sat on the monitor speakers and thought, "Fucking hell, how many more people that we know are going to come up on stage?" It was a great night.

CHARLIE: Stu died at the end of 1985. We have been fortunate to work with some great piano players, like Nicky Hopkins, but Nicky couldn't play what Stu could, and vice versa. Stu didn't possess the finesse or the musical touch that Nicky had, which was pretty amazing. Nicky

Bill celebrates his birthday in Florida, 1981.

used to play great blues, which is how I first knew him, when he was really young, before he worked with the Rolling Stones. Nicky used to play with Screaming Lord Sutch and sounded like a cross between Jerry Lee Lewis and Otis Spann, lovely blues, all top end stuff. Stu never played like that. Stu was rumbling, with his left hand going at some ridiculous speed. Stu had a very physical way of playing. He was one of those players where the piano would bounce up and down. The way he played was more like drumming.

KEITH: One of the biggest drags for us was that what we did became a sequence of two years on and then three years off. It has become a little easier now that we do more stuff in-between the road, but there was always the period of idling between tours and recording, which can screw you right up. Stu had more insight than the rest of us on that whole thing, because Stu always did what he wanted to do. He eventually ended up with his own band, Rocket 88, and did all the other things he wanted to do, like promoting all of his mates, pushing the people he thought were good, which is what he loved to do. He'd fix somebody up with some gear or get them a rehearsal room. Stu just loved the day-to-day mechanics of bands working.

Stu liked to amble through life in a totally eccentric, but totally reasonable and logical

The continuing jovial presence of Ian Stewart, the "sixth Stone", made his sudden death, on December 12 1985, all the more difficult to bear. "Who's gonna tell us off now when we misbehave?" was Keith's remark to Ronnie at Stu's funeral. Mick: A great friend. His odd but invaluable musical advice kept us on a bluesy course most of the time.

way that made all the sense in the world when you knew the man's character. It was very much part of him to be totally happy with what he was. I mean the shit he used to put me through, man. We'd be playing some town in the Midwest, like Tulsa, and we would be saying, "Oh great, some Oklahoma bitches" and all the guys would have their tongues hanging out once the show was over. We'd ask Stu, "Where are we going?" Instead of heading off into town for some fun, Stu would drive us thirty miles away into the sticks to a hotel on a golf course, because he knew the Assistant Manager at the golf course, and he wanted to get a round in first thing in the morning. It took us years to realise why we were living in these places. We thought all hotels had golf courses. We'd say, "What are we doing here, Stu?" "We got better rates… and to keep you lot out of trouble"; that was his usual reply. And in the morning you'd wake up and see Stu heading out on to the golf course, practising his swing.

> *Stu liked to amble through life in a totally eccentric, but totally reasonable and logical way that made all the sense in the world when you knew the man's character.*
>
> *Keith*

CHARLIE: Stu was a lot older than us in his head. He always wore a Lacoste shirt, jeans and carried golf clubs: he used to carry the clubs around with us on tour and we would be appalled. He never changed from the day I first knew him. He never made any attempt to acknowledge the '70s – nor did I really, but I had a go at it and looked stupid – Stu didn't bend at all towards any of it, nothing, he never changed. The first time I met him in the early '60s, he looked exactly the same as when I said goodbye to him on the steps of Fulham Town Hall, which was a day or so before he died. He was wearing jeans, loafers and a cardigan with the crocodile on, exactly the same as ever, and he was going to a golf game – just like he always did. Stu used to dump us off and leave us, and he'd be out at some golf course while we had to sit around waiting because he was finishing a round.

PETER WOLF

Peter Wolf was the lead vocalist of the Boston-based J. Geils Band, whose raw and authentic R&B sound made them an appropriate choice as special guests on the Stones' 1982 European tour. Peter has continued to release critically acclaimed solo recordings. His most recent, *Sleepless*, includes contributions from Mick and Keith.

The Stones and the J. Geils Band were label mates together on Atlantic Records starting in the late '60s. Atlantic Records was quite an amazing place. The people who created the label were still in charge of things during those years. They were not only businessmen but they also made important musical contributions to R&B and the development of rock'n'roll.

I always looked forward to my visits at Atlantic Records. Their offices were located just off Broadway in midtown Manhattan and occupied an entire floor of an office building. One side had office space and the other had several recording studios. It had a family feel between its employees and artists, not unlike what went on at Motown and Stax Records.

On any given day you never knew which artist might stop by. I remember the time I rode in the elevators with soul singer Wilson Pickett and jazz great Sonny Rollins. When the elevator door opened, Dr. John and Eric Clapton were hanging in the lobby, while saxophonist King Curtis was reviewing some arrangements with Aretha Franklin in one of the studios. The place always had a real strong, funky, street sensibility to it.

For a period of time, the Rolling Stones and J. Geils Band recorded at the same Atlantic studios. Around midnight when we finished our sessions, the Stones and their crew would start rolling in to begin their day's work. On many occasions I'd find myself lingering in the corner of the control room just to watch them. There was always a parade of colourful characters, plenty of Jack Daniels, and many other assorted amusements that created a whole, chaotic scene which seemed to have no structure or focus. After several hours, however, there'd be something that slowly began to take shape, developing like a photograph in a darkroom tray. In the midst of all this were Mick and Keith, two distinct personalities that somehow made the whole thing come together.

Mick Jagger and I first met in New York when we kept showing up at the same music events and were guests at many of the same social gatherings, frequently hosted by two charismatic eccentrics, Atlantic president Ahmet Ertegun and Rolling Stones Records label head Earl McGrath.

A lady friend of mine who was also dating Mick at the time introduced me to a man by the name of Fred Sessler. Fred was a mysterious and curious character who had immigrated from Poland. He had survived several concentration camps and when he first arrived in America he had just a few dollars to his name. By the time I met him, he had already, through his creative and unorthodox manner, earned and lost several millions of dollars. Yet his financial fluctuations never seemed to matter much to him. When people would visit Fred they ended up not staying for hours but days. That's where I first met Keith, or should I say stepped over him, as he was sprawled out on the floor of Fred's living room.

A decade earlier I had encountered the music of the Stones for the first time. I was working in record stores to make money for my art supplies — besides music, painting was an important part of my life. Most of the time I was a glorified delivery boy and would be sent to different record distributors to pick up the new releases. On one of these visits, somebody gave me a copy of the Stones' first American release. Down the street from the record store I worked at what was one of the first venues the Stones played in the States, Carnegie Hall. One evening as I was leaving work, I saw an unusual-looking group rushing out of the nearby Americana Hotel, surrounded by a bunch of young girls. One of the group walked up to me and asked for directions to a nightclub. To my surprise it was Brian Jones.

Later I moved to Boston to study painting at the Boston Museum School of Fine Arts. There I met some other students who loved the same blues and R&B music that I did. We formed a band that evolved into the J. Geils Band. We worked throughout New England and got to tour with many of the great Chicago bluesmen. It was having these similar roots that made touring with the Stones all the more meaningful.

The J. Geils Band had toured with the Stones in the States several times but the 1982 European tour was one of the most memorable. It was the first time the Stones did a major stadium tour in Europe. It was also the year the Geils Band had our first major commercial success after seventeen years of endless touring.

One of the many things I found unique about the Stones is their loyalty. Lots of people who work for the band have been with them for a very long time. Some even go back to the days when they were still battling the Beatles for the top of the charts.

Being on the road with the Rolling Stones is in many ways like being part of a huge travelling caravan, and no matter how well things are planned, there's somehow a sense of chaos and bedlam, along with an ever-changing entourage drawn

together by the seductive power of the music. On the road with the Rolling
Stones, almost anything goes, and it usually does... Here are just a few freeze-
frame memories.

The night before one of the shows in Germany, Mick and I were out dining with
a large group of people. Someone at our table mentioned that we were in the area
of a notoriously famous dance hall (and bordello) that was frequented in the era
when the Stones and Beatles first started to tour Germany. Mick thought it would
be fun to try to locate the place and see if it still existed. After a long
while of travelling through small winding streets, it suddenly appeared,
seemingly unchanged. We ventured in, only to find a large and mostly empty dance
hall. There was an old wooden balcony, lined with doors that ran around the
circumference of the room. The place was very dark, except for the dim candle
light on top of the empty tables. The walls were draped with old heavy velvet
curtains. On the far end of the dance hall was a small stage and a instrumental
lounge band from the Philippines, each dressed in a shiny purple tuxedo. Unaware
Mick was there, they coincidentally began playing the Stones song 'As Tears Go
By'. I bet Mick he wouldn't join them on stage. To my surprise, he jumped up and
started singing the song with the band. Word quickly got around, and the ladies
who worked there emerged from behind the doors on the balcony above. Mick pulled
out all the stops, turning out a risqué performance that made even those ladies'
mouths drop and left them all yelling for more.

Before another show I went with Mick to check out the sound system during one
of the opening act's performance. To be inconspicuous, we slipped into the crowd
wearing hooded sweatshirts. On our attempt to return backstage, we were
confronted by several large security guards. I was allowed back in because I had
my stage pass, but they refused Mick entrance because he wasn't wearing one. I
watched with great amusement as Mick tried to explain who he was.

It was in Sweden I learned first-hand about Mick's amazing physical
preparation. Mick always arrived at the venues very early. I decided to
investigate. When I arrived I observed him going through a rigorous routine with
his trainer. The whole concept of working out was alien to me and probably most
rock musicians at that time. Mick ran fifteen miles around the stadium,
sometimes even backwards. Then he would do a long series of stretches followed
by weights and callisthenics. I always knew Mick had incredible stamina on and
off stage. Now I was discovering one of the reasons why. I tried to emulate him,
but this was not the thing to attempt after staying up all night with Keith.

Keith and I formed an after-hours doo wop group called the 'Carltones', named
after the Carlton hotel in London, where we were staying at the time. The group
was actually called the 'Carltones Four, Five or Six', depending on how many
people showed up. It was primarily an *a cappella* group, except for Bobby Keys on
sax. Because of the echo, we found the bathroom to be the best place for our
rehearsals. City after city we would meet in Keith's room, consuming a generous
supply of Rebel Yell, a bourbon he used to like. We'd end up in the bathroom –
sometimes for days on end – taping our rehearsals. Our debut (which also turned
out to be our one and only performance) was at a birthday party for Jerry Hall,
put together by Bill Graham. I am not sure how well we did that night. Once the
'Carltones' got together, it was pretty hard to remember much of anything –
especially trying to sing in key.

Halfway during the tour the Stones decided to throw a private party for the entire crew. They rented out a large nightclub. There was plenty of food and of course an open bar. Bill Graham hired a DJ to help with the festivities. For some reason the DJ kept playing a lot of bad disco tracks. People kept coming up to him requesting some rock and R&B which he would do for only several songs before going back to disco. I was at a table with Keith and I could tell he was really starting to get pissed off. Finally Keith took his drink, walked slowly up to the DJ booth, smiled at the disc jockey, grabbed him by the neck, flashed his bowie knife, put it right up to the DJ's throat and gave him his final warning. Needless to say nobody heard any disco for the rest of the night.

I was at a bistro in the south of France with Charlie Watts and Ian Stewart, listening to them discuss their favourite jazz musicians in the most intricate detail, while we all consumed our fair share of wine. This was a great treat for me until the passionate discussion ended after I had one too many and happened to voice a contradictory opinion about some obscure jazz saxophone player they were discussing. There was a long silence. Charlie rose from his chair and hit me square in the jaw, knocking me off my bar stool right onto the floor. Once we realised how much we had drunk, we broke up laughing.

The Stones and their crew were huge soccer fans and this tour coincided with the 1982 World Cup. All along the tour travel would stop so no one would miss watching a broadcast of the games. We were in Turin during the final match between Brazil and Italy. It seemed the entire city was transfixed on the broadcast. Not being a soccer fan I was exploring the city during the match. From every window you could hear screams of encouragement as Italy was taking the lead. The streets were totally deserted. All the shops were closed. If someone tried to rob a bank no one would've noticed. When Italy finally won the mayhem exploded out into the streets. People rushed into the main piazza. There were cars, motorcycles, bicycles, goats, chickens, everyone carrying large bottles of wine. The crowd was as jubilant as if Christ himself returned for a visit. Unfortunately there was an afternoon show the next day and it was really hot. When we went on to perform the crowd was completely listless. Everybody had partied so hard we had almost nothing left for the show. We hit the crowd with everything we had and as the sun went down the Stones took the stage. Keith, who was still fresh as a daisy and ready to party on, hit the opening chords of 'Satisfaction' and the crowd finally began to rejuvenate. It was the first time we all played to an entire country that was hungover.

Many people consider the Stones to be the world's greatest rock'n'roll band. After working with them and thinking of their long legacy, it's a title that's well-deserved.

I never plan anything, which is
probably the difference between
Mick and myself.
Mick needs to know what he's going
to do to-morrow and I'm just happy
to wake up and see who's hanging
around.
Mick's ROCK, I'M ROLL!

Keith Richards

MID-LIFE CRISIS

9

On the set of the 'Harlem Shuffle' video. The band's remake of the Bob and Earl soul classic gave them a US Top 5 hit. The album it came from, Dirty Work, *while never rated a classic, reached number 4 on both sides of the Atlantic.*

RONNIE: *Dirty Work* was the most troubled period of our entire voyage. You can tell that because I've got four songs on the record – which is a clear sign that Keith and Mick's songwriting engine was not functioning properly. Things were getting increasingly worse between them, especially around the recording sessions for the album. It reached a head at that point – and it wasn't until the Jagger/Richards set-up started operating properly again that I could rest assured that the ship was going to sail correctly once more. In the meantime I was always ready to step in and help out if it was needed. I've got loads of songs round the back, as they say.

On *Undercover* I had been more or less in the hands of Mick, who would come in with his skeleton of a song, which we would then work with. On *Dirty Work* it was very different – Keith and I were very tight. Although this period was a bad one for the band, it turned out to be great for Keith and myself. It was a time when I got married to Jo, and Keith was one of my two best men – Charlie was the other one. I was renting a house in Chiswick, where I had a piano and guitars, and Keith and I spent a lot of time hanging out there, working on songs for *Dirty Work*, designing and planning and zeroing in on the riffs for the album.

Steve Lillywhite, who had been working with Peter Gabriel, U2 and Simple Minds, came in on that album as the co-producer. That was essentially the result of some of Mick's investigations: he is always on the lookout for a new producer and a new angle to develop the band's sound for whichever decade we happen to be in. Using Steve was a Mick move and, as it happened, it turned out to be a good one. Keith turned up at the studio saying, "All right, who's Mick picked this time? He'd better be good", which initially made it quite a hard interview – for want of a better word – for Steve; he was made to overcome a number of hurdles during which Keith was effectively asking, "Will this guy pass the test?" Steve did pass, and he and his wife Kirsty MacColl, who was a lovely person, ended up becoming very close to us, much in the same way as Don Was has. I think that Keith eventually took his hat off to Mick for bringing Steve into the frame, because he's still a good friend – although it's funny that we never actually worked with him again.

CHARLIE: During this period, I was personally in a hell of a mess and as a result I wasn't really aware of the problems between Mick and Keith and the danger these posed to the band's existence. I was in pretty bad shape, taking drugs and drinking a lot. I don't know what made me do it that late in life – well, to Keith, it wasn't late enough! – although in retrospect I think I must have been going through some kind of mid-life crisis. I had never done any serious drugs when I was younger, but at this point in my life I went, "Sod it, I'll do it now" – and I was totally reckless. What scared me was that I became a completely different person by going down that path, a totally different person to the one that everybody had known for over twenty years. Some people are able to function like that, but for me it was very dangerous, because I am the kind of person who could become a casualty quite easily. I just don't have the constitution. This phase lasted for a couple of years, but it took a long time for me, and my family, to get over it.

KEITH: Charlie is very strong physically, and you don't want to be on the end of a drummer's right hand. He put Mick across the table in Amsterdam once during that period. Mick and I had been out for a drink and I'd lent Mick my wedding jacket. Mick got pissed, and when Mick gets pissed he gets sloppy. We went back to the hotel and Mick wanted to talk to Charlie: he said something on the phone like "Where's my drummer?"

CHARLIE: He annoyed me, so I went storming upstairs and told him not to say things like that.

KEITH: There's a knock at the door and there's Charlie Watts, dressed in a Savile Row suit, tie, hair done, shaved, cologne. He walks across to Mick, grabs him and says, "Never call me your drummer again" – bang. On this table is a great silver platter of smoked salmon. Mick was on his back on the silver platter, which started to shoot down the table towards the open window. I'm sitting there. I'm

> *Given the state of the band at the time, it was probably very good that we hadn't done any touring for a while. We wouldn't have been able to do anything: we were struggling internally, and externally.*
>
> *Mick*

Keith backstage.

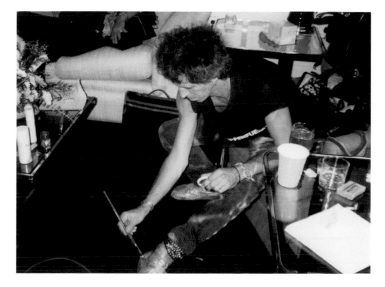

watching Mick and I'm going to let him go, but then I thought, "That's my fucking wedding jacket", so I grabbed him!

CHARLIE: The bottom line is, don't annoy me. It's not something I'm proud of doing and if I hadn't been drinking I would never have done it.

RONNIE: Despite the problems within the band while we were recording *Dirty Work*, there were some special moments, especially when Bobby Womack and Don Covay added their vocals to 'Harlem Shuffle'. The Stones had done that cover version of Don's 'Mercy Mercy' at Chess Studios in '64, and Bobby, apart from being a great vocalist, had been in the Valentinos when they had recorded his song 'It's All Over Now', which was the Stones' first hit. On that track we were paying respect to both of them. I particularly got off on that because Bobby and Don have always been very special and very close to me – Bobby was a collaborator on my solo albums – so for me personally it felt like a very special achievement to have been part of getting them involved, which was partly my doing and partly Mick acquiescing to work with them. It seemed pretty much like a joint decision to select 'Harlem Shuffle' – we've always loved that song – because somebody in the studio suggested the idea of doing it and we more or less went straight into it.

The mid-'80s were the toughest time for me. That's when I was going through what Keith was going through in the '70s.

Charlie

Bobby and Don helped add a little bit of magic to 'Harlem Shuffle', with all the history adding to the tonal qualities of their voices. There is a little bit of Don Covay in Mick's voice: it's something that Mick doesn't realise so much – I think we all do more than he does. There is something similar in the make-up of their voice box, a very similar ring. Bobby's voice was always wonderful and that definitely helped get the song off the ground, and I think he gave Mick some advice on the vocals for a number of the other songs on *Dirty Work* – 'Back To Zero', 'Winning Ugly' and 'One Hit', as well as 'Harlem Shuffle'. Mick would ask me, "Do you think Bobby would help me?", and I'd say, "He'd *love* to".

On 'Too Rude', I got to play the drums. That was when Charlie was going through a terrible time with Shirley. They were having lots of heavy arguments and so Charlie was often late, or Shirley would come into the studio and forcibly drag him out. On one of those nights Keith said, "All right, you're on drums, Ronnie". I have always loved playing the drums, so I sat down and had been playing away for hours and hours when Charlie came back in to the studio. I stopped playing and said, "Charlie, here's your sticks", but he said, "No, come on, let me watch you". So we did the song a few more times and he was standing behind me when we did the take that we actually used on the album. I said, "Are you sure, Charlie?" and he said, "No, I really like what you're playing – and I can't play it". The drum sound was very dynamic: I ended up sounding like Solomon Burke's drummer. I was very proud of it, actually.

There was a certain amount of interchanging of roles at the time. I may have been playing bass on a few of the tracks as well: I honestly don't remember seeing much of Bill during those sessions. He'd be in and out, say, "I'm going out to dinner", then head out for a long meal and come back after midnight.

Keith's version of the Chuck Berry duck walk.

Ronnie: Whopping Keith's arse at snooker is the only way I can keep him in trim. He does win from time to time, but usually he wins by default, by me making mistakes. I tell him, "Remember the rules, get down, have a look, and stay down when you play the shot, get the pace right". It's a very good way to get your brain functioning for a show.

After the album came out, there was some talk of touring *Dirty Work*, but there was an equal amount of discussion about that whole idea being quashed. A great deal of time was spent debating the pros and cons, and then we got the message that it was not going to happen.

CHARLIE: While the Stones weren't on the road, I got together an orchestra that consisted of all the musicians I liked, but who I'd never played with, as well as people that I had played with, and I ended up with this huge band. It's something I could never have done if I hadn't been in that state, but I'm very pleased I did, because I was able to work with some of the great people I had loved since I was a kid. So my bad period had its downside and its good side. I just wish that I had been more together when I did it because it would have been better than it was but, on the other hand, without the drugs I would never have had the courage to ask these guys to play with me.

Those jazz musicians have something that I do not have, which is the facility to work off notated music – that's how they live and work. I listen to what they do and try and fit my part in, but it will take me three gigs or three hours' rehearsal to do the part. The jazz guys do it in three minutes, write it all down and never forget it *because* it's written down, whereas my way of working is totally through memory. Although I have some very crude notations with notes for each song – whether I need to use the mallets, brushes or sticks, that kind of thing – my main way of working is to watch Keith for this, watch Ronnie for that, and now I tend to watch Chuck Leavell for the changes.

The band worked at Ronnie Scott's – we had a two-week residency there and we worked in America twice. Compared to when the Stones play club gigs, working at Ronnie Scott's is much more relaxed. You can just walk on, start the set and at the end there will be some dancing and you can go home. When the Stones play in a club it can be a real nightmare.

The jazz orchestra was a good band in the end – during the period we were playing I had cleaned up, so the first phase was completely barmy and the second phase was totally straight: it was the first band I had played with for years where I was completely straight. It was a bit like Ronnie when we started the *Forty Licks* tour: he was very frightened, wondering how he could get through it. All I could say to him was, "Just do it and you'll realise in two hours' time that you've done it," but it's very difficult when you actually have to go out there and do it.

RONNIE: Mick was putting out his first couple of solo albums, which gave me a slight cause for concern. It worried me a bit that if Mick proved to be really popular as Mick Jagger, he might not have wanted to come back to the Rolling Stones. It was like, "Whoops, we may never see him again". But luckily it was a learning process for him, just as Charlie's jazz turned out to be a great thing for Charlie's development and enjoyment. I bring together various conglomerations of musicians, as does Keith – and Keith had a lot of songs that he could get off his chest through his own solo albums – and so does Mick. Mick's solo tours worked nicely for him and they were a good outlet for him, but it never became over-successful to the point that he didn't want to come back to the Stones, and so it didn't worry me again after that. And other good things came out of Mick's solo work, like the musical relationship with Bernard Fowler.

MICK: I was surprised when Keith was so upset when I wanted to do something outside the band – because he'd already done his thing with the New Barbarians. Keith can be really authoritative and helpful, and have lots of ideas, and sometimes he can be completely narrow-minded and bigoted. But I know him well enough that I know he's not going to be like that all the time. People are very complex and they don't play the same roles the whole time. So I might be quite flaky one week and somebody else will have to take over a job. Those roles shift a lot.

RONNIE: While all this was going on I had got onto another boat. I started painting in earnest and during the 1980s had moved out to New York and then back to England by the time of *Dirty Work*, but I was always getting into different things and always keeping things going in the studio. While I was out in New York, I had been recording a lot of stuff that I never released, with Bob Dylan and Billy Idol's band, and Al Green's band. I'd invited Al's band along when I saw them at the show: "Come down and see me". Al had gone back to Memphis and left them all back in New York. So they came down to my

Keith by Claude Gassian.

studio, recorded all night, and then slept in the studio as well!

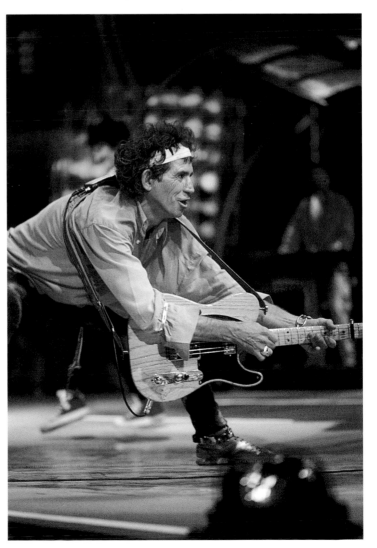

Working with all these other musicians – I also did a club tour with Bo Diddley – gave me a lot of additional confidence in myself, although a lot of that came through drugs. I didn't know whether I was coming or going, but I certainly had a lot of confidence! Looking back on those days it's a wonder that I'm still alive; I hardly used to sleep. But it was all part of the learning experience.

KEITH: I call this period World War III – it was a hiatus in the story of the Rolling Stones. I had got extremely pissed with Mick for taking his solo record deal with Columbia Records and stitching it onto a Stones deal without telling anybody, which at the time I thought was really slimy. I said, "That is not on and that is when I pulled out. Excuse me, old chap. That doesn't go down this gullet like that. Go ahead and make your solo album. You ain't going to get one out of me". It then got carried on in the press: "He said this, and he said that". I love Mick dearly. He's my mate and I'll protect him to the end. But sometimes you think, "Where's the

The view from the drum stool has changed over the years from Richmond's Crawdaddy Club to the world's biggest stadia.

Charlie and his wife Shirley by Claude Gassian.

comeback? Where's the reciprocation?". Maybe I fucked it in those ten years when I was on the dope and there is no reciprocation.

When I look back on all of that now – and a little part of me probably thought this even then – I think, "Well we'd been working together since 1962 through to the mid-1980s, we'd been jammed up each other's jacksies for ever, so it's hardly surprising that one of us would feel, "Is this all there is?" It happened to be Mick who went for it first.

Now, the last thing I ever wanted to do was to break this band up and equally the last thing I had ever wanted to do was to go and think about doing my own solo stuff, but Mick did me a favour without knowing it, because it meant that I got together with a new bunch of musicians, and that was an enlightenment to me.

That was simply because I had to do something. I got forced into it because I couldn't sit around and wait for Mick to finish his album. And although I had no intention of going out to create a new band, various things fell into place, and during that period I got to work with some other great musicians, an incredible ensemble of musicians who just arrived. I began to write with Steve Jordan and the likes of Charlie Drayton, Ivan Neville and Waddy Wachtel, which became the X-Pensive Winos, with Steve and Charlie Drayton sharing bass and drum duties, Ivan on keyboards and Waddy playing guitar, and which was probably one of the best rock'n'roll bands in the world – a great band, very much like the early Stones. There's nothing on those two albums that I wouldn't proudly display at my funeral. I had to be the front man for the band, which meant that I learned a lot about what Mick's job is.

During the same period, all of us learned a number of things. I guess Mick in his own way found out that you can't hire the Rolling Stones, and that it doesn't matter if you hire in the best musicians in the world, they don't necessarily make a band. At the same time Charlie found out that he could organise a band and discovered what it actually means to take a big jazz band all over the damned world. At the end of the day when it eventually did all come back together again we returned with a slightly better appreciation of each other's task within the Rolling Stones. In the long run I look upon it as a learning process: it was either going to come back together again, or we'd have had to say, "It's only a rock'n'roll band, it's only rock'n'roll!"

CHARLIE: I think that Mick on his own would have lost his way years ago if he hadn't had Keith to bounce off – and vice versa. Mick and Keith are like brothers, always arguing but also always getting on. It's a lovely conflict, a loving conflict.

KEITH: Mick and my friendship exists on the basis of a certain amount of space. I have a feeling that I'm not supposed to have any friend except him. He doesn't have many close male friends apart from me, and he keeps me at a distance. There is something of a siege mentality, so that whenever anyone comes up to Mick, he's thinking, "What do they want out of me?" But the only way to find whether a guy's worth anything is to take a risk. Sometimes friends let you down, sometimes they don't. But you take the chance, otherwise you get nothing at all. This is my personal opinion. Mick is very difficult to reach. Mick will be walking down the plane looking straight ahead, and you'll say, "Hey Mick remember me?" – but that's Mick, and you accept it.

RONNIE: It was just awful during the time when it looked like Mick and Keith weren't ever going to talk again, but I did manage to get them talking on the phone. I wasn't going to let the institution of the Stones fall down, and I thought, "If there's any way I can save it, I'm going to do it". As soon as I realised that I had been in the band longer than Brian Jones and Mick Taylor combined, I thought, "This must mean something". I think Charlie and Bill just decided to stay out of it and felt, "Well, we never thought it would last this long". I don't think they viewed it with the same level of enthusiasm that I did, and didn't have quite the same sense I had that: "This must carry on, we can't have this breaking up, let's keep it going".

I never set out to be a mediator, but I do like good things to continue. If I look back I've done it all my musical career: when Jeff Beck left the Yardbirds I thought, "I hope he's not going to disappear, he's a great guitar player". I rang him up and he said, "Oh, I'm not doing anything, fancy forming a band?" I'd thought he'd be too busy to talk to me, but he was happy to, and that led to the formation of the Jeff Beck Group.

The same thing happened when Steve Marriott left the Small Faces in 1969 and formed Humble Pie – I could never understand the reason why he did that. Rod Stewart and I used to love listening to the Small Faces' *Ogden's Nut Gone Flake* album and thought the Small Faces were a great team, so when Steve left the band, Rod and I said to each other, "What are the other three, Mac and Kenney and Ronnie, going to do? We can't have them sinking into oblivion".

I called up Ronnie Lane and said, "I hope you are going to do something". Ronnie said, "Well, we haven't got a vocalist any more. We're orphans". I told him, "I'll get something together", and Ronnie said, "Oh, would you?" – "Yeah". He said, "We'll come over" and we started playing together, which went on for months and months, using the Stones' Bermondsey rehearsal studio, thanks to Ian Stewart. While the Stones were away, the mice were at play. We were playing songs by the Meters and Booker T.; doing them instrumentally because the boys had this attitude of, "They're fucking terrible, these lead vocalists, we don't want to know another one". I told them, "Well, I've got this guy called Rod Stewart, man, he's all right". "Yeah, but he'll probably turn out to be another Steve Marriott, bossing us all around." I said, "No, Rod's upstairs now, he's very shy…" – which Rod was in those days. Kenney Jones finally asked Rod to come down and he really was completely shy, wouldn't take his coat off, but the others managed to break the ice and that's how the Faces came about.

CHARLIE: This was a particularly difficult time for the band; Keith was wanting one thing and Mick was pulling totally in another direction. Maybe Mick wanted to do some of his own things that he'd never done before. But when Mick and Keith were having their differences, Mick wasn't able to ask me any questions about it, and I certainly wasn't capable of answering him. Keith was in America, which meant that he and I didn't get to talk much, although that was just par for the course for us, because Keith very rarely uses the phone to talk when we're off the road and back at home. He'll fax you, but he'll hardly ever ring, whereas Mick will always call you. They're very opposite in that way.

RONNIE: It was one of those things the band had to go through. This period was the head of the boil. Shortly after that it erupted and then the healing process could begin. And the band is much stronger for it. My God, you wouldn't have planned having such an eruption point because it got near, so near, to falling apart. And that's when I had to do my stuff to keep Mick and Keith talking.

Mick called me up and he said, "Woody, Keith just doesn't want to talk to me; he hates me". I said, "I've just got off the phone with Keith. He doesn't hate you, there's just been a misunderstanding". Mick went, "Oh yeah, Woody", so I said, "You stay where you are for fifteen minutes and I guarantee I'll have Keith ring you and then you ring me back after Keith's spoken to you", and he was going, "Oh, Woody, are you sure?"

So I rang Keith and after a bit of chit chat I told him, "Mick has got this stupid idea that you hate him" to which he said, "Well, so what?" and I went, "Yeah, OK, talk to him". Keith was saying, "Oh, come on, it's only what the papers are doing, they're magnifying this and putting it all out of proportion". I said, "Well, ring him up and tell him", so Keith said, "All right, where's his number?" I told him, "Make sure you ring him right now", and he said, "OK, I will" and he did. Mick rang me back and said, "It worked,

Charlie performs with his jazz band.

251

Claude Gassian captures Mick's performance (and overleaf) and life backstage.

Woody" – and I thought, "Da dah, I've done my good deed for the decade". It was a good feeling because I knew that underneath anything else that might have happened they had that old love – and that old love/hate – for each other from back in the sandpit.

It couldn't have been very long after those phone conversations – a matter of a month or so – before Mick and Keith went away to Barbados and started writing together for a few weeks, putting together the groundwork for the new album, which was *Steel Wheels*.

KEITH: What Mick had done by himself was not particularly successful and what I had done was a fair success. And where else was there to go? There's the magnetic pull, the electromagnetics. From the day Mick and I got back together, it was a dream.

MICK: Keith and I have a very complicated relationship. I don't pretend to understand it. I find it quite tricky. He is a very inward person and he was always a very quiet and meditative type of person, so to bring out what he really wants to say is, I think, quite a problem for him sometimes. I'm a very outgoing person and very gregarious. Keith isn't, really, although he's learned to be somewhat more gregarious than he used to be.

CHARLIE: The funny thing about Mick is that he is very easy, and within that very complex. He longs to have big status records, number ones, and when he gets them he's the first to put them down and deride them. Or if we're doing a video, it's never right, he can never just leave it alone, he has to go in and spend another £4,000.

RONNIE: It happens though the music. You just start playing and then everything makes sense. Otherwise we're just a bunch of extremely different guys who are going off at extremely different tangents. The Rolling Stones is a vehicle that only works when we actually put it into motion.

CHARLIE: We're like 75% separated but 100% together. It's very weird; I don't know what

it is. I play with a lot of very good, brilliant, musicians – which is great – but this lot are just something special. I've never wanted to play rock'n'roll with anyone else.

KEITH: Mick is my wife! But we can't get divorced. If we never wanted to see each other again we'd have to deal with what we've done, all the babies...When we brought it back together, we knew that we were going to be a little rusty. You can't just shove something back together after five years and expect it to fit perfectly, but luckily it was, as it always has been, intriguing enough and promising enough for us to say, "Yeah, we want to keep on doing this, and I don't mind the money and the birds, because there's that side to rock'n'roll as well!"

I never doubted that we could do it, really. My take is, "This is what I do and I'm going to stick around", but at the same time I can understand the outside perception being totally different, people saying, "Oh, they've really screwed it now". The hardest bit from that period, from around 1989 onwards, was the fact that we, the Stones, were thinking, "We're putting it back together again, we're very determined to do it and anyway why

not?" and at the same time we had to deal with the sledgehammer of people talking about "the wrinkled old rockers" and all of that bullshit.

It's a question of how to deal with the music business and the press conception of what you are supposed to do at a certain age. There is also a certain amount of being wished to death, a certain amount of jealousy. And also this is what these boys want to do. I couldn't pull this off, nor could Mick or Charlie or Ronnie, individually, but we keep looking at each other and saying, "We don't care what they think, they're not looking for 'Satisfaction' again. We've been there, done that".

Keith by Mikio Ariga.

MICK: We have a pretty reasonable relationship with the press. But you can't really trust anybody , which is a drag. You always have to be on your guard because as soon as you let your guard down, they tend to pounce.

CHARLIE: I don't care what people say about me. But I do care what they say about my family. So I don't really talk to the press.

KEITH: We had a whole new generation listening to our music. There are twelve-year-old kids I used to play to on the *Steel Wheels* or *Voodoo Lounge* tours, who are now making hit records. Bands like the Hives and the Strokes. What are you going to do? On a musician's gravestone all you can have is "He passed it on". It's the best accolade you can get.

RONNIE: When we got back together for *Steel Wheels*, the atmosphere was kind of kid gloves, but there was nevertheless a happy feeling. You could see everybody breathing a sigh of relief that Mick and Keith were getting on again. Thank God!

KEITH: We recorded *Steel Wheels* at Air Studios in Montserrat. Working in a city is not always the best thing for a band. On a little island with nowhere to go you get a lot more done, and more quickly.

MICK: I was surprised that we got the recording of *Steel Wheels* done so quickly. But if you've got weeks, you can always make excuses and leave it to another day.

KEITH: Nobody had kept a band together this long. I wouldn't have dreamt of it, but now it's become a challenge. As long as the juices are flowing, I've got to follow this thing down the line. When we were working at Olympic Studios in London, Mick had Bernard Fowler and Pierre de Beauport with him. They'd been out in Australia with Mick and pissed him off because they played *Talk Is Cheap* all the time. I was playing 'Slipping Away' with Bernard Fowler, and it was the first time we'd sung together. I told Bernard, "Shit, man, I didn't *want* to like you, because you're his man". And now I probably couldn't do anything on the guitar without Pierre.

At the same time I knew that album was about starting over. The important thing was to do it, not how good it was or wasn't. Either that was where the thing was going to break and all the wheels would fall off forever or we'd survive and carry on. The next ten years for me were just trying to reinvent and re-establish the Stones in a new way, considering what we'd all gone through.

MICK: Given the state of the band at the time, it was probably very good that we hadn't done any touring for a while. We wouldn't have been able to do anything: we were struggling internally, and externally. But then we came up with a big tour in 1989, which turned out to be very successful and great fun to design and put a team together for.

> *Ronnie is a great morale booster because he never looks on the dark side of life and sometimes you'll be thinking, "Shut up, Ronnie, we don't want to be happy". You know, he's irresistible.*
>
> *Keith*

RONNIE: Before we went to Japan, on the *Steel Wheels* tour, my pals Charlie and Bill stood up for me. They said, "Are you earning as much as we are?" and I said, "No". So they said, "Unless you earn as much as us, we're not going to carry on". They brought this up at a meeting and I thought, "Thank you very much!". Bill and Charlie were very supportive. They made a stand for me without me having to beg and say, "I'm being unfairly treated". They said, "Ronnie's slaved away as hard as we have and he's not getting as much as us". And the rest of the band said, "Right, OK, we'll finally end your apprenticeship, you're finally part of the band".

The great thing about Bill is that he was a real humanitarian. He said, "I'm going to look after my friend, Ronnie, I'm going to make sure that he is taken care of". Whereas everyone else would probably have glossed over it and said, "Oh, if Ronnie didn't get it, fuck him", when Bill would say, "Hang on a minute, he deserves a chance here".

MICK: The logistics of the *Steel Wheels* tour were fantastic. The show was enormous and the steel framework for it was huge. This was the first time that we had worked on that scale for a whole tour. We had done a lot of stadium shows, but never so many together,

Jajouka, North Africa, 1989. Revisiting a project begun by Brian Jones in July 1968. Brian's original idea had been twofold: to capture the magic of the Master Musicians of Jajouka and to expand the Stones' music.

Ronnie: We went to Morocco to do the video for 'Continental Drift' with the local musicians that Brian had worked with. The same old boys met us at the airport and it was a real experience for me: they were so polite, carrying our bags while playing and singing all the time — nice people.

and we had never done them so lavishly, so big or so expensively. Even Mark Fisher and I were shocked when we finally got to put it up for the first time: it took about five days. That was never going to work, because it had to be put up in some thirty-six hours or so – it was a disaster. We had this huge thing, but when we got it up there, apart from all the teething troubles, and saw it at night with all the smoke coming out of it, we said "What the hell is this thing we've built, we don't really know".

We started trying to make some intellectual sense out of it. We asked other people who said that – depending on where they were sitting – it represented a factory or something out of *Blade Runner*. It meant a lot of things to different people. What it taught us, I think, was that people like to try and figure out what the staging represents.

We created another version of it for Europe – the *Urban Jungle* tour – and designed a whole set of fresh visuals featuring lots of dogs. We couldn't use all the steel we had used on the *Steel Wheels* tour, because we couldn't afford it for Europe – the ticket prices wouldn't support it – and so we had to scale it down somewhat.

I always want the band to earn a lot of money for their efforts. I don't want them to go round and do a long tour for a year or more and then not earn any money, because we did that a lot. But then you have to spend something on the show. Most of the cost is not the actual material, but the cost of transporting it around, getting it into the trucks, moving it and putting it up again, all of which is expensive. It's great, though, to see fifty-four trucks in the parking lot and going, "This is our show. Yeah! Fifty-four trucks!"

KEITH: For Mick, who's the guy out in the front, everything is designed as a safety net for him, especially on those big stages when you've got echoes and you're virtually a quarter of a mile away from each other at times. You're still having to play to give the singer the confidence that it doesn't matter what he does: he can screw everything up, and we'll twist the beat around and catch him on the other end. Ideally the singer will never know that he messed up – which is one of the things I think Mick found out when he started to do his own shit: there was no safety net. Charlie and I will make Mick look great to our own detriment: "Oh, he's missed the beat. It doesn't matter, let's switch it and he won't even realise that we've caught him". It's intuitive – some of it comes from experience, but in fact we've been like that from the beginning. Charlie says the same thing. This is the singer, whatever he's doing, follow him, and if he screws up you recapture him, you don't leave him out there dangling. That's not on.

MICK: What happens is that you are nervous and make mistakes. I know I'm going to make mistakes. Everyone makes their share of them, but you hope that your mistake doesn't fuck the whole thing up. I have to watch out because if I make a mistake and go to the wrong part of a

Mick and Jerry on a video shoot.

song, half of the band will follow me and the other half will go with the right version, and the whole thing can come to a messy, grinding halt. Normally, though, the band do find me if I go wrong.

CHARLIE: The *Steel Wheels* stage was huge. Mick used to run about four miles a night. When he first started doing that I felt as if I was the only one on stage because Keith also started heading off along the wings, and Ronnie would be off somewhere else. Of course Matt Clifford was there on the keyboards – and Bill was there, because he never moved, but I still felt very isolated because I had no front men. Eventually I grew used to it and now it feels quite normal.

MICK: If you're working in an arena or a stadium, most people think it's enormous, but I think it's quite small. Everybody can see you all of the time that you're on the stage. You can't even blow your nose on there without somebody noticing.

KEITH: When the lights are on, and the music's playing, you look upon it as home. That's where you are totally in control. You are Zeus, the emperor of the world. And anything that is going to happen, God willing, it's going to be because you have decided it is going to happen.

We started working with the video screens on that tour – Jesus Christ, who would have

The band in performance by Ken Regan.

thought of carrying all of that around with us – and slowly we began to develop how to use them. The first time they showed me the video screens I thought, "Oh no, now we're just like little puppets, and it will be as though everybody's watching a movie". But it didn't take me long to realise that I was wrong about that, because it actually helped make the place feel more intimate. If you are standing at the far end of the stadium we look like matchsticks without the screens. I'm 5' 10" and there's nothing much we can do about that. So the screen was not the distraction I had expected,

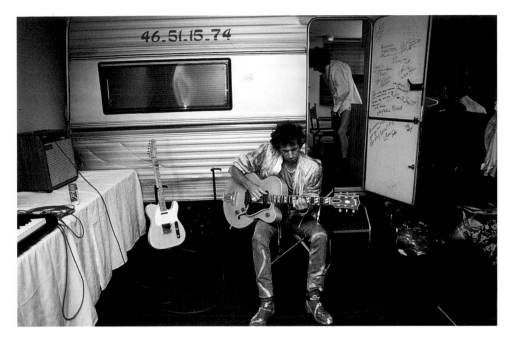

Keith, Paris, by Claude Gassian.

Ronnie, Barcelona, by Claude Gassian.

although it was weird getting used to the fact that the audience were looking over your head at something you couldn't see, or which you might glimpse on the odd occasion you turn round for a few seconds. Now the screens have turned into a travelling backdrop. They change the way that you deal with a big show because instead of only working the front row and the space out there, now you have to learn how to deal with the camera. In fact, you never stop learning, because every time you come back out on tour, there's always something new in the technology: the screens are bigger or the PA is better or there's a new system to try out. Whatever it is, you're always out in front of it, which is what makes it interesting. It's like being a pilot and getting the new fighter plane before anybody else.

RONNIE: We had the Uptown Horns with us on the *Steel Wheels* and *Urban Jungle* tours. That's something that grew out of Mick touring with his own band and us using some of the musicians he worked with, and Keith working with people like Charlie Drayton and Steve Jordan: just keeping an open mind to other talent. Having the brass is a useful element, like

It was just awful during the time when it looked like Mick and Keith weren't ever going to talk again, but I did manage to get them talking on the phone. I wasn't going to let the institution of the Stones fall down.

Ronnie

the fact that Blondie Chaplin is a singer as well as a guitar player – he comes in useful for fattening out various effects on different songs. It doesn't limit what we do, it changes it. It gives you another level of freedom if a particular area of a song is covered by brass or by background vocals. It gives you the space to put in maybe just one note that's important or a particular riff, knowing that you have that hole covered behind you. It gives you the feeling that "That's safe, I can either not play anything in there, or I can put a nice note in or a riff and it will add to it. It's kind of interesting".

KEITH: *Steel Wheels* was a hell of a long tour. A major enterprise. But if that's what keeps her majesty happy, let's try the big blow-ups and lah di dah. I always prefer to make a set look like a jazz club.

The hardest thing is how to make this 50,000 audience feel like there's only 500 or 50 of them. How can we turn this football stadium into a club? Playing a football stadium is not your optimum arena. God joins the band every day in the form of wind, heat, light and rain and you can't wag your finger at him and say, "Stop it".

CHARLIE: What's really surprising is that we *have* stayed together, with all the egos and the lack of it and whatever it is that make people what they are. And the fact that people still like you is staggering.

KEITH: At the end of the *Urban Jungle* tour Bill said he was leaving the band. I got really pissed with him. I threatened to do everything in the world to him, including death at dawn – as I always say, "Nobody leaves this band except in a coffin". But he'd made up his mind: he'd really started to hate flying, he developed a real fear of flying. Now, this was pretty strange after twenty-five years, but it happens to people. He was having to drive to every gig, which was knackering him, and sometimes people get to the end of their tether.

> *After all, the only thing Bill did was to leave the band and have three babies and one fish-and-chip shop!*
>
> *Keith*

RONNIE: Bill had been heading that way for years, and the more planes we got on the worse it got. In the end he'd taken too many plane flights. In fact the last flight he took with us, he said, "Hey, look out here". I looked out of the window and he said, "See that stuff coming off the wing?" I said, "Yeah, that's condensation", but Bill said, "No it's not, that's fuel. It's leaking". I think in his own mind his time was up and, for a change, Keith let someone leave without a big deal being made of it.

KEITH: After all, the only thing Bill did was to leave the band and have three babies and one fish-and-chip shop!

CHARLIE: Bill had got to the point where he was of a certain age; he had just got married and had started a family and he didn't want to be in the band or tour any more. He was extremely paranoid about flying, which I hadn't realised, although he drove everywhere on the *Urban Jungle* tour that we did in Europe. I thought it was just him going off on one of his own things.

RONNIE: Bill said, "Fuck you lot, you didn't use any of my songs" and Keith was going, "Haven't you sussed that they're useless songs?!"

KEITH: I love Bill dearly. He's a very funny guy, with a very dry wit. He's got some wicked jokes out of South London – I think they're carved in concrete somewhere – and a very steady temperament. When you listen to what Bill says, he's incredibly subtle, which you might not expect from what you see on the surface.

It was a huge surprise when he actually said, "I'm going to leave the group". Nobody says that – that's a kind of *Spinal Tap* line – but I eventually had to accept it. I didn't let him off the hook for ages about it, because we've got this unit and whatever it is we do somehow seems to work well. The idea of taking a slice out of something that only has five elements in it in the first place is difficult. You can't do anything about people dying, but apart from that…

Also Bill was my rhythm section. As far as I was concerned he and Charlie were joined at the hip, musically. He had an affinity with Charlie Watts that was quite amazing, and good rhythm sections don't come around that often.

RONNIE: I miss Bill as a sparring partner because he was always on stage looking at girls' tits, always on the look out for gazongas. He'd say, "Hey, Woody, see that huge pair?"

CHARLIE: When Brian left the band, he had not been a very pleasant person for some time, so in many ways the decision wasn't hard to make in that way, but it was not a decision that we made quickly. And when Bill left, it wasn't that he left and didn't turn up a week later. He said he was leaving at the end of one tour and when we discussed going on the road again, which was a couple of years later, we asked him if he was serious, so he actually had two years in which to consider his decision. If at that point he'd said he wanted to stay, we would have said, "OK". But he said he was going, and that was that. But finding another bass player was bloody hard work, my goodness.

Richard Branson plays host as the Jaggers, Richards and Woods celebrate the band signing a three-album deal with Virgin Records in late 1991.

EDNA GUNDERSEN

Edna Gundersen, pop music critic at *USA Today* since 1986, began reporting on the Rolling Stones in Texas in the 1970s and '80s and has written about every tour and album since 1972's *Exile on Main Street*. She has interviewed the band collectively and individually since 1988, most recently in September 2002.

As a budding flower child in high school, I grooved on Jimi Hendrix and idolised Bob Dylan, but it was the mystique of the Rolling Stones that steered me towards a career in rock journalism. I immediately grasped the sunny appeal of the cute Beatles with their shaggy coifs and lucid pop. That was the British Invasion's love boat. Navigating darker waters was an ominous pirate galleon steered by a pair of swashbuckling contradictions. Mick Jagger's sly charm and feline yowl seemed at odds with Keith Richards' uncultivated cool and raw riffs. Yet somehow these mismatched misfits crafted some of rock's sturdiest classics.

The spotlight only magnified the distinctions, as I discovered when I first saw the Stones in Albuquerque, New Mexico, on June 15, 1972. I was a teen shutterbug 300 miles from home clutching a scalped ticket for a seat in a distant tier of the arena. That didn't stop me from weaseling to the front row with a smuggled camera. Lobbing grenades like 'Rip This Joint' and 'Midnight Rambler', the band played with astonishing force and finesse. I again was captivated by the off-kilter dynamics: Keith's staggering gait, Mick's carnal ballet; Keith's guerrilla garb, Mick's purple eye shadow; Keith's lurching guitar spasms, Mick's vocal flamboyance.

Sonically and vocally, the Stones embodied harmonious disharmony. Were there also duelling philosophies, diametric personalities? Impossible, I thought.

I thought wrong. The clashing colours ran deeper than fashion, and the cockeyed coexistence finally cracked. None of the perils plaguing the Rolling Stones in the treacherous '80s, from Charlie Watts' heroin habit to the tabloid frenzy surrounding Bill Wyman's teen squeeze, could finish off a legendary band that seemed to regard chaos and controversy as simply more coal for its creative engines.

Even the infamous drunken brawl in Amsterdam, where Charlie belted an inebriated Mick for a dismissive dig, produced few repercussions beyond a collective hangover.

Only the lingering rift between Mick and Keith seemed grave enough to bury the band. The feud started when Mick chose to record a solo album rather than tour after 1986's *Dirty Work*. Keith was crushed, and the fraternity fractured, with Ron Wood joining Bo Diddley on tour, Charlie booking dates with an orchestra and Bill undertaking charity work. Clearly seeking to distance himself from the Stones, Mick unleashed the kinetic and clever *Primitive Cool* in 1987, proclaiming on 'Kow Tow': "The future looms, so damn the past".

When I interviewed Keith a year later, he was still feeling the sting of betrayal but also relishing revenge with the release of his solo debut, the gloriously ragged *Talk Is Cheap*, which addresses the grudge on 'You Don't Move Me'. Reacting to Mick's willingness to reconvene the Stones after two modest-selling solo albums, Keith snarls, "Now you want to throw the dice; you already crapped out twice".

When I met Keith on a September afternoon in an LA hotel suite, I didn't know whether to expect Mick's friend or foe. I found both. The rumpled and gregarious guitarist vacillated from cranky to conciliatory as he sipped a tall glass of Jack Daniels and ginger ale. ("After you've kicked heroin, everything else is baby's milk", he pointed out.)

Splintering off to record *Talk Is Cheap* "wasn't my idea", he told me. "I was forced to because I wanted to work. I wasn't the one who said I'm going to go out alone. As I said to Mick, 'Darling, the Stones are bigger than both of us'. One way or another, I'm determined to beat some sense into him."

And yet Keith was reluctant to relinquish his own turn in the spotlight.

"Not yet", he said with a hoarse laugh. "I'm enjoying this too much. It's been good for me to leave the bubble. It's given me more confidence. And I know I'm no longer totally dependent on the Rolling Stones as a way of life."

The Jagger/Richards codependency had morphed into a schoolyard standoff. Keith accused Mick of touring with the "ersatz" Stones. Mick in turn appeared loath to commend Keith's detour. With a sour smile, Keith recounted how Mick chattered nonstop during his first exposure to *Talk Is Cheap*. Later, Keith spied him dancing to a track.

"I saw him leaping around the room to the music", he said proudly. "If it got him on his feet, he must have liked it. Yet he didn't want to admit it to me at the time. He's a funny boy. Our own personal relationship is a little complex. We have our quarrels and differences. It's growing pains. I feel he needs to get over this Peter Pan complex so we can get down to work."

Keith resisted absolving Mick for sins of arrogance, but his new position as front man for the X-Pensive Winos gave a fresh appreciation of the difficulties facing a lead singer.

"It's hard," he said. "Onstage, you have to believe you're semi-divine. The problem comes when that belief sticks with you offstage."

The sniping provoked by this trial separation eventually gave way to soul-searching, reconciliation and a triumphant return to form. The truce produced 1989's *Steel Wheels*, the band's meatiest work since 1978's *Some Girls*.

In August, between the album's release and the kick-off of the record-breaking *Steel Wheels* tour, the Stones huddled for rehearsals at a boarding school in tiny Washington, Connecticut. After years of wondering about the sorcerer's glue that kept them intact, I finally got my chance to grill Mick and Keith in person. But not in tandem. Despite their studio détente, the two were still poised on the battlefield. I was invited to interview them separately, a Swiss referee dispatched to mediate the Cold War. One of the band's publicists encouraged a diplomatic posture, noting that maintaining neutrality was crucial in adapting to a camp already stressed by an album roll-out and tour preparations.

Finding Mick and Keith in their respective corners, ensconced at separate estates in the nearby hills, again accentuated the polar personalities that form their unlikely alliance.

Keith, his hair a riot of tangles, was shoeless and sporting a faded polka-dot shirt as he chain-smoked Marlboros on the back porch of his cluttered house. While he could still muster resentment over the estrangement, he recognised Mick's reason for retreat.

"He probably felt a need for a break from duelling with me constantly", Keith said. "We were sitting on each other's backs for too long. When you've known someone forty years and work becomes a pressure cooker, little things annoy you intensely."

Yet irritations were vaporised in the spontaneous combustion of creating *Steel Wheels*, a process Richards described with delight and pride. After calling a ceasefire in February, the two met in Barbados to write songs for the band's thirty-fourth album, a daunting landmark for a partnership craving novel ideas. The baggage accrued during three decades of high-profile fellowship vanished in the adolescent glee of building songs from scratch. Lyrics and hooks and melodies gelled with amazing speed.

A mile away in the Connecticut countryside, Mick could be found relaxing in his antique-appointed parlour. His hair cropped short, he was coolly elegant in shades, crisp slacks and Moroccan slippers. On the topic of recent hostilities, his tone turned icy.

"He was very rude", Mick confided, referring to potshots Keith delivered via the media. "Keith is not known for his good manners. He just doesn't have any manners. I tried to lay off saying what I thought about Keith because it's potentially damaging. You don't like to say, 'Well, my brother is an idiot, but I have to get on with him.' Those aren't things you talk about publicly. I thought Keith was just an unnecessary loudmouth."

He paused and added crisply, "As I don't hold grudges, it's quite easy for me to forget about it for the purposes of this tour".

He was also readjusting to teamwork after three years of autocratic rule in his solo career.

"I have to be much more democratic about how I impose my authority," he said with a smile. "It is difficult being so diplomatic, which is boring."

Boredom serves as a vital catalyst in channelling the partnership's volatility towards healthy quests. The band's low threshold for monotony and allergy to rust were amply evident in the gleaming *Steel Wheels,* an ambitious blend of exoticism, pop smarts and *Exile*-era garage rock. Friction that would have ground weaker unions into dust only sharpened their edges.

That sizzle translated to the stage, confounding detractors who expected an autopilot oldies revue. News of the *Steel Wheels* tour was greeted with cynicism and contempt in some corners of pop's fickle universe. Not surprisingly, a comeback staged by forty-something rockers in an era reeking of teen spirit drew taunts and pronouncements about obsolescence and osteoarthritis. The "steel wheelchairs" cracks quickly faded once the juggernaut got rolling after a breathtaking launch in Philadelphia. The production, a glitzy spectacle of jaw-dropping proportions, never overshadowed the sweaty brilliance of the band.

Like every album and tour before *Steel Wheels*, the Stones savoured the moment but didn't linger. They returned to wives and children while contemplating the band's next growth spurt. After sparring like wild horses, Mick and Keith settled into a post-*Wheels* state of genial patience and even pooled energies in a vain attempt to thwart an internal calamity: Bill's departure.

"Nothing worked," a dismayed Mick told me in 1991. "He just wanted out. He never wavered."

Initially irate, Keith later decided Bill's exit was appropriate. "You have to want to do this more than one hundred per cent," he insisted when I pressed him to characterise the bassist's burn-out. "Bill didn't have that extra five per cent in him anymore."

That level of commitment has been key to the band's survival and evolution, along with impressive chops and a shared devotion to high-voltage, blues-drenched musical integrity. The antagonism between Mick and Keith was less a reflection of incompatibility than a determination to raise the bar and uphold the band's reputation. That persisted in the early '90s, when hints of rancour resurfaced on occasion.

When I spoke to him in 1993, on the eve of releasing his third solo album *Wandering Spirit* (five months after Richards' sophomore disc, *Main Offender*), Mick confessed indifference to his cohort's opinion.

"We don't take much notice of each other's work," he sniffed. "We have a good relationship, but it's a very English relationship, where not a lot is said."

Forays afield again resulted in collective radiance, unleashed in 1994 as *Voodoo Lounge*, a deep-grooved, *Sticky Finger*-painting of rock euphoria and hedonism. This conjured balance of craft and primal force underscored the limitless possibilities of harnessing a personality clash. The sardonic sophisticate with the menacing yelp and the disorderly outlaw with the funk-baited hooks found common ground in a mutual passion for sonic adventure.

"What we went through in the '80s was a slow realisation that we were working for a monster we created instead of it working for us", Keith explained to me. "When Mick and I couldn't vent our frustration at the invisible enemy, we turned to each other. All the bad blood's past. I think Mick is enjoying the fruits of comradeship, and things are not annoying him as much."

In fact, by the mid-'90s, the chief annoyance came from late-night TV hosts, who delighted in reporting that Mick, the swivel-hipped, rubber-lipped rock god, was older than President Clinton ("But younger than the secretary of state!" Mick retorted). The attacks only fuelled the band's defiance, with Keith advising comics "to get over it, boys, 'cause we're still gonna be here when nobody's listening to your jokes".

At the band's thirty-year milestone, Keith expressed undimmed confidence in the Stones' ability to persevere with dignity.

"There's a possibility of another very interesting golden era for the Stones," he said. "We're going down a road nobody has taken before."

That road is bound to be littered with obstacles, he conceded. And any peace treaties between Mick and Keith will likely crack in the collision of views and visions.

In the Stones' case, when sparks fly, they ignite the imagination. The unstable alchemy in the Rolling Stones ensures a place for ingenuity and skill to blaze with Darwinian efficiency. Unquestionably, the band's regenerating hipness and enduring relevance owes more to push-pull dynamics and the Glimmer Twins' sibling rivalry than to cosy compliance. When I asked Keith to consider the role of independent ambition within the Stones, he said cautiously, "If there's competition, it's very subliminal."

And potentially sublime.

The difficult days had gone. The camaraderie and the bonding was back. The Rolling Stones were rocking. and going from strength to strength.

Ronnie Wood

SOME KIND OF MIRACLE

10

*The band,
Indianapolis, 1994.*

RONNIE: We had some fun in New York auditioning bass players to find a replacement for Bill. We had a feeling that we should move on and see what the future held, and maybe get a little bit funky instead of holding everything down, like Bill did.

Bill had his own special style of playing bass. It wasn't a very adventurous style, but it was always locked right in with Keith and Charlie, and that's what had created the disjointed feel of the Stones from the very earliest days – that push and pull thing – so we thought we didn't want to find somebody who was going to be too perfect, because that would have tidied it up too much. Whoever we were going to choose would have to walk a fine line between being a good bass player and having just enough raggedness.

For weeks before the auditions, I'd ring up Mick and say, "Oh, we should try so and so" – the same as the others in the band were doing – and eventually we had enough names on the list to say, "OK, we've got twelve coming in today and twelve tomorrow". Each of them came in and played three songs with us. It was good fun, because there was such a different atmosphere with each new guy.

KEITH: When Bill left we had to get a new bass player, a totally different bass player from a new generation. There was not a shabby bass player in the house. What was important was finding who clicked with Charlie.

RONNIE: One of the songs we would play with a bass player coming to audition with us would be a blues jam, but we'd leave that to the end, after starting with a couple of numbers like 'Brown Sugar' and 'Miss You'. The jam was important because it gave us the opportunity to see how solid they were and how well they kept with Charlie.

CHARLIE: It felt as though we auditioned a few thousand players and that I was sitting at my drums for about nine days. It was unbelievable – we had a list of guys to try out, and they were all good. Each of them came with their own recommendations. There was one particular guy who Keith had worked with and liked a lot; there was another Mick liked a lot: Dougie Wimbish, who's a fabulous player.

RONNIE: I had a book running, a little red notebook, where I wrote down a little story about every single one of the bass players who came to try out: it's very interesting; I keep it in my archive in Kingston. It lists everybody's name, their background, which songs we played with them, my rating out of 10 and their popularity among the band, plus a few comments like, "This guy can't sing with us" or "What a creep he was – next!" It was very hard for these extremely talented people to be treated like that, but they all understood that we had a big job on our hands. We had so many applicants. All these people were coming out of the woodwork once they heard we were auditioning, from Noel Redding out of the Jimi Hendrix Experience to all these young whippersnappers.

The decision was more or less made by a look between us all that said, "We feel comfortable with this guy, he is talented". Eventually it came down to a handful of possibilities, maybe two or three guys. It was no problem for me that Darryl Jones got the gig, because he's perfect. I used to do this thing where, when each of the bass players walked in through the door, I would ask them, "Would you like a Guinness?" as my opening line! Darryl always says that he'll never forget the moment he walked into the studio and I said, "Would you like a Guinness, mate?" Darryl got the job because he said, "Yeah, I'll have a Guinness". Everyone is suffering from a little bit of nerves in that kind of situation, even if they're not showing it, and that little interchange about the Guinness with Darryl immediately got rid of any tension.

> *The thing that's most important when you're selecting a musician for this band is that you have to be able to live with them as people, which is as important as that person being a great player.*
>
> *Charlie*

CHARLIE: Eventually it came down to Dougie Wimbish and Darryl as well as this guy that Keith had worked with. It was an extremely close-run thing between the three of them, but Darryl was so easy to work with that in the end he got a unanimous decision.

KEITH: I saw Charlie's face when he started playing with Darryl. It was the jazz connection, and also the fact that Darryl is incredibly accomplished.

CHARLIE: Darryl is such a good bass player and he fits in to things so well. He is able both to be part of the rhythm section, but also very much a front man – I've seen him perform both roles with different bands, including his jazz fusion line-up. He's very rhythmic, and driving. So he can do a lot of things musically, but the thing that's most important when you're selecting a musician for this band is that you have to be able to live with them as

Two studies of Ronnie.

people, which is as important as that person being a great player. I mean, I love hearing Darryl telling me stories about working with Miles Davis, but it must have been a nightmare sometimes to have had Miles as your leader. I wouldn't like it that much.

Darryl has beautiful hands as a bass player, but he's also a seriously strong man. It made me realise that Bill in comparison was almost an effeminate kind of player, although he played some great bass lines, fabulous lines in fact – I think that was because he came from the guitar, in the same way that Ronnie can play great bass, although Ronnie drives harder than Bill did. Bill was totally unlike a bass player. When we were in Toronto rehearsing for the *Forty Licks* tour I was listening back to a lot of the songs that Bill and I had played together – and I found myself thinking that he was a lot better than I had remembered. I suppose that I had never really thought about it before: Bill had been a bass player who I worked with, and a friend, and I had never sat down and considered his actual bass playing. So we might have been rehearsing 'Mother's Little Helper' with Darryl and playing the original version over and over again, and I'd think, "That's pretty inventive" while seeing, in my mind's eye, Bill's tiny little hands going over the neck of his bass.

RONNIE: Watching from afar when I was working with Bill in the band, I could see the way that Charlie, Bill and Keith interacted: it was the result of this time lapse between Keith's riff, Charlie hitting the beat and Bill hitting it slightly later, which is what gave the original shuddering effect to the songs. Bill had some simple magic going on in there within the structure of the way the rhythm section sounded. Darryl, being such a complete virtuoso player, still makes that work, but he also makes it work even more efficiently now. Charlie is a very happy man. And it tends to make me play with more thought, more sparingly, so that what I do play actually means more. Equally I think about what and when I'm *not* playing. I used to do a hell of a lot of talking about that idea – "Oh yeah, it's what you don't play that counts" and then I'd get on stage and play the whole way through everything, but still imagining I had left some gaps. That's just something that came with experience.

KEITH: As well as Darryl joining us on bass, we had a new producer working with us on *Voodoo Lounge*. Don Was has incredible diplomacy and great musical insight. He's very, very good at working between the cracks – which is Mick and myself – and then when things really come down to the crunch, we ask Charlie: he's the final arbiter. Don will say, "Don't push it now – it's very good, but not now. Timing is everything and Charlie, you're the timekeeper".

You are inevitably influenced by everybody you work with. If you're onto something and you think it's really great, but Don Was is going, "Well, maybe it ain't that great", you

*Three studies of Keith.
Second right,
performing at
Indianapolis, 1994.*

take the judgement for what it is – nobody has to say anything. Or he says, "It needs a bit more work, but OK, I'll leave that alone". Either you pick up those messages on the spot or you're lost for ever.

RONNIE: Don Was is like a Steve Lillywhite. Steve would always be there watching, not saying much, and you could go to him and get an opinion, maybe asking him, "Should I do this? Do you think this needs a twelve-string or an acoustic?" and he'd say, "No, you're fine where you are on the six-string…", just little pieces of advice like that.

Don is much the same. He has an unwritten understanding with the band that he doesn't interfere too much, but that he's there if you need any direction, which means that we are able to operate pretty quickly and efficiently with his help: he's a very easy man to work with. Most of the time the feedback I get from Don is, "No, you're doing fine, just carry on doing exactly what you're doing". He might come up to me and say, "You can let rip on this one, this one's for you" or, "I really like that line you were playing – play some more of that". And I think that Mick gets a lot of bounce-back from Don in terms of the arrangements, because Don's a very good arranger.

Apart from that Don just sits there during the take, giving the odd cue, but not intervening very often. He is also on hand in the studio, being a fellow musician and an excellent bass player. His right-hand man, Ed, who goes everywhere with Don, handles the sound so that Don can be out in the studio with us, whereas Chris Kimsey, for example, was in the booth all the time working with the sound; Steve Lillywhite also had an engineer, which meant he could come in and out of the booth. Don is out there with us virtually the whole time; he very rarely stays in the booth when we're doing a take.

Chris and Steve would always put in their twopennyworth, whatever they could do, but they were operating much more under the orders of Mick and Keith, who would be telling them, "Right, we're going to do this this way, and we want you to handle it this way", whereas they tend to give Don more of an open hand in what he is doing, more of his own choice about the direction he wants the song to go in. In fact, it's quite amazing for me to see them take orders from somebody like Don Was; I think, "OK, if they're

happy this way, then cool". He's positive and knowledgeable, he's someone who we can confide in and trust without too much being discussed or analysed. He just fits in.

KEITH: I like to work with Don Was: he's a great musician, like Jimmy Miller was. It is not always necessary that a producer plays an instrument – some guys go entirely by sound, but you can still communicate – but on a day-to-day basis it *is* easier to work with a producer who does.

CHARLIE: Don will try out a number of things with us. In the studio one day we had a go at something that Don suggested, where he asked me to drum along to Dr Dre's album *The Chronic*. I think that the idea was for the guys behind the glass to have some complete tracks of me playing in case they needed it at some point, some drum patterns that they could pull out and use later on. They put the CD on the system and I simply played along with the whole album. Don was amazed that I could do that, but in fact the tracks were actually all the same and very simple. Sometimes you can play along to tracks and they will be very difficult, but this wasn't one of those. It wasn't done to catch me out, though, it was to get me on tape, although I'm not sure that we ever used anything that came out of that exercise.

MICK: When I am writing songs, I get a great deal of fun out of it. I don't think, "What kind of impact is this going to have?" I wouldn't be able to write anything otherwise. Most songwriting of the kind that I do expresses what you think at the time. You could write a song one week and not believe in it the week after; you could be in love with a girl this week and not in love with her next week – and that's the transitory nature of any writing, not just songwriting.

KEITH: I've never even thought about writing songs, I've always thought of songs as gifts that just arrive. I've never sat down in my life and said I'm going to write this or that... I mean, after all, I'm the guy that wrote 'Satisfaction' in my sleep. It wouldn't even exist if I hadn't had that little tape recorder and pushed it in and pushed it back again, and maybe that's a blessing to me because I've never thought of myself as having to hammer something into shape. It's just a feeling, an intuition.

On an album like *Voodoo Lounge* there are songs that people won't get for ten years... and then suddenly they realise what I've been doing. 'Thru And Thru' was exactly like that. It took off when it was put on the soundtrack of *The Sopranos* along with 'Make No Mistake' from the X-Pensive Winos. Suddenly everybody was saying "What's that wonderful record?" and I'd say, "Well, it's the last track on *Voodoo Lounge*".

I know these songs. I'm not writing them to hit you between the eyes, right now – you can do that with a shooter – but to see if you get it in a bit, once you've had a couple of babies and you've laid down with a babe... Whether people get the song or not is not important for me any more. I don't have to churn another hit out every eight weeks like we had to do in the 1960s. Now I can stretch out and do what I want to do – and if you don't get it now, you don't get it in ten years, or you don't get it until after I croak, it doesn't matter to me – you'll get it one day.

> *I wake up in the morning and sometimes think, "Oh, this one goes like this" with very little thought involved. One note against another: that's my theory about a song.*
>
> Keith

Musically I've never laid down a lie. I'll lie to everybody else – especially judges! – but I won't lie to my audiences: what I put out I do in the hope that I can make your heart throb a little better or bring a little tear to your eye or make you smile. When it comes down to it, what are you going to play music for otherwise? I just wish to transmit the joy I feel to somebody else, and if I can do that, I've done my gig.

RONNIE: The guitar interplay between Keith and myself on a track like 'Sweethearts' is something that just evolves without words. It is done during the playing thanks to some kind of miracle that is born in the two of us. If it doesn't happen we don't pursue the song, but nine times out of ten our parts just click in without either of us having to say anything. Keith will go down to the bottom of the neck, and I will go up to the top, or the other way round, or we both hover around the middle, like we did on 'Beast Of Burden', when we were both playing on a similar part of the guitar neck, crossing over, so that we don't know which part is which.

KEITH: I just sit down and say, "I feel like playing 'Maybe Baby' by Buddy Holly", or I'll sit down at the piano and try a bit of Bach, which I know I'm useless at, but I can still try and figure it out. Then, after about ten or fifteen minutes, something else creeps in; it's the old antennae. That way you avoid the writer block bullshit; you can tinker around with something and then transmit it.

When we get in the studio, I'll say, "OK, I haven't seen you for three or four months, maybe longer, and we have to do something, what have you got?" Mick might say, "I've got a riff", "Oh, funnily enough I've got one very similar", and he'll say, "Yeah, but I'm missing the bridge, the middle part", "Well, I've got a lousy beginning, but I've got a great bridge..." With the Stones we have always been able to come up with just a thread of an idea and see what the band will do with it.

Keith raises a smile in the studio.

MICK: When we start looking at touring, sometimes other people will put the money up and sometimes we do. There is obviously a break-even point that is usually quite a long way into the future: you may have to do 30 shows before you break even. We do try not to spend too much money on the whole show. We make an effort to keep it within bounds, but it is always expensive. Trying to keep the construction work under budget is particularly difficult, especially in an industry which is not noted for its thriftiness. Very few show business events, like movies or rock shows, are known for keeping within their budgets, so you tend to be over budget before you even start.

CHARLIE: Taking some time off between tours does make a massive difference. One of the things that I think has sustained us – apart from being very good visually – is that we've had these great big gaps, so that when we do go back out on the road, it becomes a real event, and we try and make it an occasion. Sometimes the gap is quite long because of internal circumstances, but in general it's a couple of years, which we need, to get everything together.

Darryl Jones (top) bass guitar.

The decision to go on tour usually comes to a head when all of us have done everything else we want to do – solo work or whatever – or Michael Cohl comes up with a plan for us to look at. Rupert Loewenstein will say, "Do you want to go to work?" and

Chuck Leavell (below) keyboards.

a band meeting will be called; they're fantastic. Where the meeting is held depends on which part of the world Mick and Keith are in, so it could be somewhere like Bali, but usually we meet in London. We all sit round a table and that first meeting will be a bit *mañana* because it all seems a long way away – usually more than a year – but the basic shape is pencilled in and Rupert has written that down, so we know it's going to happen.

Then Mick starts to worry and eventually everything comes together. It starts very early for someone like Mick, who will ask me to get involved – and there's so much to do. Designing the stage starts a year or so before the tour. You just think, "Oh God, here we go – what can we do now? We can put the stage in the middle of the arena, add some curtains, what else can we do?" And by a few months before the tour, you've got the stage design in hand, hundreds of questions to be answered, bits of paper coming in from all sides asking what size everything needs to be. Then suddenly the stage is built and when you try to work around it, weaving in and out and under, people are banging their heads and Keith's saying, "Who built this?" and you're hiding in case it was you.

MICK: What the audiences want are a lot of lights and pizzazz with bangs and whistles – and I will be thinking of the show in terms of three or four acts and trying to establish the mood of each of those acts. In practice that means that something actually has to happen: maybe a screen that comes round which you hadn't seen before and which then disappears. If we have too many gimmicks I can always take them away, although it's a real hassle putting them in to the stage, getting these big objects constructed, and then realising, "Wait a minute, this is useless". On the *Voodoo Lounge* tour we had this huge lamp-post structure stuck in the middle of the stage. It was very good-looking, but by the time we got twenty-five minutes into the show, and then an hour, the lamp-post was still standing there doing nothing. We had to invent a whole feature with these Mexican inflatables, which were interesting, although slightly odd. They were done in a way that made them look as though they were dolls in some strange kind of religious shrine.

There is a theatrical aspect to the shows, but because there is no libretto, no book to the show, no characters emerging and having moments of conflict, and no dénouement – all the things that we accept with the theatre – it's up to the audience to make their own sense of whatever architecture we create, and what it all means. In a way I wish we could have had a Peter Hall character, someone who only has to think about the conceptual aspect of the show. It would be a great role, but I've never found anybody to do it.

So Mark Fisher and I had to talk ourselves into the aesthetic of how the inflatables and the lamp-post worked for *Voodoo Lounge*, because we always feel that the shows must make some sort of sense to us intellectually. We don't care if nobody else ever gets the

Bobby Keys, sax, with Keith.

concept, but it has to work for us, so that should we have to explain the staging to a really serious critic – someone who might come up and say, "OK, what is this show really about? What the hell is this lamp-post doing there?" – then we've got the answer ready. But no one ever does.

A rock concert is a very fluid kind of theatre, but the problem you have is that you're dealing with the same people on stage, more or less, so you are limited in the number of elements that you are able to change. And it's partly a problem specific to rock music. If you are putting on a show like Britney Spears or Madonna, every time you go out with her you can change everything about the show. You can change the way she looks, the band she has, all the dances she performs, so if we call that pop, you can design the show to do anything you want. With a rock show there is a completely different set of aesthetics that you can't mess with much, because then you detract from a lot of what you're supposed to be delivering as a rock show, as far as the audience's expectations are concerned.

RONNIE: On the *Voodoo Lounge* tour, the band was pretty settled, including the additional musicians, who ended up doing all the following tours with us – Darryl on bass, Chuck Leavell on keyboards, Bobby Keys with the horn section, and Bernard Fowler, Lisa Fischer and Blondie Chaplin providing the backing vocals.

MICK: It wouldn't be the same show without Lisa. She worked with me for the first time on my solo tour of Australia. Although I don't think that any of the extra musicians, apart from the keyboards, are in the strictest sense essential, it is nice to have them there and good to have some additional visual hooks.

RONNIE: Lisa is wonderful. She looks great and she moves great – and her singing is fabulous. She has her own signs in the audience saying, "We love Lisa". I point them out to her: "Look down there, that's not there for nothing, babe; you know they love you". Bernard is also very close to my family, he loves my kids and he calls me "Pop" and Jo "Mama".

MICK: Having extra musicians does help, but the problem is that you have to be very careful that you don't over-use them – they'd be on stage all the time if they could! You'd be surprised.

RONNIE: Once again the band exceeded my expectations. The Rolling Stones caters for all my needs, churning out rock'n'roll. I'm only happy when the band is really churning it out.

CHARLIE: Chuck Leavell has a completely different way of playing from the other pianists and keyboard players we've worked with: he has a really intriguing style, when you hear him playing on his own, sitting there doodling. He plays a very weird mixture of southern country and jazz – very interesting. It's a style that could only happen in America, where you get all the mixtures blending together and then coming out quite naturally as something completely different.

RONNIE: Chuck Leavell's role in the band is as a kind of book-keeper, the keeper of the songs. He keeps detailed notes on all the strategies of the songs: how we did it last time and how we did it the time before. He's there as our immediate reference point; if there's any kind of argument about the way in which a song should be played, Chuck can say, "No, it says here, da, da, da" – problem solved. It's always useful to have someone like

Keith: Mick is my wife, but we can't get divorced...

Mick in mid-performance. Charlie: Mick's probably the best entertainer in the world.

*Mick and Keith on
stage, by Anton Corbijn.*

that around. And although there is a click track, Chuck counts in most of the songs that need a count.

MICK: Chuck keeps the book with all the arrangements – which of course no one can ever remember – so when we come to rehearsals he's very helpful in keeping it all together, and he and I also prepare the set list for each show together. He helps a lot with the musical direction, keeping everything in line, otherwise it can get a bit chaotic because no one else is going to keep control of the tempos.

RONNIE: The click track is something that took many years to wean Keith onto. He used to say, "If I hear that tick-tock machine again, I'm going to kill somebody". We had years of that! At first I also thought, "Fucking click, clack", but I soon got used to it. It is vital if you are ever going to use part of a song for a film or in an advert – anything that has to be synched. On stage it's only used for the intro – and in any case Charlie's like a metronome once the song's taken off: he very rarely veers away from that original click – but it is good to have it there. If you start a song off too fast or too slow, then you're screwed for the rest of it, especially when you're in a stadium or you're in a panic situation. Without the click track it can be, "1, 2, 3 and oh no, it's too fast". It's good to be able to take a breath and go, "Click, clack, 3, 4…".

CHARLIE: It's great for us to have Chuck counting us in – we need that – but Keith is not like that at all, he's never played like that. Keith is how he is when he does it, and I'm very much like that as well, so we're liable to be incredibly right or incredibly wrong! We both play by ear, which is the way we learned to play: it's not a counting thing, it's an ear thing.

MICK: When we're putting a show or a set list together, the songs don't determine the theatrics completely, but I do keep in mind that there are some songs which lend themselves to a certain kind of visual treatment; a song which you might not lean towards too much musically but which offers a possibility visually. You have to think about what is going to work in the context of the show. So if a song has a great look to it, and a video that goes with it, and it's different to the others, even though about the song itself you might say, "It doesn't sound that great", you might still use it. However, although there are a few of those, normally the set is not really driven by the theatrics; you make the theatrics work with the tunes. When I do the set lists I have to keep both of those aspects in mind, because if you talk to a musician about a set, they think the only reason that people come is to listen to their guitar-playing.

CHARLIE: My favourite way of hearing our records is either if somebody else plays one really loud, at a party, and you think, "Oh, that's nice" or if a track is played on the radio, and you can hear in context with something else, all jumbled up.

KEITH: I have nothing to do with the selection of songs for a show. There's a singer out there and he has to choose the songs and say, "I want to sing these because of my throat". You might disagree with the order they're in and you might throw in an idea, but in general it seems like he has his own reasons for saying, "I want to sing these songs today" and we wouldn't have a violent disagreement. You can have an argument, but it very rarely happens. It's just sheer logistical common sense – the singer doesn't want to sing it. You don't want to make a guy sing something he doesn't want to sing.

Keith by Pennie Smith.

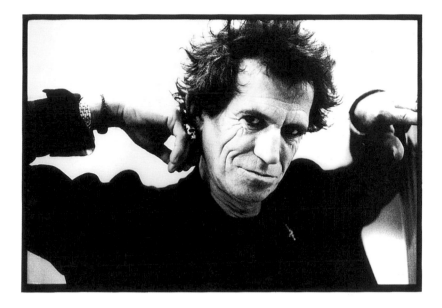

MICK: There have been a few scary times during performances, people running on stage, the occasional loony. It takes you by surprise when you're in the middle of some ballad, really emoting, and some guy comes up, puts his arms around your neck and tries to throw you to the ground.

KEITH: I've seen murders. I've seen dogs come on stage trying to savage people. I've turned round and found a pool of blood where the piano player should be! I've been struck by sharpened pennies. But you can't really do anything about that. It's just a part of the gig.

RONNIE: On one tour I learned how to fly. I tripped and suddenly found myself going headlong with my guitar into some iron scaffolding. Everything went floating by. But I didn't miss a chord...

KEITH: Probably the most frightening incident I had on stage was one I knew nothing about. My guitar touched the microphone stand and my mouth hit the microphone and all I saw was a flash and some smoke. I woke up an hour later in Sacramento General hospital with a doctor saying, 'They either come around or they don't'.

RONNIE: Backstage in the guitar room before the show, Keith and I will go back to our Barbecue Bob method of swapping ideas and riffs, weaving this way and that, which sets us up for the show. We will also go right back to the history of Jamaican music; we have a lot of very good reggae albums, which also contributes to our weaving: the reggae and the old blues. And we play snooker together, which is very important for the head. We always

Scenes from the Voodoo Lounge tour.

Charlie and his drums on the Voodoo Lounge *tour. The kit he played with Alexis Korner was from Ludwig, a kit he still owns. He bought a Gretsch kit while on tour in the US in the mid-60s. He now plays with a Gretsch set-up he has had since he did a record with Ronnie in the 1970s.*

have a frame or two before we go on, and we'll be listening to those records and then go to the guitar room to have a little tinkle on our lovely old Gibsons, which are purely for playing backstage or in the studio; we never use them on stage. We only need to do five or ten minutes of that and we've got the rapport going, which will transfer straight onto the stage.

Sometimes we might work on a solo we haven't played for a while, but which we know we're going to be doing that evening and which we want to brush up, or we'll run through an intro with Chuck. Keith will say, "Is it three times?" and we'll say, "No, it's four". Rather than playing it, we might just hum it through together. There's a lot of good camaraderie in that situation.

When I was in the Faces, we used to write a lot of songs in dressing rooms – songs like 'Stay With Me' and 'Cindy Incidentally'. The difference was that I was the only guitarist in the band, which Rod Stewart reminds me of every time he sees me. He says, "Remember, you were the only guitar player in the Faces. If we ever go touring again, I don't want another guitarist, I just want you to do it".

Keith and I used to spend a lot more time playing in the room together. In the 1970s, we'd always be sitting around – and instead of talking we'd be playing all day long and all night long for the duration of whatever album we were making or whichever tour we were on. We'd come off stage and immediately go

> *One of the things that I think has sustained us – apart from being very good visually – is that we've had these gaps so that when we do go back out on the road, it becomes something of an event.*
>
> Charlie

back to the room, where we could carry on playing and evolving new songs, loads of which still haven't seen the light of day. Keith and I have this song called 'Munich Hilton', which was obviously written in that hotel, and which sums up that kind of era. One day we might take that further on through its paces because there's a really good song in there. All of that work proves useful now. We can dip in and pick little bits out of this huge

Mick:What the audience wants are lots of lights and pizzazz with bangs and whistles.

Charlie:When you are out there in this vast stadium you are physically tiny up on stage, so that's why we started using video screens. Mick is the one who really has to project himself over the footlights.

melting pot of reggae and rock'n'roll or Mozart, everything that's in there, and just take a piece out and apply it to whatever we're doing on stage or whatever approach we're bringing to an album.

CHARLIE: One of the best records we've made in the past few years was the album called *Stripped*. I think that's one of the most interesting records we've done, the best-played record we've made for years. *Stripped* was supposed to be recorded when it was fashionable to do an *MTV Unplugged* session, and then for some reason the record company decided they didn't want to do it, or the money wasn't there or we got cold feet or something – one of the three. Mick might have thought it was a bit old-fashioned, which it was, to do it in 1995. So we thought about how we could do it differently, and the finished article was one of the best things we've done: the version of 'Not Fade Away' is fantastic.

RONNIE: *Stripped* gives a good idea of a typical session. It's a very overlooked album, I think. The video and the album really capture the way we work with Don in the studio and how Darryl interacts with us: it shows how the modern band works.

KEITH: People said that the band in the '90s had more energy than ever before. It was probably more a focus of the energy which had always been there. What had changed was the efficiency and quality of the sound systems and monitoring, so that we could hear much better what we were doing while we were performing, and there was less confusion on stage. It really helps if a band is confident that what they're playing and the idea they have of what they should be sounding like is pretty much what's going out there to the audience. In some ways the Rolling Stones was the same band, the same guys, but it was also a new band. *Steel Wheels* was not a bad getting back together, and *Voodoo Lounge* had been a pretty good follow-on. But with *Bridges To Babylon*, it was a chance to refuel the band, to take some chances and to go into some different areas. I'm amazed by all of it. Something exists between everybody out there and us that strikes a chord. I guess that's music. I can't imagine anything else.

DON WAS

Don Was co-produced the Stones' albums *Voodoo Lounge*, *Stripped* and *Bridges To Babylon* and the new material on *Forty Licks*. He has also worked with Bob Dylan, Roy Orbison, Willie Nelson and Bonnie Raitt (for his work on her *Nick Of Time* he received four Grammy awards) and founded, with David Was, the band Was (Not Was).

The Rolling Stones are Giants. They transcend the boundaries of human skin — their personalities loom larger than the inflatable characters that once graced their live stages. A few years back, we were working in Studio One at Ocean Way Recorders — an enormous room where, thirty years earlier, Sinatra recorded 'It Was A Very Good Year' with an 80-piece orchestra — a space three stories high. Charlie and Mick and Keith were in there alone, discussing football. Although their combined weight is less than 400 lbs, these guys completely filled the largest studio in LA — there was no space for anyone else.

Man... this world is desperate for heroes like the Rolling Stones! These are tough times for our species: evolution is trailing sociology by about 30,000 years. We're still tribal creatures with a deep-seated need for security, stability and community. Instead, we get fired and divorced, priests go to jail, our Presidents get impeached, families scatter and we're digesting more Prozac than vegetables.

But should this world forsake you, you can always come home to the Rolling Stones. They'll never, ever let you down. You are safe leaving your unrealised hopes and dreams in their care. They can walk out on a stage and soothe the souls of 100,000 people — each of whom has their own unique set of troubles. Two hours later they all leave feeling emotionally whole and linked to a global community of millions. Whatever else is happening in the world, you can always count on the Rolling Stones to show up and play the shit out of 'Satisfaction' for you. In these times, they may provide the most solid foundation this life has to offer. Isn't that what heroes do?

I became part of that audience when I was eleven years old. It was June 1964, and the Stones were playing in Detroit at Olympia Stadium, the Red Wings' hockey arena. I took a bus to one of the worst neighbourhoods in town at 3 am to make sure I had a good seat. What were my parents thinking? Today they'd be arrested by social workers. The Stones were only a few dates into their first ever US tour, so they were playing to no more than 200 people, but they were amazing. No one knew who they were, but the rebellious subtext that reinforced the music had a dramatic impact on me. I have been very lucky. I've been able to live out my dreams. And that's due in part to the courage the Stones gave to kids like me by saying, "Don't let anyone stamp you out into some mould. You're not a piece of steel on the assembly line. It's OK to be different – in fact, it's *better* to be different." Since then, I don't believe I have missed a single Stones tour, and I bought every record they released on the day it came out, right up until *Voodoo Lounge*, when I finally got my own advance copy.

It was well over twenty-five years after that gig in Detroit when Mick contacted me and asked me to come and meet the band with an eye towards producing what would become *Voodoo Lounge*. They were auditioning bass players to replace Bill Wyman. I walked in, the Stones were on stage playing their greatest hits and there was nobody else there, except for Pierre and Chuch. It was pretty incredible. I don't think Keith knew that I was coming, who I was or that anyone was even considering hiring a producer. I am certain that he hated the idea. He simply said to me, "I don't need someone to tell me how to play guitar." I replied, "That's true".

I sat down on the sofa with Mick on one side and Keith on the other, and they both spoke constantly at me for fifteen minutes. Constantly. They never once yielded a second of silence to the other. It was like a tennis match – I was trying to nod my head at both of them – until Keith finally said, "Are you sure you want to be the meat in this sandwich?" I thought, "There's no way I'm getting this job, but I've got a good story to tell my children..."

After ten years working with them, I have a better insight into the Stones' sibling rivalry. At one point I had thought that it was my responsibility to control it, and my childish ego thought I might even have some effect on it. But I realised that it is the fuel that keeps the Stones going. I once said to Keith, "If you guys didn't bicker, if there wasn't a little tension there, if everyone was full of integrity and perfect all the time, you'd be about as exciting as REO Speedwagon". I thought to myself, "That's going too far, man" and I held my breath... Keith laughed and didn't stab me. He didn't need me to point this out to him – I'm sure that he and Mick reached the same conclusion thirty years ago.

The first time I played bass with them was while they were writing B-sides for *Voodoo Lounge*. Darryl Jones had gone home, so I picked up a bass and we cut some tracks. My whole perspective on the band was different after that day. What I had never picked up listening to their records or watching their shows was how much fun they have and how relaxed and jocular the interplay is. They might be playing the hardest rock'n'roll you've ever heard in your life, but if you look at Charlie, he's enthroned like Art Blakey, with the sticks down at his waist. Stand beside his kit and it sounds as if he's playing very lightly. Walk five feet in front of the drums and you can feel how powerful the sound is.

As a bass player, I have a theory about playing with Charlie that I call the "fruit bowl" theory. Imagine a big, old vertical line that represents what a drum machine, or a mathematician or, say, a very stiff white man would define as the exact beat. When computers are badly programmed, the drums play exactly on this line and all the dancers sit down. Drummers who really swing — guys like Charlie, Al Jackson, Elvin Jones, Benny Benjamin, Jim Keltner, — are human beings, and, as such, experience a slight disparity, consisting of a few milliseconds, between where each limb perceives the aforementioned vertical line to be. That disparity defines each individual drummer's unique "feel". Now, put a mark ahead of the line — that is where Charlie feels the hi-hat. Then, make another mark slightly behind that line, which is where the bass drum lives. And just behind that, is the sublime spot where he hits the snare drum. If you drew a fruit bowl and allowed these dots to define the width of the bowl, you'd find a nice, wide beautiful piece of funky kitchenware. If, as a bass player, you think of yourself as a guy holding an apple, you can lob your bass part — your "apple" — into this huge fruit bowl that Charlie has created. There is such a deep pocket you can't miss. If the fruit bowl is too wide, there would be no groove, but Charlie swings like a motherfucker. On the other hand, playing with a drum machine would be like trying to lob the apple into a champagne glass — which, for those of you who've never tried it, becomes a total bore after about thirty seconds.

There is also huge generosity in their playing. They really listen to each other and they react immediately. No one hogs the space. On another occasion I was playing bass on 'Already Over Me' from *Bridges To Babylon*. Charlie usually played "boom...boom boom" on the bass drum, but sometimes he would just play "boom...boom", and the bass would stand out really awkwardly. I was trying to work out what the pattern was, trying to understand Charlie's sensibility. I finally figured it out at the end of the second day. Charlie was listening to the singer. I took my eyes off his bass drum, listened to Mick, and I locked with Charlie. Any way that Mick phrased the song, Charlie would just answer him conversationally. I had been sitting there watching his bass drum foot when I should have been listening to the singer. It was a wonderful lesson.

Keith is the best guitar player I know of. He doesn't try to dazzle you with technique. He knows that something rooted in honest feeling is ultimately more valuable and more meaningful than bowling you over with flash. He interacts primarily with Charlie's hi-hat and, though he probably won't admit it, Mick's vocal and harp. And he feeds the others with blocks to build on. Keith feeds Darryl, Ronnie and Charlie — he gives something to all of them. To use a baseball analogy, every note Keith plays is like a ball lobbed right into your glove. All you have to do is put your glove out there and respond; you've got to be clumsy not to catch what he throws you.

Playing with Keith one night dramatically altered my life. Keith doesn't write songs by sitting alone with a sequencer; he likes to work live in the studio so he can explore the song's different corners and hidden passageways. We were playing 'How Can I Stop', repeating the final four chords over and over like a mantra. I knew there was this ideal in music where you lose all self-consciousness and play in the moment, but I'd never experienced it. I was playing a Wurlitzer piano; Keith was playing an electric guitar on the other side of the room. It was a musical conversation, utterly effortless, like transcendental meditation. I said to myself, "This is what I've been searching for. I've just never played with a master musician before." After we finished I went into the control room and asked them to play some of it back, imagining it was about five minutes. The engineers said, "Which reel?" — we'd been playing for over an hour.

Mick Jagger is probably one of the most famous people in the world. He is also incredibly sane and well-adjusted to dealing with celebrity. He gets out and experiences life — not just exclusive, hip clubs. I'm talking about shopping malls and cineplexes. In order to move about like that, he has learned to contain and conceal his huge, charismatic persona. So, when Mick, the shopper, arrives at the studio it takes a little while for him to turn in to Mick Jagger, the character. After a couple of takes he'll get his white shirt off, strip down to his tanktop: his whole musculature changes and his lips get bigger; suddenly he looks forty years younger. It is so intense that I feel like I'm gawking at him the way a tourist would and I get so embarrassed that I can't even look. He'll record four or five passes where he is so deeply inside the character that we have a wealth of material to choose from.

During the *Bridges To Babylon* tour I ran the distance from one wing of the stage to the other and was out of breath after going back and forth once. Mick subsequently ran the same distance dozens of times — singing in tune and performing for two hours. The guy is superhuman. It is both a freaky athletic phenomenon and a malfeasance of justice — he can eat whatever he wants, perform like that and, to top it off, he gets all the models.

I was a big fan of Ronnie's solo records before he even joined the Stones. What I hadn't realised was that he not only plays with great taste but he is utterly fearless about pursuing a creative spark. He would risk making a glaring mistake to produce something brilliant and totally original. I was stunned by his versatility and his innate musicality. He is such a valuable utilitarian player, and there is a profound intuitive lock between him and Keith.

Getting sober and staying that way right before an album and a tour took real balls. Musically, the results are staggering: the Stones are a guitar band once again, better than they've ever been. And Ronnie's musicality has inspired Keith to raise the stakes. In what is primarily a hopeless world, it's beautiful to see a sweet soul like Ronnie — who doesn't have a mean or vengeful bone in his body — hit a grand slam in the 10th inning and win the game.

There's a point in each session with the Rolling Stones where what we're striving for appears to be elusive. Then — just when you least expect it — the hand of God reveals itself and these four disparate personalities seamlessly merge into something awesome. To be sitting in the middle of that room when lightning strikes is the most exhilarating feeling I've ever experienced.

I don't particularly want to stop playing. I have this fear of stopping and becoming old. I'm sure we'll always do a week's residency in Bognor Regis or somewhere.

Charlie Watts

11

ACQUIRING THE PATINA

MICK: For the tour that was going to follow *Voodoo Lounge*, we got to a point where we still hadn't settled on any kind of theme, and I was screaming and banging my head trying to find one. I had been going on about bridges for a while – I have always been obsessed with bridges – and I was particularly interested in the beautiful bridges that Santiago Calatrava was building in Seville and elsewhere. When we were designing the staging for the *Voodoo Lounge* tour I had said to Mark Fisher, "I want to have this bridge; we'll have the stage there and then we can have a bridge to here, here and here". Mark just said, "Oh, what a useless idea", and I'd said, "No, I really like Calatrava. His bridges are great – you should go and look at them".

So when this new tour came round, and we found ourselves short of an idea, that was when Mark threw my own idea back at me. He said, "OK. If you give me one million dollars now, I can make a bridge that will emerge from the stage and land on the B-stage". I just said, "You've got it, but it's got to be ready by September 1st". Of course, two weeks before the due date, I got the phone call, which part of me had been expecting, saying "The bridge won't be ready!" Can you imagine? The structure didn't work because it had a similar problem to the Millennium Bridge in London: it wouldn't hold up without moving about. People were very worried that the audience underneath the bridge would get hurt if the bridge collapsed when we walked on it and there were all these instructions like "Only one person at a time" and "Don't run too fast, Mick". The band was quite nervous about going on it at all, but, in the end, after we'd done it fifty times on the tour, there we all were running along and banging across the bridge.

We didn't have a title for the tour until we'd built the model and I asked Tom Stoppard to come and look at it and to give his opinion as somebody from outside the rock world. It's funny how people can come in from other parts of theatre, take a look at something that you've been looking at for weeks and go, "You shouldn't have that thing in there". Tom started to talk about Babylon and came up with a number of incredibly long titles. I shortened one and ended up with the *Bridges To Babylon* title for the tour and the album.

I do try not to overwhelm the performance with the staging, but you never know where that boundary is because you're not watching the show. I'm not paying to come in the show; I'm on the other end of it. So I try to think of the punters and go, "OK, this guy's paid to come to see this. What is he going to want?"

KEITH: For the recording of *Bridges to Babylon*, Mick and I agreed that instead of us coming together, he would cut some tracks his way and I'd cut some tracks my way. We hadn't tried that before; I wanted to see how Mick would take that idea and he took it a lot further than I expected. I had no idea that Mick thought that meant he had a licence to have a different producer for every song. Which was not quite what I had in mind. There seemed to be producers coming and going all the time. Meanwhile I was just working with Don Was. It was an interesting experiment and I like the album – you can sense the diversity and the division – but it did create a bit of a rickety bridge between us. But there's always a point in each album where we have a bridge to cross.

CHARLIE: Jim Keltner took part in the sessions for *Bridges To Babylon*. Jim is a great drummer, but with us he usually plays percussion, doing something quite outrageous but very good. We would never dream of having Jim sitting in the middle bashing away – he sits on the edge, feeding in ideas. During those sessions I also worked with Jim on a project of our own, which was a lot of fun. In that situation Jim was playing endless gadgets and loops, which he is fantastically clever at, while I played the straight rhythm. I also worked on a soundtrack for a Francis Ford Coppola movie, *The Rainmaker*, which was based on the John Grisham novel. It was set in the southern States and we put together this fantastic track with Don Was on bass, Billy Preston and Taj Mahal and a really good Brazilian percussionist and slide guitar player. Taj is a fabulous player – like a one-man band really – and Billy was producing a great Booker T. sound, and what we produced felt like the right music for the deep south; unfortunately the track didn't get used in the movie. They used some string arrangement instead.

RONNIE: On *Bridges To Babylon* we had three studios. Keith had one going, Mick had another lot of producers, like the Dust Brothers, coming into another studio. So I ended up opening one up down the corridor for my own stuff, where Charlie and I worked on some cuts while the other two were getting on with their ideas. Luckily, following *Bridges To Babylon* the shield was dropped again and Mick and Keith got together like they always should be, began writing like they used to and working like a band.

> *On the last few albums it has been great having Mick and Keith back to the sandpit days, old buddies again, although there will always be a couple of moments on tour, where if looks could kill...*
>
> *Ronnie*

CHARLIE: Mick and Keith never really argue. What happens is that other people create these things. A lot of the times it's a question of too many cooks, and that's the reason these rumours happen. The only real disagreements they had during the recording of *Bridges To Bablyon* – and I do mean honest disagreements – was because of the way the different producers we asked to get involved wanted to make records; all the newer, younger producers, because Keith and I have never made records like that. The way that record was made, you'd sit down, Keith would play a song, you'd wait until you got the right tempo and then you'd play it three or four times. These tracks are made late at night with nobody around. I'd be in there playing the drums and the producers would tape me and then do whatever they liked to it. In fact, I enjoyed doing it because I had never worked like that before. But although I found it really interesting, I knew that I would hate to make records like that on a permanent basis, because then it becomes a producer's game – it's got nothing to do with the musicians at all. So if the producers don't like the feel of what you've played, they'll just blank it out, sample a bit off somebody else and drop in it instead. Which ends up being more fun for them than it is for me. I think that the Dust Brothers did very well. John King and Mike Simpson are very nice guys, and I think they did a good job on the songs we gave to them, as did Danny Saber. But it was all very alien to the way that I normally work. That was really the only contention, because of the different ways that Keith and Mick like to work.

KEITH: *Bridges To Babylon* is another album that has one of my time bombs tucked on the end: 'How Can I Stop', which I will let re-surface in due course. It's got Wayne Shorter playing on it, for Christ's sake. Some jazz musicians look upon what I do as "dudey" music, and I'll say to them, "That's up to you, guys", because I really hate jazz snobbery: "Excuse me, if you play music, you want people to listen to it, right? There's no point playing into a vacuum".

RONNIE: On the last few albums it has been great having Mick and Keith back to the sandpit days, old buddies again, although there will always be a couple of moments on tour, where if looks could kill… It could be somebody coming in at the wrong moment, or Mick forgetting the arrangement and suddenly going to the middle eight, when you can see Keith mouthing, "What the hell is he doing?" But those temporary explosions are all part of what keeps the band so vibrant.

CHARLIE: There is a big difference between the songwriters and players in any band. Usually the songwriters create the music and the other musicians are there to interpret it and to make it work. It's the same with the Stones, except that in this band the musicians have an awful lot of say, and we also have Keith, who has a foot in both camps: he's very proud of being a songwriter and of being able to play the guitar. I hear the songs totally differently to Mick and Keith because I don't have to go through any of the problems involved in writing a bloody song – I think it's a horrendous thing to have to do.

KEITH: When we started compiling the selection for *Forty Licks*, part of me felt, "These tracks have been released so many times, who'd want to buy them again?", but I guess people must have worn their other copies out. The important thing about that album is that there are four new songs on it. Whether or not anyone likes them is up to them.

RONNIE: We recorded a lot of new material in Paris in 2002, the sessions which produced 'Don't Stop' and the other three new tracks on *Forty Licks*, including 'Stealing My Heart', which is a really good blended effort by Mick and Keith. We came away with another 24 songs. We had the basis for a while for a new album, but we didn't have time before we got caught up in the *Forty Licks* tour to do the overdubs and polish the songs off.

Keith by Chris Wahl.

(opposite) Bassist David Green lived next door to Charlie; they have known each other since they were three years old, and learnt to play music together. David still works with Charlie in his jazz band.

Things were ticking over quite nicely during those sessions. With the rift between Mick and Keith having healed up, I was quite happy that they were getting on and that the songs were flowing. I could sit back and concentrate on playing my best. Mick will pull me to one side and say, "I want you to do a nice melodic part here", and he will even hum it for me, so that I can get a sense of what he has in mind. In fact he's done that ever since I've known him, and I will do the same for him vocally – "Why don't you do this?", which he can either use or not.

In the mid-80s I would see these huge holes in the albums because Mick and Keith's songwriting was not functioning, and if I suggested one of my songs, nine times out of ten they would be receptive. I'd soon know if they weren't receptive – whenever they told me to piss off!

When we were in the studios in Paris Mick and Keith would say, out of the blue, "All right, let's have one of Ronnie Wood's songs". They'd ask me, "Have you got one?". I'd say "Yeah". They'd say, "How does it go?" – bang, like this. There's a good few sitting there on the back burner.

'Don't Stop' is a classic Mick song. I could see that Mick had designed it to come across well in large venues, a 'Start Me Up'-style crowd song, with a simple kind of message and a straightforward structure. Because Mick is playing guitar, there isn't so much room for Keith, but he did manage to find a way of stabbing away at it, so that he was semi-happy with the result. I took on the stronger guitar part, because I was covering for Keith and also delivering what Mick was expecting from the way he had written the song: he wanted a trademark Woody guitar solo.

'Losing My Touch', on the other hand, was a Keith song, and he immediately had a picture in his mind of what I could play: "Ronnie, please play a pedal steel line. Imagine you're playing pedal steel on it".

Mick (above) and Ronnie (opposite) portrayed in action by Fernando Aceves.

CHARLIE: Mick and Keith simply have different ways of working, ways that they are comfortable with. For the new songs on *Forty Licks* I had spent time in the studio with Mick before we went over to Paris, helping him prepare demos of his songs. Mick likes to have the songs well worked out in advance. Keith is much more into leaving some room to see what happens when we all get into the recording studio.

Mick does see and hear exactly what he wants and that vision is what he is striving to get. He is more interested in the finished product, which is quite nice because you can see the end point and you become focused on that; it's much more cut and dried. But the other way of working is just as nice. Keith is much looser about things. He is quite happy for something to sit around for years, to marinate, although he does have some tapes with fragments and ideas that he has recorded on his own or with Blondie Chaplin, which are usually fantastic, magical little moments. Keith is very easy to play with – he's the *easiest* person in the world to play with.

Another difference between the two of them is that I don't think Keith looks on Ronnie as somebody who is coming in to put a guitar solo on his record, whereas Mick does. Keith sees it as Ronnie joining in on this venture of making a song together. Both approaches mean that you end up with a track that has a solo guitar on it, so both methods work, but they represent very different ways of working.

The magic of the band is when Mick and Keith are doing it together. What would be wonderful is if they ever sat down together and started writing together from scratch. It may be that they don't necessarily need to do that from the off, but it would be great to go back to the days of Keith sitting on the end of a bed with his guitar and a cassette recorder, making songs up with Mick, with me playing brushes on a book…

MICK: 'Don't Stop' is probably not as good a song as something like 'Satisfaction', but as long as it fits in the show it works. What is interesting is that unlike those songs from the 1960s, it will never, in our lifetime, get played as much and acquire the patina of age. But a lot of the songs that we play live were not important songs when they came out.

On the *Forty Licks* tour, when we were preparing the set list for a show in Yokohama, Chuck Leavell suggested we play 'Loving Cup', the ballad from *Exile On Main Street*. I didn't want to play the tune and I said, "Chuck, this is going to die a death in Yokohama. I can't even remember the bloody song, and no one likes it. I've done it loads of times in America, it doesn't go down that well,

> *Ronnie got it together, like I did after my ten years in my personal laboratory. It is all part of growing up. We promise that once we get mature, we'll go far…*
>
> *Keith*

Mick with Lisa Fischer.

Lenny Kravitz between Keith and Ronnie.

it's a very difficult song to sing, and I'm fed up with it!" Chuck went, "Stick in the mud!" so I gave in and put it in the set-list. Lo and behold, we went out, started the song and they all began applauding... Which just proves how, over time, some of these songs acquire a certain existence, or value, that they never had when they first came out. People will say, "What a wonderful song that was", when it was virtually ignored at the time it was released. And a tune like 'Don't Stop' might – or might not – one day acquire the same patina. What is certain is that if you don't play a song on stage, it will never have a chance to be anything.

KEITH: I've said that the strength of the Stones is that we just do what we do and that we shouldn't go and check out what somebody else is listening to and on the basis of that formulate what we're going to write. I often have considerable difficulty with Mick on that angle. Sometimes he's right, sometimes he's wrong. I can live without 'Undercover Of The Night' or 'Emotional Rescue'. I can probably live without 'Don't Stop', although I enjoyed playing it – it's a pretty little thing and you can sizzle it off, but there's not much substance to it. That's where Mick and I will differ, but at the same time many things we don't disagree about, and when we do things together that are right, it's more than worth its weight in gold.

RONNIE: I generally stayed out of the selection process for *Forty Licks* because a lot of the tracks were from before my time. I think the real root of the Stones lies in that period of *Beggars Banquet*, *Sticky Fingers* and *Exile On Main Street*, which is why I was really pleased to be playing songs like 'Stray Cat Blues' and 'Can't Hear Me Knocking' on the *Forty Licks* tour. When it came to choosing the tracks for the half of the album that I *had* been involved with, I thought, "I won't complicate the issue", though I did ring up Mick once and say "Have you forgotten 'Dance'?" He said, "Let's just run with the selection like it is; it's enough of a headache already and we've got a pretty good cross-section. Shall we just go with it?" I said, "Yeah, all right, but don't forget I said that" – and Mick went, "Yeah, we'll put it on the next one!" When we were rehearsing for *Forty Licks*, there were songs like 'Can't You Hear Me Knocking', which the band had never been able to make work, so it was quite a surprise when I suggested we try it and they said, "Do you really want to do that?" I said, "Of course" – it was one of my favourite songs – "Let's just do it" and Mick was saying, "Well, OK, but I'm not sure this is going to hold up". He had a point: it had never worked in the past. Keith said they tried it once in Scotland and it had ground to a painful halt. He said it was one of the most embarrassing moments they had ever had.

CHARLIE: A lot of the work preparing for a tour is brought upon ourselves, particularly by me and Mick, and especially by Mick: there are so many things that need to be addressed before we go on the road. The working surface, what it looks like, the programme, the T-shirts. They all take a lot of time to get right and the seven weeks of rehearsing are part of doing that, physically getting yourself there again after not working for a while. I had just come off a jazz tour, but that was a different kind of strain, just as intense but not the same wear and tear on your body. Jazz musicians would die if they did two hours straight, you don't do that in a club, and because that was my band, it could be done at my tempo, whereas the Stones is done at everybody's tempo.

MICK: There was no theme for the *Forty Licks* tour. We had three different sizes of stage, but no unifying concept. I really could not find an overriding theme for the three shows apart from the fact it was three shows by the Rolling Stones! So we created the artwork with the three tongues and worked with that, and in the end I just said, "I really like the stage and the theme is original".

As with the other tours it was a group design experience, with myself, Charlie, Mark Fisher, the stage designer, and Patrick Woodroffe, who's the lighting designer. We talk our way through everything, with a certain amount of pulling and pushing and screaming. We don't really have that many rows, but I am always worried that there is not enough content. I had a problem where there wasn't enough video content. We were talking to some people in the business and I got a reply saying, "You should talk to the guy who did Aerosmith's tour when they had a content crisis", which basically means you haven't got enough video. It's always much better to have a lot of video, as long as it's not

Chuch Magee, backline technician, who died during rehearsal for the Forty Licks *tour.*

Ronnie: He had a massive heart attack and died on his flight case, with all of his tools, amongst all of his friends with his favourite band. We'd just done a wicked version of 'Stray Cat Blues' and he went with a smile on his face.

(overleaf left) Clockwise from top left: Mick; Lisa Fischer and Darryl Jones; the horn section, from left to right Tim Ries (sax), Kent Smith (trumpet) and Michael Davis (trombone); Blondie Chaplin; Keith; Bobby Keys.

(overleaf right) Clockwise from top left: Bernard Fowler; Ronnie; Lisa; Charlie; Chuck Leavell; Darryl Jones.

305

prohibitively expensive, because then you can just cut it back really hard at the last minute rather than having to come up with new stuff.

CHARLIE: It's always the same when you're developing a show: you'll have the first leisurely meetings and come up with a really interesting idea, which then slowly evolves, but there's also usually one big disaster. The problem is showing people ideas while you're in the middle of developing them, while they're still not right, which means you have to wait until they're nearly finished. So sometimes, if somebody hasn't shared the process of getting there, they take one look at it and have no idea what it's meant to be, although, on the other hand, that is great because, like the audience they see it without preconceptions.

On the *Forty Licks* show, it was the first Jeff Koons backdrop, which was only ever meant to be a temporary item while we waited for the real thing, but when we tested the staging the first time it just didn't work. It was the same on the *Urban Jungle* tour: we started the tour off in a football stadium in Rotterdam, and at the dress rehearsal we glanced round and Mick and I looked at each other as if to say, "Bloody awful…" Keith, who is generally quite happy with a workable and flat stage – that's what he really wants – is very good at protecting the band from making a mistake in what is going on behind us or above us. When he saw the temporary Jeff Koons backdrop, he was adamant that it shouldn't go up, but unfortunately it had to go up because we had nothing else to use. There was an image of some corn, some maize, in the artwork and he got a bee in his bonnet about the fact that he objected to us being associated with corn… I kept telling Keith that it was only until Jeff Koons got his other backdrop together – but if Keith hadn't pushed we would probably have still been waiting for it. He got so mad that people panicked and that certainly speeded up getting the proper backdrop in place. If Keith has a legitimate criticism of something, it won't go there – that's how he sees it – and he'll have very good reasons why that is so.

KEITH: When I saw the first version of the backdrop, I went ballistic. There was an image of Mick's mouth with a lot of corn spewing out of it. I studied advertising at art school. What were people going to say when they saw that juxtaposition: the Stones are a load of old corn. It was already in the works and the thing took weeks to change. So I simply wanted to know how it had slipped by. It was only when I pointed it out that people said, "Yeah that's horrible".

> *In a way I wish we could have a Peter Hall character, someone who only has to think about the conceptual aspect of the show. It would be a great role, but I've never found anybody to do it.*
>
> *Mick*

CHARLIE: The stage for *Forty Licks* was very beautiful, like a sleeker version of the one we had for *Steel Wheels*, which was fantastic to look at. The problem with the *Forty Licks* tour was that it was very hard to imagine what we could do – we spent a lot of time in Mick's apartment going over and over it. Fortunately technology moves on, which usually gives you a starting point, just as long as you can associate the technology with a particular song, otherwise it remains simply a technical feat. It's like the circus: you have to have an immediate connection with an audience. I am a great one for being too clever…

*Mick, and, opposite,
Keith, by Chris Wahl.*

But whatever you do has to be immediately obvious to everybody in the venue. It can't only work for eight blokes down the front. We settled on a very stripped-down stage apart from the huge screen overhead, which was all very nice, but we had to decide what was going to be shown on this bloody great big screen. It's an idea I would like to develop more. If you use the screen as a stage set, it could create a totally different environment for each song. It could become a ballroom in Versailles or a black screen with doors and windows opening for another mood.

RONNIE: The *Forty Licks* stage was great because it was like carrying a theatre with you up on the screens; great for atmosphere. The images on the screens could take you to your front room or to an amphitheatre; you could be in the middle of the street with all the traffic or be serene in the middle of green fields… They could take you anywhere.

KEITH: The way the tour panned out, it became what we called the *Fruit Of The Loom* tour – small, medium and large – with shows in clubs, arenas and stadiums. It was essentially one show that came in three different disguises, and if the three shows hooked together in any one town, then we'd delivered one great show.

MICK: For the *Forty Licks* set of shows, pacing what happened was a little easier because I was able to figure that if we were going to play these big shows, we would only play quite well-known songs and not go too far off the deep end. In the small theatres we could do more or less what we wanted, and in the arenas we could put together a combination of the two. What tends to happen if you just play in arenas is that you get too locked into one set list, which becomes automatic and difficult to change, and is very constricting.

KEITH: The small shows make it possible to do a tour and keep it interesting and alive, because you are able to try a new idea or a new song out. If it really works, you can bump it up to the medium show, and if it really, really works, then you bump it up to large. We did rehearse a lot of songs for *Forty Licks* and I was always pushing Mick to use them: "Why did we rehearse all these songs, Mick, if you're not going to sing them on the road?" Mick's general inclination is to stick on the safe side of what he knows, whereas I usually like to take a few more chances, and so the small gigs give us the opportunity to say to him, "Go on, throw it out to the wind".

MICK: I did some work with a voice coach, Don Lawrence, for the tour. It was a more scientific way of preparing for the show because you really do need a proper warm-up routine for your voice, in the same way that you need one for your body. And as well as the warm-up element, I wanted to be able to sing for a two-hour-plus show without breaking down – which is very hard to do – and to give myself some extra back-up so that I didn't start getting bad throats and miss shows. The problem is that when you get a really bad cold it can completely throw you. You can do the show, but you're always on the edge – a nightmare really. On the *Bridges To Babylon* tour I had missed a few shows,

James, Elizabeth, Jerry, Georgia May, Mick and Gabriel Jagger by Mario Testino, 2000.

and that was nearly always to do with a cold, so I wanted to avoid that on *Forty Licks*.

I also did some dance work with Stephen Galloway, a ballet dancer from the Frankfurt Ballet, who also does choreography, but not the kind used in rock and pop, which is much more to do with carefully worked out moves, the kind of routine that Michael and Janet Jackson were putting together in the 1980s. I enjoyed working with Steve because he was a different kind of dancer – much more freestyle. His job was to teach me some of the moves that he liked, but also to pick out moves that I did which he liked, which was useful because I can't remember the moves. If you're not a trained dancer, it's like not being a trained musician or a trained singer; you can't remember what you do that's good. Steve could tell me, and remember, what was really good, what not to do, and help me avoid becoming repetitious. I came away with a much larger movement vocabulary.

KEITH: Before the *Forty Licks* tour, Ronnie really straightened himself out. Right up until the beginning of 2002, Ronnie was still living on road time from the *Bridges To Babylon* tour: up at four in the afternoon and lying down at ten in the morning. In other words, he hadn't got off the road since the end of *Bridges To Babylon* even though he was back at home. The rest of us had made a conscious attempt to say to ourselves, "I'm going to be at home, and I'm going to get up with the kids", which is not easy to do, believe me, but it's not cold turkey either.

The amazing thing was that Ronnie actually did it. He had incredible stamina and tolerance, because most people would think, "Oh my God, Ronnie's going to stop doing all that stuff, but he's going to be the most boring person". And the great thing is that after he got straightened out he was totally the same guy, except that he concentrated much better. He was just as funny, just as loony, but he looked in your eyes when you spoke to him, and when we were playing together, he was so much more imaginative. He got it together, like I did after my ten years in my personal laboratory. It is all part of growing up. We promise that once we get mature, we'll go far...

CHARLIE: Ronnie started playing really well once he was straight, because he used to be silly before: his performance would get in the way of his playing. That either proves how badly Ronnie played when he wasn't straight, or just how good he is when he is straight, the latter, I think. He would still clown around, but he did it in the right places, so he could concentrate on his playing. Ronnie's problem is that he is not very good at concentrating on anything, because most things come so easily to him. He was one of those people who didn't bother concentrating because he knew he was able to do whatever was necessary, but one of the things about being in a band like this and playing every other night of the week is that you do have to do it all again tomorrow night and again the night after. That is "touring", which is far more tiring than actually playing.

RONNIE: It was a new era for me, an amazing period – not doing a bottle-and-a-half of vodka a day – even though it was very hard! There were times when I really would have liked a drink, but the feeling soon passed. And the support of my family was vital.

MICK: The kids make you very grounded; they are just fun to have around. They always laugh, so when you get bored, if you have four children around, there's always something. I didn't spend as much time with my older children as I should have done. I think that's

Leah, Jesse, Ronnie, Jo, Jamie and Tyrone Wood at Leah's 21st birthday party, 15th May 2000.

Alexandra and Theodora Richards.

Keith with Marianne Faithfull and his son Marlon.

Keith dances with his daughter Angela at her wedding.

just a function of age. We were much wilder and madder than we are now and I think it was too much to have children around when we were that crazy.

RONNIE: My earliest memory of Leah on the road was when she came up to me on stage during 'Honky Tonk Woman' when she was about two, dressed in a ballet tutu. You get the whole thing from your kids. Ty said to me one night, "Nice playing, Dad" and I said, "Ty, I didn't even bribe you!"

KEITH: There's a certain period of adjustment required between the last show of a tour finishing and suddenly finding yourself back home, where there's no motorcycle escort and you still forget that the red lights mean "Stop". Usually I don't go straight back home, but take off by myself or with the family, maybe to Jamaica for a month or so, where I can kick back. At the end of the *Bridges To Babylon* tour, for example, I made a conscious effort to be back at home, and instead of getting up at three or four in the afternoon, I'd get up at seven in the morning and drive the kids to school, readjusting my schedule. Family's family, and it's good just to be in the same time synch. When you're living at home, especially with three women, you'd better snap to.

Charlie's daughter Serafina with her daughter Charlotte.

CHARLIE: My wife and daughter may come out on tour, but Shirley's always had other things outside of this band. She's a great fan of the Stones, though. I'm not; it's what I do. Mick and Keith and Ronnie are my friends and the band is a very good one, but that's it. But Shirley actually plays our records. I don't.

KEITH: You can travel and move and still keep a family together. Otherwise there wouldn't have been gypsies or nomads. Sometimes there are gaps, but I don't know if anybody's

better off from having their dad come home at exactly six o'clock every evening and disappear again at seven the next morning. I don't think a constant hands-on thing with families is necessary, as long as you know where the heart lies. They can always find me and I can always find them; everybody's got enough confidence to be able to deal with that. Families are the first importance, but then I've got this other family which is *far* harder to bring up, called the Rolling Stones...

Mick's son Lucas.

SHERYL CROW

Sheryl Crow, after a successful career as a backing vocalist, notably with Michael Jackson, released her debut album *Tuesday Night Music Club* in 1994, followed by *Sheryl Crow*, *The Globe Sessions*, *Sheryl Crow And Friends Live At Central Park* and *C'mon C'mon*, an album which paid tribute to the rock'n'roll of the 1970s. She supported the Rolling Stones on both the *Bridges To Babylon* and *Forty Licks* tours.

PART ONE

It is spring of 1979 and I have just gotten my driver's license. Disco is still ruling the airwaves and in my small town of Kennett, Missouri, rock'n'roll is where it's at. Lynyrd Skynyrd, Allman Brothers, southern rock in general is the soundtrack to our escapades but in the middle of it all is the Rolling Stones with their song 'Miss You'. The song that everytime it's played, everyone in the car starts grooving and feeling his or her young sexuality.

PART TWO

I grew up in the rural outback of southern Missouri (or Missourah, as we say) among cotton fields and dusty back roads. The mighty Mississippi, in all its mythical glory, winds down toward New Orleans just twelve miles from home. The legend of bluesmen and the lore of southern strife is still a part of the consciousness of those parts and in the music of these country and blues singers, we have always found our identity.

For a young girl itching to get out into the world and experience all it has to offer, the images painted in songs like 'Miss You' and 'Brown Sugar', as well as

'Gimme Shelter' and 'Street Fighting Man', were romantic, threatening, evocative, and alluring. My afternoons were spent pouring over the pages of *Rolling Stone* and *Creem* magazines at Blakemore Drugstore, imaging what it must be like to know the larger-than-life heroes in these mythical black and white photos, or better yet, what it would be like to be one of them.

The radio stations in my small town played mostly country music... real country. Willie, Waylon, Johnny, Patsy, Loretta, the Carters, and Jimmy Rogers, to name a few. I never "cottoned" much to that style of music, but I sure understood it and it was definitely a huge influence on the music I would later on write. It was the stations in Memphis and Chicago that had the great Sunday night programmes, like *King Biscuits Flower Hour* and album rock programming, that brought the Stones to life for me. It would be much later that I would realise the importance of the Stones influence in tying country music to rock music for me as a writer and lover of rock'n'roll.

PART THREE

Let's cut to 1995. I am in Hamburg, Germany, touring my first record, which is just beginning to receive notice. It is 4:30 in the morning and the phone rings in my very inexpensive hotel room. The person on the other end of the phone says he is Mick Jagger. I, of course, hang up only to be awoken again by this mystery caller still claiming to be Mick Jagger. He is asking me if I'd be interested in performing with the Rolling Stones on a pay-per-view Thanksgiving weekend in Miami in front of 65,000 fans. He asks me if there is anything I'd like to sing and I say, "Well, how about something uptempo that rocks." His reply is, "How about 'Wild Horses'. That's a nice song." Nice song, indeed, is my thought. The next thing I know, I am on a private plane getting ready to land in Miami where I will be met and have Thanksgiving dinner with the Rolling Stones (or the Rolling Stones Group, as Bobby Keys refers to them). I meet the lads and Keith says to me, "So you're going to sing 'Live With Me', huh. Bold choice, little sister!" I have been "little sister" ever since.

I spend the entire day of rehearsal, which consists of one run-through and a lot of hanging out, as well as a huge Rolling Stones style Thanksgiving feast where I get to absorb some of the wily Ronnie Wood energy and the stoic, classiness of Charlie Watts along with family and crew members. It isn't until the next day that the nerves heavily kick in to the point that I am throwing up and shaking. Even at gig time, I am still losing whatever food I had enjoyed the day before. As I am walking up to the stage to sing, I am clearly still wracked with nerves and it is at which point I am handed the mike to face not only 65,000 people in the stadium and millions on pay-per-view but also Mick Jagger, that Bobby Keys offers me a swig from his very large personal bottle of tequila. Within moments I am on stage being dragged from one end to the other with the man I have dreamed of meeting, as well as being, my whole life. I know my lips are moving and sound is coming out and that I am, in fact, holding his hand and moving around this giant stage but it is my mind that has gone back to that little drug store and the black and white pictures of the Rolling Stones in all of their debauchery and their glory. I am that 14-year-old girl sitting on my bed scouring the album artwork on *Sticky Fingers*. I am that 17-year-old imagining Mick and Keith standing on a street corner in romantic New York City and saying, "what's a matter withchoo boy!" In that moment, in Joe Robbie Stadium, there is no one in the world but me and Mick, Keith, Ronnie, and Charlie. The question I'd wondered so many years before of what would it be like to be one of the Rolling Stones... well, I will never know the answer but I got to step into that world and look around a little... and there is no place like it.

PART FOUR

I have since had the great fortune of being invited into the world of the Rolling Stones on many different occasions. It matters not whether it is opening up for the Greatest Rock Band to ever live or to imply "sit in" with them in a club, it is always a good ol' fashioned schooling for someone who longs to be great and to have longevity... the kind that they enjoy. Every tour I have done with the Stones as an opening act has been different but always exciting. I will never know what it is like to be the kind of rock star the Stones are. They simply wrote the book and the rest of us are imitators. My generation cannot have the kind of following that rockstars from the early era of rock'n'roll enjoy because they wrote the soundtrack to our lives and the careers of today are much more fleeting, for many reasons. Stepping into the backstage area of, say the *Bridges To Babylon* tour, gives one a glimpse into the extravagance of a real rock show tour. Expense is not spared to provide comfort and inspiration for the band. I love the memory of first entering the inner sanctum of Ronnie and Keith, with the snooker table, red wine, Muddy Waters blasting on the stereo, and random vintage guitars for getting inspired.
I felt as though I was being let into the back room of a juke joint and that it was invitation only. A step across the hall would lead one into Mick's world, a more gentle atmosphere of tea and wardrobe and a piano for warming up. I was frequently blessed with the great fortune of getting to sing with Mick during the Stones' set. Our ritual was that I would come back and spend a little time with Mick working out whatever song we might do, whether it be 'Wild Horses', 'Honky Tonk', 'Dead Flowers', etc. (this time, of course, without all the throwing up!). One of the great lessons I've learned by being around the Rolling Stones is the importance of being authentic. There are many ways to debate why the Stones have remained vital and have enjoyed the kind of longevity they have had but for me, it is about authenticity. They simply could not do what they are doing without it. You see it when you spend any time at all with them.

They are still turned on by the music they love and the music they make. They do not put on a costume and become the Rolling Stones. They are those people we have counted on to give voice to our emotions and our experiences. They know who their "peeps" are and they write for us. And we listen and go there with them. But most importantly, we believe them because they don't let us down by recreating themselves for the sake of commerce. (I laugh now that the "rock stars" of my generation cannot be discerned from the roadies. It is the era of the anti-rock star. The days of the clever, quick-witted lad who could manipulate the press, who could use the media for gain and discard them at a whim, who presided in a world of mystery and pageantry, no longer exist in the rock stars of today. And sadly, this absence of sense of humour and a point of view is apparent in the music of today.)

I always like to explain to folks how exhilarating it is to be onstage with the Band who wrote the book on Rock but it is a difficult task. Is there a way to describe what it is like to have Mick Jagger flirt with you on stage as if you were alone in a bedroom? Is there a way to give weight to the impact of standing next to Keith grinding through his serial number 00002 or 00006 amp to the uniquely pulsing groove laid down by the best drummer ever? Or to feel you are being accepted into a secret club of bad boys when leaning on Ronnie's shoulder or leaning on Keith in rock fashion? I have a few memories that I am reticent to share, like getting to hear the first mixes of the live album with Ronnie and Keith in Keith's hotel room in Hamburg or getting to try on some of Mick's cool stage clothes in his dressing room. One I will share, because it's funny, happened on the recent tour in San Francisco. Mick, being particularly flirtatious with me during 'Honky Tonk Women' one night, grabbed me by my left butt cheek and lifted me up on his hip. The most humorous part of the story comes after the song ends and I'm leaving the stage, when I hear Mick say into his mike to an audience of 30,000 fans, "Sheryl, you look fetching in those trousers!"

I can only say that being invited into the inner sanctum is something not to forsake for there are nuggets of wisdom to be attained there. There is a way to approach music with the kind of respect and honour it deserves by nature of those who introduced it to us and the reverence that tradition demands. I see this love and respect for the great blues masters coming from the Stones and in their music. It is the kind of reverence I feel for those who introduced me to the same great architects of the music I love and so I feel a responsibility to artists like the Stones and Clapton and Dylan to be the best I can be and to handle my art with love and care and honour.

It's a wonderful gift:
The Rolling Stones for young
and old. For the old it brings
back memories. For the young
it brings new discoveries.

Ronnie Wood

NEVER STOP
GROWING

12

*The Rolling Stones
by Mario Testino,
Los Angeles, 2003.*

MICK: When we played at the Palais Royale in Toronto as a warm-up for the *Forty Licks* tour, the rest of the Rolling Stones were incredibly nervous. I had never seen them so nervous. I tried to calm them down because they were so intense: "It's going to be great guys, we sound great". And they made tons of mistakes, tempos flying everywhere, which was the result of nerves, but you're thinking, "How many times have we rehearsed this tune?" It was very ragged, but I guess that Keith and the rest of the band hadn't been on stage in a long while. I do find it useful when we have time off between tours to go and walk onto someone else's stage and do a couple of numbers with them, with somebody like Lenny Kravitz – it helps take the edge off the feeling that you haven't been on the stage for four years.

CHARLIE: The Palais Royale gig was awful! It was so hot and so loud my ears… I couldn't hear a bloody thing. It was the most uncomfortable set I'd ever played in my life. I hit the drums, but I didn't play a note. I had a headache after two numbers, a splitting headache. I was nearly sick up there.

KEITH: The first full show of the tour was in Boston, where we did three shows. On previous tours, if we'd played a couple of different-sized stages there, we'd have played at the most twenty-eight songs: the shows would have been pretty much the same, with maybe three or four changes between the shows. Because of the way we approached the *Forty Licks* tour, we were able to play sixty songs in Boston.

From right out of the gate, from those first gigs onwards, there was an amazing feeling on the tour. Charlie Watts and Darryl Jones were on their third tour together and had forged this immense rhythm section – and the band as a whole was continuing to evolve, to find itself. I think the Stones are still looking for the ultimate Stones. It's like the Holy Grail, whether we ever find it or not is immaterial; it's the quest that is important.

Each song is a coat hanger, and every night you can put a different shirt on it. I have still not discovered all the myriad possibilities of 'Midnight Rambler' or 'Satisfaction', so I never have that feeling of, "Here we go again, what a grind". I could play 'Jumpin' Jack Flash' all night if my hand would bear it. The songs are flexible enough to play them in a subtly different way every single night. Maybe only the band will recognise how a particular version differs, but it is enough to keep us guessing – though at the same time you're thinking, "I wish I'd put that on the record"!

RONNIE: On the *Forty Licks* tour we changed the set list every night, throwing in songs and often going back to the drawing board; Keith would say, "Oh shit, get my five-string in here, we're going to revise this one". We all got off on the challenge of a new surprise every day.

The variety and the choice of the songs helped contribute to keeping the liveliness of the band alight, plus the fact that we were still doing a sound check before every new show. Wherever we are in the world, Chuck Leavell is able to look at his notes and tell us which songs we played in that city the previous time and the times before that. He'll say, "We don't want to do 'Undercover' because we played that the last time we were here – we've got to give them something new".

KEITH: In general I would let Mick decide the set lists because he's the one who has to sing the songs, and his decision depends on how he feels on any particular day, but sometimes if I thought he was flaking me, I would push him. I'd have to make a decision between Mick's natural conservatism and the fact that the band would get bored if there wasn't enough variety. The band would always play the set list as well as they could, but we didn't rehearse 145 songs in Toronto in order to play only thirty of them on the road. It was a matter of working out how to break Mick out of his shell. For instance, Mick would want to open the shows with 'Start Me Up' because he'd say it was totally obvious, and I would say, "Yeah, that's what's wrong with it, it *is* totally obvious!" That is the difference between our brains. That's Mick and me.

> *The Rolling Stones could have imploded many times, especially with everybody being such different personalities. But one reason the band has never completely fallen apart is that we don't spend enormous amounts of time sitting around asking too many questions.*
>
> *Ronnie*

CHARLIE: The live band is where Keith loves being – and our records have never, ever reflected that. We've produced some very good, very clever, records, but they've never had the fire of the live performance. That's partly because an album is designed and

Ronnie paints his fellow band members.

produced to be listened to over and over again, while a live show is done and then it's gone.

KEITH: When I look back I always find a thread, a constant thread all the way through – it's other people's time warps, not mine.

RONNIE: What impressed me was that not only was there a new generation of kids coming to the shows, but they knew what they were listening to. They would pick out individual numbers and say, "We loved the version of 'Can't You Hear Me Knocking'" or "I love the way you played on 'Midnight Rambler'", which I found mind-blowing. I'd be thinking, "Oh, you got it? You heard it? You listened? You weren't talking to your friends or you weren't going off to have a bite to eat?"

CHARLIE: We did a live HBO special during the second leg of the US tour dates, which added another level of pressure. Although in principle the show was just another show, anything can go wrong when you're playing live and the thought of it all being shown on live television can drive you mad. You might have played something two hundred times and it has always been fine, but you only need not to hear Keith on one song and you've had it. On one of the other shows I misread one of Keith's directions and the song went completely wrong at a very important time, for just a few seconds or so, but it would have been quite noticeable on a live broadcast. These are mistakes that happen because we work loosely within the overall structure, and which is exactly the same reason that the great moments happen. It is part of playing live, which is what Keith likes. I find it quite nerve-racking, though – I'm not a great thrill person like that. But I do love it when everything goes right; it's what keeps you doing it, really.

RONNIE: We put a camera on the head of one of the guitars, pointing back down the neck. At first I thought, "This will soon wear off", because I never saw the results up on the big screens – and Keith was saying, "What the hell are you doing prancing around with that bloody camera?", but I decided to go along with the idea to see if it worked, and especially having seen the HBO special, I was glad I had. I gradually became more adept at using it, by having a quick look up at the video screens, I could aim the camera at the others or at the crowd – and it became great fun to do. Christine, who is the girl backstage, told me, "Ronnie, you're really getting it down now". I said, "How do I know?" because the screen's so far over my head it's impossible for me to see it, but Christine told me, "You're feeling the right parts".

CHARLIE: I have resigned at the end of every tour since 1969. I thought the *Forty Licks* tour might be the last tour we would undertake of that size and that length, but then I said the same thing at the end of the *Bridges To Babylon* tour… Keith won't ever stop. He'll always be playing a guitar somewhere, but as a band performing that kind of show, I think there will come a time when we will call it a day. In the meantime, though, we have the combination of Keith's spirit and Mick's drive. Without his drive I don't think we would have been able to do this for so long. Although I can help drive the band on stage, I can't provide the "Let's have a meeting and talk about this" kind of drive. And Keith isn't like that either. Keith isn't a meeting person: he's like me – he gets a piece of paper and says, "Oh, what?", so without Mick being there and delivering that momentum, we probably wouldn't have bothered.

KEITH: There is still a feeling that there is more for us to do, and that this is no time to get off the bus, because the feeling of desolation of getting off the bus and watching it carry on careering down the road would be more than any of us could bear. I think that this is the only band in the world that can shape what a rock'n'roll band is – we're the only ones who have been doing it this long, nobody else knows – and we're enjoying it, which is the real trick. All of us are still willing to schlep from hotel to hotel and spend endless hours in planes. Maybe we're creatures of habit. There's also the possibility that we're addicted to it, yet at the same time beyond that we share the feeling that we still enjoy playing up on stage and there are thousands of people who are enjoying it with us, which means – I don't know if it's an obligation – but it's like "Hey, what would the world be without the Rolling Stones?" The important thing about the Rolling Stones now is to see how far it can go.

The fact is that I am sixty years old and twenty-year-old chicks are still throwing panties at me! It's ludicrous, really. What do I tell the old lady about these? "I need them to decorate my room, they're very nice." But there is no way of talking about the music and divorcing it from the vaudeville and circus aspects of show business, of walking the boards. One of the most important things about the Stones is that this band really likes to get up on stage and we know how to work a crowd. We've never been booed off, although sometimes we've had very polite applause!

Crowd control is the other part of my gig. I can handle 500,000 or 600,000 – the more the merrier – and I can make them swing because I know what's happening out there, that they want to lose themselves and to become one single entity like an amoeba. All you have to do is be the glue: "Come in love, let's forget the problems, and get down for a couple of hours". There's nothing to it – it's only rock'n'roll, right?

Ronnie and Jo Wood.

Charlie by Mikio Ariga.

RONNIE: During one of the interviews I did on the tour, I was asked by a Japanese journalist, "Why do you think you've come so far" – and I said, "Maybe it's because we're all different personalities". There's Charlie, the engine, sitting there drumming and keeping out of trouble, Mick going, "Leave me alone" and Keith saying, "Fuck you!"

You go on stage and you take the risk of having a guitar wrapped around your head by Keith. He's always going, "Raah, I'll smash your head in" – "Oh yeah? Don't you start on me, you might get it back". On one show, Keith looked at me and shouted at me, "I was meant to do that bit" and Charlie was sitting there laughing saying, "You nearly got punched, you nearly had the guitar round your head". After one row on the tour, I walked into Keith's dressing room the next day – and this probably sums up one truth about the Stones – and Keith said to me, "What a difference a day makes". The day before Keith had been mad, telling me "I'll kill you, but your wife would hate the mess she'd have to clean up", and the next day we came in and we were immediately like brothers.

CHARLIE: I don't think we're particularly ahead of the game. I think the world's changed an awful lot. The first time we played in Japan, one of the most amazing things was that everyone came in their suits, and changed into their rock'n'roll t-shirts, with their shirts sticking out from under the sleeves and their ties underneath. They all clapped and went home, and this time it's truly different. Nowadays in Japan nobody was in their seats from the first song onwards.

RONNIE: There was a moment on the *Forty Licks* tour where Keith told us he'd woken up with this pain in his arm, and had been worried it was a heart attack, until he realised it was only cramp. Mick said, "Do you remember the other time that happened", and Keith said, "When I fell asleep on the console? I couldn't get the use of my arm back". Keith had woken up and his arm was completely numb, it wouldn't move; it was his strumming arm and he needed to go and do a gig or something more in the studio. So Mick said to Keith, "The bad news is that it only gets better one millimetre at a time", and Keith's going, "How long is that?", so I told him, "Oh, about three weeks or something."

KEITH: The Stones are a jazz band masquerading as a rock'n'roll band. We don't go into the studio or write songs in a way that is pre-planned or cut and dried. If I have a song, I'll say, "Here's the skeleton, let's put the skin on it, dress it up and see where the band will take it". The band doesn't need to know where it's going. This band is at its best when everybody has loosened up and they think they're not working, when it's a free-for-all and the tape is rolling. You won't get the best out of them if you tell them exactly how the song is meant to go. I just say what the chords are and see what happens. Charlie will sit down and give me a totally different beat to the one I had been expecting, but at the same time it is far better than what I was expecting. Mick and I sometimes look at each other and go, "That was only an idea, listen to it now!", because the band has taken it to another place and shown us where to take it. That's what I mean about the Stones being a jazz band.

CHARLIE: By the time a song gets to me and I add my part, what I can bring to the table is a different slant to the place it came from. My approach to what I do is different to the one Mick and Keith have, but it's not an academic approach, it's a heard one. So I can comfortably fit in with Keith and converse with Mick about the track. It's an amateurish process, but one we've made very professional.

Charlie and Shirley at their farm in Devon.

KEITH: For me the name of the game is that I can instinctively write a song for Mick to sing better than he can write songs for himself to sing. Mick writes some great songs, but they're not necessarily the best ones for him to sing. I know how to write for him, because that

Keith by Chris Wahl.

The live band is where Keith loves being — and our records have never, ever reflected that. We've produced some very good, very clever records, but they've never had the fire of the live performance.

Charlie

was how I learnt to write. Give Mick Jagger 'Midnight Rambler' and nobody else in the world can do what he can do with it. He can take that song and fly. My job in writing songs for the Rolling Stones is to come up with the right feel. The question then is always whether Mick will bite on it.

CHARLIE: There are a number of reasons why the Stones have been able to continue for forty years. Personally, I could never have done it without Shirley. Another factor is that one needs the money, or wants the money. As Bill Wyman pointed out on numerous occasions, he and I didn't really make any money when we weren't working. I actually make my money from playing and although I love playing and I love playing with this band, it's a very difficult life when you're away from your home and your family, and it's hard work playing for two hours each show. However, I make my living by doing this – albeit I only do it once every four years – but that's why I do it. People sometimes don't like to hear that reason. And also it is very moving to see so many people at a show enjoying the music. Sometimes I look at a set list and I think, "Fucking hell, apart from one Motown cover, Mick and Keith wrote all of these songs that all these people are singing" – it's amazing.

I used to say, "We've been together for twenty years, but Duke Ellington was together for forty years". Now we're level with Duke Ellington! You shouldn't read history backwards, but it's very weird, because the equivalent of a song like 'Street Fighting Man' is like me being a teenager and listening to Louis Armstrong. I used to love the music, but to me at the time it used to sound very old.

MICK: My instinct tells me that one of the reasons the Rolling Stones are still a draw is not purely because of the reasons that people often give – "We've always liked the Stones, they're lovely; the songs are old tunes; we can't wait to see it all; and what fabulous musicians they are" – but because the showmanship element is very important, especially if you're playing in a huge venue and you need to reach the person who is sitting at the back. I think that musicians like Ronnie, Charlie and Keith don't ever want to admit that, and if they do, it's always admitted rather begrudgingly. At the beginning of every tour they will say that they would like the staging to be very simple, and what they mean is that there shouldn't be too much of a show, just the music.

CHARLIE: We are very fortunate because we have a great lead man. Mick's probably the best entertainer in the world. Michael Jackson was possibly his only rival at one point, I think: Michael dancing at his peak, during his 'Thriller' and 'Billy Jean' period, would probably have beaten Mick at that particular style of dancing. But in terms of having an audience in your hand, Mick is the best. He's amazing. Anybody else would be lynched: eighteen wives and twenty children and he's knighted, fantastic! The radical decision would have been to give Keith a knighthood as well; I thought they should have given it to both of them.

KEITH: I've always felt totally blessed. I've never said "Yes sir" since I left school and people have paid me to do it. Sometimes you feel like you've been given this licence to lead a life that everybody else wants to lead or thinks they want to lead if they could and

Keith in his library in Connecticut.

Mick as producer on the set of Enigma, *directed by Michael Apted.*

they want to pay you inordinate amounts of money in order to do it.

There is just a certain chemistry between Mick, myself and Charlie and Ronnie that just works. If I could bottle it, I'd be selling it.

RONNIE: Mick is a fabulous front man: I always tease Rod Stewart by saying, "You'll be a front man when you can be as good as Mick Jagger", and Rod will go, "What the hell are you talking about?"

KEITH: I get two songs a night when Mick is changing his clothes. I try and keep the people entertained. The audience is an instrument. It's not something just to be yelled at, you can make them breathe, you can kiss them, you can stroke them, you can do anything as long as you take the time. I start going into Max Miller routines: "It's nice to be here – it's nice to be anywhere". It's just a moment of release and I know they need a breather: you can feel the mass exhalation.

CHARLIE: As with a lot of great artists, what Mick does looks very easy and nonchalant, but actually there's a lot of hard work required. For the tours he has to do a couple of hours of dancing a day to get back into it, so that he can reach a loose and natural style of dancing. When he's on peak form and we're pushing him along, he's not doing set steps or routines. It just comes spontaneously, and that's when Mick will do something unbelievably natural but great.

KEITH: I am probably able to play like I do because of Charlie Watts. Without knowing it, the first drummer I ever really, really worked with happened to be one of the very best. That is how I can chop up rhythms and have the freedom to come up with risks that defy people's imagination, because I know that Charlie is there. I can just watch Charlie's left hand and I know what's happening. A lot of what happens in the Stones is down to the shared experience that Charlie Watts and I have. We can toss mistakes at each other in the middle of a show just to see if the other one will pick it up. It's like juggling sometimes. If we know that Mick's arse is covered, and everything is safe for a moment, we can afford to mess around with each other, and that keeps us on our toes.

RONNIE: It is rare to have a couple of playmates like Keith and me who are lucky enough to share such a wonderful rapport. It's a valuable gift. Playing and working with Keith is like doing a painting with someone else who thinks exactly the same way as you do – and I've never really found that with another artist. I imagine that it was a little like that in the old days when an artist like Leonardo da Vinci or Michelangelo was working with other artists, and they'd say, "OK, Boris you're good at skies, Trevor you do the trees…" As Chuck Berry once said to me, "We ain't doing nothing that Mozart ain't already done".

KEITH: Rock'n'roll is only about the same age as we are. I'll throw on a bit of Bach and say, "Well, if only he'd had a good drummer!"

RONNIE: The Rolling Stones could have imploded many times, especially with everybody being such different personalities. But one reason the band has never completely fallen apart is that we don't spend enormous amounts of time sitting around asking too many questions or examining and analysing the set list after the show. We'll say, "OK, that was a good gig, let's get on with the next one". I think a lot of bands tend to disappear up their own backsides because they look too closely into everything and become emotionally involved with each other's personal lives. Within the Rolling Stones there is a lot of space which we have to maintain so that everyone can come together when we need to, but outside the Stones, there is also a massive expanse of space for our own personal lives.

KEITH: You can never remember everything about the past, but you always uncover fragments of it every time you think back. And it all comes together like a broken mirror, it's like a little mirrorball spinning: you just get a glimpse every now and again of what happened.

MICK: I'm not a historian. I have no idea about our history. I don't even know which songs appear on which albums. I have to go and look it up. It's like that famous test when you show a group of people a video of an accident and then ask them each to describe what happened in the accident – everybody has a different interpretation of the same events. So we all have different memories of what happened forty years ago. People distil their stories over time and they polish them up. And after a while you don't know whether they're true or not.

KEITH: My dad said to me on his death bed, "We never stop growing…" That was the last thing he said, and then I closed his eyes. He always said that younger people think older people know everything, but older people know they don't know shit from shit anyway. Nobody stops growing, otherwise there's no point in doing the trip in the first place.

Mick with Andy Garcia, his co-star in The Man From Elysian Fields.

CARL HIAASEN

Carl Hiaasen, born and raised in South Florida, has worked for the *Miami Herald* since 1976 as an investigative reporter and columnist. In the 1980s he started writing satirical fiction – he has been called "the Mark Twain of the crime novel" – including the novels *Tourist Season*, *Skin Tight*, *Basket Case* and *Strip Tease*.

When I'm writing I work beneath a large black and white photograph of the Rolling Stones taken in Time Square in 1964. My wife found it tucked underneath a piece of canvas in a photo gallery, and brought it home for my wall. Mick and the boys are standing there on 4th and Broadway, beneath a giant marquee advertising Canadian Club, looking as though they had snatched three hours' sleep maximum, but still managing to project an attitude that is splendidly sullen. All around them are passers-by who obviously have no idea who these alien beings in their midst are. They are looking at the Stones in an inquisitive way as though they are a circus act. Half of them probably thought they were the Beatles.

It is a snapshot of the USA at a time of great innocence and wonder. The onlookers in Time Square could have been my parents. They had been fairly sceptical of the Beatles, but once the Stones hit big, they would have bought me any of the Beatles' albums, just so long as I avoided anything to do with the Stones. My mother was the daughter of a conservative Catholic family from Chicago. In her eyes, the Rolling Stones' hair and Mick's facial expression alone were enough to convince her that the band represented the vanguard of a satanic invasion of the United States. Despite the 'Pelvis' tag, nobody had really felt threatened by Elvis, but here were five of them, and they weren't proposing to hold your daughter's hand, they wanted to spend the night together. Oh God.

At eleven years of age, I had to close the door if I wanted to indulge in the sinful recreation of playing a Stones record, and I could only raise the volume to the level where my younger – and therefore eminently more impressionable – brother and sister would not be tainted by the music. The music was great, the beat and the vocals exciting, the suggestiveness of the lyrics just made it better.

Things came to a head when the Stones appeared on the *Ed Sullivan Show*. Watching Ed Sullivan was a Sunday evening ritual, not just in our house but across the States. The show was, in general, safe family fare – Russian dancers, puppet acts, crooners like Rosemary Clooney or Robert Goulet – although Ed was prepared to include the cutting edge offered by the young Woody Allen or George Carlin. He had hosted Elvis and when he heard about the Beatles had been canny enough to realise he would be foolish not to bring them over. But with the Stones he had booked a slab of dynamite with the fuse already lit.

The show was aired in the aftermath of America's transition to a nation of TV junkies, a change catalysed by the killing of John Kennedy in November 1963. As the first fractured reports of the assassination (a term that previously we had only known from history books) were aired on the radio, we shifted our gaze to the images on television: the footage of the motorcade, LBJ being sworn in on the presidential plane, alleged assassin Lee Harvey Oswald being shot to death on live TV. Instantly we were TV freaks, watching history unfold on the screen.

This was the environment in which news about the Stones' appearance on the *Sullivan Show* broke. DJs on AM radio were talking about it all week. There was a buzz at school: "the Stones are going to be on Ed Sullivan" – "They'll never let them play that". Sunday evening came around. We gathered in the living room *en famille* – there was no way we were going to be able to watch the show without our parents. I can still recall the mortified look in my father's eyes as the Stones played 'Satisfaction'.

The whole scene sounds corny now, four decades on, in an era when we are saturated by MTV and VH1. But the impact of the Stones beamed through our TV in 1964 was electrifying. Even now, when my mother, in her seventies, comes to visit, she sees the photo above my desk and has to smile. Carl survived exposure to the demons.

If somebody had said to me at the time that the Rolling Stones would still be selling out arenas on the *Forty Licks* tour in 2002 and 2003, I would have told them they were out of their mind. I remember reading interviews with the Beatles in which they said they would try and get a couple of good years out of the business. My father, of course, told me it wouldn't last. The Beatles managed eight years. The Stones hit forty and kept on rolling. How they do it I have no idea. I can't think of anything more gruelling, especially, how shall I put it, in one's middle years. The dynamic between Mick and Keith must be part of the lifeforce. Because what they do defies the actuarial tables. Holy moly. Whatever Keith has in his DNA should be distilled and made immediately available to the general public.

From a journalist and writer's perspective I find a clue in Keith's observation that he will still get up in the middle of the night if a lick occurs to him, and he will wonder why he didn't think of that riff thirty years earlier. A new idea can still excite him and that lick will become the spine of a song. It's a handy mantra for all of us: "It's a new day and I can do better."

I try and avoid distractions when I'm writing. I have a natty pair of Ruger shooting earmuffs which I put on to cut out extraneous noise (the result of a deafening level of construction work going on when I moved into my current house, along with the arrival a young baby). But all I need to do is look up at the Stones in Time Square and I can hear all the inspiration I need.

TIM RICE

Tim Rice's first published song, 'That's My Story', appeared in 1965. With Andrew Lloyd Webber he created *Joseph And The Amazing Technicolour Dreamcoat, Jesus Christ Superstar* and *Evita*. He has received three Oscars and worked with Björn Ulvaeus and Benny Andersson of ABBA on *Chess* and Elton John on *The Lion King*.

On 29 September 1963 I saw the Rolling Stones for the first time, at the New Victoria Theatre, London. They were half way down the bill, well below the act I had paid 12/6d to see, the Everly Brothers. The highly influential and gifted country-rock duo were on the way down - not in terms of talent or class, which is permanent, but in terms of popularity, and the tour (which also featured Bo Diddley, the Flintstones, Mickie Most and Julie Grant) struggled economically in its early stages. Little Richard was hastily drafted in after a few dates to boost ticket sales. The Stones performed just four numbers in the middle of the first half, none of them original compositions, one being their moderately successful début single, Chuck Berry's 'Come On'. During their short, lively, raucous set (they wore cute matching outfits) I do not recall thinking that I was witnessing the growing pains of one of the 20th century's greatest entertainment phenomena.

Neither, I am certain, did the Stones themselves. They were quoted at various times in the early and mid-'60s to the effect that the group (not a band then) might last for another two or three years. Simultaneously, John Lennon noted that he didn't want to be singing 'Twist And Shout' on stage when he was thirty. No one knew then (with the possible exception of Danny and the Juniors) that rock'n'roll really was here to stay and that its greatest practitioners would develop and mature with the music. And even the Rolling Stones, after a string of swaggeringly brilliant recordings in their first three years, floundered a little until finding the confidence to return to their roots with *Beggars Banquet*. In the early '70s they were totally back on course, professionally at least. Not only making their greatest albums, their live performances and tours were breaking new ground, becoming spectacular, theatrical, inter-continental, big (on and off stage). Showmanship was shown to be compatible with great rock music; the Stones' music was so strong it never suffered under the weight of spectacle or extravagance. Who in their right mind would write a rock musical for the legitimate theatre when such magnificent rock theatrics were careering around the globe courtesy of the Rolling Stones and those who followed in their wake?

On 15 and 16 March 2003 I saw the Rolling Stones at the Tokyo Dome, two of their five Japanese dates on the *Forty Licks* tour. Forty years on from the New Victoria, some things had changed. No worried promoter would be on the phone to Little Richard. Some 45,000 fans were crammed into the stadium each night and the Stones were the opening act, the middle of the show and the closing act. They were flawless and not for the first time I found myself questioning the received wisdom that the band (not a group any more) were to be seen at their best in a small venue. This was emotional and physical communication with a huge number of people and all the more exciting and moving because of the sheer size of it. Barriers of culture and language were swept aside; had the Stones moved with the times or had they moved the times?

Back then they were loathed by anyone over forty; now almost the only age group which snipes at them in the press is the forty-somethings, livid that the Stones are still alive, let alone parading their magnificent wares, doubtless seething with envy that their own generation has failed to produce an act of remotely comparable musical stature. What is it about being forty than means you just don't get it? But then even the Stones nearly lost the plot in their forties.

To spend the best part of a week involved with the Rolling Stones on the road was a wonderful experience for me, particularly as that week was in Japan, where I had spent a year of my life as a child. The band and the entourage were an oasis of sanity in the midst of craziness around them, which I dare say has been the way they've seen it for forty years, exactly the opposite of the way the media likes to portray it – the Stones are the madhouse, we are the voices of reason. The *Forty Licks* company was a huge family, incorporating real families, all ages, many nationalities. If you were there for a reason, and there with enthusiasm, or a recent Prime Minister of the United Kingdom, you were welcomed in, not only to the shows and the back-stage hospitality, but to the birthday parties, art galleries, dinners and beers. A tour newsletter appeared under your door every morning.

The four men at the centre, upon whose energy, and willingness (and need) to perform, so many depend, preside with good humour and considerable charm over the vast and complex structure, Mick Jagger magisterially, Keith Richards iconoclastically, Charlie Watts laconically, Ronnie Wood impulsively; in turn depending upon their team literally keeping the show on the road. They live in contrasting styles in the hotels – the united artistes on stage operate in different kinds of bunker between performances; Mick organised, mobilised, *The Spectator*; Keith impromptu, spontaneous, 'The Nearness Of You'; Charlie minimalist, Ronnie accessible, open, ubiquitous. Large screens for the cricket for two out of four.

Theodora Richards' 18th birthday party, at which her father delivered a note-perfect (and word-perfect) vocal rendition of the Platters' 'Only You', was memorable indeed, as was Ronnie Wood's exhibition of paintings and drawings. But the concerts were remarkable. The drive that sustained the band through four blues standards in 1963 just before Bo Diddley came on, was still there all night in Tokyo, 2003. When Keith strikes the opening chords of another show time dissolves and we are, as their song says, "imagining the world has stopped". Thank you, chaps.

BACK CATALOGUE

ACKNOWLEDGEMENTS

DORA LOEWENSTEIN – I would like to dedicate this book to my immediate family – to Margherita, Aliotto and Manfredi – who have endured the stresses and strains of this project and my repeated absence from home while completing the task ahead. Of course there are many more people to thank, many of whom appear in the list below (abject apologies for any omissions) in conjunction with those of my co-editor Philip Dodd. I must, though, mention here my gratitude to Philip for agreeing to embark on this crusade with me and to stick with it through thick and thin; without him there would be no book. The patience and faith of Michael Dover at Weidenfeld & Nicolson and his team must not go unmentioned, as well as that of Dan Einzig of Mystery? Design and Emily Hedges. My office, in particular Miranda House and Sally Renny for being a tower of strength and organisation receive endless thanks. Last, but not least, I must thank my mother and father, Prince and Princess Rupert Loewenstein, for their support, and above all my father for being the driving force behind the initiative.

PHILIP DODD – I would like to thank Prince Rupert and Dora Loewenstein for inviting me to take part in this project in the first place, and for all their work behind the scenes to make even the most complicated logistics fall neatly into place. A huge thanks to my wife Wan and our daughter Wan Mae, who were cheerfully supportive whenever the demands of this book required me to jump on a plane to another continent or hemisphere. I also want to thank Michael Dover and everybody at Weidenfeld, Dan Einzig and the Mystery? posse for producing the design we all imagined at the start of the project, Emily Hedges for yet another great picture selection, and for their help at critical moments: Ed Caraeff, John Cork, Dawn Eden, Miranda House, Margot Lester, Sally Renny and Norman Seeff.

Jointly we would like to thank: first - and always foremost - the Rolling Stones, David Bailey, Kate Bonham-Carter, Rob Bowman, Scott Brisbin, Duncan Calow, Fiona Campbell, Christine Carswell and all at Chronicle Books, Frances Chantly, Marshall Chess, Pauline Clark, Aline Claude, Sheryl Crow, Cameron Crowe, Fran Curtis, Sherry Daly, Steve Daly, Marilyn Demick, Bernard Doherty, Alan Dunn, Arnold Dunn, Ahmet Ertegun, Deborah Evans, Jan Favié, Andy Fischer, David Fox, Christopher Gibbs, John Giddings, Giorgio Gomelsky, Edna Gundersen, Jerry Hall, Michael Heatley, Eileen Heinink, Carl Hiaasen, Adèle Herson, Paige Kevan, Tony King, Shelley Lazar, Richard Leher, Earl McGrath, Carol Marner, Alie Mayne, Iain Mills, Marissa Parry, Miranda Payne, Lisa Portman, Peter Rinaldi, Tim Rice, Angela Richards, Patti Richards, Doris Richards, Helen Robert, Linda Rootes, Jane Rose and Delilah, Tony Russell, Annamarie Sep, Mike Sexton, Joyce Smyth, Bethany Smith Staelens, Brigitte Sondag, Meilyn Soto Chapman, Christine Strand, Jacqui Thomas, Clare Turner, Isabel Vicente, Don Was, Lisa Watkins, Serafina Watts, Shirley Watts, Scooter Weintraub, Pam Wertheimer, Alan Williams, Peter Wolf, Jamie Wood, Jo Wood and Donna Worling.

The Rolling Stones would like to say a special thanks to all those who have worked with and for them over the years, especially the guys on their backline who have supported them throughout: Chuch Magee (in memoriam), Pierre de Beauport, Mike Cormier, Dave Rouze, Russell Schlagbaum, Johnny Starbuck and Peter Wiltz.

WHO'S WHO

Mick Avory
Drummed with the embryonic Stones, most notably on first Marquee Club date in July 1962 before Charlie's arrival; went on to find fame with the Kinks.

Jeff Beck
Ex-Yardbirds guitarist whose first group in 1968 featured Ronnie Wood (on bass) and Rod Stewart, who would reunite in the Faces. Briefly a candidate to replace Mick Taylor, he continues a sporadic and highly respected solo career playing mostly jazz-flavoured instrumental music.

Geoff Bradford
Blues guitarist who played with Alexis Korner and Cyril Davies in 1958. Worked with Keith, Mick and Brian early on, but split due to relatively purist musical views and pursued a low-key career thereafter.

Tony Chapman
Drummer with Bill Wyman's pre-Stones group, the Cliftons, who also worked with him as rhythm section for hire. Took Bill to his Stones audition and briefly played with the band.

Ken Colyer
British jazz pioneer who worked with the likes of Chris Barber and also briefly embraced skiffle. Ran a London club at Studio 51 which the Stones often played early in their career.

Don Covay
Legendary US singer and member of the Soul Clan (with Solomon Burke, Ben E King, etc) whose 1964 single 'Mercy Mercy' was an early Stones cover. Appeared as backing vocalist on 'Dirty Work'.

Recommended CD: Ooh! My Soul. Official 5565
This is the only covay CD in print. Featuring 26 recordings from the late 1950s and early 1960s including the original recording of 'Mercy Mercy'.

Cyril Davies
A seminal influence on British R&B, harmonica-player Davies split from Alexis Korner to form his own All Stars, playing Chicago-style blues. Died tragically young from leukaemia in 1964 when barely into his thirties.

Charlie Drayton
Drummer/bass player who worked extensively with Keith, alternating rhythm-section roles with Steve Jordan. Contributed percussion to Dirty Work.

The Dust Brothers
Pseudonym of John King and Mick Simpson, renowned 1990s remixing team whose sampling techniques and production work featured on releases by Tone Loc, Young MC and Beck. They co-produced three tracks on the Stones' *Bridges To Babylon* album.

Eric Easton
Showbiz agent and manager of the old school who shared duties with Andrew Oldham until ousted in 1965 at same time as Allen Klein came on board.

Jules Fisher
Much-respected Broadway lighting designer whose work with the Stones set new standards and led to commissions from Kiss, David Bowie and others.

Giorgio Gomelsky
Film-maker of French-Russian descent who managed the Stones unofficially in early 1963 until superseded by Andrew Oldham. Later masterminded the Yardbirds' career.

Nicky Hopkins
Keyboard-player extraordinaire, one of Cyril Davies' All Stars, who featured on many classic Stones albums from *Between The Buttons* onwards, and on stage between 1968-73. Poor health hampered his career in later years, and he died in 1994.

Brian Jones
Founding member of the Rolling Stones, a passionate blues and R&B fan, who excelled at slide guitar and was a talented multi-instrumentalist. After parting company with the Stones in June 1969, he died – in circumstances still not fully explained – the following month.

Darryl Jones
Former Miles Davis bassist who moved into rock backing Sting. His debut performance with the Stones on *Voodoo Lounge* was followed with a world tour, and he remains the post-Wyman bassist of choice.

Steve Jordan
Co-producer, co-writer and musical confidant of Keith (they first worked together on Aretha Franklin's video of 'Jumpin' Jack Flash') who played drums and sometimes bass with X-Pensive Winos. Previously with the Blues Brothers and David Letterman's house band.

Chris Kimsey
One-time Olympic Studios man who worked on *Sticky Fingers* as assistant engineer and, by *Undercover*, had graduated to co-producer. The Glimmer Twins' chief sounding board after Jimmy Miller.

Alexis Korner
Godfather of British blues whose Blues Incorporated, founded in 1961, included Charlie Watts on drums and introduced the likes of Jack Bruce, Ginger Baker and Long John Baldry to the scene. After finding unlikely pop success in the early 1970s with CCS, Korner died in 1984.

Recommended CD: Sky High. Indigo 2012
Unfortunately, there are no extant recordings of Korner's influential early 1960s ensembles. *Sky High* is a reissue of a 1969 LP and provides at least a sense of Korner's aesthetic and talents.

Steve Lillywhite
U2/Simple Minds overseer who took over as Stones co-producer from Chris Kimsey for 1986's *Dirty Work*. Was supplanted by his predecessor for one subsequent album. Wife Kirsty MacColl supplied backing vocals.

Carlo Little
Drummer with Screaming Lord Sutch's Savages who played with Mick, Stu and Dick Taylor. Also deputised on a failed Stones BBC audition fate when Charlie was working.

Harvey Mandel
Ex-Canned Heat/John Mayall guitarist who enjoyed brief solo success and appeared on *Black And Blue* ('Hot Stuff' and 'Memory Motel') when a possible replacement for Mick Taylor.

Jimmy Miller
American producer/drummer whose work with Traffic impressed the Stones so much they engaged him to produce their albums from 1968 to 1973. Died in 1994.

Chip Monck
Lighting and stage production guru, famous for his announcements at Woodstock, who worked with the Stones on their 1969 and early 1970s tours.

Ivan Neville
Multi-instrumentalist son of Neville Brother Aaron who'has worked with Don Henley and Robbie Robertson. Contributed to Stones albums *Dirty Work* and *Voodoo Lounge* as well as becoming one of Keith's X-Pensive Winos.

Andrew Oldham
Teenage hustler who assumed managerial control from Giorgio Gomelsky in April 1963 and guided the Stones' fortunes, both on and off record, until a parting of the ways in late 1967.

Jimmy Page
Former Immediate label session guitarist who joined Stones' R&B rivals the Yardbirds in 1966, developing their ideas into heavy-metal supergroup Led Zeppelin. Appeared on one track of *Dirty Work*.

Gram Parsons
Born Cecil Ingram Connors, this American musician left the Byrds to form influential country-rockers the Flying Burrito Brothers who were first to record 'Wild Horses'. Hung out with the Stones, especially Keith, in 1970-71 and died a drug-related death in 1973.

Recommended CD: Anthology: Sacred Hearts and Fallen Angels Rhino R2 76780
2 CD set spanning Gram's career. In addition to material from Gram's two solo LPs, this set includes tracks by The International Submarine Band, The Byrds, The Flying Burrito Brothers. Stunning.

Harold Pendleton
Manager of London's Marquee Club who founded the annual Richmond (later Windsor, Reading) Jazz and Blues Festival.

Wayne Perkins
Guitarist with Texan soft-rockers Smith, Perkins and Smith who played on several *Black And Blue* tracks. Losing out to Ronnie Wood as Mick Taylor's successor, he has since played with Levon Helm, Glenn Frey and others.

Billy Preston
American keyboardist and vocalist who reprised his 'fifth Beatle' status with the Stones in the 1970s by appearing both on album (*Sticky Fingers* through to *Tattoo You*) and on stage.

Jimmy Reed
Hugely influential Mississippi-born singer, harmonica player and guitarist, who moved up the river to Chicago where, from the early 1950s, he produced a string of blues/R&B standards including 'Big Boss Man' and 'Honest I Do'. Reed's music is the quintessence of relaxed, rhythmic, infectious blues. His harmonica style, guitar sound and his drummer Earl Phillips all had a major influence on the Rolling Stones in their formative days.

Recommended CD: Classic Recordings. Rhino 71660.
Three-CD set featuring the best of Reed's Vee-Jay recordings. Includes such seminal examples of post-war Chicago blues as 'Bright Lights, Big City', 'Honest I Do', 'Big Boss Man', 'Baby What You Want Me To Do', and 'You Don't Have To Go'.

Ian Stewart
Excluded from the official Stones line-up at Andrew Oldham's insistence for not looking the part, Stu remained on the scene as friend, road manager and stage (sometimes studio) pianist until his sudden death in late 1985.

Sugar Blue
New York-born harmonica-player, real name James Whiting, who played on *Some Girls* (most notably 'Miss You') and *Emotional Rescue*. Occasionally jammed on stage with the band in the 1980s.

Hubert Sumlin
Legendary guitarist with Howlin' Wolf. Prominent on many of Wolf's Chess recordings.

Recommended CD: My Guitar & Me. Evidence 26045
The best of Sumlin's many solo efforts, this release features superb accompaniment by Lonnie Brooks, Willie Mabon, Dave Myers and Fred Below. Along with the expected high-wire electric guitar playing are four solo acoustic tracks.

Dick Taylor
Keith's fellow Sidcup art school student and original guitar partner who quit the embryonic Stones in 1962 to return to his studies. Later founded the Pretty Things.

Mick Taylor
Ex-Gods, Bluesbreakers guitarist who replaced Brian Jones in the Rolling Stones in 1969. Quit the band five years later, joining Jack Bruce, but failed to make the expected mark in his own right. Still tours and records with his own band.

Waddy Wachtel
US session guitarist well known for his work with the likes of James Taylor and Jackson Browne who contributed to a Ronnie Wood solo album and later became one of Keith's X-Pensive Winos. Played on *Bridges To Babylon*.

Little Walter
Born Marion Jacobs, Little Walter was one of the first blues musicians to amplify the harmonica. One of the giants of the post-war Chicago blues scene, Walter was initially a member of Muddy Waters' band before embarking on a solo career in 1952. Walter's pioneering style of playing horn-like lines on the harmonica remains the dominant approach to blues harmonica playing fifty years later.

Recommended CD: His Best. Chess CHD 9384.
Twenty classics recorded for Chess Records in the 1950s and early 1960s. Collectively these tracks define the sound of post-war blues harmonica playing.

Muddy Waters
Arguably the most important post-war Chicago Blues man. It was Muddy's recording, 'Rollin' Stone', that inspired Brian Jones to name his new group the Rollin' Stones.

Recommended CD: The Chess Box. Chess CHD3 80002
3 CD set presenting a comprehensive overview of Muddy's recordings from 1947 to the early 1970s. These recordings define the sound of post-war Chicago blues and feature sidemen such as Little Walter, Jimmy Rogers and Fred Below.

Howlin' Wolf
One of the most dynamic bluesmen ever to record and a seminal influence on The Rolling Stones. Wolf recorded the original version of "Little Red Rooster" and was selected by the Rolling Stones to appear with them on the American television show shindig in 1965

Recommended CD: The Chess Box. Chess CHD3 9332
3 CD's presenting an overview of Wolf's career from his first recording session in 1951 through his last Chess session in 1973. Sidemen include Willie Dixon and Hubert Sumlin.

CHRONOLOGY

1936

24 October – Bill Wyman born William Perks in Penge, London.

1941

2 June – Charlie Watts born in Neasden, London.

1942

28 February – Brian Jones born in Cheltenham, Glos.

1943

26 July – Mick Jagger born in Dartford, Kent.

18 December – Keith Richards born in Dartford, Kent.

1947

1 June – Ron Wood born in Hillingdon, Middlesex.

1960

October – Keith Richards and Mick Jagger meet on the train from Dartford to London. LSE student Mick has four or five R&B albums under his arm. A friendship is rekindled…

1962

17 March – Alexis Korner's Blues Incorporated play their first gig with Charlie Watts on drums.

7 April – Mick, Keith and bass player Dick Taylor go to see Blues Incorporated and fall in with their guitarist, Brian Jones (aka Elmo Lewis).

12 July – With Blues Incorporated playing a radio session, the Stones fill their usual Marquee slot. The line-up comprises Mick, Keith, Brian, Dick Taylor, Ian Stewart and future Kinks drummer Mick Avory.

7 December – Bill Wyman auditions for the band, playing his first gig at Putney Church Hall eight days later.

1963

January – Charlie Watts joins the Stones on the advice of Alexis Korner. His first gig is at Soho's Flamingo Jazz Club on the 14th

24 February – First date of a regular Sunday-night residency at Richmond's Station Hotel.

28 April – 19-year-old Andrew Oldham, formerly a PR man for Brian Epstein, checks out the band and within a week has snatched their management from Giorgio Gomelsky.

9 May – Decca Records sign the Stones and rush them into Olympic Studios with Oldham the following day. First single, the Chuck Berry-penned 'Come On' is released on 7 June.

7 July – The Stones' first TV exposure sees them perform their single on *Thank Your Lucky Stars*. Their *Ready Steady Go!* debut follows on 28 August.

10 September – The band finishes recording 'I Wanna Be Your Man', an unreleased Lennon–McCartney composition which will be their first UK Top 20 hit.

29 September – A first 30-date UK tour with the Everly Brothers, Bo Diddley and, later, Little Richard. Brian, Bill and Charlie back Diddley on an October radio session.

1964

2 January – The Stones take their bow on the first ever edition of BBC-TV's *Top Of The Pops*, broadcast from Manchester. Two UK tours follow in successive months.

2 May – First album *The Rolling Stones* reaches UK Number 1 after only eight days on sale. A gig in Rochdale is abandoned when the audience riots.

1 June – The band fly out for their first US tour, which opens at San Bernardino on the 5th. A session at the legendary Chess Studios in Chicago sees them meet Chuck Berry, Muddy Waters and Willie Dixon. A Chess-cut track, 'It's All Over Now', will become their first singles chart-topper.

19 September – 'As Tears Go By', written by Jagger for girlfriend Marianne Faithfull, makes the Top 10 as the Stones tour the UK again.

25 October – Two months after the Stateside version of their first album, *England's Newest Hit Makers*, reaches US Number 11, an *Ed Sullivan Show* TV appearance sparks an audience riot. "We won't

book any more rock'n'roll groups," Sullivan vows.

28-29 October – The Stones record the TAMI (Teen Age Music International) show at Santa Monica

3 December – 'Little Red Rooster', penned by Chess bluesman Willie Dixon, goes straight to Number 1 in the UK thanks to 300,000 advance sales.

1965

21 January – A first Australasian/Far East tour kicks off with a 3,000-fan riot at Sydney Airport. Roy Orbison, Rolf Harris and Dionne Warwick look on.

6 February – *The Rolling Stones No 2* tops the UK album chart.

18 March – 'The Last Time' deposes Tom Jones to reign at UK Number 1 for three weeks. The same day, three of the Stones are caught using the wall of a London petrol station as a urinal: £5 fines result.

23 April A third North American tour opens in Montreal as *The Rolling Stones Now!* hits US Number 5. Ed Sullivan lets the band film behind closed doors.

1 August – The Stones make their debut at the London Palladium, the Walker Brothers and the Moody Blues among the supporting acts.

August – Their first album in stereo, *Out Of Our Heads*, shoots to US Number 1 as Allen Klein is apointed co-manager.

4 September – The Stones fly from Ireland to LA in the same month that '(I Can't Get No) Satisfaction', already a US Number 1, reaches the top in Britain. A sixth UK tour begins.

October – The US-recorded *Out Of Our Heads* is held off the UK Number 1 spot by The Sound Of Music film soundtrack. LA-recorded 'Get Off Of My Cloud' will go one better in November.

1966

19 February – '19th Nervous Breakdown' ends a run of five successive UK Number 1s by stalling behind Nancy Sinatra.

April – *Aftermath*, the first album totally penned by Jagger and Richards, spends eight weeks at UK Number 1. 'Paint It Black' follows it to the top.

July – As they tour the States with the Standells and

McCoys, two Jagger/Richards songs hit at home: 'Sittin' On A Fence' by Twice As Much and 'Out Of Time', a UK chart-topper for Chris Farlowe.

October – The group dress in drag and Bill Wyman is pictured in a wheelchair for publicity photos for 'Have You Seen Your Mother, Baby', a UK Number 5.

1967

15 January – 'Let's Spend The Night Together' is censored by US television, Jagger singing 'Let's Spend Some Time Together'.

5 February – As *Between The Buttons* heads for UK Number 3, US Number 2, the Stones sue the *News Of The World* newspaper after they allege drug use.

12 February – Redlands, Keith's country house in Sussex, is raided and he and Mick are charged with drug offences.

June – Brian attends the Monterey Festival.

29 June – Mick and Keith spend a night apiece in jail before receiving bail, and eventually a conditional discharge/acquittal.

29 September – The Stones and Andrew Oldham finally part company.

30 October – Brian is sentenced to nine months' imprisonment on drugs charges, but this is rescinded in December.

1968

January – *Their Satanic Majesties Request*, the Stones' self-produced psychedelic album, reaches UK Number 3/US Number 2.

June – 'Jumpin' Jack Flash' gives the band their first UK Number 1 single for nearly two years.

September – 'Street Fighting Man' is banned by US radio, only reaching Number 48 as a consequence

5 December *Beggars Banquet*, a UK Number 3 hit, appears in a white sleeve rather than the originally planned 'toilet wall' artwork.

11–12 December – *The Rock And Roll Circus* TV special is recorded with the Lennons, Eric Clapton, Jethro Tull, Marianne Faithfull and the Who, but is not screened due to the Stones' dissatisfaction with the result of the shoot.

CHRONOLOGY

1969

8 June – *The Daily Sketch* headlines 'Brian Jones Quits The Stones as Group Clash Over Songs'. Mick Taylor is appointed four days later.

3 July – Brian is found dead in the swimming pool of his house. Bill, Keith and Charlie attend his funeral, held on the 10th in his home town of Cheltenham.

5 July – The Stones play Hyde Park as the chart-topping 'Honky Tonk Women' is released. They dedicate the day to Brian.

6 December – A late date on the band's sixth US tour at the Altamont speedway circuit in Northern California, writes its name into rock infamy as an 18-year-old audience member, Meredith Hunter, is fatally stabbed by Hell's Angels.

20 December – *Let It Bleed* reaches UK Number 1.

1970

29 July – The band announces that Allen Klein has no authority to negotiate recording contracts on their behalf. Two days later they fulfil their commitment to Decca with the delivery of 'Cocksucker Blues'. (Decca will release the live *Get Yer Ya-Ya's Out* in September.)

1 August – The movie *Performance*, starring Mick Jagger, James Fox, Anita Pallenberg and Michele Breton, premieres.

5 October – The band hire Prince Rupert Loewenstein to co-ordinate their business affairs.

1971

6 April – With the band now tax exiles, the formation of Rolling Stones Records is announced with Marshall Chess and the Stones themselves overseeing operations.

May – *Sticky Fingers*, produced by Jimmy Miller, tops the transatlantic album chart as 'Brown Sugar', the band's first UK hit in two years, heads for Number 2 (Number 1 Stateside).

12 May - Mick marries Bianca Perez Moreno de Macias in St Tropez. As well as the Stones, guests include Ronnie and Krissy Wood, Ringo Starr, Paul McCartney, Eric Clapton, Ronnie Lane and Stephen Stills. A daughter, Jade, is born on 21 October.

1972

26 May – The release of the Stones' first and only double vinyl studio album, *Exile On Main Street*, heralds a two-month North American tour.

December – As French police issue warrants for Keith and Anita, Mick and Bianca fly to earthquake-hit Nicaragua on a mercy mission. A Los Angeles Forum gig in January '73 raises funds.

1973

31 July – Redlands is severely damaged by fire but Keith, Anita and children escape. He later has it rebuilt to its original plans.

September – The band tours Britain and Germany as *Goats Head Soup*, the Stones' last Jimmy Miller production, heads for UK/US Number 1 with assistance from hit single 'Angie'.

1974

May – Bill Wyman's debut solo LP 'Monkey Grip' appears, featuring the likes of Dr John and Lowell George as guest musicians.

October – *It's Only Rock'n'Roll*, with production credited to the Glimmer Twins (Mick and Keith), is trailed by a London graffiti campaign. It will top the US chart, while the bubble-filled video for the single title track remains memorable.

12 December – Mick Taylor quits the band after five and a half years. "My attitude towards the other four members is one of respect...but now is the time to move on and do something new," he says.

1975

14 April – Ron Wood is named as fifth Stone for the summer tour, but the Faces split (eventually announced in December) is not yet confirmed.

1 May – The Stones drive by their own Greenwich Village press conference in a flatbed truck, playing 'Brown Sugar', to promote their tour.

1 June – The US tour opens in Louisiana, debuting a specially designed petal-shaped stage. The Memphis Vice Squad later threaten arrest if the band perform 'Star Star' (aka Starfucker), but back down.

1976

April – As *Black and Blue* heads for Number 2 in the UK charts (US Number 1), promoter Harvey Goldsmith announces one million ticket applications for the forthcoming London shows – enough to fill Earl's Court 67 times.

June – Keith and Anita's son Tara dies in the Geneva hospital where he was born, aged ten weeks.

21 August – The Stones play a circus-themed outdoor gig at Knebworth House in Hertfordshire to 200,000.

1977

12 January – Keith is found guilty of possessing cocaine, a substance having been discovered when he crashed his Bentley on the M1 the previous May.

24 February – As the Stones decamp to Canada to complete a live album recording Keith and Anita are stopped at Toronto Airport and later arrested

4-5 March – The band plays to a 300-strong invited audience at Toronto's El Mocambo Club including Prime Minister's wife Margaret Trudeau. (Mick issues a press statement denying any affair.) The double album *Love You Live* will emerge in September, one vinyl side dedicated to the second concert.

April – Having switched distribution from Warners to EMI for the rest of the world, Rolling Stones Records re-signs with Atlantic for the US.

1978

10 June – The album *Some Girls* and disco-styled single 'Miss You' both head for the top of the US chart as the band head off on a ninth Stateside tour. Furores break out over the cover (featuring Raquel Welch and Lucille Ball, among others) and lyrics to the tongue-in-cheek title track.

9 July – While in Chicago, the band (except Bill) jam with Muddy Waters at the Quiet Knight club. Bill, meanwhile, breaks a knuckle in a fall the next day but plays nine gigs with a taped-up left hand.

October – As Keith is given one year's probation by the Toronto court, Mick duets with reggae star (and Rolling Stones Records signing) Peter Tosh on a re-cut of Smokey Robinson's '(You Gotta Walk) Don't Look Back'.

1979

February – Keith releases his first ever solo single, combining covers of Chuck Berry's 'Run Rudolph Run' and Jimmy Cliff's 'The Harder They Come'.

April – Keith leads his New Barbarians (including Ron Wood, Ian McLagan, Stanley Clarke and Bobby Keyes) at a benefit concert for the blind as part of his drugs sentence. The Stones also appear, while the New Barbarians reconvene in August to play Knebworth.

2 November – The Jaggers divorce.

1980

April – *Emotional Rescue* is released and will top both the UK and US charts for one and seven weeks respectively. All the Stones except Keith attend a launch party at the Duke of York's Barracks in Chelsea.

July – Keith and Anita Pallenberg separate.

1981

February – Mick drops out of Fitzcarraldo after co-star Jason Robards falls ill on location in the Amazon jungle, causing filming schedules to be altered.

August – Bill Wyman enjoys his first solo hit single with '(Si Si) Je Suis Un Rock Star'', which stalls just one place short of the UK Top 10 but hits bigger across Europe.

September – *Tattoo You*, largely compiled from previous sessions but promoted as a new album, nevertheless tops the US charts, makes Number 2 in Britain and spawns a transatlantic Top 10 single in 'Start Me Up'. Meanwhile, a 50-date tenth US tour plays to two million: Mick Taylor jams in Kansas City.

1982

26 May – A European tour opens in Aberdeen as *Still Life*, recorded on the previous year's US tour, is days away from release.

1 September – Redlands is again engulfed by fire.

CHRONOLOGY

1983

November – *Undercover* becomes the first Stones album to be distributed by CBS, who take over from EMI. The title track video, directed by sometime Sex Pistols collaborator Julien Temple, causes controversy for its violent content.

December – Keith marries Patti Hansen in a secret ceremony on his 40th birthday; Mick is present.

1984

2 March – Elizabeth Scarlett, first of four children to Mick and Jerry Hall, is born.

14 June – The Madison Square Garden includes the Stones in their Hall of Fame, as well as giving them their first platinum ticket for the 1981 concerts. Meanwhile Mick guests alongside Michael on the Jacksons' 'State Of Shock' single.

1985

March – Mick's debut solo album *She's The Boss* appears, with an all-star cast including Pete Townshend and Jeff Beck. Bill, Charlie and Ron are video'd fundraising for Multiple Sclerosis at Fulham Town Hall as Willie And The Poor Boys.

13 July – Mick performs solo for the first ever time at Live Aid in Philadelphia, joining with Tina Turner for 'State Of Shock' and (on video) David Bowie for 'Dancing In The Street'. This will, in August, become a UK Number 1 (US Number 7) single.

18 November – Charlie Watts debuts his 29-strong Big Band at Ronnie Scott's club in London. Mick, Keith and Stu attend the residency's opening night, Bill later in the week.

12 December – Ian 'Stu' Stewart dies of a heart attack while visiting a West London clinic. He was 47. All the Stones attend his funeral on the 20th, along with many big rock'n'roll names.

1986

23 January – Keith inducts Chuck Berry into the Rock and Roll Hall of Fame, saying "I lifted every lick he ever played."

25 February – Eric Clapton presents the Stones with a Lifetime Achievement Grammy, two days after they played London's 100 Club as a tribute to Stu.

March – 'Harlem Shuffle' precedes the release of new album 'Dirty Work', co-produced with Steve Lillywhite. It is a transatlantic Number 4 hit.

July – Bill and Ron Wood play with Rod Stewart and the Faces in a reunion gig at Wembley Stadium.

August – The UK tabloid press reveals Bill Wyman's affair with teenager Mandy Smith.

December – 'Live At the Fulham Town Hall' is released by the Charlie Watts Orchestra as they play a mini North American tour.

1987

26 September – Mick's second solo album *Primitive Cool*, co-produced with Eurythmics' Dave Stewart, enters the chart at UK Number 26. A tour falls through when Jeff Beck pulls out, though Japanese dates are played in March '88.

November – Ron and Bo Diddley tour the States, billed as the Gunslingers. Charlie Sexton replaces Diddley for dates in Dallas and Memphis.

1988

20 January – Mick inducts the Beatles into the Rock and Roll Hall of Fame, joining George Harrison and Bruce Springsteen for a performance of 'I Saw Her Standing There'.

18 May – A band meeting at London's Savoy Hotel – the first for two years – irons out personal differences and pencils in a new album and tour for 1989.

October – Keith's debut solo album *Talk Is Cheap* appears. It will be promoted from late November by his new solo band, the X-Pensive Winos, including guitarist Waddy Wachtel and Ivan Neville on keyboards.

1989

18 January – The Stones are inducted into the Rock and Roll Hall of Fame, though Charlie and Bill elect not to attend. Mick Taylor augments the remaining trio.

March – A contract is signed with Michael Cohl of Concert Productions International guaranteeing the Stones $65-70,000,000 for 50 North American dates.

May – Bill opens his Sticky Fingers restaurant in Kensington, London, and a month later (on 2 June) marries 19-year-old Mandy Smith.

31 August – The *Steel Wheels* tour opens in Philadelphia, where 55,000 people see each of two shows, as the album heads towards UK Number 2, US Number 3.

1990

18 May – The tour, now renamed the *Urban Jungle* tour, opens in Rotterdam.

July – Keith's infected finger causes three UK dates to be cancelled – the first Stones gigs ever pulled due to injury.

12 November – Ron Wood breaks both legs after being hit by traffic on the M4; his car had crashed en route from his father in law's funeral. Ten days later, Bill announces his marriage is over, while Mick and Jerry Hall undergo a Hindu marriage service in Bali.

1991

April – *Flashpoint*, a live album from the previous year's tour, is launched as Keith flies to San Francisco to record with John Lee Hooker. Charlie releases his latest solo album, *To One Charlie*, dedicated to Charlie Parker.

2 May – Bill and Ron collect the band's Ivor Novello Outstanding Contribution to British Music Award.

20 November – The Stones sign a three-album deal with Virgin, including their post-1971 back catalogue. Bill Wyman is not a signatory.

1992

January – Mick attends the New York premiere of his latest film, *Freejack*, as Keith inducts guitar/amplifier-maker Leo Fender into the Rock'n'Roll Hall of Fame.

14 February – The concert film *Rolling Stones At The Max* is premiered on a 52x64-foot screen.

October – As Ron promotes solo album *Slide on This* with a US tour, Keith releases his second effort *Main Offender* and prepares to tour.

1993

6 January – Bill Wyman confirms he is now an ex-Stone on the *London Tonight* TV programme: "I thought the last two tours were the best we have ever done, so I was quite happy to stop." He will marry third wife Suzanne Acosta in April.

February – Mick Jagger's third solo album, the Rick Rubin-produced *Wandering Spirit*, is released on Atlantic/East West.

2 June – Jagger and Richards are inducted into the Songwriters Hall of Fame in New York, with Keith present.

1994

1 August – *Voodoo Lounge*, with Don Was co-producing and Darryl Jones on bass, heads for UK Number 1 and US Number 2 as the tour opens in Washington DC.

September – The Stones announce their own logo'd Mastercard and Visa credit cards.

23 October – Jimmy Miller, producer of such classic Stones albums as *Beggars Banquet* and *Sticky Fingers*, dies.

18 November – The Stones' concert in Dallas become the first to be broadcast over the Internet.

1995

January – Sell-out shows in Mexico City mark the start of a Central and Latin American tour. First Australian dates since 1973 follow in March.

25 May – Mick bids successfully for a reel-to-reel tape of the first Jagger-Richards recordings.

August – Microsoft announce that they will use 'Start Me Up' as the theme for their Windows 95 computer operating system, while Volkswagen cars get a 150,000 sales boost due to a tour tie-in.

November – *Stripped*, a collection of pared-down live performances, is released and will hit Number 9 in both Britain and the States.

1996

March – The *Voodoo Lounge* tour starts its final leg in Bombay.

12 October – The *Rock And Roll Circus* TV special filmed in 1968 is finally screened prior to video release.

1997

June – The Verve are obliged to credit Jagger and Richards for their Top 5 single 'Bitter Sweet Symphony' after sampling the orchestral version of 'You Can't Always Get What You Want'.

23 September – The *Bridges To Babylon* tour opens at Chicago's Soldier Field as the album, co-produced with Don Was, the Dust Brothers and Danny Saber, heads for UK Number 6/US Number 3.

1998

8 April – Ron Wood is saved by paparazzi when the pleasure boat he's on explodes off the Brazilian coast. The band have just played with Bob Dylan in Buenos Aires and will go on to play Rio and Sao Paulo.

16 May – Keith injures his ribs and chest falling off a ladder in his library, necessitating rescheduling of tour dates.

June – Four UK concerts are postponed until June 1999 because of tax reforms that would have landed the Stones with a reported £12 million bill. The current leg of the tour ends in Istanbul in September, two months before the release of the live *No Security*.

1999

January – Extra US dates are added to the *No Security* tour, with the likes of Bryan Adams, the Corrs, Jonny Lang and Goo Goo Dolls playing support.

June – A rescheduled UK tour includes a secret show at the Shepherds Bush Empire. Over-running by 55 minutes leads to a £25,000 fine, which the venue pays to charity.

July – Mick and Jerry Hall's 1990 marriage is annulled, ending 22 years together.

2000

28 May Andrew Oldham publishes his autobiography, *Stoned*.

2001

29 March – Mick reportedly scraps Stones plans to tour the US and UK as his film company, Jagged Films, takes off. Latest project, *Enigma*, starring Kate Winslet, premiered in the States in January.

December – Mick's solo album *Goddess In The Doorway*, released on 19th November, debuts at Number 2 in Germany, three in Austria, five in Sweden and eight in Switzerland.

2002

15 June – Mick wins a knighthood for Services to Music in the Queen's Birthday Honours.

3 September – The band's World Tour opens in Boston's Fleet Center, first of 40 shows in 15 cities in an itinerary that stretches to February 2003.

1 October – *Forty Licks*, a career-spanning retrospective of 36 hits on two digitally remastered CDs, includes four new songs. Meanwhile, Universal mount a reissue campaign for the band's 1963-70 albums.

3 November – The Stones unveil a new line of branded clothing created by Agent Provocateur, Buddhist Punk and Chrome Hearts.

2003

18 February – The tour continues with 50 shows planned in 25 cities across the world, including Australia, Europe, China, Japan, South America and Mexico.

1 April – The Stones first visit to China is called off and two concerts at Shanghai and Beijing scrapped due to the SARS epidemic

4 June – European leg of the tour starts at Munich's Olympiahalle.

23 August – First of two UK shows at Twickenham rugby ground outside London, close to where Mick Jagger still has a home.

DISCOGRAPHY

THE ROLLING STONES
Released (UK): April 1964

Route 66 (Troup) • I Just Want To Make Love To You (Dixon) • Honest I Do (Reed) • I Need You Baby (Mona) (McDaniels) • Now I've Got A Witness (Like Uncle Phil And Uncle Gene) (Phelge) • Little By Little (Phelge-Spector) I'm A King Bee (Moore) • Carol (Berry) • Tell Me (You're Coming Back) (Jagger-Richard) • Can I Get A Witness (Holland-Dozier-Holland) • You Can Make It If You Try (Jarrett) • Walking The Dog (Thomas).

Record label: Decca. Producer: Impact Sound (Andrew Loog Oldham and Eric Easton). Recorded at: Regent Sound Studios. UK chart position: 1. Song credits: as above.

Musicians: Mick Jagger, Brian Jones, Keith Richards, Charlie Watts, Bill Wyman, Ian Stewart (Piano, organ), Phil Spector (Percussion), Gene Pitney (Piano).

ENGLAND'S NEWEST HIT MAKERS
Released (US): May 1964

Not Fade Away (Petty-Hardin) • Route 66 (Troup) • I Just Want To Make Love To You (Dixon) • Honest I Do (Reed) • Now I've Got A Witness (Like Uncle Phil And Uncle Gene) (Phelge) • Little By Little (Phelge-Spector) I'm A King Bee (Moore) • Carol (Berry) Tell Me (You're Coming Back) (Jagger-Richard) • Can I Get A Witness (Holland-Dozier-Holland) • You Can Make It If You Try (Jarrett) • Walking The Dog (Thomas)

Record label: London. Producer: Impact Sound (Andrew Loog Oldham and Eric Easton). Recorded at: Regent Sound Studios US chart position: 1. Song credits: as above

Musicians: Mick Jagger, Brian Jones, Keith Richards, Charlie Watts, Bill Wyman, Ian Stewart (Piano, organ), Phil Spector (Percussion), Gene Pitney (Piano)

12X5
Released (US): October 1964

Around And Around (Berry) • Confessin' The Blues (Brown-McShann) • Empty Heart (Nanker-Phelge) • Time Is On My Side (Meade-Norman) • Good Times, Bad Times (Jagger-Richard) • It's All Over Now (B Womack-S Womack) • 2120 South Michigan Avenue (Nanker-Phelge) • Under The Boardwalk (Resnick-Young) • Congratulations (Jagger-Richard) • Grown Up Wrong (Jagger-Richard) • If You Need Me (Pickett-Bateman-Sanders) • Susie Q (Hawkins-Lewis-Broadwater).

Record label: London. Producer: Andrew Loog Oldham. Recorded at: Regent, IBC, London and Chess, Chicago. US chart position: 3. Song credits: as above.

Musicians: Mick Jagger, Brian Jones, Keith Richards, Charlie Watts, Bill Wyman.

THE ROLLING STONES NO. 2
Released (UK): January 1965

Everybody Needs Somebody To Love (Russell-Burke-Wexler) • Down Home Girl (Leiber-Butler) • You Can't Catch Me (Berry) • Time Is On My Side (Meade-Norman) • What A Shame (Jagger-Richard) • Grown Up Wrong (Jagger-Richard) • Down The Road Apiece (Raye) • Under The Boardwalk (Resnick-Young) • I Can't Be Satisfied (Waters) • Pain In My Heart (Redding-Walden) • Off The Hook (Nanker-Phelge) • Susie Q (Hawkins-Lewis-Broadwater)

Record label: Decca. Producer: Andrew Loog Oldham. Recorded at: Chess Chicago, RCA Hollywood, Impact Sound London. UK chart position: 1. Song credits: as above.

Musicians: Mick Jagger, Brian Jones, Keith Richards, Charlie Watts, Bill Wyman, Ian Stewart (Piano, organ), Jack Nitzsche (Piano, Nitzsche-phone).

THE ROLLING STONES NOW!
Released (US): February 1965

Everybody Needs Somebody To Love (Russell-Burke-Wexler) • Down Home Girl Leiber-Butler) • You Can't Catch Me (Berry) • Heart Of Stone (Jagger-Richard) • What A Shame (Jagger-Richard) • I Need You Baby (Mona) (McDaniels) • Down The Road Apiece (Raye) • Off The Hook (Nanker-Phelge) • Pain In My Heart (Redding-Walden) • Oh Baby (We Got A Good Thing Goin') (Ozen) • Little Red Rooster (Dixon) • Surprise Surprise (Jagger-Richard)

Record label: London. Producer: Andrew Loog Oldham. Recorded at: Chess Chicago, RCA Hollywood, Impact Sound London. US chart position: 5. Song credits: as above.

Musicians: Mick Jagger, Brian Jones, Keith Richards, Charlie Watts, Bill Wyman, Ian Stewart (Piano), Jack Nitzsche (Piano, Nitzsche-phone).

OUT OF OUR HEADS
Released (US): July 1965

Mercy Mercy (Covay-Miller) • Hitch Hike (Gaye-Stevenson-Paul) • The Last Time (Jagger-Richard) • That's How Strong My Love Is (Jamison) • Good Times (Cooke) • I'm Alright (Nanker-Phelge) • (I Can't Get No) Satisfaction (Jagger-Richard) • Cry To Me (Russell) • The Under Assistant West Coast Promotion Man (Nanker-Phelge) • Play With Fire (Nanker-Phelge) • The Spider And The Fly (Nanker-Phelge) • One More Try (Jagger-Richard).

Record label: London. Producer: Andrew Loog Oldham. Recorded at: Chess Chicago, RCA Hollywood. US chart position: 1. Song credits: as above.

Musicians: Mick Jagger, Brian Jones, Keith Richards, Charlie Watts, Bill Wyman, Ian Stewart (Piano), Jack Nitzsche (Piano, Nitzsche-phone).

OUT OF OUR HEADS
Released (UK): September 1965

She Said Yeah (Jackson-Christy) • Mercy Mercy (Covay-Miller) • Hitch Hike (Gaye-Stevenson-Paul) • That's How Strong My Love Is (Jamison) • Good Times (Cooke) • Gotta Get Away (Jagger-Richard) • Talkin' 'Bout You (Berry) • Cry To Me (Russell) • Oh Baby (We Got A Good Thing Goin') (Ozen) • Heart Of Stone (Jagger-Richard) • The Under Assistant West Coast Promotion Man (Nanker-Phelge) • I'm Free (Jagger-Richard).

Record label: Decca. Producer: Andrew Loog Oldham. Recorded at: Chess Chicago, RCA Hollywood. UK chart position: 2. Song credits: as above.

Musicians: Mick Jagger, Brian Jones, Keith Richards, Charlie Watts, Bill Wyman, Ian Stewart (Piano, percussion), Jack Nitzsche (Piano, organ, percussion), JW Alexander (Percussion).

DECEMBER'S CHILDREN (AND EVERYBODY'S)
Released (US): December 1965

She Said Yeah (Roderick-Christy-Jackson) • Talkin' 'Bout You (Berry) • You Better Move On (Alexander) • Look What You've Done (Morganfield) • The Singer Not The Song (Jagger-Richard) • Route 66 (Troup) • Get Off Of My Cloud (Jagger-Richard) • I'm Free (Jagger-Richard) • As Tears Go By (Jagger-Richard-Oldham) • Gotta Get Away (Jagger-Richard) • Blue Turns To Grey (Jagger-Richard) • I'm Moving On (Snow)

Record label: London. Producer: Andrew Loog Oldham. Recorded at: Various. US chart position: 4. Song credits: as above.

Musicians: Mick Jagger, Brian Jones, Keith Richards, Charlie Watts, Bill Wyman.

BIG HITS (HIGH TIDE AND GREEN GRASS)
Released (US): March 1966

(I Can't Get No) Satisfaction (Jagger-Richard) • The Last Time (Jagger-Richard) • As Tears Go By (Jagger-Richard-Oldham) • Time Is On My Side (Meade-Norman) • It's All Over Now (B Womack-S Womack) • Tell Me (You're Coming Back) (Jagger-Richard) • 19th Nervous Breakdown (Jagger-Richard) • Heart Of Stone (Jagger-Richard) • Get Off Of My Cloud (Jagger-Richard) • Not Fade Away (Petty-Hardin) • Good Times, Bad Times (Jagger-Richard) • Play With Fire (Nanker-Phelge).

Record label: London. Producer: Andrew Loog Oldham. Recorded at: Various. US chart position: 3. Song credits: as above.

Musicians: Mick Jagger, Brian Jones, Keith Richards, Charlie Watts, Bill Wyman.

AFTERMATH

Released (UK): April 1966

Mother's Little Helper • Stupid Girl • Lady Jane • Under My Thumb • Doncha Bother Me Goin' Home • Flight 505 • High And Dry • Out Of Time • It's Not Easy • I Am Waiting • Take It Or Leave It • Think • What To Do.

Record label: Decca. Producer: Andrew Loog Oldham. Recorded at: RCA Hollywood. UK chart position: 1. Song credits: Jagger-Richard. Musicians: Mick Jagger, Brian Jones, Keith Richards, Charlie Watts, Bill Wyman, Ian Stewart (Piano, percussion), Jack Nitzsche (Piano, organ, percussion).

AFTERMATH

Released (US): July 1966

Paint It Black • Stupid Girl • Lady Jane • Under My Thumb • Doncha Bother Me • Think • Flight 505 • High And Dry • It's Not Easy • I Am Waiting • Goin' Home.

Record label: London. Producer: Andrew Loog Oldham. Recorded at: RCA Hollywood. US chart position: 2. Song credits: Jagger-Richards. Musicians: Mick Jagger, Brian Jones, Keith Richards, Charlie Watts, Bill Wyman, Ian Stewart (Piano, percussion), Jack Nitzsche (Piano, organ, percussion).

BIG HITS (HIGH TIDE AND GREEN GRASS)

Released (UK): November 1966

Have You Seen Your Mother, Baby, Standing In The Shadow? (Jagger-Richard) • Paint It Black (Jagger-Richard) • It's All Over Now (B Womack-S Womack) • The Last Time (Jagger-Richard) • Heart Of Stone (Jagger-Richard) • Not Fade Away (Petty-Hardin) • Come On (Berry) • (I Can't Get No) Satisfaction (Jagger-Richard) • Get Off Of My Cloud (Jagger-Richard) • As Tears Go By (Jagger-Richard) • 19th Nervous Breakdown (Jagger-Richard) • Lady Jane (Jagger-Richard) • Time Is On My Side (Meade-Norman) • Little Red Rooster (Dixon).

Record label: London. Producer: Andrew Loog Oldham. Recorded at: Various. US chart position: 3. Song credits: as above. Musicians: Mick Jagger, Brian Jones, Keith Richards, Charlie Watts, Bill Wyman.

GOT LIVE IF YOU WANT IT!

Released (US): December 1966

Under My Thumb • Get Off Of My Cloud • Lady Jane • Not Fade Away (Petty-Hardin) • I've Been Loving You Too Long (Redding-Butler) • Fortune Teller (Neville) • The Last Time • 19th Nervous Breakdown • Time Is On My Side (Meade-Norman) • I'm Alright (Nanker-Phelge) • Have You Seen Your Mother, Baby, Standing In The Shadow? • (I Can't Get No) Satisfaction .

Record label: London. Producer: Andrew Loog Oldham. Recorded at: Royal Albert Hall, London, by Glyn Johns. US chart position: 6. Song credits: Jagger-Richard except where noted.

Musicians: Mick Jagger, Brian Jones, Keith Richards, Charlie Watts, Bill Wyman.

BETWEEN THE BUTTONS

Released (UK): January 1967

Yesterday's Papers • My Obsession • Back Street Girl • Connection • She Smiled Sweetly • Cool, Calm And Collected • All Sold Out • Please Go Home • Who's Been Sleeping Here? • Complicated • Miss Amanda Jones • Something Happened To Me Yesterday

Record label: Decca. Producer: Andrew Loog Oldham. Recorded at: Olympic Studios, London. UK chart position: 3. Song credits: Jagger-Richard.

Musicians: Mick Jagger, Brian Jones, Keith Richards, Charlie Watts, Bill Wyman.

BETWEEN THE BUTTONS

Released (US): February 1967

Let's Spend The Night Together • Yesterday's Papers • Ruby Tuesday • Connection • She Smiled Sweetly • Cool, Calm and Collected • All Sold Out • My Obsession • Who's Been Sleeping Here? • Complicated • Miss Amanda Jones • Something Happened to Me Yesterday.

Record label: London. Producer: Andrew Loog Oldham. Recorded at: Olympic Studios, London. US chart position: 2. Song credits: Jagger-Richard.

Musicians: Mick Jagger, Brian Jones, Keith Richards, Charlie Watts, Bill Wyman.

FLOWERS

Released (US): July 1967

Ruby Tuesday • Have You Seen Your Mother, Baby, Standing In The Shadow? • Let's Spend • The Night Together • Lady Jane • Out Of Time • My Girl (Robertson-White) • Back Street Girl • Please Go Home • Mother's Little Helper • Take It Or Leave It • Ride On Baby • Sittin' On A Fence.

Record label: London. Producer: Andrew Loog Oldham. Recorded at: Olympic Studios, London, RCA Hollywood. US chart position: 3. Song credits: Jagger-Richard except My Girl (Robinson-White).

Musicians: Mick Jagger, Brian Jones, Keith Richards, Charlie Watts, Bill Wyman.

THEIR SATANIC MAJESTIES' REQUEST

Released (UK/US): December/November 1967

Sing This All Together • Citadel • In Another Land • 2000 Man • Sing This All Together (See What Happens) • She's A Rainbow • The Lantern • Gomper • 2000 Light Years From Home • On With The Show.

Record label: Decca/London. Producer: The Rolling Stones. Recorded at: Olympic Studios, London. UK chart position: 3. US chart position: 2. Song credits: Jagger-Richard except In Another Land (Wyman).

Musicians: Mick Jagger, Brian Jones, Keith Richards, Charlie Watts, Bill Wyman.

BEGGARS BANQUET

Released (UK/US): December/November 1968

Sympathy For The Devil • No Expectations • Dear Doctor • Parachute Woman • Jigsaw Puzzle • Street Fighting Man • Prodigal Son • Stray Cat Blues • Factory Girl • Salt Of The Earth.

Record label: Decca/London. Producer: Jimmy Miller. Recorded at: Olympic Studios, London UK chart position: 3. US chart position: 5. Song credits: Jagger-Richard except Prodigal Son (Wilkins).

Musicians: Mick Jagger, Brian Jones, Keith Richards, Charlie Watts, Bill Wyman, Nicky Hopkins (Piano) 'and many friends'.

THROUGH THE PAST DARKLY (BIG HITS VOL 2)

Released (UK): September 1969

Jumpin' Jack Flash • Mother's Little Helper • 2000 Light Years From Home • Let's Spend The Night Together • You Better Move On • We Love You • Street Fighting Man • She's A Rainbow • Ruby Tuesday • Dandelion • Sittin' On A Fence • Honky Tonk Women .

Record label: Decca. Producer: Andrew Loog Oldham, Jimmy Miller, the Rolling Stones. Recorded at: Various. UK chart position: 2. Song credits: Jagger-Richard except You Better Move On (Alexander).

Musicians: Mick Jagger, Brian Jones, Keith Richards, Charlie Watts, Bill Wyman

THROUGH THE PAST DARKLY (BIG HITS VOL 2),

Released (US): September 1969 .

Paint It Black • Ruby Tuesday • She's A Rainbow • Jumpin' Jack Flash • Mother's Little Helper • Let's Spend The Night Together • Honky Tonk Women • Dandelion • 2000 Light Years From Home • Have You Seen Your • Mother, Baby, Standing In The Shadow? • Street Fighting Man (Jagger-Richard).

Record label: London. Producer: Andrew. Loog Oldham, Jimmy Miller, the Rolling Stones. Recorded at: Various. US chart position: 2. Song credits: Jagger-Richard.

Musicians: Mick Jagger, Brian Jones, Keith Richards, Charlie Watts, Bill Wyman.

LET IT BLEED

Released (UK/US): December/November 1969

Gimme Shelter • Love In Vain • Country Honk • Live With Me • Let It Bleed • Midnight Rambler • You Got The Silver • Monkey Man • You Can't Always Get What You Want.

Record label: Decca/London. Producer: Jimmy Miller. Recorded at: Olympic Studios, London. UK chart position: 1. US chart position: 3. Song credits: Jagger-Richard except Love In Vain (Payne).

Musicians: Mick Jagger, Keith Richards, Mick Taylor, Charlie Watts, Bill Wyman, Merry Clayton, Madeline Bell, Doris Troy, Nanette Newman (Vocals), Nicky Hopkins (Piano, organ), Jimmy Miller (Drums, percussion), Al Kooper (Piano, French horn), Byron Berline (Fiddle), Ry Cooder (Mandolin), Leon Russell (Piano), Ian Stewart (Piano), Bobby Keyes (Sax), Rocky Dijon (Percussion), London Bach Choir (Vocals).

GET YER YA-YA'S OUT!

Released (UK/US): September 1970

Jumpin' Jack Flash • Carol • Stray Cat Blues • Love In Vain • Midnight Rambler • Sympathy • For The Devil • Live With Me • Little Queenie • Honky Tonk Women • Street Fighting Man.

Record label: Decca/London. Producer: The Rolling Stones and Glyn Johns. Recorded at: Madison Square Garden, New York. UK chart position: 1. US chart position: 6. Song credits: Jagger-Richard except Carol and Little Queenie (Berry), (Love In Vain (Trad, arr).

Musicians: Mick Jagger, Keith Richards, Mick Taylor, Charlie Watts, Bill Wyman, Ian Stewart (Piano)

STONE AGE

Released (UK): April 1971

Look What You've Done (Morganfield) • It's All Over Now (B Womack-S Womack) • Confessin' The Blues (Brown-McShann) • One More Try (Jagger-Richard) • As Tears Go By (Jagger-Richard) • The Spider And The Fly (Nanker-Phelge) • My Girl (Robertson-White) • Paint It Black (Jagger-Richard) • If You Need Me (Pickett-Bateman-Sanders) • The Last Time (Jagger-Richard) • Blue Turns To Grey (Jagger-Richard) •Around And Around (Berry).

Record label: Decca. Producer: Andrew Loog Oldham. Recorded at: Various. UK chart position: 4. Song credits: as above.

Musicians: Mick Jagger,. Keith Richards, Mick Taylor, Charlie Watts, Bill Wyman, Ian Stewart (Piano).

STICKY FINGERS

Released (UK/US): April/June 1971

Brown Sugar • Sway • Wild Horses • Can't You Hear Me Knockin' • You Gotta Move
Bitch • I Got The Blues • Sister Morphine • Dead Flowers • Moonlight Mile.

Record label: Rolling Stones. Producer: Jimmy Miller. Recorded at: Olympic Studios, London, and the Rolling Stones Mobile. UK chart position: 1. US chart position: 1. Song credits: Jagger-Richard except You Gotta Move (McDowell)

Musicians: Mick Jagger, Keith Richards, Mick Taylor, Charlie Watts, Bill Wyman, Nicky, Hopkins (Piano, organ), Jimmy Miller (Percussion), Billy Preston (Organ), Ry Cooder (Guitar), Jimmy Dickinson (Piano), Ian Stewart (Piano), Bobby Keyes (Sax), Rocky Dijon (Percussion), Jim Price (Trumpet, piano), Jack Nitzsche (Piano).

GIMME SHELTER

Released (UK): August 1971

Jumpin' Jack Flash (Jagger-Richard) • Love In Vain (Payne, adapted by Jagger-Richard) • Honky Tonk Women (Jagger-Richard) • Street Fighting Man (Jagger-Richard) • Sympathy For the Devil (Jagger-Richard) • Gimme Shelter (Jagger-Richard) • Under My Thumb (Jagger-Richard) • Time Is On My Side (Meade-Norman) • I've Been Loving You Too Long (Redding-Butler) • Fortune Teller (Neville) • Lady Jane (Jagger-Richard) • (I Can't Get No) Satisfaction (Jagger-Richard).

Record label: Decca. Producer: Andrew Loog Oldham and Jimmy Miller. Recorded at: UK chart position: 19. Song credits: as above.

Musicians: Mick Jagger, Brian Jones, Keith Richards, Charlie Watts, Bill Wyman.

HOT ROCKS 1964-1971

Released (US): January 1972
Released on CD (UK): June 1990

Time Is On My Side • Heart Of Stone • Play With Fire (Nanker-Phelge) • (I Can't Get No) Satisfaction • As Tears Go By • Get Off Of My Cloud • Mother's Little Helper • 19th Nervous Breakdown • Paint It Black • Under My Thumb • Ruby Tuesday • Let's Spend The Night Together • Jumpin' Jack Flash • Street Fighting Man • Sympathy For The Devil • Honky Tonk Women • Gimme Shelter • Midnight Rambler • You Can't Always Get What You Want • Brown Sugar • Wild Horses.

Record label: London. Producer: Andrew Loog Oldham and Jimmy Miller. Recorded at: Various. UK chart position: 3 (in 1990). US chart position: 4. Song credits: Jagger-Richard except Time Is On My Side (Meade-Norman), As Tears Go By (Jagger-Richard-Oldham)

Musicians: Mick Jagger, Keith Richards, Mick Taylor, Charlie Watts, Bill Wyman, Various.

EXILE ON MAIN STREET

Released (UK/US): May 1972

Rocks Off • Rip This Joint • Shake Your Hips • Casino Boogie • Tumbling Dice • Sweet Virginia • Torn And Frayed • Sweet Black Angel • Loving Cup • Happy • Turd On The Run • Ventilator Blues • I Just Want To See His Face • Let It Loose • All Down The Line • Stop Breaking Down • Shine A Light • Soul Survivor .

Record label: Rolling Stones. Producer: Jimmy Miller. Recorded at: Rolling Stones Mobile in Villefranche, France. UK chart position: 1. US chart position: 1. Song credits: Jagger-Richard except Shake Your Hips (Slim Harpo), Stop Breaking Down (Trad, arr).

Musicians: Mick Jagger, Keith Richards, Mick Taylor, Charlie Watts, Bill Wyman, Bill, Plummer (upright bass), Ian Stewart (Piano), Nicky Hopkins (Piano), Clydie King, Vanetta Fields, Tammi Lynn, Kathy McDonald, Shirley Goodman (Vocals), Mac Rebennack (Vocals), Joe Green (Vocals), Al Perkins (Steel guitar), Jim Price (Trumpet, trombone, organ), Jimmy Miller (Percussion), Bobby Keys (Sax), Billy Preston (Organ), Jerry Kirkland (Vocals).

ROCK'N'ROLLING STONES

Released (UK): October 1972

Route 66 (Troup) • The Under Assistant West Coast Promotion Man (Nanker-Phelge) • Come On (Berry) • Talkin' 'Bout You (Berry) • Bye Bye Johnny (Berry) • Down The Road Apiece (Raye) • I Just Want To Make Love To You (Dixon) • Everybody Needs Somebody To Love (Russell-Burke-Wexler) • Oh Baby (We Got A Good Thing Goin') (Ozen) • 19th Nervous Breakdown (Jagger-Richard) • Little Queenie (Berry) • Carol (Berry).

Record label: Decca. Producer: Andrew Loog Oldham. Recorded at: Various. UK chart position: 41. Song credits: as above.

Musicians: Mick Jagger, Brian Jones, Keith Richards, Charlie Watts, Bill Wyman.

MORE HOT ROCKS (BIG HITS AND FAZED COOKIES)

Released (US): December 1972
Released on CD (UK): November 1990

Tell Me (You're Coming Back) (Jagger-Richard) • Not Fade Away (Petty-Hardin) • The Last Time (Jagger-Richard) • It's All Over Now (B Womack-S Womack) • Good Times Bad Times • I'm Free (Jagger-Richard) • Out Of Time (Jagger-Richard) • Lady Jane (Jagger-Richard) • Sittin' On A Fence (Jagger-Richard) • Have You Seen You Mother, Baby, Standing In The Shadow? (Jagger-Richard) • Dandelion (Jagger-Richard) • We Love You (Jagger-Richard) • She's A Rainbow (Jagger-Richard) • 2000 Light Years From Home (Jagger-Richard) • Child Of The Moon (Jagger-Richard) • No Expectations (Jagger-Richard) • Let It Bleed (Jagger-Richard) • What To Do (Jagger-Richard) • Money (Gordy-Bradford) • Come

On (Berry) • Fortune Teller (Neville) • Poison Ivy (Leiber-Stoller) • Bye Bye Johnny (Berry) • I Can't Be Satisfied (Morganfield) • Long Long While (Jagger-Richard).

Record label: London. Producer: Andrew Loog Oldham and Jimmy Miller. Recorded at: Various. US chart position: 9. Song credits: as above.

Musicians: Mick Jagger, Brian Jones, Keith Richards, Charlie Watts, Bill Wyman, Various.

GOATS HEAD SOUP

Released (UK/US): August 1973

Dancing With Mr. D • 100 Years Ago • Coming Down Again • Doo Doo Doo Doo Doo (Heartbreaker) • Angie • Silver Train • Hide Your Love • Winter • Can You Hear The Music • Star Star .

Record label: Rolling Stones. Producer: Jimmy Miller. Recorded at: Dynamic Sound Studios, Jamaica. UK chart position: 1. US chart position: 1. Song credits: Jagger-Richard.

Musicians: Mick Jagger, Keith Richards, Mick Taylor, Charlie Watts, Bill Wyman, Nicky Hopkins (Piano), Billy Preston (Piano, clavinet), Ian Stewart (Piano, jangles), Bobby Keys (Sax), Jim Horn (Sax, flute), Chuck Finley (Trumpet), Jim Price (Horns), Jimmy Miller, Pascal, Reebop (Percussion).

NO STONE UNTURNED

Released (UK): October 1973

Poison Ivy (Leiber-Stoller)• The Singer Not The Song (Jagger-Richard) • Child Of The Moon (Jagger-Richard) • Stoned (Nanker-Phelge) • Sad Day (Jagger-Richard) • Money (Gordy-Bradford) • Congratulations (Jagger-Richard) • I'm Moving On (Snow) • 2120 South Michigan Avenue (Nanker-Phelge) • Long Long While (Jagger-Richard) • Who's Driving Your Plane? (Jagger-Richard).

IT'S ONLY ROCK'N'ROLL

Released (UK/ US): October 1974

If You Can't Rock Me • Ain't Too Proud To Beg • It's Only Rock'n'Roll (But I Like It) • Till The Next Goodbye • Time Waits For No One • Luxury • Dance Little Sister • If You Really Want To Be My Friend • Short And Curlies • Fingerprint File.

Record label: Rolling Stones. Producer: The Glimmer Twins (Jagger-Richard). Recorded at: Musicland, Munich, Germany, Ron Wood's Studio. UK chart position: 2. US chart position: 1. Song credits: Jagger-Richard except Ain't Too Proud To Beg (Whitfield-Holland).

Musicians: Mick Jagger, Keith Richards, Mick Taylor, Charlie Watts, Bill Wyman, Willie Weeks (Bass), Kenney Jones (Drums), Billy Preston (Piano, clavinet), Nicky Hopkins (Piano), Ian Stewart (Piano), Charlie Jolly (Tabla), Ray Cooper (Percussion), Blue Magic (Vocals).

MADE IN THE SHADE

Released (US/UK): June 1975

Brown Sugar • Tumbling Dice • Happy • Dance Little Sister • Wild Horses • Angie • Bitch • It's Only Rock'n'Roll (But I Like It) • Doo Doo Doo Doo Doo (Heartbreaker) • Rip This Joint.

Record label: Rolling Stones. Producer: The Glimmer Twins and Jimmy Miller. Recorded at: Various. UK chart position: 14. US chart position: 6. Song credits: Jagger-Richard.

Musicians: Mick Jagger, Keith Richards, Mick

Taylor, Charlie Watts, Bill Wyman.

METAMORPHOSIS
Released (UK): June 1975

Out Of Time (Jagger-Richard) • Don't Lie To Me (Jagger-Richard) • Some Things Just Stick In Your Mind (Jagger-Richard) • Each And Every Day Of The Year (Jagger-Richard) • Heart Of Stone (Jagger-Richard) • I'd Much Rather Be With The Boys (Oldham-Richard) • (Walkin' Thru) Sleepy City (Jagger-Richard) • We're Wastin' Time (Jagger-Richard) • Try A Little Harder (Jagger-Richard) • I Don't Know Why (Wonder-Riser-Hunter-Hardaway) • If You Let Me (Jagger-Richard) • Jiving Sister Fanny (Jagger-Richard) • Downtown Susie (Wyman) • Family (Jagger-Richard) • Memo From Turner (Jagger-Richard) • I'm Going Down (Jagger-Richard).

Record label: Decca. Producer: Andrew Loog Oldham and Jimmy Miller. Recorded at: Various. UK chart position: 45. Song credits: as above.

Musicians: Mick Jagger, Brian Jones, Keith Richards, Charlie Watts, Bill Wyman, Various.

METAMORPHOSIS
Released (US): June 1975

Out Of Time (Jagger-Richard) • Don't Lie To Me (Jagger-Richard) • Each And Every Day Of The Year (Jagger-Richard) • Heart Of Stone (Jagger-Richard) • I'd Much Rather Be With The Boys (Oldham Richard) • (Walkin' Thru The) Sleepy City (Jagger-Richard) • Try A Little Harder (Jagger-Richard) • I Don't Know Why (Wonder-Riser-Hunter-Hardaway) • If You Let Me (Jagger-Richard) • Jiving Sister Fanny (Jagger-Richard) • Downtown Susie (Wyman) • Family (Jagger-Richard) • Memo From Turner (Jagger-Richard) • I'm Going Down (Jagger-Richard).

Record label: ABKCO. Producer: Recorded at: US chart position: 8. Song credits: as above

Musicians: Mick Jagger, Brian Jones, Keith Richards, Charlie Watts, Bill Wyman, Various.

ROLLED GOLD
Released: November 1975

Come On (Berry) • I Wanna Be Your Man • (Lennon-McCartney) • Not Fade Away (Petty-Hardin) • Carol (Berry) • It's All Over Now (B Womack-S Womack) • Little Red Rooster (Dixon) • Time Is On My Side (Meade-Norman) • The Last Time • (I Can't Get No) Satisfaction • Get Off Of My Cloud • 19th Nervous Breakdown • As Tears Go By (Jagger-Richard-Oldham) • Under My Thumb • Lady Jane • Out Of Time • Paint It Black • Have You Seen Your Mother, Baby, Standing In The Shadow? • Let's Spend The Night Together • Ruby Tuesday • Yesterday's Papers • We Love You • She's A Rainbow • Jumpin' Jack Flash • Honky Tonk Women • Sympathy For The Devil • Street Fighting Man • Midnight Rambler • Gimme Shelter.

Record label: Decca. Producer: . Recorded at: . UK chart position: 7. Song credits: Jagger-Richard except where noted.

Musicians: Mick Jagger, Brian Jones, Keith Richards, Charlie Watts, Bill Wyman, Various.

BLACK AND BLUE
Released (UK/US): April 1976

Hot Stuff • Hand Of Fate • Cherry Oh Baby • Memory Motel • Hey Negrita • Melody • Fool To Cry • Crazy Mama

Record label: Rolling Stones • Producer: The Glimmer Twins • Recorded at: Musicland, Munich, Rolling Stones Mobile in Rotterdam, Montreux Casino. UK chart position: 2. US chart position: 1. Song credits: Jagger-Richard except Cherry Oh Baby (Donaldson).

Musicians: Mick Jagger, Keith Richards, Charlie Watts, Ron Wood , Bill Wyman, Harvey Mandel (Guitar), Wayne Perkins (Guitar), Billy Preston (Piano, organ, synthesiser), Ollie E. Brown (Percussion), Nicky Hopkins (Piano, organ).

LOVE YOU LIVE
Released: September 1977

Intro (Fanfare For The Common Man) (Copland) • Honky Tonk Women (Jagger-Richard) • If You Can't Rock Me (Jagger-Richard) • Get Off Of My Cloud (Jagger-Richard) • Happy (Jagger-Richard) • Hot Stuff (Jagger-Richard) • Star Star (Jagger-Richard) • Tumbling Dice (Jagger-Richard) • Fingerprint File (Jagger-Richard) • You Gotta Move (McDowell-Davis) • You Can't Always Get What You Want (Jagger-Richard) • Mannish Boy (London-McDaniel-Morganfield) • Crackin' Up (McDaniel) • Little Red Rooster (Dixon) • Around And Around (Berry) • It's Only Rock'n'Roll (But I Like It) (Jagger-Richard) • Brown Sugar (Jagger-Richard) • Jumpin' Jack Flash (Jagger-Richard) • Sympathy For The Devil (Jagger-Richard).

Record label: Rolling Stones. Producer: The Glimmer Twins. Recorded live at: Avetoire, Paris, and El Mocambo Club, Toronto. UK chart position: 3. US chart position: 5. Song credits: as above.

Musicians: Mick Jagger, Keith Richards, Charlie Watts, Ronnie Wood, Bill Wyman, Billy Preston (Keyboards, vocals), Ian Stewart (Piano) , Ollie Brown (Percussion).

GET STONED - 30 GREATEST HITS, 30 ORIGINAL TRACKS
Released (UK): October 1977

Not Fade Away (Petty-Hardin) • It's All Over Now (B Womack-S Womack) • Tell Me (You're Coming Back) • Good Times, Bad Times • Time Is On My Side (Meade-Norman) • Little Red Rooster (Dixon) • The Last Time • Play With Fire (Nanker-Phelge) • (I Can't Get No) Satisfaction • Get Off Of My Cloud • I Wanna Be Your Man (Lennon-McCartney) • As Tears Go By (Jagger-Richard-Oldham) • 19th Nervous Breakdown • Mother's Little Helper • Have You Seen Your Mother, Baby, Standing In The Shadow? • Paint It Black • Lady Jane • Let's Spend The Night Together • Ruby Tuesday • Dandelion • We Love You • She's A Rainbow • 2000 Light Years From Home • Jumpin' Jack Flash • Gimme Shelter • Street Fighting Man • Honky Tonk Women • Sympathy For The Devil • Wild Horses • Brown Sugar.

Record label: Arcade. Producer: Various. Recorded at: Various. UK chart position: 13. Song credits: Jagger-Richard except where noted.

Musicians: Mick Jagger, Keith Richards, Mick

Taylor, Charlie Watts, Ronnie Wood, Bill Wyman, Various.

SOME GIRLS
Released (US/UK): June 1978

Miss You • When The Whip Comes Down • Just My Imagination • Some Girls • Lies • Far Away Eyes • Respectable • Before They Make Me Run • Beast Of Burden • Shattered.

Record label: Rolling Stones. Producer: The Glimmer Twins. Recorded at: EMI Studios, Paris, and the Rolling Stones Mobile. UK chart position: 2. US chart position: 1. Song credits: Jagger-Richard except Just My Imagination (Whitfield-Strong).

Musicians: Mick Jagger. Keith Richards, Charlie Watts, Ronnie Wood, Bill Wyman, Ian, McLagan (Piano, organ), Mel Collins (Sax), Sugar Blue (Harmonica).

TIME WAITS FOR NO ONE - ANTHOLOGY 1971-1977
Released (UK): June 1979

Time Waits For No One • Bitch • All Down The Line • Dancing With Mr. D • Angie • Star Star • If You Can't Rock Me • Get Off Of My Cloud • Hand Of Fate • Crazy Mama • Fool To Cry.

Record label: Rolling Stones. Producer: The Glimmer Twins and Jimmy Miller. Recorded at: Various. UK chart position: Did not make the charts. Song credits: Jagger-Richard.

Musicians: Mick Jagger, Keith Richards, Mick Taylor, Charlie Watts, Ronnie Wood, Bill Wyman.

EMOTIONAL RESCUE
Released (UK/US): June 1980

Dance • Summer Romance • Send It To Me • Let Me Go • Indian Girl • Where The Boys Go • Down In The Hole • Emotional Rescue • She's So Cold • All About You.

Record label: Rolling Stones. Producer: The Glimmer Twins. Recorded at: Pathe-Marconi Studios, Paris, Compass Point Studios, Nassau, and Rolling Stones Mobile. UK chart position: 1. US chart position: 1. Song credits: Jagger-Richards except 'Dance' (Jagger-Richards-Wood).

Musicians: Mick Jagger, Keith Richards, Charlie Watts, Ronnie Wood, Bill Wyman, Ian Stewart (Piano), Bobby Keys (Sax), Sugar, Blue (Harmonica), Michael Shrieve (Percussion), Max Romeo (Vocals).

SUCKING IN THE SEVENTIES
Released (UK/US): March/April 1981

Shattered • Everything Is Turning To Gold • Hot Stuff • Time Waits For No One • Fool To Cry • Mannish Boy • When The Whip Comes Down (Live) • If I Was A Dancer (Dance Pt. 2) • Crazy Mama • Beast Of Burden.

Record label: Rolling Stones. Producer: The Glimmer Twins. Recorded at: Various. UK chart position: Did not make the charts. US chart position: 15/. Song credits: Jagger-Richards except Mannish Boy (London-McDaniel-Morganfield)

Musicians: Mick Jagger, Keith Richards, Mick Taylor, Charlie Watts, Ronnie Wood, Bill Wyman.

TATTOO YOU

Released (UK/US): August 1981

Start Me Up • Hang Fire • Slave • Little T&A • Black Limousine • Neighbours • Worried About You • Tops • Heaven • No Use In Crying • Waiting On A Friend

Record label: Rolling Stones. Producer: The Glimmer Twins. Recorded at: Compass Point, Nassau, Pathé Marconi, Paris, Electric Lady, New York, RSM Rotterdam, Musicland, Munich, Dynamic Sound, Kingston, Atlantic Studio, New York, Village Recorders, Los Angeles (Culled from various sessions). UK chart position: 2. US chart position: 1. Song credits: Jagger-Richards except Black Limousine, No Use In Crying (Jagger-Richards-Wood)

Musicians: Mick Jagger, Keith Richards, Charlie Watts, Ron Wood, Bill Wyman, Mick Taylor (Guitar)★ (legal action!!), Sonny Rollins (Sax), Ian Stewart (Piano), Billy Preston (Keyboards), Nicky Hopkins (Keyboards), Wayne Perkins (Guitar), Jeff Beck (Guitar), Pete Townshend (Guitar).

STILL LIFE (AMERICAN CONCERT 1981)

Released (UK/US): June 1982

Intro (Take The A-Train) (Strayhorn) (Performed by the Duke Ellington Orchestra) • Under My Thumb (Jagger-Richards) • Let's Spend the Night Together (Jagger-Richards) • Shattered (Jagger-Richards) • Twenty Flight Rock (Fairchild) • Going to a Go-Go (Robinson-Tarplin-Rogers-Moore) • Let Me Go (Jagger-Richards) • Time Is On My Side (Meade-Norman) • Just My Imagination (Running Away With Me) (Whitfield-Strong) • Start Me Up (Jagger-Richards) • (I Can't Get No) Satisfaction (Jagger-Richards) • Outro (Star Spangled Banner) (Trad, arr Hendrix) (Performed by Jimi Hendrix).

Record label: Rolling Stones. Producer: The Glimmer Twins. Recorded at: Various US venues. UK chart position: 4. US chart position: 5. Song credits: as above

Musicians: Mick Jagger. Keith Richards. Charlie Watts. Ron Wood. Bill Wyman. Ian Stewart (Piano). Ian McLagan (Keyboards). Ernie Watts (Sax)

STORY OF THE STONES

Released (UK): November 1982

(I Can't Get No) Satisfaction • It's All Over Now (B Womack-S Womack) • Time Is On My Side (Meade-Norman) • Play With Fire (Nanker-Phelge) • Off The Hook (Nanker-Phelge) • Little Red Rooster (Dixon) • Let It Bleed • Have You Seen Your Mother, Baby, Standing In The Shadow? • Paint It Black • The Last Time • We Love You • You Better Move On (Alexander) • Under My Thumb • Come On (Berry) • I Just Want To Make Love To You (Dixon) • Honky Tonk Women • Jumpin' Jack Flash • Route 66 (Troup) • I Wanna Be Your Man (Lennon-McCartney) • Mother's Little Helper • You Can't Always Get What You Want • Carol (Berry) • Let's Spend The Night Together • Get Off Of My Cloud • 19th Nervous Breakdown • Not Fade Away (Petty-Hardin) • Walking The Dog (Thomas) • Heart Of Stone • Ruby Tuesday • Street Fighting Man.

Record label: K-Tel. Producer: Andrew Loog Oldham and Jimmy Miller. Recorded at: Various. UK chart position: 24. Song credits: as above.

Musicians: Mick Jagger, Keith Richards, Charlie Watts, Ron Wood, Bill Wyman, Various.

UNDERCOVER

Released: November 1983

Undercover Of The Night • She Was Hot • Tie You Up (The Pain Of Love) • Wanna Hold You • Feel On Baby • Too Much Blood • Pretty Beat Up • Too Tough • All The Way Down • It Must Be Hell.

Record label: Rolling Stones. Producer: The Glimmer Twins and Chris Kimsey. Recorded at: Compass Point, Nassau, and EMI Studios, Paris. UK chart position: 3. US chart position: 4. Song credits: Jagger-Richards except Pretty Beat Up (Jagger-Richards-Wood).

Musicians: Mick Jagger, Keith Richards, Charlie Watts, Ron Wood, Bill Wyman, Moustapha Cisse, Brahms Coundoul, Martin Ditcham, Sly Dunbar (Percussion), Ian Stewart (Piano, percussion), David Sanborn (Saxophone), Chuck Leavell (Keyboards), Jim Barber (Guitar), CHOPS (Horns).

REWIND (1971-1984)

Released: July 1984

Miss You • Brown Sugar • Undercover of the Night • Start Me Up • Tumbling Dice • Hang Fire • It's Only Rock'n'Roll (But I Like It) • She's So Cold • Miss You • Beast Of Burden • Fool To Cry • Waiting On a Friend • Angie • Respectable

Record label: Rolling Stones. Producer: The Glimmer Twins. Recorded at: Various. UK chart position: 23. US chart position: 86. Song credits: Jagger-Richards

Musicians: Mick Jagger, Keith Richards, Mick Taylor, Charlie Watts, Ron Wood, Bill Wyman,

DIRTY WORK

Released (UK/US): March 1986

One Hit (To The Body) (Jagger-Richards-Wood) • Fight (Jagger-Richards-Wood) • Harlem Shuffle (Relf-Nelson) • Hold Back (Jagger-Richards) • Too Rude (Roberts) • Winning Ugly (Jagger-Richards) • Back To Zero (Jagger-Richards-Leavell) • Dirty Work (Jagger-Richards-Wood) • Had It With You (Jagger-Richards-Wood) • Sleep Tonight (Jagger-Richards) • Trouble In Mind (Jones).

Record label: Rolling Stones. Producer: The Glimmer Twins and Steve Lillywhite. Recorded at: Pathé Marconi Studios, Paris. UK chart position: 3. US chart position: 4. Song credits: as above

Musicians: Mick Jagger, Keith Richards, Charlie Watts, Ron Wood, Bill Wyman, Chuck Leavell (Keyboards), Jimmy Page (Guitar), Kirsty MacColl , Beverley D'Angelo, Bobby Womack, Jimmy Cliff, Tom Waits, Don Covay, Patti Scialfa, Janis Pendarvis, Dolette McDonald (Vocals), Ivan Neville (Keyboards, bass), Anton Fig (Percussion)(Unconfirmed)★ Steve Jordan, Charley Drayton, Philippe Saisse, Dan Collette, John Regan, Alan Rogan, Ian Stewart (no instruments specified).

ROLLING STONES SINGLES COLLECTION - THE LONDON YEARS (3CD BOX)

Released (US): August 1989

Come On (Berry) • I Want To Be Loved (Dixon) • I Wanna Be Your Man (Lennon-McCartney) • Stoned (Nanker-Phelge) • Not Fade Away (Petty-Hardin) • Little By Little (Phelge-Spector) • It's All Over Now (B Womack-S Womack) • Good Times, Bad Times (Jagger-Richard) • Tell Me (You're Coming Back) • I Just Want To Make Love To You (Dixon) • Time Is On My Side (Meade-Norman) • Congratulations • Little Red Rooster (Dixon) • Off The Hook (Nanker-Phelge) • Heart Of Stone • What A Shame • The Last Time • Play With Fire (Nanker-Phelge) • (I Can't Get No) Satisfaction • The Under Assistant West Coast Promotion Man (Nanker-Phelge) • The Spider And The Fly (Nanker-Phelge) • Get Off Of My Cloud • I'm Free • The Singer Not The Song • As Tears Go By • Gotta Get Away • 19th Nervous • Breakdown • Sad Day • Paint It Black • Stupid Girl • Long Long While • Mother's Little Helper • Lady Jane • Have You Seen Your Mother, Baby, Standing In The Shadow? • Who's Driving Your Plane? • Let's Spend The Night Together • Ruby Tuesday • We Love You • Dandelion • She's A Rainbow • 2000 Light Years From Home • In Another Land • The Lantern • Jumpin' Jack Flash • Child Of The Moon • Street Fighting Man • No Expectations • Surprise Surprise • Honky Tonk Women • You Can't Always Get What You Want • Memo From Turner • Brown Sugar • Wild Horses • I Don't Know Why • Try A Little Harder • Out Of Time • Jiving Sister Fanny • Sympathy For The Devil

Record label: ABKCO. Producer: Andrew Loog Oldham and Jimmy Miller. Recorded at: Various. US chart position: 88. Song credits: Jagger-Richard except where noted

Musicians: Mick Jagger, Brian Jones, Keith Richards, Mick Taylor, Charlie Watts, Bill Wyman, Various.

STEEL WHEELS

Released (US/UK): August/September 1989

Sad Sad Sad • Mixed Emotions • Terrifying • Hold On To Your Hat • Hearts For Sale • Blinded By Love • Rock And A Hard Place • Can't Be Seen • Almost Hear You Sigh • Continental Drift • Break The Spell • Slipping Away.

Record label: Rolling Stones. Producer: The Glimmer Twins and Chris Kimsey. Recorded at: AIR Studios, Montserrat. UK chart position: 2. US chart position: 3. Song credits: Jagger-Richards except Almost Hear You Sigh (Jagger-Richards-Jordan)

Musicians: Mick Jagger, Keith Richards, Charlie Watts, Ron Wood, Bill Wyman, Chuck Leavell (Piano, organ), Kick Horns , Bernard Fowler, Sarah Dash, Lisa Fischer (Vocals), Luis Jardim (Percussion), Matt Clifford (Keyboards), Phil Beer (Fiddle, mandolin), Roddy Lorimer (Trumpet), Master Musicians of Joujouka.

FLASHPOINT

Released (UK/US): April 1991

Continental Drift (Intro) • Start Me Up • Sad Sad Sad • Miss You • Rock And A Hard Place (CD bonus) • Ruby Tuesday • You Can't Always Get What You Want • Factory Girl • Can't Be Seen (CD bonus) • Little Red Rooster • Paint It Black • Sympathy For The Devil • Brown Sugar • Jumpin' Jack Flash • (I Can't Get No)

Satisfaction • Highwire (Studio track) • Sex Drive (Studio track)

Record label: Rolling Stones. Producer: Chris Kimsey and the Glimmer Twins. Recorded at: Various venues in the USA, Japan, England, Spain and Italy. UK chart position: 6. US chart position: 16. Song credits: Jagger-Richards except Little Red Rooster (Dixon)

Musicians: Mick Jagger, Keith Richards, Charlie Watts, Ron Wood, Bill Wyman, Bobby Keys (Sax), Chuck Leavell (Keyboards), Matt Clifford (Keyboards, French horn), Bernard Fowler, Lisa Fischer, Cindy Mizelle, Tessa Niles, Katie Kissoon (Vocals), Eric Clapton (Guitar), Uptown Horns, Kick Horns.

JUMP BACK - THE BEST OF THE ROLLING STONES 1971-1993
Released (UK): November 1993
Start Me Up • Brown Sugar • Harlem Shuffle • It's Only Rock'n'Roll (But I Like It) • Mixed Emotions • Angie • Tumbling Dice • Fool To Cry • Rock And A Hard Place • Miss You • Hot Stuff • Emotional Rescue • Respectable • Beast Of Burden • Waiting On A Friend • Wild Horses • Bitch • Undercover Of The Night

Record label: Rolling Stones. Producer: . Recorded at: . UK chart position: 16. Song credits: Jagger-Richards except Harlem Shuffle (Relf-Nelson).

Musicians: Mick Jagger, Keith Richards, Mick Taylor, Charlie Watts, Ron Wood, Bill Wyman, Various.

VOODOO LOUNGE
Released (UK/US): July 1994
Love Is Strong • You Got Me Rocking • Sparks Will Fly • The Worst • New Faces • Moon Is Up • Out Of Tears • I Go Wild • Brand New Car • Sweethearts Together • Suck On The Jugular • Blinded By Rainbows • Baby Break It Down • Thru And Thru • Mean Disposition (CD bonus).

Record label: Rolling Stones. Producer: Don Was and the Glimmer Twins. Recorded at: Windmill lane Studios, Dublin, Ron Wood and Don Was's Studios, A&M Studios, Los Angeles. UK chart position: 1. US chart position: 2. Song credits: Jagger-Richards.

Musicians: Mick Jagger, Keith Richards, Charlie Watts, Ron Wood, Darryl Jones (Bass), Chuck Leavell (Keyboards), Bernard Fowler (Vocals), Ivan Neville (Organ), David McMurray (Brass), Mark Isham (Brass), Lenny Castro (Percussion), Louis Jardim (Percussion), Bobby Womack (Vocals), Frankie Gavin (Fiddle), Pierre De Beauport (Guitar), Flaco Jimenez (Accordion), Max Baca (Bajo sexto), Phil Jones (Percussion).

STRIPPED
Released (UK/US): November 1995
Street Fighting Man • Like A Rolling Stone (Dylan) • Not Fade Away (Petty-Hardin) • Shine A Light • The Spider And The Fly (Nanker-Phelge) • I'm Free • Wild Horses • Let It Bleed • Dead Flowers • Slipping Away • Angie • Love In Vain (Payne, adapted by Jagger-Richards) • Sweet Virginia • Little Baby (Dixon).

Record label: Rolling Stones. Producer: The Glimmer Tiwns and Don Was. Recorded at: Toshiba-EMI Studios, Japan (Slipping Away studio track), Brixton Academy, London,

Olympia Theatre, Paris. UK chart position: 9. US chart position: 9. Song credits: Jagger-Richards except where noted.

Musicians: Mick Jagger, Keith Richards, Charlie Watts, Ron Wood, Darryl Jones (Bass), Chuck Leavell (Keyboards), Bernard Fowler (Vocals), Lisa Fischer (Vocals), Bobby Keys (Sax), Andy Snitzer (Brass), Michael Davis (Brass), Kent Smith (Brass).

ROCK AND ROLL CIRCUS
Released (UK/US): October 1996
Song For Jeffrey (Jethro Tull) • A Quick One (The Who) • Ain't That A Lot Of Love (Taj Mahal) • Something Better (Marianne Faithfull) • Yer Blues (Dirty Mac) • Whole Lotta Yoko (Yoko Ono) • Jumpin' Jack Flash • Parachute Woman • No Expectations • You Can't Always Get What You Want • Sympathy For The Devil • Salt Of The Earth .

Record label: ABKCO. Producer: Jimmy Miller, Jody Klein, Lenne Allik. Recorded at: Olympic Mobile and Intertel Studios, London. UK chart position: 12. US chart position: 92. Song credits: (Stones songs only) Jagger-Richard.

Musicians: Mick Jagger, Brian Jones, Keith Richards, Charlie Watts, Bill Wyman, Nicky Hopkins (Piano), Rocky Dijon (Percussion), The Who, John Lennon and Yoko Ono, Eric Clapton (Vocals).

BRIDGES TO BABYLON
Released (UK/US): September 1997
Flip The Switch • Anybody Seen My Baby? • Low Down • Already Over Me • Gun Face • You Don't Have To Mean It • Out Of Control • Saint Of Me • Might As Well Get Juiced • Always Suffering • Too Tight • Thief In The Night • How Can I Stop.

Record label: Rolling Stones • Producer: The Glimmer Twins, Don Was, Danny Saber, the Dust Brothers. Recorded at: Ocean Way Recording Studios, Hollywood. UK chart position: 6. US chart position: 3. Song credits: Jagger-Richards except Anybody Seen My Baby? (Jagger-Richards-Lang-Mink), Thief In The Night (Jagger-Richards-De Beauport)

Musicians: Mick Jagger, Keith Richards, Charlie Watts, Ron Wood, Waddy Wachtel (Guitar), Benmont Tench (Keyboards), Doug Wimbish (Bass), Jim Keltner (Percussion), Darrell Leonard (Sax), Joe Sublett (Sax), Wayne Shorter (Sax), Bernard Fowler (Vocals), Clinton Clifford (Keyboards), Danny Saber (Keyboards), Blondie Chaplin (Vocals, piano), Jeff Sarli (Bass), Jamie, Muhoberac (Bass, keyboards), Don Was (Keyboards), Darryl Jones (Bass), Pierre De Beauport (Keyboards, bass), Me'shell N'degeocello (bass)

NO SECURITY
Released (UK/US): November 1998
Intro • You Got Me Rocking • Gimme Shelter • Flip The Switch • Memory Motel • Corinna • Saint Of Me • Waiting On A Friend • Sister Morphine • Live With Me • Respectable • Thief In The Night • The Last Time • Out Of Control.

Record label: Rolling Stones. Producer: The Glimmer Twins. Recorded at: Amsterdam, St Louis, Nuremberg, Buenos Aires, MTV. UK chart position: 67. US chart position: 34. Song credits: Jagger-Richard except Corinna (Mahal, Davis), Sister Morphine (Jagger-Richard-

Faithfull), Thief In The Night (Jagger-Richards-De Beauport).

Musicians: Mick Jagger, Keith Richards, Charlie Watts, Ron Wood, Chuck Leavell (Keyboards), Bernard Fowler, Lisa Fischer, Blondie Chaplin (Vocals), Darryl Jones (Bass), Dave Matthews (Vocals), Taj Mahal (Vocals), Joshua Redman (Sax), Andy Snitzer (Keyboards), Tim Ries (Keyboards), Johnny Starbuck (Percussion), Michael Davis, Bobby Keys (Sax), Kent Smith, Pierre De Beauport (Piano), Leah Wood (Vocals).

FORTY LICKS
Released (UK/US): October 2002
Street Fighting Man • Gimme Shelter • (I Can't Get No) Satisfaction • The Last Time • Jumpin' Jack Flash • You Can't Always Get What You Want • 19th Nervous Breakdown • Under My Thumb • Not Fade Away (Petty-Hardin) • Have You Seen Your Mother, Baby, Standing In The Shadow? • Sympathy For The Devil • Mother's Little Helper • She's A Rainbow • Get Off Of My Cloud • Wild Horses • Ruby Tuesday • Paint It Black • Honky Tonk Women • It's All Over Now (B Womack-S Womack) • Let's Spend The Night Together • Start Me Up • Brown Sugar • Miss You • Beast Of Burden • Don't Stop (New song) • Happy • Angie • You Got Me Rocking • Shattered • Fool To Cry • Love Is Strong • Mixed Emotions • Keys To Your Love (New song) • Anybody Seen My Baby? (Jagger-Richard-Lang-Mink) • Stealing My Heart (New song) • Tumbling Dice • Undercover Of The Night • Emotional Rescue • It's Only Rock'n'Roll (But I Like It) • Losing My Touch (New song).

Record label: Rolling Stones. Producer: Various (New songs produced by Don Was and the Glimmer Twins). Recorded at: Various. UK chart position: 2. US chart position: 2. Song credits: Jagger-Richard except where noted

Musicians: Mick Jagger, Brian Jones, Keith Richards, Charlie Watts, Mick Taylor, Ron Wood, Bill Wyman, Various.

INDEX

Note: Headings in italics refer to albums unless otherwise indicated, those in single speech marks refer to single releases or tracks from albums. Page numbers in italics refer to illustrations.

INDEX

PICTURE CREDITS

Weidenfeld & Nicolson would like to thank the following sources for their kind permission to reproduce the photographs in this book:

Endpapers: Ronnie Wood; 4 Anton Corbijn; 6-7 Mark Hayward/Philip Townsend; Chapter One: 10-11 Private Collection; 12 Private Collection; 14 Lynn Goldsmith; 16 Redferns/Michael Ochs Archive; 17 Redferns/Michael Ochs Archive; 18 Private Collection; 19 Christopher Sykes; 21 Rex Features/Dezo Hoffmann; 22 Christopher Sykes; 25 Jane Rose; Chapter Two: 26-27 Mark Hayward/Philip Townsend; 28 Mark Hayward/Philip Townsend; 31 Mark Hayward/Philip Townsend; 32 Pictorial Press; 33 Mark Hayward; 36 Redferns/David Redfern; 37 Mark Hayward/Philip Townsend; 38 Mark Hayward/Philip Townsend; 42 Mark Hayward/Andrew Milton; 45 Mark Hayward/Philip Townsend; 46, 47 The Collection of Marilyn Demick; 48 Redferns/Jeremy Fletcher 51 Redferns/NIKPOP; Chapter Three: 52-53 Redferns/Jeremy Fletcher; 54 Photo 12/Jean-Marie Périer; 56 Rex Features/Ian Fleming 57 Val Wilmer; 58-59 Mark Hayward/Philip Townsend; 60 Val Wilmer; 61 Val Wilmer; 62 The Collection of Marilyn Demick; 64 Val Wilmer; 65 Val Wilmer; 66 Terry O'Neill; 67 Mirrorpix; 69 Rex Features/Terry O'Neill; 71 Michael Ochs Archives; 72 Mirrorpix; 74-75 Rex Features/ Terry O'Neill; 76 Mirrorpix; 77 Michael Ochs Archives; 78 Terry O'Neill 81 David Bailey; Chapter Four: 82-83 Photo 12/Jean-Marie Périer; 84 Gered Mankowitz © Bowstir Ltd. 2003; 85 Gered Mankowitz " Bowstir Ltd. 2003; 86 Rex Features/Dezo Hoffmann; 87 Photo 12/Jean-Marie Périer; 89 Gered Mankowitz © Bowstir Ltd. 2003; 90 Gered Mankowitz © Bowstir Ltd. 2003; 91 The Collection of Marilyn Demick/Belfast Telegraph; 92 Photo 12/Jean-Marie Périer; 93 Gered Mankowitz © Bowstir Ltd. 2003; 94 The Collection of Marilyn Demick; 96-97 Gered Mankowitz © Bowstir Ltd. 2003; 98 Gered Mankowitz © Bowstir Ltd. 2003; 99 Photo 12/Jean-Marie Périer; 101 Gered Mankowitz © Bowstir Ltd. 2003; 102-103 The Collection of Marilyn Demick; 104 Redferns/Chuck Boyd; 105 The Collection of Marilyn Demick; 106 Photo 12/Jean-Marie Périer; Chapter Five: 110-111 Hulton Archive; 112 Redferns/Michael Ochs Archive; 115 Rex Features/David Magnus; 116 Hulton Archive; 117 Munro Sounds; 118 Mirrorpix; 120 Mark Hayward/Peter Whitehead; 121 Mirrorpix; 122 Hulton Archive; 123 Mark Hayward/Dave King; 126-127 Munro Sounds; 130 top Hulton Archive; 130 bottom Ken Regan/Camera 5; 131 top Rex Features/Mike Randolph, 131 bottom Rex Features/Mike Selby; 132 Mirrorpix; 133 Mark Hayward; 134 Ken Regan/Camera 5; 135 Rex Features/Brian Moody; 136 © Michael Cooper from The Raj Prem Collection; 139 Rex Features; Chapter Six: 140-141 Ken Regan/Camera 5; 142 Norman Seeff; 144-145 Pennie Smith; 146 Ken Regan/Camera 5; 147 Redferns/David Redfern; 148 Dominique Tarlé; 149 top Mirrorpix; 149 bottom left and right Corbis/Hulton-Deutsh Collection; 150-151 Dominique Tarlé; 153 Ken Regan/Camera 5; 154 Ken Regan/Camera 5; 155 Ed Caraeff; 156-157 Photo 12/Jean-Marie Périer; 158 Munro Sounds; 159 Ken Regan/Camera 5; 160-161 Norman Seeff; 163 Photo 12/Jean-Marie Périer; 164-165 Ken Regan/Camera 5; 166-167 Jim Marshall; 168 Jamar Chess; Chapter Seven: 172-173 Ken Regan/Camera 5; 174 Mirrorpix; 177 Pennie Smith; 178 Michael Ochs 179 top Ken Regan/Camera 5; 179 bottom left Terry O'Neill; 179 bottom right Ken Regan/Camera 5; 180 Retna Ltd./Michael Putland; 181 David Bailey; 183 Christopher Sykes; 184 Joe Sia; 185 left Retna Ltd./Michael Putland; 185 right © The Andy Warhol Foundation for the Visual Arts, Inc./ARS, NY and DACS, London 2003; 186 Ken Regan/Camera 5; 187 Christopher Sykes; 188 Christopher Sykes; 189 Ken Regan/Camera 5; 190 Christopher Sykes; 191 top four Christopher Sykes; 191 bottom Ken Regan/Camera 5; 192 Ken Regan/Camera 5; 193 Christopher Sykes; 194 top Ken Regan/Camera 5; 194 left and right of centre Christopher Sykes; 194 bottom left Retna Ltd./Michael Putland; 194 bottom right Christopher Sykes; 195 Christopher Sykes; 196-197 Ken Regan/Camera 5; 198 Jane Rose; 199 Ken Regan/Camera 5; 200 Joe Sia; 203 Ken Regan/Camera 5, 204 top Christopher Sykes; 204 bottom Ken Regan/Camera 5; 205 top Ken Regan/Camera 5; 205 bottom Ken Regan/Camera 5; 206 Ken Regan/Camera 5; 209 Jean Pigozzi; Chapter Eight: 210-211 Ken Regan/Camera 5; 212 Munro Sounds/Dimo Safari; 214 Michael Halsband; 215 Terry O'Neill; 216 Ken Regan/Camera 5; 217 Ken Regan/Camera 5; 218 Corbis/Wally McNamee; 219 Ken Regan/Camera 5; 220 Ken Regan/Camera 5; 221 Michael Halsband; 222 top Ken Regan/Camera 5; 222 bottom Private Collection; 223 Pennie Smith; 224-225 Ken Regan/Camera 5; 226-

227 Michael Halsband; 228 Ken Regan/Camera 5; 229 Munro Sounds/Denis O'Regan; 230 Ken Regan/Camera 5; 231 Brian Aris; 232 top Jane Rose; 232 centre and bottom Ken Regan/Camera 5; 233 Jane Rose; 234 Michael Halsband; 235 Retna Ltd./Michael Putland; 236 Corbis/Lynn Goldsmith 239 Lynn Goldsmith; Chapter Nine: 240-241 Gered Mankowitz " Bowstir Ltd. 2003; 242 Jane Rose; 243 Jane Rose; 245 Munro Sounds; 246-247 Munro Sounds/Claude Gassian; 248 Munro Sounds/Claude Gassian; 249 Claude Gassian; 251 Munro Sounds; 252-253 Munro Sounds/Claude Gassian; 254-255 Munro Sounds/Claude Gassian; 256 Munro Sounds/Mikio Ariga; 258 Munro Sounds/P. Rider; 259 top Jane Rose; 259 bottom Ken Regan/Camera 5; 260-261 Munro Sounds/Claude Gassian; 262 Munro Sounds/Claude Gassian; 263 Rex Features/Richard Young; 264 Edna Gundersen; Chapter Ten: 268-269 Michael Halsband; 270 Munro Sounds/Kevin Mazur; 272 Munro Sounds/Mikio Ariga; 273 Munro Sounds; 274 left Munro Sounds/Mikio Ariga; 274 right Munro Sounds/Kevin Mazur; 275 Ken Regan/Camera 5; 277 Munro Sounds/Mikio Ariga; 278 top Munro Sounds/Claude Gassian; 278 Jane Rose; 279 Jane Rose; 280 Munro Sounds; 281 Munro Sounds; 282-283 Anton Corbijn; 285 Pennie Smith; 286 Munro Sounds; 287 Munro Sounds/Kevin Mazur; 288 Munro Sounds/Claude Gassian; 289 Munro Sounds/Kevin Mazur; 290, 293 Jane Rose; Chapter Eleven: 294-295 Munro Sounds/Claude Gassian; 296 Luis Sanchis; 299 Fernando Aceves; 300 Chris Wahl; 301 Munro Sounds/Jack English; 302 Fernando Aceves/rockarchive.com; 303 Fernando Aceves; 304 Chris Wahl; 305 Dimo Safari; 306 top left Chris Wahl; 306 top right Jane Rose; 306 centre left and right Jane Rose; 306 bottom left Chris Wahl; 306 bottom right Jane Rose; 307 top left Jane Rose; 307 top right Chris Wahl; 307 centre left and right Jane Rose; 307 bottom left Jane Rose; 307 bottom right Chris Wahl; 308 Fernando Aceves/rockarchive.com; 310-311 Chris Wahl; 312 Mario Testino; 313 Rex Features/Dave Hogan; 314 top Private Collection314 bottom left Lynn Goldsmith; 314 bottom right Private Collection; 315 top Private Collection; 315 bottom Private Collection; 316 Jane Rose; 319 Retna Ltd./Neil Massey; Chapter Twelve: 320-321 Jane Rose; 322 Mario Testino; 324 Scream Art 2002; 325 Jane Rose; 326 Munro Sounds/Mikio Ariga; 327 Rex Features/Jeremy Williams; 328 Chris Wahl; 329 The Interior Archive/Christopher Simon Sykes; 330 Jaap Buitendijk; 331 Rex Features/JHS; 332 Suzanne Le Mehaute; 334 Arabella Warburton; 336 Chris Wahl; 348 All record covers " Promotone B.V. except for those " ABKCO Records, detailed as follows, reprinted by permission. All rights reserved. ENGLAND'S NEWEST HIT MAKERS – 1964 (Photo: Nicolas Wright); 12X5 —1964 (Cover Photo: David Bailey); THE ROLLING STONES NO. 2 - 1965; THE ROLLING STONES, NOW! – 1965 (Cover Photo: David Bailey); OUT OF OUR HEADS - 1965 - UK Version (Cover Photo: Gered Mankowitz); OUT OF OUR HEADS - US Version (Cover Photo: David Bailey); DECEMBER'S CHILDREN - 1965 (Cover Photo: Gered Mankowitz); AFTERMATH - 1966 - UK Version (Photography: Guy Webster/Jerrold Schatzberg, Original Cover Design: Sandy Beach); AFTERMATH - US Version (Photography: David Bailey, Jerrold Schatzberg, Cover Design: Stephen Inglis); BIG HITS (HIGH TIDE AND GREEN GRASS) – 1966 (Cover photo: Gered Mankowitz, Original Cover Design: Andrew Loog Oldham); GOT LIVE IF YOU WANT IT! – 1966 (Cover Photograph: Gered Mankowitz, Cover Design: Stephen Inglis); BETWEEN THE BUTTONS - 1967 (Cover Photo: Gered Mankowitz); FLOWERS – 1967 (Photography: Guy Webster, Original Graphics: Tom Wilkes, Original Design Execution by The Corporate Head); THEIR SATANIC MAJESTIES REQUEST – 1967 (Original album designed and photographed by Michael Cooper); BEGGARS BANQUET – 1968 (Cover Photo: Barry Feinstein, Original Design: Tom Wilkes); THROUGH THE PAST, DARKLY – 1969 (Cover Photography: Ethan Russell); LET IT BLEED – 1969 (Cover Photo: Don McAllester, Original Cover Design: Robert Brownjohn); GET YER YA-YA'S OUT! – 1970 (Cover Photo: David Bailey, Original Design: John Kosh & Steve Thomas Associates); HOT ROCKS 1964-1971-1972 (Cover Photo: Ron Rafaelli, Original Design: Michael Gross); MORE HOT ROCKS – 1972 (Photograph: Gered Mankowitz, Original Cover Concept: Lenne Allik); METAMORPHOSIS – 1975; THE ROLLING STONES SINGLES COLLECTION - THE LONDON YEARS – 1989; FORTY LICKS – 2002 "ABKCO Records and Promotone B.V;. THE ROLLING STONES ROCK AND ROLL CIRCUS 1995(Cover Illustration: Marvin Mattelson); BEGGAR'S BANQUET - ORIGINAL BANNED DECCA COVER (Cover Illustration: Marvin Mattelson); 360 Mark Hayward/Philip Townsend.

First published in the United Kingdom in 2003 by Weidenfeld & Nicolson, a division of the Orion Publishing Group

Edited by: Dora Loewenstein and Philip Dodd
Consulting Editor: Charlie Watts

Interviewers: Rob Bowman, Philip Dodd, Dora Loewenstein, Tim Rice.

Contributed essays: David Bailey, Robert Bowman, Marshall Chess, Sheryl Crow, Ahmet Ertegun, Christopher Gibbs, Giorgio Gomelsky, Edna Gundersen, Carl Hiaasen, Prince Rupert Loewenstein, Tim Rice, Don Was, Peter Wolf. Essay by Peter Wolf © Peter Wolf 2003. Reproduced with permission.

Designed by Dan Einzig, assisted by Sara Ramazanoglu & Greg Macdonald, Mystery? Design
Design Director for Weidenfeld & Nicolson: David Rowley
Picture Research: Emily Hedges
Editorial: Jo Godfrey Wood, Claire Marsden, Nikki Sims, Claire Wedderburn-Maxwell
Interviews transcribed by Adèle Herson and Jacqui Thomas
Reference section and captions compiled with the help of Michael Heatley
Index: Derek Copson

Additional interview material from "25 x 5", produced and directed by Andrew Salt © 1989 Promotour U.S., Inc.; and from the documentary directed by Michael Apted, currently entitled "The Rolling Stones Licks World Tour Documentary", © 2003 RST Concerts, Inc.

Tongue and lips logo is a registered trade mark reproduced with permission of Musidor b.v.

Printed and bound in Italy by Printers SRL and LEGO

A CIP catalogue record for this book is available from the British Library.

ISBN 0 297 84332 X

Weidenfeld & Nicolson
Wellington House
125 Strand
London WC2R 0BB

Endpapers painted by Ronnie Wood